Li Zheng, Yuan Dong, Fang Yang
C++ Programming

Also of Interest

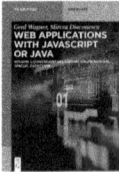

Web Applications with Javascript or Java, vol. 1
G. Wagner, M. Diaconescu, 2017
ISBN 978-3-11-049993-3, e-ISBN (PDF) 978-3-11-049995-7,
e-ISBN (EPUB) 978-3-11-049724-3

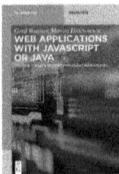

Web Applications with Javascript or Java, vol. 2
G. Wagner, M. Diaconescu, 2017
ISBN 978-3-11-050024-0, e-ISBN (PDF) 978-3-11-050032-5,
e-ISBN (EPUB) 978-3-11-049756-4

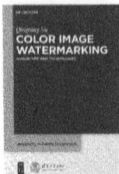

Color Image Watermarking
Q. Su, 2016
ISBN 978-3-11-048757-2, e-ISBN (PDF) 978-3-11-048773-2,
e-ISBN (EPUB) 978-3-11-048763-3, Set-ISBN 978-3-11-048776-3

Trusted Computing
D. Feng, 2017
ISBN 978-3-11-047604-0, e-ISBN (PDF) 978-3-11-047759-7,
e-ISBN (EPUB) 978-3-11-047609-5, Set-ISBN 978-3-11-047760-3

Li Zheng, Yuan Dong, Fang Yang

C++ Programming

DE GRUYTER

清華大学出版社
TSINGHUA UNIVERSITY PRESS

Authors
Dr. Li Zheng
Tsinghua University
Dept. of Computer Science and Technology
Haidian District, 30 Shuangqing Road
100084 Beijing, China

Dr. Yuan Dong
Tsinghua University
Dept. of Computer Science and Technology
Haidian District, 30 Shuangqing Road
100084 Beijing, China

Dr. Fang Yang
Tsinghua University, Dept. of Foreign Languages
Haidian District, 30 Shuangqing Road
100084 Beijing, China

ISBN 978-3-11-046943-1
e-ISBN (PDF) 978-3-11-047197-7
e-ISBN (EPUB) 978-3-11-047066-6

Library of Congress Control Number: 2018941441

Bibliographic information published by the Deutsche Nationalbibliothek
The Deutsche Nationalbibliothek lists this publication in the Deutsche Nationalbibliografie;
detailed bibliographic data are available on the Internet at http://dnb.dnb.de.

© 2019 Walter de Gruyter GmbH, Berlin/Boston
Cover image: tostphoto/iStock/thinkstock
Typesetting: le-tex publishing services GmbH, Leipzig
Printing and binding: CPI books GmbH, Leck

www.degruyter.com

Preface

This book draws on the author's extensive teaching experience on C++ and takes its current form after incorporating valuable advices from colleagues and students.

1. Background of Writing This Book

C++ is an object-oriented programming language, which is evolved from C. C++ has two main characteristics: one is its full compatibility with C and the other is that it supports object-oriented methods.

The object-oriented program design encapsulates both data and related operations to form an interdependent and indivisible whole – an object. By abstracting common features of objects of the same category, we can get a **class**. Most data in a class can only be processed by the methods encapsulated in the class. A class communicates with the outside world through a simple external interface, and objects communicate with each other through messages. In this way, we can have simple relationships among program modules, and module independency and data security can be ensured. Meanwhile, through inheritance and polymorphism, codes can be well reused, which facilitates both the development and maintenance of software.

Because of the outstanding qualities of object-oriented methods, they have now become the major ways to develop large-scale software, and C++ is one of the most widely used object-oriented programming languages.

C++ has long been considered hard to use, and is seldom used as an introduction language for teaching. Are C++ and object-oriented program design indeed hard to learn? The answer is no. In fact, when C was first created, it was only used by a few professional developers. However, along with the development of computer science, computer technologies have permeated research and applications of different subjects. Now C has been widely used by various engineers and technicians, and it has also been used as the introduction programming language in many schools. C++ is fully compatible with C, although it provides a stricter and more secure grammar. In this sense, C++ is primarily a better C.

C++ is an Object-Oriented Programming (OOP) language. OOP has once been considered a comparatively advanced technology. This is because before the theories of Object-Oriented Analysis (OOA) and Object-Oriented Design (OOD) were developed, in order to write a good object-oriented program, programmers would first learn to use object-oriented methods to understand and describe problems. Now, since the work of understanding problem domains and designing system components are done during the phases of system analysis and system design, the work of OOP becomes much easier – it is just to write every component of an OOD model with an object-oriented programming language.

https://doi.org/10.1515/9783110471977-201

The emergence of object-oriented methods is in fact a process where the program design gets back to its roots. Essentially, software development aims to correctly understand problems that the software needs to handle and to accurately describe the understandings. The fundamental principle that object-oriented methods emphasize is to develop software directly facing the objective existence, and to apply the ways of human thinking and human expressions to software development. Thus, software development can return back to the real world from past methods, rules and skills that are extravagantly specialized.

Thus, do we need to learn C before learning C++? No. Although C++ is evolved from C, C++ itself is an integral programming language, and it has a completely different design philosophy from C. Our learning course does not need to exactly follow the development course of science and technology. Only by mastering the latest theories and technologies quickly can we stand on the shoulders of giants.

Thus, we think that C++ can be taught as an introduction programming language.

2. Features of this book

This book is comprehensive, tries to explain problems in simple terms, and has abundant complementary materials.

This book is for programmer beginners. Since the publication of the first edition in 1999, the book has been used by different majors in many universities including Tsinghua University, and has achieved good effects.

Using C++ as the introduction programming language for college students, this book not only details the language itself, but also introduces data structures, algorithms, object-oriented design ideas and programming, and the Unified Modeling Language (UML). In each chapter of this book, we first introduce the related object-oriented programming ideas and methods, and then expound the necessary grammar through practical examples, explaining its meaning and usage primarily from the aspect of programming methodology. The purpose of this book is to make readers be able not only to master the C++ language itself, but also to use computer languages to describe simple practical problems and their solutions. However, to describe complex problems, readers still have to learn other object-oriented courses such as object-oriented software engineering.

As a book for programming beginners, this book aims at explaining complicated subjects in simple terms.

3. Content Abstract

Chapter 1: Introduction

From a development perspective, this chapter first introduces the history and the characteristics of object-oriented programming language, as well as the origin and the primary basic concepts of object-oriented methods. Then it makes a brief introduction on object-oriented software engineering. Finally, the chapter takes a look at how information is represented and stored in computers and the development procedure of programs.

Chapter 2: Elementary C++ Programming

This chapter focuses on the basic knowledge of C++ programming. It first introduces the history and the characteristics of the C++ language; then it discusses the basic elements that construct a C++ statement – character sets, keywords, identifiers, operators, etc. The chapter also introduces basic data types and user-defined data types in C++, and three main control structures in algorithms: sequential, case, and loop structures.

Chapter 3: Functions

This chapter focuses on the functions in C++. In object-oriented programming, function is the basic unit of module division, the basic abstract unit of problem-solving processes, and also the abstract of functionalities. Using functions offers support for code reuse. From an application perspective, this chapter mainly introduces the definitions and usages of various functions, especially the usages of system functions.

Chapter 4: Class and Object

This chapter first introduces the basic idea of object-oriented program design and its main characteristics: abstraction, encapsulation, inheritance, and polymorphism. Then, revolving around encapsulation, the chapter focuses on the core concept of object-oriented methods – class, including the definition and the implementation of class, and how to use class to solve practical problems. Finally, it briefly introduces using Unified Modeling Language (UML) to describe the characteristics of class. Later chapters will always use UML to describe the relationships between class and object.

Chapter 5: Data Sharing and Protecting

This chapter introduces the scope and visibility of identifiers, and the lifetime of variables and objects. We can see how to use local variables, global variables, data members of classes, static members of classes, and friends to achieve data sharing and the protection of shared data. Finally, the chapter introduces using multifile structures to organize and write programs to solve complex problems.

Chapter 6: Arrays, Pointers, and Strings

This chapter focuses on arrays, pointers, and strings. Array and pointer are the most commonly used compound (structure) data types. They are the primary means by which we organize and represent data and objects, and are the useful tools for manipulating math operations. This chapter first introduces the basic concepts of arrays and pointers, and discusses dynamic memory allocation. Then, revolving around the organization issues of data and objects, the chapter focuses on how to use arrays and pointers to link and coordinate data, functions, and objects. Finally, the chapter introduces the concept of strings and two methods to process strings: using character arrays and using the class *string*.

Chapter 7: Inheritance and Derivation

This chapter focuses on the inheritance characteristic of class. Revolving around the derivation process, the chapter primarily discusses the access control issues of base class members under different inheritance modes, as well as how to add the constructor and destructor in a derived class. Then, the chapter discusses the issues of unique identification and the access of class members in comparatively complex inheritance relations. Finally, the chapter gives two instances of class inheritance – "Use Complete Gaussian Pivoting Elimination Method to Solve Linear Equations" and "Personnel Information Management Program for a Small Company."

Chapter 8: Polymorphism

This chapter introduces another important characteristic of class – polymorphism. Polymorphism refers to how a same message can result in different actions when received by different kinds of objects. Polymorphism is a re-abstract of specific function members of a class. C++ supports many forms of polymorphism, and the main forms include overloading (include function overloading and operator overloading) and virtual functions, which are also the learning focus. Finally, the chapter gives two instances of class polymorphism – "Variable-Step Trapezoid Integral Algorithm" and "Improvement of Personnel Information Management Program for a Small Company."

Chapter 9: Collections and the Organization of Collection Data

A collection refers to a set of data elements. Collections can be divided into two main categories: linear collections and nonlinear collections. This chapter mainly introduces some commonly used collection class templates.

The organization issues of collection data refer to the sorting and searching methods of the data elements in a collection. Sorting is also called classification or reorganization. It is a process of making an unordered array ordered. Searching is the process of finding specific data elements in an array by some specific method.

Chapter 10: Generic Programming and Standard Template Library

Generic Programming is writing programs as general as possible without loss of efficiency. This chapter briefly introduces some concepts and terms that are involved in the C++ Standard Template Library (STL), as well as the structure of STL and the usage of its primary components. We focus on the basic applications of containers, iterators, algorithms, and function objects, in order to give readers a conceptual understanding of STL and generic programming.

Chapter 11: I/O Stream Library and Input/Output

This chapter introduces the concept of stream, as well as the structure and usage of the stream library. Like C, there is no Input/Output statement in C++. However, the compiler of C++ has an object-oriented I/O software packet, which is the I/O stream library.

Chapter 12: Exception Handling

This chapter focuses on the exception handling. Exception is a kind of program-defined error. In C++, exception handling refers to a set of implementation mechanisms that handles predicted errors in the runtime of programs. *Try*, *throw* and *catch* statements are the mechanisms in C++ to implement exception handling. With the exception handling of C++, programs can deliver unexpected events to execution contexts at higher levels, and thus better recover from these exceptions.

4. User's Guide and Related Resources

The author assigns 32 class hours for teaching with this book, 32 class hours for experiments, and 32 class hours for computer practice outside class. Thus, there are 96 class hours in and out of class, and each class hour has 45 minutes. We recommend distributing the teaching hours as follows:

Chapter 1: 2 class hours; Chapter 2: 4 class hours; Chapter 3: 2 class hours; Chapter 4: 4 class hours; Chapter 5: 2 class hours; Chapter 6: 4 class hours; Chapter 7: 4 class hours; Chapter 8: 2 class hours; Chapter 9: 4 class hours; Chapter 10: 2 class hours; Chapter 11: 1 class hours; Chapter 12: 1 class hour.

The readers can download the learning resources from the Tsinghua University Press website.

5. Acknowledgement

Chapters 1–3, 9, 11, and 12 are written by Zheng Li; Chapters 4–8 are written by Dong Yuan, Zheng Li and Zhang Ruifeng; and Chapter 10 are written by Zhang Ruifeng and Zheng Li. Yang Fang took great efforts to rewrite this book in fluent English prose. Additionally, Zhou Zhiwei, Dai Nike, Wang Jing, Shan Liang, Mai Haohui, Liu Yintao, Xu Chen, Fu Shixing, Tian Rongpai, Meng Hongli, Meng Wei, Zhang Wenju, Yang Xingpeng, and Wang Xuan participated in parts of the writing work.

Thank you to the readers for using this book; any criticisms or suggestions are warmly welcomed. In your note, please specify your email address. The email address of the author is: zhengli@tsinghua.edu.cn

Contents

1 Introduction

This chapter briefly introduces the history and characteristics of object-oriented programming languages, the origin of the object-oriented method and its basic concepts, and the definition of object-oriented software engineering. Additionally, we will introduce how information is represented and stored in a computer and the development process of a program.

1.1 The Development of Computer Programming Languages

A language is a system with a set of grammatical and morphological rules. Language is a tool for thinking, and thoughts are expressed by languages. A computer programming language is a language that can be recognized by computers. It describes **solutions to problems**, which can be **read** and **executed by computers**.

1.1.1 Machine Language and Assembly Language

Since the birth of the first digital computer in the world – ENIAC, in February 1946, computer science has developed rapidly in the past 50 years. Computers and their applications have penetrated into various areas of society, effectively promoting the development of the whole information society, wherein the computer has become an essential tool.

A computer system consists of software and hardware. It is not only the strong hardware but also the software system that makes a computer system so powerful. The software system consists of all the programs a computer needs for running, as well as the relevant documents. The work of a computer is controlled by programs, and a computer can do nothing without a program. A program is a set of instructions. Software engineers translate their solutions to problems and their procedures into a series of instructions, which make up programs, and input these programs into the computer storage system. The computer executes the instruction sequence to complete the scheduled task.

The so-called instructions are commands that can be recognized by computers. We know that every ethnic group has rich languages for expression, communication, and recordation, while these languages are difficult for a computer to recognize. The only instruction types that a computer can recognize are simple combinations of 0s and 1s. The set of instructions that can be recognized by the hardware system of a computer is called the instruction system.

All binary instructions that can be recognized by the hardware system constitute the machine language. Undoubtedly, though machine language is easy for

https://doi.org/10.1515/9783110471977-001

a computer to recognize, it is too obscure for human beings to understand, let alone to remember. However, in the early years of computers software engineers could only use the machine language to write programs. At that time, there was a huge gap between natural human language and the computer programming language. It took great difficulty and long cycles for software developing, while the developed software had simple functions and unfriendly interfaces.

Before long, **assembly language was developed to map the machine instructions onto some mnemonic symbols,** such as ADD and SUB. The gap between the programming language and human language is somewhat reduced, while the machine language is still far from the human mind. Since machine language is pretty weak in abstraction, programmers still need to consider a great many machinery details.

Nevertheless, it is still a big progress from the machine language to assembly language. It means that it is not necessary for human beings and the computer hardware system to share a same language. Programmers can use languages that suit man's ways of thinking, while the computer hardware system only needs to recognize machine instructions. Then, how to realize the communication between the two languages? A translation tool (software) is needed. The translator for an assembly language is called an assembler, which transforms the mnemonic symbols written by programmers into machine instructions, and then the computer can recognize and execute these instructions.

1.1.2 High-level Language

The emergence of high-level language is a great progress in programming language. It **masks** the details of a machine, and raises the level of abstraction. In programs we can name variables with specific meanings and use statements that are easier to understand. Through this we can correlate the specific objects a program describes when we write the program.

Structured programming language that emerged in the late 1960s further enhanced the language level. Concepts such as structured data, structured statements, data abstraction, and procedure abstraction made programs more easily reflect the structures and logic meanings of objects. This further reduced the gap between the programming language and natural language, while their differences remained non-negligible. The main problem was the separation between data and operation in a program, making it difficult to create program components that could closely correspond to objects in the real world.

Today there are several widely-used high-level programming languages, including Fortran, BASIC, Pascal, C, etc. The C++ programming language this book introduces is also a high-level programming language, although it has some fundamental differences from other procedure-oriented languages.

1.1.3 Object-oriented Language

The fundamental difference between an object-oriented language and formerly used programming languages is that it is designed to describe real objects in the world and their relationships more directly.

We develop software to solve problems. The business scope a problem involves is called the **problem domain**. Object-oriented programming language treats things in the real world as objects with attributes and behaviors (or services), and then classifies objects with common attributes (static features) and behaviors (dynamic features) through abstraction, calling them a **class**. By using class inheritance and polymorphism, we can easily realize code reuse, significantly shorten the software development cycle, and make the software style unified. Therefore, an object-oriented programming language can make a program directly reflect the real problem domain, and software developers can thus use normal ways of human thinking to develop software.

Object-oriented programming language has experienced a long stage of development. For instance, LISP-family's object-oriented language, Simula67, Smalltalk, CLU, Ada, and Modula-2 are all programming languages that more or less use the concept of "object oriented", among which Smalltalk is the first "true" object-oriented programming language.

However, the most widely used object-oriented (OO) programming language is C++, which is extended from C. Since C++ is compatible with C and C is already familiar to most programmers, C++ has naturally become the most widely used OO programming language.

1.2 Object-oriented Method

A programming language is a tool for writing programs, so the progress of a programming language reflects the progress of program design methods. Here we will first introduce the basic concepts of the object-oriented method. We believe that after reading this book, you may have a sound and complete comprehension of object-oriented method.

1.2.1 The Origin of Object-oriented Method

Before the emergence of object-oriented method, we had been using a procedure-oriented design method. In the early days computers were tools for mathematic computations, such as computing a ballistic trajectory. To complete the computation, people had to design a method, or procedure. Therefore, the main work for software design was to figure out a procedure to solve the problem.

Along with the rapid development of hardware systems, computers have become more and more powerful and widely used, not only limited to mathematic computations. Because of the increasing complexity of the problems we want to solve, programs have become much larger and more complex. The structured design method that emerged in the 1960s provided an effective way for procedure-oriented programming to solve complex problems. As a result, from the 1970s to the 1980s, structured programming was adopted by programmers in every field of software design. The main idea of structured programming is **top-down** and **stepwise refinement**. Its program structure is divided into several basic modules by different functionalities, and these modules form a tree structure. The relationships among the modules are kept as simple as possible and the function of each module is relatively independent. Each module consists of three basic structures – sequential structure, branch structure, and loop structure. The concrete way to realize modularization is to use subroutines. Due to the use of modular decomposition, function abstraction, and top-down and stepwise refinement, structured programming can effectively decompose a complex program system into several subtasks that are easier to control and handle, so as to facilitate development and maintenance.

Whatever advantages structured programming may have, it is still a kind of procedure-oriented design method, which separates data and its processing operations. When a data structure changes, all relevant processing procedures need corresponding modifications. Any new method for an old problem may entail extra costs, making the program hard to reuse. Besides, due to the use of GUI (Graphical User Interface), software has become easier to use while being more difficult to develop. Good software should be responsive to any user operation, rather than ask its users to follow some specific steps. For example, we are all familiar with the word processor. A good word processor should be able to be used easily and at liberty, and fixed operation orders should never appear in a software specification. Therefore, it is very difficult to use procedures to describe and implement the functions of the software. If we continue to take the procedure-oriented method, both development and maintenance will be difficult.

Then, what is object-oriented method? First, it puts together the data and its operation as an interdependent and inseparable whole, which is called an **object**. Secondly, it abstracts common characters from objects of the same kind and groups those objects into a class. Most of the data in a class can only be processed by the methods of this class. A class communicates with the outside world through a simple external interface, while objects communicate with messages. Through this way, the relationships among program modules become much simpler, and the independence of modules and data safety can be better guaranteed. Besides, class inheritance and polymorphism, which will be introduced in the following chapters, may further improve code reusability and facilitate the development and maintenance of software.

There are so many advantages in the object-oriented method, and yet one may wonder whether it is easy for beginners to understand and master. The answer is yes.

The emergence of object-oriented method is in fact a process of the development of programming design method returning to nature. The goal of software development, in essence, is to get a proper understanding of the problem domain it needs to solve, and to correctly describe the understanding. The fundamental principle the object-oriented method emphasizes is to develop software directly according to existing objects, and to bring human ways of thinking and expressing into software development. Through this, we can turn software development from those over-specialized methods, rules, and techniques back to human ways of thinking.

1.2.2 Basic Concepts of Object-oriented

Now we will introduce some basic concepts in the object-oriented method. We cannot expect to understand all these concepts through only a few such statements. The following chapters of this book will help us to get a better understanding of these concepts to finally achieve proficiency.

1. Object

Generally speaking, objects are things that really exist. They can be either material (like a car) or immaterial (like a plan). An object is an independent unit that makes up the world. It has static features (can be described by certain data) and dynamic features (the behaviors an object presents or its functionalities).

The Object in OO (object-oriented) method is an entity system used to describe objective things. It is an elementary unit for constructing a system. An object consists of a group of attributes and a group of behaviors. Attributes describe the static features of an object while behaviors are the operation sequences that describe an object's dynamic features.

2. Class

People tend to sum up their understanding of the world and put them into categories. **The principle for such classification is abstraction**, which means ignoring minor issues and only focusing on essential characteristics that relate to our current goals. In this way, we can find out the shared characteristics and sort out those things with common characteristics and put them into a class. Then we can have an abstract concept, such as a stone, tree, car, or house, which are all concepts that people abstracted from humanity's long-term life experiences in production and practice.

A "class" in the OO method is a set of objects with the same attributes and behaviors. It provides abstract descriptions for all objects of the class and is mainly composed of two parts: attribute and behavior. The relationship between class and object is similar to that between a mold and cast. An object of a class is called an instance of that class.

3. Encapsulation

Encapsulation is an important principle in the OO method. It means assembling the attributes and services of an object into an independent unit and concealing the internal details of the object as much as possible. Here encapsulation has two meanings. The first meaning is assembling all the attributes and services of an object into an inseparable entity; the second meaning, also called "information hiding", is creating a boundary (or barrier) to hide internal details and making the object interact with the outside world only through limited external interfaces.

4. Inheritance

Inheritance is one of the most important factors that make the OO method improve software development efficiency. If objects of a particular class possess all attributes and services of its common class, we call this an inheritance of a particular class from the common class.

The practical significance of inheritance is that it simplifies people's understandings and descriptions of objective things. For example, once we know all the features of "ship", we consider "passenger ship" and know that it is a kind of "ship". We may conclude that "passenger ship" has all the features of "ship", so we only need to focus on those features specialized in "passenger ship".

Inheritance has significant importance for software reuse. A particular class inheriting a common class is in itself a kind of software reuse. In addition, if we put a developed class in the component library as a component, we can directly use it or inherit it when trying to develop a new system.

5. Polymorphism

Polymorphism refers to how the attributes or behaviors defined in a common class can have different data types or behaviors after they are inherited by a particular class. This makes the same attribute or behavior possess different semantics in the common class and in various particular classes.

For example, we can define a common class of the "geometric figure". The class has a behavior of "draw" but with no specific meaning, that is, we don't know to draw the figure in execution (because we don't know what the figure is). Next, we can define some particular classes of "geometric figure", such as "ellipse" or "polygon". Since both of them inherit the common class "geometric figure", they are within the behavior of "draw". Thereafter, we can redefine "draw" according to the particular class and make it possible to draw ellipse and polygon accordingly. Furthermore, we can define a particular class "rectangle" that inherits from "polygon" and implements the function of drawing a rectangle in "draw". That is what polymorphism is in the OO method.

1.3 Object-oriented Software Development

In the whole process of software development, programming is a relatively small part. The pacing factor of software development comes from raising problems in early stages but not resolving the problems in later stages. Once we recognize, understand, and express the essence of the problem correctly, we can design and program to solve it.

The problems we want to solve in early days are simple, so it is not very difficult to recognize the problem and solve it by programming. With the extension of the application fields of computers, the problems we want to solve become more complex, and the scale and complexity of software systems increase to an unprecedented level. This leads to the situation that the complexity of the software and the bugs in it reach an extent that programmers cannot control, known as the "software crisis" in the 1960s, which speeds up the emergence and development of software engineering.

To learn object-oriented programming we should first know the overall process of software development and maintenance. So, what is object-oriented software engineering? It is the application of the object-oriented method in the field of software engineering, including object-oriented analysis (OOA), object-oriented design (OOD), object-oriented programming (OOP), object-oriented test (OOT), and object-oriented software maintenance (OOSM), etc.

1.3.1 Analysis

By describing a problem, we can build up a model of a real situation to illustrate the important features of the system. To understand the problem, system analysts should work with their clients. In the analysis stage, we should abstract what the system should do precisely, rather than care about implementation.

Object-oriented system analysis builds objects in a model directly with the objective existence in the problem domain. Thus, separate objects as well as their relationships can be well preserved with no transformation or any recombination that violates the original boundary, so as to reflect the objective existence effectively.

1.3.2 Design

The design stage aims at a concrete implementation of the system and uses the OO method. It includes two different jobs: one is to move the OOA model directly into OOD as its component; the other is to add some related work according to the factors of the concrete implementation, such as data storage, task management, and human-computer interface.

1.3.3 Programming

Programming is a very important stage in the final implementation of object-oriented software development. Before the emergence of OOA and OOD theories, programmers should learn to understand the problem domain with the object-oriented method in order to write a good object-oriented program. Therefore, OOP is considered an advanced technique. Nowadays OOP is much easier, since the work of understanding the problem domain and designing system components have already been accomplished in the stage of OOA and OOD. The work left for OOP is to write down every component in the OOD model using an OO programming language.

Nevertheless, we still emphasize the basic thinking process of object-oriented program design, rather than only mastering the programming skills. So, even though this book is for beginners of programming, and mainly concerns the C++ programming language and object-oriented programming approach, we still take some space to introduce design methods through examples.

1.3.4 Test

The task for the test is to detect bugs in the software. Any software product should be strictly tested before being released. Continually using the concepts and principles of object-oriented in the test of OO software, and deeming the class as the basic test unit, can detect bugs more accurately and furthermore improve the test efficiency.

1.3.5 Maintenance

No matter how strict the tests are, which the software may undergo, it may still have bugs. Therefore, maintenance is necessary in software development.

In the software developed by the OO method, the problem domain is consistent with the program, and the presentations in every stage of the software engineering are consistent, so that it is easier for the maintainer to understand the software. Whether we may discover a bug in the program or demands may change; tracing back to the program will not be very hard. Besides, impacts due to changes in other objects have been reduced because of the encapsulation of the object. Thus, software maintenance efficiency can be highly increased through the object-oriented method.

As readers may see, examples in this book are very simple, and they always come with clear descriptions of the problems encountered. Thus, it is not easy for the readers to understand the effect of software engineering. However, we still recommend designing the object before programming. This book is mainly for programming methods, yet we suggest that readers learn OO software engineering after you have mastered C++ programming language.

1.4 Representation and Storage of Information

Computers can process data information, although it is conducted by control information. So the information in computers can be classified into two categories:

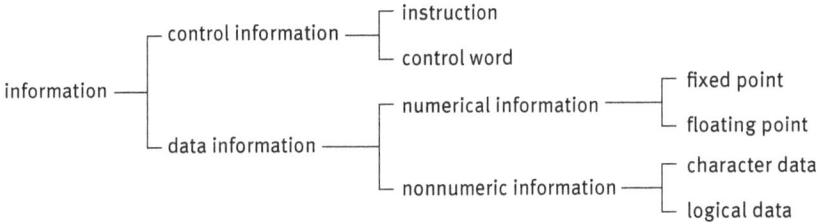

This chapter focuses on data information. Please refer to related books on hardware for details on control information.

1.4.1 Digital System of Computers

People are familiar with the decimal numeral system. However, almost all computers use the binary system. Computers cannot transfer, store, or process data until it is coded into binary digits. When programming, we usually transfer binary system into the octal system or hexadecimal system. A feature common to all these numeral systems is that they are positional numeral systems.

Generally speaking, if there are R basic symbols in a numeral system, we call it an R-based numeral system. R is the "base" of the numeral system and each position in the numeral system has a value called "weight".

The coding of positional numeral system complies with the "standing-on-R" rule, which means their weight is the power based on R. Any number can be expanded to a polynomial according to the weight. For example, a decimal number 256.47 can be expanded into the polynomial as follows:

$$256.47 = 2 \times 10^2 + 5 \times 10^1 + 6 \times 10^0 + 4 \times 10^{-1} + 7 \times 10^{-2}$$

For any R-based number x, its value $V(x)$ can be presented as:

$$V(x) = \underbrace{\sum_{i=0}^{n-1} x_i R^i}_{\text{Integral}} + \underbrace{\sum_{i=-1}^{m} x_i R^i}_{\text{Decimal}}$$

Here m and n are integers, and R^i is the weight in Position i. X_0 and X_{-1} are separated by a decimal point. Usually, X_i should satisfy the following condition:

$$0 \leq X_i < R$$

Tab. 1.1: Some positional numeral systems.

Radix	Base	Carry Principle	Basic symbols
Binary	2	every 2 carries 1	0,1
Octal	8	every 8 carries 1	0,1,2,3,4,5,6,7
Decimal	10	every 10 carries 1	0,1,2,3,4,5,6,7,8,9,
Hexadecimal	16	every 16 carries 1	0,1,2,3,4,5,6,7,8,9,A,B,C,D,E,F

Note: A–F in the hexadecimal numeral system correspond to 10–15 in the decimal numeral system.

In other words, R-based numeral systems use $0 \sim (R - 1)$ numerical notations.

Table 1.1 presents some common numeral systems.

In the binary numeral system, the base is 2 and the weight of each position is a power of 2, following the principle of "every 2 into 1". There are two basic symbols: 0 and 1. Here is an example of a number in the binary numeral system:

$$1011.01 .$$

Nearly all computers use the binary numeral system for coding because of its following advantages:

1. Convenient for Physical Implementation
There are many physical devices with two different stable states, such as on and off states of gate circuit, high level, and low level of voltage. These states exactly correspond to the two symbols of 0 and 1. However, if the decimal numeral system is adopted, it would be really difficult if we tried to make a physical circuit with ten stable states.

2. Easy Mathematical Operations
It is proven that there are $R(R + 1)/2$ arithmetic rules for summation and quadrature in an R-based numeral system. So if we use the decimal numeral system, we will have 55 different arithmetic rules while there are only three different rules if we use the binary numeral system, which furthermore simplifies the designs of physical devices such as Arithmetic Logical Unit (ALU).

3. High Reliability
Since the voltage level (high or low) and current existence (with or without), etc. are all related to qualitative change with two distinct states, information coded by the binary numeral system has strong anti-inference capability in transmission and high reliability for information discrimination.

4. Versatility
The binary numeral system suits not only numerical information encoding but also non-numerical information encoding. Particularly, since the only two symbols of 0 and 1 correspond exactly to the two values in logical position – "true" and "false", it is very convenient for computers to implement logical computation and logical judgment.

Although computers internally use binary numeral system to encode information, the communication between computers and the outside world is still through forms that are human familiar and easy to read, such as texts, pictures, and decimal data. The transformation between the two is completed by computer hardware and software.

It is self-evident that there are some disadvantages in the binary numeral system such as its small capacity. Using the binary numeral system requires more digits to encode a number than other numeral systems.

1.4.2 Conversions among Numeral Systems

1. *R*-based to Decimal

We can get the decimal value of an R-based number only by multiplying each digit of the number by its weight, then calculating the sum of all the products. For example:

$$(11111111.11)_2 = 1 \times 2^7 + 1 \times 2^6 + 1 \times 2^5 + 1 \times 2^4 + 1 \times 2^3 + 1 \times 2^2 + 1$$
$$\times 2^1 + 1 \times 2^0 + 1 \times 2^{-1} + 1 \times 2^{-2}$$
$$= (255.75)_{10}$$

$$(3506.2)_8 = 3 \times 8^3 + 5 \times 8^2 + 0 \times 8^1 + 6 \times 8^0 + 2 \times 8^{-1} = (1862.25)_{10}$$
$$(0.2A)_{16} = 2 \times 16^{-1} + 10 \times 16^{-2} = (0.1640625)_{10}$$

From the above examples we know: when an R-based number is to be converted into a decimal number, we can convert its integral part and decimal part respectively by starting the conversion from its decimal point both leftward and rightward. For the binary numeral system, we just need to add the weights of those 1-valued positions together, and the sum will be its equivalent decimal value. Therefore, binary-decimal conversion is the simplest and most widely used numeral system conversion.

2. Decimal to *R*-based

When we try to convert a decimal number into its equivalent R-based number, we can convert the integral part and decimal part separately and then merge the two parts together.

a) Decimal integer to *R*-based integer

When a decimal integer is to be converted into an R-based integer, we can divide it by R continuously, and the remainders are the corresponding coefficients of the digits of the R-based number. This method is called the "R divide method".

We know that any decimal integer N can be represented by an R-based number:

$$N = X_0 + X_1 R^1 + X_2 R^2 + \cdots + X_{n-1} R^{n-1}$$
$$= X_0 + (X_1 + X_2 R^1 + \cdots + X_{n-1} R^{n-2})R$$
$$= X_0 + Q_1 R$$

Therefore, if we divide N by R, the quotient is Q_1 and the remainder is X_0. Similarly, we have

$$Q_1 = X_1 + Q_2 R$$

Divide Q_1 by R, the quotient is Q_2 and the remainder is X_1, and so on:

$$Q_i = X_i + (X_{i+1} + X_{i+2} R^1 + \cdots + X_{n-1} R^{n-2-i}) R$$
$$= X_i + Q_{i+1} R$$

Divide Q_i by R, so the quotient is Q_{i+1} and the remainder is X_i

Continue the division until the quotient is 0. Then the remainders array X_0, X_1, $X_2 \ldots X_{n-1}$ that we get constitutes the resulting R-based number.

For example, we can convert the decimal value 68 into a binary number like this:

```
2 | 68                          Remainder
  2 | 34  ... ... ... ... ... 0      low order digit
    2 | 17  ... ... ... ... ... 0
      2 | 8  ... ... ... ... ... 1
        2 | 4  ... ... ... ... ... 0
          2 | 2  ... ... ... ... 0
            2 | 1 ... ... ... ... 0
                0 ... ... ... ... 1    high order digit
```

so $68_{10} = 1000100_2$

To convert 168_{10} into an octal number, we can divide it by 8 and get the remainders:

```
8 | 168                         Remainder
  8 | 21 ... ... ... ... ... 0       low order digit
    8 | 2... ... ... ... ... 5
        0  ... ... ... ... ... 2     high order digit
```

So $168_{10} = 250_8$

b) Decimal fraction to R-based fraction

When a decimal fraction is to be converted into an R-based number, we can multiply the decimal fraction by R continuously, and the integer array we get constructs the resulted R-based fraction. This method is named "multiply by R and get the integers":

We can convert a decimal fraction to the R-based fraction like this:

$$V = \frac{X_{-1}}{R^1} + \frac{X_{-2}}{R^2} + \frac{X_{-3}}{R^3} + \cdots + \frac{X_{-m}}{R^m}$$

Multiplying both sides of the equation by R, we get:

$$V \times R = X_{-1} + \left(\frac{X_{-2}}{R^1} + \frac{X_{-3}}{R^2} + \cdots + \frac{X_{-m}}{R^{m-1}} \right) = X_{-1} + F_1$$

X_{-1} is the integral part, which is the first digit of the R-based fraction, F_1 is the decimal part. We can multiply F_1 by R again:

$$F_1 \times R = X_{-2} + \left(\frac{X_{-3}}{R^1} + \frac{X_{-4}}{R^2} + \cdots + \frac{X_{-m}}{R^{m-2}} \right) = X_{-2} + F_2$$

X_{-2} is the integral part, which is the second digit after the decimal point of the R-based number.

Continue the multiplication until the decimal part is 0 or we obtain a required precision (the decimal part may never be 0).

For example, we can convert 0.3125_{10} into a binary number by doing as follows:

```
                               ┌──────────────── high order digit
0.3125 ×2 = 0 .625
0.625  ×2 = 1 .25
0.25   ×2 = 0 .5
0.5    ×2 = 1 .0
```

So $0.3125_{10} = 0.0101_2$

Note that usually a decimal fraction cannot be converted into a binary number (or other R-based number) precisely, where deviation must exist.

If we want to convert the decimal value 68.3125 into binary number, we can convert the integral part and decimal part respectively and then join them together:

$$68.3125_{10} = 1000100.0101_2$$

3. Conversions Between Binary, Octal, and Hexadecimal Numeral Systems

There are some internal relationships between the weights of binary, octal, and hexadecimal numeral systems, that is, each digit in an octal number can be represented by three binary numbers ($2^3 = 8$), and each digit in a hexadecimal number can be represented by four binary numbers ($2^4 = 16$). Let's see the following examples:

As to a binary number, we start from the decimal point and group every three (or four) digits into a unit leftward and rightward. By converting each binary unit into an octal (or hexadecimal) number, we achieve the conversion from the binary number to its octal (or hexadecimal) form. Notice that in conversion, the unit grouping centers on the decimal point and extends leftward and rightward, so the 0's in the middle cannot be omitted. We need to fill some 0's if there are not enough on either end.

Every digit in an octal (or hexadecimal) number can be converted into three (or four) binary digits. Notice that except the leftmost significant bit, there should be exactly three (or four) binary digits for each octal (or hexadecimal) digit or we need to fill some 0's. For example:

$$(1000100)_2 = (\underline{1}\ \underline{000}\ \underline{100})_2 = (104)_8$$
$$(1000100)_2 = (\underline{100}\ \underline{0100})_2 = (44)_{16}$$
$$(1011010.10)_2 = (\underline{001}\ \underline{011}\ \underline{010}\ .\underline{100})_2 = (132.4)_8$$
$$(1011010.10)_2 = (\underline{0101}\ \underline{1010}\ .\underline{1000})_2 = (5A.8)_{16}$$
$$(F)_{16} = (\underline{1111})_2$$
$$(7)_{16} = (\underline{0111})_2$$
$$(F7)_{16} = (\underline{1111}\ \underline{0111})_2 = (11110111)_2$$

1.4.3 Storage Units of Information

All information in the computer is stored in the binary-encoded form. Here we will introduce the data storage units:
The data units we usually use are "bit", "byte", and "word".
Bit: the smallest unit of measurement, representing a binary data.
Byte: a byte consists of 8 bits, which is the conventional elementary unit of information storage.

Usually, memory capacity is represented by the number of bytes. Common units include:

kilobytes	1 K = 1024 byte
M bytes	1 M = 1024 K
G bytes	1 G = 1024 M

Word: a word is the combination of bits and is used as an independent data unit. A word is also called a "computer word", and its exact meaning depends on machine types, word length, and user requirements. Common word lengths can be 8 bits, 16 bits, or 32 bits, etc.
A data unit is used to describe the computer's internal data form, i.e., the data arrangement inside the computer. For example, single-byte data and variable-length data (data forms of different length in bytes), etc. are kinds of data units.
Machine word length is another hardware-related data unit. Machine word length usually refers to the number of binary bits those registers that are involved in arithmetic have. It represents the precision of a machine and can be 32 bits, 64 bits, etc.

1.4.4 Binary-coded Representation

The representation of a number in a machine is called the "machine number" and its value is called the "true value" of the machine number.

As mentioned before, data information in computers is represented in binary code. Since a number can be positive or negative, how does one signify the sign of a number in computers? Generally, the leftmost bit of the number indicates the sign of the value represented, where "0" indicates the positive sign and "1" indicates the negative sign. For example:

An 8-bit binary number $A = (+1011011)$ and $B = (-1011011)$ can be represented in a computer as follows:

A:	0	1	0	1	1	0	1	1
B:	1	1	0	1	1	0	1	1

The leftmost bit is the sign bit; it forms the number together with the rest of the bits.

Once the data information has been digitized, it can be recognized and represented by a computer. In order to simplify the computation of signed numbers and then make ALU simpler, people have invented many binary-coding methods, whose substantial difference lies in the coding methods of **negative numbers**.

Now we will introduce some common coding methods: true code, ones-complement code, and complement code.

1. True Code

True code makes the separate sign bit 0 or 1 and combines the absolute value of the number with the other bits to achieve the coding. It is also called "sign–absolute value represented" coding.

Firstly we will show how to represent a signed integer in true code:

Suppose we use one byte in memory to store an integer, and its true code is like this:

$$X = +0101011 \qquad [X]_{\text{true}} = 00101011$$

$$X = -0101011 \qquad [X]_{\text{true}} = 10101011$$

Here $[X]_{\text{true}}$ are the machine number, and X is called its true value.

For decimal fraction, the sign bit in the true code is the one to the left of the decimal point. For example:

$$X = 0.1011 \qquad [X]_{\text{true}} = 0.1011$$

$$X = -0.1011 \qquad [X]_{\text{true}} = 1.1011$$

True code is simple and intuitive, and the conversion between it and its true value is convenient. However, true code has several shortcomings:

Firstly, the true code representation for 0 is not unique, since:

$$[+0]_{\text{true}} = 000\ldots0 \qquad [-0]_{\text{true}} = 100\ldots0$$

The ambiguity of 0 can cause trouble when computer makes verdicts on 0.

Secondly, when we use true code to do arithmetic operations, the sign bit should be handled independently and the operation rule is complicated. Take addition as an example: if the two addends have the same signs, the sum will have exactly the same sign. Otherwise, we have to subtract the small number from the big number and the result will inherit the sign of the bigger number. Furthermore, it is difficult for computer hardware to implement operations such as borrowing. Because of the shortcomings true code has, people try to find other better representations.

2. Ones-complement code

Ones-complement code is rarely used, but it may help us understand the meaning of complement code, so we introduce it here.

The ones-complement code of a positive number is the same as true code.

The ones-complement code of a negative number is like this:

The sign bit is the same as the one in true code (1), and the other bits are reversed $(0 \rightarrow 1, 1 \rightarrow 0)$, for example:

$$X = +1100110 \qquad [X]_{true} = 01100110 \qquad [X]_{ones\text{-}comp} = 01100110$$

$$X = -1100110 \qquad [X]_{true} = 11100110 \qquad [X]_{one's\ comp} = 10011001$$

$$X = +0000000 \qquad [X]_{true} = 00000000 \qquad [X]_{one's\ comp} = 00000000$$

$$X = -0000000 \qquad [X]_{true} = 10000000 \qquad [X]_{one's\ comp} = 11111111$$

Like true code, in ones-complement code we have positive zero and negative zero.

The ones-complement code of a decimal fraction is as follows:

$$X = 0.1011 \qquad [X]_{true} = 0.1011 \qquad [X]_{one's\ comp} = 0.1011$$

$$X = -0.1011 \qquad [X]_{true} = 1.1011 \qquad [X]_{one's\ comp} = 1.0100$$

3. Complement code
a) Modulus

In physics, a modulus is the capacity of a certain measurement. For example, the counter of a clock we daily use is reset to zero after it reaches 12 (discarding one 12), and thus the modulus of the clock is 12. This is a kind of mod operation in mathematics. C++ uses "%" as the mod arithmetic operator. For example:

$$14 \% 12 = 2$$

If the current time is 6 o'clock while your watch shows 8, then how do you adjust the watch? You can either subtract two hours from your watch or add 10 more hours, and the result is the same:

$$8 - 2 = 6$$

$$(8 + 10) \bmod 12 = 6$$

In the modulus system:

$$8 - 2 = (8 + 10) \bmod 12$$

The above equation holds since 2 and 10 are mutual complements in modulus-12 $(2 + 10 = 12)$.

Thus, we can get such a conclusion: in the modulus system, subtracting A from B, or adding a negative number $-B$ to A, is the equivalent to adding the complement of B to A:

$$8 + (-2) = (8 + 10) \bmod 12$$

We call 10 the complement of -2 in modulus-12. Once we use complement code to represent negative numbers, we can use addition to substitute for subtraction.

In a computer system, the word length is fixed. So for an n bit number, the modulus is $111 \ldots 11(n$ bits$) + 1$. In fact, the value of the modulus has exceeded the value that a single machine word can represent. Therefore, the modulus cannot be represented in the machine (we will introduce the range of the value computer can represent in Chapter 1.4.6). So if an operation result is larger than the modulus, the modulus will be discarded, which in fact is a modulus operation.

The modulus of an n-bit (including the sign bit) integer is 2^n, while the modulus of an n-bit decimal fraction (the sign bit is prior to the decimal point) is 2.

b) Complement code
From the above discussion we can know that for a negative binary number, we can get its complement code by adding its modulus) to its original value (i.e., subtracting the absolute value of the number from its modulus). For example

$$X = -0110 \quad [X]_{complementcode} = 2^4 + (-0110) = 1010$$
$$X = -0.1011 \quad [X]_{complementcode} = 2 + (-0.1011) = 1.0101$$

Since there is no original value stored in the computer, it is not easy for the computer to implement the above formula. Anyhow, we can derive another simple method:

For a negative number, we can increase its ones-complement code by 1 to get its complement code.

For example: $X = -1010101$

$$[X]_{true} = 11010101$$
$$[X]_{ones-complementcode} = 10101010$$
$$[X]_{complementcode} = 10101011$$

For example: $X = -0.1011$

$$[X]_{true} = 1.1011$$
$$[X]_{ones-complementcode} = 1.0100$$
$$[X]_{complementcode} = 1.0101$$

For a positive number, the three code forms are the same.

An important feature of complement code is that the representation of 0 is unique:

$$[+0] = 0\,0\,...0 \qquad [-0] = 1\,1\,...1 + 1 = \boxed{1}\,\boxed{0\,0...\,0}$$

$$\underbrace{}_{\text{n digits}} \qquad \underbrace{}_{\text{n digits}} \qquad \underbrace{}_{\text{n digits}}$$

Auto discarded

The above method of getting complement code is usually called "ones-complement plus 1". We will not prove this method here. Readers only need to get a basic understanding of complement code and not to get bewildered by the data storage form in memory in further studies.

c) Arithmetic rules in complement code operation

Another advantage of complement code is that it is the simplest representation method when numerical information is taken apart in arithmetic operations. Firstly, **the sign bit can be treated as part of the value** in operations and we can still get the correct sign of the result. Secondly, **subtractions can be converted into additions**, which lead to simpler arithmetic circuits.

For example, let's see how to calculate $67 - 10$ in a computer (here the number's carry system is indicated by subscripts):

$$[+67_{10}]_{\text{true}} = 01000011_2 \qquad [+67_{10}]_{\text{complementcode}} = [+67_{10}]_{\text{true}}$$
$$[-10_{10}]_{\text{true}} = 10001010_2 \qquad [-10_{10}]_{\text{complementcode}} = 11110110_2$$

$$
\begin{array}{r}
0\,1\,0\,0\,0\,0\,1\,1_2 \\
+\quad 1\,1\,1\,1\,0\,1\,1\,0_2 \\
\hline
1\quad 0\,0\,1\,1\,1\,0\,0\,1_2 = 57_{10}
\end{array}
$$

$[+67_{10}]_{\text{complementcode}}$

$[-10_{10}]_{\text{complementcode}}$

∟ The carry bit is discarded

Since the word length is only 8 bits, the carry bit of the most significant bit in addition is automatically discarded, in order to get the effect of mod operation (discarding a modulus).

Note that **the result of arithmetic operations on complement code is still complement code.** In the example above, we can know from the sign bit that the result is positive, and thus the complement code is the same as its true code, which is the decimal number 57.

If the result is negative, then the result is the complement code of the negative number:

For example: $10 - 67 = ?$

$$[+10_{10}]_{\text{true}} = 00001010_2 = [+10_{10}]_{\text{complementcode}}$$
$$[-67_{10}]_{\text{true}} = 11000011_2 \quad [-67_{10}]_{\text{complementcode}} = 10111101_2$$

$$0\,0\,0\,0\,1\,0\,1\,0_2$$
$$+\quad 1\,0\,1\,1\,1\,1\,0\,1_2$$
$$\overline{\qquad\qquad\qquad}$$
$$1\,1\,0\,0\,0\,1\,1\,1_2$$

$[\text{Result}]_{\text{complementcode}} = 1\,1\,0\,0\,0\,1\,1\,1_2 \qquad [\text{Result}]_{\text{true}} = 1\,0\,1\,1\,1\,0\,0\,1_2$

The true value of the result is -0111001, which is the decimal number -57.

Can we conclude from the examples above that arithmetic operations on complement code are always correct? Let's see the following example:

$$85_{10} + 44_{10} = ?$$
$$0\,1\,0\,1\,0\,1\,0\,1_2$$
$$+\quad 0\,0\,1\,0\,1\,1\,0\,0_2$$
$$\overline{\qquad\qquad\qquad}$$
$$1\,0\,0\,0\,0\,0\,0\,1_2$$

From the sign bit we know that the result is negative, while the sum of two positive numbers can never be negative. Where is the problem? It is caused by "overflow", i.e., the result exceeds the range of numbers that certain bits of binary number can represent (we will introduce this problem in 1.4.6).

1.4.5 Fixed Point Number and Floating-Point Number

Numerical data can be positive or negative, integer or decimal. In this section we will introduce how to represent decimal data. In computers we commonly use a floating point to represent decimal data.

A number N can be represented using a floating point (i.e., scientific notation) like this:

$$N = M \times R^E$$

R is the base. Once the base is set in a computer, it cannot be changed. So the value of the base is implicit in data representation. In manual computation we usually use the decimal system (i.e., the base is 10), while in computers we usually use the binary system (i.e., the base is 2).

E is the power of R. We also call it the exponent of N. The exponent specifies the position of the decimal point of N, and the length of the exponent specifies the range of the value.

M contains all significant digits of N, and is called the mantissa of N. The length of M reflects the precision of the data.

Exponent and mantissa are both signed values, and they can be represented by using different code systems. For example, mantissa often uses true code or complement code, while exponents often use complement code.

The specific format of a floating-point number varies among different computers. Suppose we have a 16-bit machine; then a binary number may have 4 bits for its exponent and 12 bits for its mantissa.

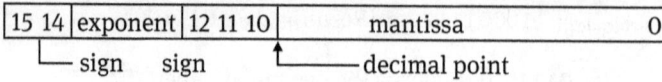

| 15 14 | exponent | 12 11 10 | mantissa | 0 |

sign   sign   decimal point

Here is a practical example, where the exponent and the mantissa are represented by complement code and true code respectively.

| 0 | 010 | 1 | 110............. 0 | represents $(-0.11 \times 10^{10})_2$

| 1 | 101 | 0 | 110............. 0 | represents $(0.11 \times 10^{-11})_2$

1.4.6 The Number Range that can be Represented

The number range that can be represented in a computer depends on the data bits and the representation used. An M bit integer (including the sign bit) can be as large as $2^{m-1}-1$ and as small as $-(2^{m-1}-1)$ when represented by true code or ones-complement code; if it is represented by complement code, it can range from -2^{m-1} to $2^{m-1}-1$.

One thing we should mention is that the representation of 0 by complement code is unique, so $[X]_{complementcode} = 100 \ldots \ldots 0$ corresponds to the original value of -2^{m-1} (note that the complement code $100 \ldots \ldots 0$ is a special case, the value 1 on the bit that has weight 2^{n-1} represents both sign and value). Here we do not prove the number range that complement code can represent, but you can prove it yourself if interested.

For example, suppose $M = 8$, then the number range that true code can represent is $127 \sim +127$. The case in ones-complement code is the same as true code, while for complement code it is $-128 \sim +127$. For an n-bit fixed point decimal number, the bit to the left of the decimal point is the sign bit. The number range that true code or ones-complement code represents is $-(1 - 2^{-n}) \sim (1 - 2^{-n})$, while for complement code it is $-1 \sim (1 - 2^{-n})$.

The range of a floating-point number that can be represented depends on the number of bits in the exponent and mantissa.

Suppose the exponent is an R-bit integer (represented by complement code), and the mantissa is an n-bit fixed point decimal number (represented by true code); then the range of floating-point number is:

$$-(1 - 2^{-n}) \times 2^{(2^{r-1}-1)} - 1 \quad \sim \quad +(1 - 2^{-n}) \times 2^{(2^{r-1}-1)}$$

If we want to enlarge the number range that can be presented, we should increase the number of bits in the exponent. Each 1-bit increase in the exponent will double the number range. If we want to increase the precision, we should increase the number of bits in the mantissa. In computers that have fixed word length, the proportion of bits for exponents and bits for the mantissa should be appropriate. However, if we want to satisfy requirements both in range and in precision, we usually use a double word or even more words to store a floating-point number.

1.4.7 Representation of Non-numerical Information

In computers, non-numerical information is also encoded using 0 and 1. Here we will focus on the coding schemes for Chinese and Western characters.

The most popular coding scheme for western characters is "American Standard Code for Information Interchange", shortened as ASCII code. It includes 10 numbers, 95 printable characters including upper and lower case English characters and specific characters, and 33 control characters. ASCII code uses 7 bits of a byte to represent a character and can represent at most $2^7 = 128$ characters.

Since ASCII code does not use the most significant bit in a byte, many systems use this bit as the check bit to improve the transmission reliability.

Aside from ASCII, there is another code called EBCDIC code (Extended Binary Coded Decimal Interchange Code), which uses 8 bits to represent a character. EBCDIC can thus represent at most 256 characters.

So how can we represent Chinese characters in computers? There are many more Chinese characters (at least thousands of ordinary characters) compared to English characters, and obviously one byte (of eight digits) is far from enough. Now we have two-byte, three-byte or even four-byte code schemes for Chinese characters and the most popular one is "Chinese Standard Code for Information Interchange" (GB2312-80), shortened as GB code. GB code is a two-byte code scheme, and it uses seven bits of each byte to encode a Chinese character.

Chinese character coding and Western character coding coexist in a computer. How to distinguish them is important, because different types of information have different process modes. One method is to set the most significant bits in each pair of bytes in GB2312-80 as "1", while keeping the most significant bit in each byte in ASCII code as "0". Then software (or hardware) can distinguish them.

1.5 The Development Process of Programs

Before we start learning programming, let's first get a basic understanding of the development process of a program and learn some elementary terms. In the following chapters, readers may gain a deeper comprehension of the knowledge.

1.5.1 Elementary Terms

Source program: program written in source language and needing to be translated. It can be an assembly language or high-level programming language (such as C++).

Object program: program translated from source program. It can be represented by machine instructions (thus it is also called "object code"), assembly instructions, or other intermediate languages.

Translator: program that translates a source program into its equivalent object program. To a translator, source program is the input and object program is the output. There are three kinds of translators: assembler, compiler, and interpreter.

Assembler: assembler translates a source program written in assembly language into the object program formed by machine instructions. Thus, the source program written in assembly language should be processed by the assembler first to turn into the equivalent object program.

Compiler: translate a source program written in high-level programming language into the object program. If the object program consists of assembly instructions, we still need to run the assembler to translate them into machine instructions.

Interpreter: another translator that translates source program written in high-level programming language into machine instructions. Its difference from a compiler is that the interpreter executes programs during translation. That is, it reads a statement, translates it, and executes it. This action sequence is repeated until all statements have been translated and executed. An interpreter does not generate a whole object program. For some statements inside the loop body, the interpreter needs to translate and execute them many times. Therefore, compared with a compiler, it is slower in execution and less efficient.

1.5.2 The Development Process

The process of developing a C++ program includes editing, compiling, linking, running, and debugging. In editing we put the source program into the computer and save the code as a .cpp file. Compiling converts the source program into machine instructions. However, the compiled program cannot be executed directly, and we need to link multiple target files together with some files in the library to create an executable file suffixed with .exe. In the end we also need to run and debug the program.

When a compiler is compiling and a linker is linking, they will check the program and show all the errors in the screen. Errors found in the compiling stage are grammar errors and those found in the linking stage are link errors. That is the development process of a C++ program.

Figure 1.1 is the development process of a C++ program.

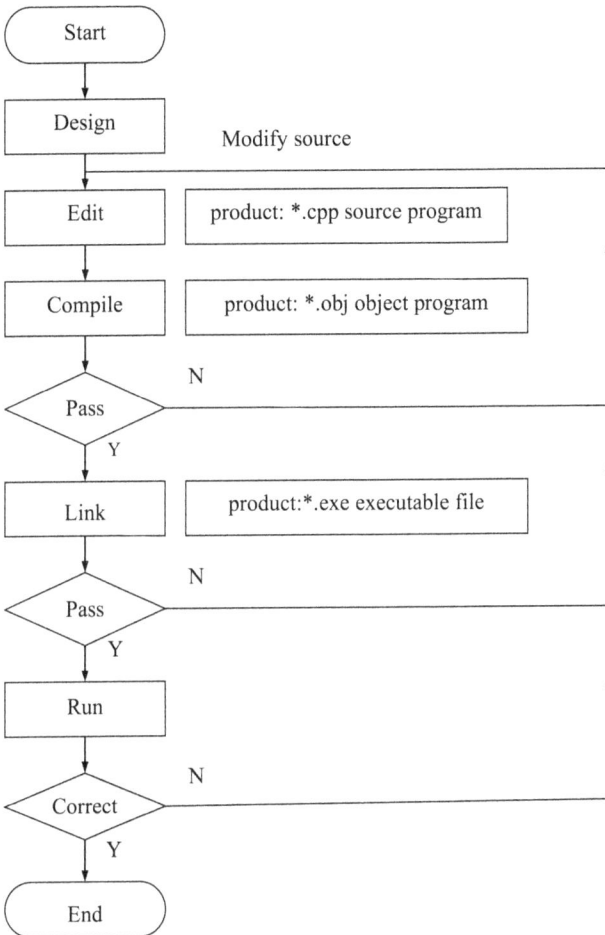

Fig. 1.1: The development process of a C++ program.

1.6 Summary

A language is a system with a set of grammars and lexical rules. It is a tool of thinking, and ideas are expressed by languages. Programming languages are languages that can be recognized by a computer and are used for describing the solutions for problems. Programming languages can be classified as machine languages, assembly languages, high-level programming languages and object-oriented programming languages. This book focuses on the C++ programming language, which is the most widely used OO programming language.

Object-oriented software engineering is the application of the object-oriented method in software engineering. It consists of object-oriented analysis (OOA), object-oriented design (OOD), object-oriented programming (OOP), object-oriented test (OOT), and object-oriented software maintenance (OOSM), etc.

Computers can process data information, while their operation is conducted by control information. All the information in computers is encoded using a binary numeral system, while different data types may have different notations, which is also one of the concerns of this book.

Exercises

1.1 Describe the development process of computer programming languages.

1.2 What are the features of an object-oriented programming language?

1.3 What is structured programming? Describe the advantages and disadvantages.

1.4 What does "object" mean? What is an object-oriented method? Describe the features of this method.

1.5 What does encapsulation mean?

1.6 What does object-oriented software engineering contain?

1.7 Describe the categories of information in computers.

1.8 What is a binary numeral system? Describe the advantages and disadvantages of this numeral system.

1.9 Convert the following decimal values into binary and hexadecimal complement codes.
a) 2   b) 9   c) 93
d) −32   e) 65535   f) −1

1.10 Convert the following representations into decimal values.
a) $(1010)_2$ b) $(10001111)_2$ c) $(0101111111000011)_2$
d) $(7F)_{16}$ e) $(2D3E)_{16}$ f) $(F10E)_{16}$

1.11 Make a simple comparison between true code, ones-complement code, and complement code.

2 Elementary C++ Programming

The chapter begins with a brief look at the history of C++ the language and its characteristics. Then we look at the basic elements that construct a C++ statement – character sets, keywords, identifiers, operators, etc. Program design mainly includes data structure design and algorithm design. Data types, data type conversion, and simple data input/output are the basic knowledge elements of data. The chapter introduces basic C++ data types and user-defined data types. Algorithms consist of a series of control structures. The sequential, case, and loop structures described in this chapter are the most fundamental control structures in program design, and they are also the basis of complex algorithms.

2.1 An Overview of C++ Language

2.1.1 Origins of C++

C++ originates from the C language. Thus, to understand C++ better, the history of the C language should be reviewed first. The C language was first realized on a DEC PDP-11 computer in 1972. Dennis Ritchie, working in Bell Laboratory, created it based on the B language. After that, continuous improvements have been made and nowadays the comparatively popular C languages are based on ANSI C.

The C language has many advantages, such as its simplicity and agility, its abundant operators and data structures, its structured controlling statements, and its high efficiency when executing programs. It combines the advantages of both high-level languages and assembly language: compared with other high-level languages, the C language can access physical address directly; while compared with assembly language, it has better readability and portability. Because of all these features, the C language has been widely used by numerous programmers, and there are many C library codes and developing environments.

However, since the C language is a procedure-oriented programming language, like other procedure-oriented languages, it cannot meet the needs of software development that uses object-oriented methods. C++ was then created from C to support object-oriented programming. It is a general-purpose language. It was created by Bjarne Stroustrup, a doctor at AT&T Bell Labs, in 1980.

Since the primary objective in creating the C++ language was to make it a better C, C++ has successfully solved all the problems in C. Another important goal of C++ was to support object-oriented programming, and thus **class** was introduced. The initial name for C++ was "C with Class", and later in 1983 it was formally renamed as **C++**. The standardization of C++ began in 1989 and an ANSI C++ standardization draft was made in 1994. In the following years, continuous improvements were made before it was

https://doi.org/10.1515/9783110471977-002

approved by the ISO (International Standardization Organization) as an international standard in November, 1998, known then as the current C++.

2.1.2 Characteristics of C++

The C++ language has two main characteristics: it is fully compatible with C and it supports object-oriented methods.

First of all, C++ is indeed a better C. It keeps some features of C, such as C's simplicity, high efficiency, and closeness with assembly language. Furthermore, it reforms and expands the type system of C, making it safer and its compiling system more capable of detecting type errors than C.

As C++ is compatible with C, many C codes can be used in C++ without any modification. Many library functions and utility software written in C can be used in C++. In addition, the widespread use of the C language promotes the spread of both C++ and object-oriented techniques.

However, from another perspective, C++'s compatibility makes it not a pure object-oriented language. It supports both procedure-oriented programming and object-oriented programming.

The most meaningful feature of C++ is that it supports object-oriented programming. Although its compatibility with C makes it have dual characteristics, conceptually speaking it is totally different from C. Thus we had better write C++ with an object-oriented way of thinking.

If you already have some procedure-oriented programming experience, we suggest that you pay more attention to the object-oriented feature of C++ and less attention to its similar parts with C, for C and other procedure-oriented high-level programming languages are similar in design methods.

However, beginner programmers cannot overlook the compatible parts of C++ with C, although they are not the main content of C++. This is because that many elements such as data types, controlling structures of algorithms, functions, etc. are not only basic components of procedure-oriented programming, but also fundamental knowledge for object-oriented programming. In object-oriented programming, objects are the basic units for a program, while their static attributes always need to be represented by certain data type, and their dynamic attributes need to be realized by their member functions whose implements are, after all, the design of algorithms.

2.1.3 C++ Programming Examples

The following is an example of C++ programming. Since the characteristics of object-oriented programming have not been discussed, Example 2.1 is only a procedure-oriented program, by which we can find out what a computer program looks like and how to use it to control the operations of a computer.

Example 2.1: A simple C++ program.

```
//2_1.cpp
#include<iostream>
using namespace std;
int main()
{
    cout<<"Hello!\n";
    cout<<"Welcome to c++!\n";
}
```

Here, *main* is the main function name, and its function body is enclosed in a pair of braces {}. Function is the smallest functional unit in C++ programs. In a C++ program there must be one and only one function named *main()*, which denotes the starting point of the execution of the program. The *int* before *main()* is the type of the return value of the function (the return value of function will be detailed in Chapter 3). Inside the function body there are statements, and each of them is ended by a semicolon (;). *cout* is an output stream object. It is a predefined object in the C++ system and contains many useful output functions. Output operations are implemented by the operator "<<", whose function is to direct the character string inside the following double quotation marks to the standard output device (monitor). Chapter 9 will detail the output stream and here readers just need to know that "*cout<<*" is used to achieve outputs.

The following words in this program

```
#include<iostream>
```

tell the C++ compiler to read the source codes in the *iostream* file into this text file when it preprocesses the program. Here *#include* is called a compiling directive. The file *iostream* declares the information needed by the input and output operations of a program, and also the information about cout and <<. Files of this kind are **referred to as header files**, for they are always embedded at the beginning of a program. If some system functions are used in a C++ program, relative header files must be included.

The expression using namespace is a directive concerning namespace whose concept will be covered in Chapter 5. Beginner programmers are only required to add the following statement after including the iostream file:

```
using namespace std;
```

When we finish writing a program text, we need to store it as a .cpp file, which is called a **C++ source file**. It will generate an **executable file** suffixed with .exe after compiling and linking through the compiling system. All the examples used in this book are developed in the integrated environment of Microsoft Visual C++ 6.0. For more information about developing programs in this environment, please refer to matching books of exercises and experiment guidance.

Example 2.1 has an output on the screen as follows:

```
Hello!
Welcome to c++!
```

Header files that the C++ compiler system provides can be divided into two categories. One is header files from the standard C++ libraries, which have no suffixes, such as <iostream> used in the above example; the other follows the C language style and has a suffix ".h", such as <iostream.h>. Examples and exercises in this book use header files from standard C++ libraries (i.e., without any suffix). However, some other textbooks and examinations may still use the latter kind of header files with a suffix ".h".

2.1.4 Character Set

The character set is the basic element of the C++ language. When programming with C++, all the components are made up of characters except for character data. Character set of C++ is made up of the following characters:

Alphabetic characters: A~Z, a~z
Numerical characters: 0~9
Special characters:

space	!	#	%	^	&	*	_(underscore)
+ =	–	~	<	>	/	\	
' "	;	.	,	()	[]	{}	

2.1.5 Lexical Tokens

The lexical token is the smallest lexical unit. Here we will introduce the keywords, identifiers, characters, operators, separators, and blanks in C++.

1. Keywords
A keyword in C++ is a word that is predefined and reserved for some specific usage. C++ now has the following keywords:

auto	bool	break	case	catch	char	class
const	const_cast	continue	default	delete	do	double
dynamic_cast	else	enum	explicit	extern	false	float
for	friend	goto	if	inline	int	long
mutable	namespace	new	operator	private	protected	public
register	reinterpret_cast	return	short	signed	sizeof	static
static_cast	struct	switch	template	this	throw	true
try	typedef	typeid	typename	union	unsigned	using
virtual	void	volatile	while			

Further introduction of their meanings and usages will be covered later in this book.

2. Identifiers

Identifiers are defined by programmers. They are used to name entities in the program body such as functions, variables, classes, and objects. Rules to make up a C++ identifier are as follows:

- Start with upper cases, lower cases or underscore (_).
- Must consist of upper cases, lower cases, underscore (_) or numbers (0~9).
- Upper cases and lower cases stand for different identifiers.
- Should not be C++ keywords.

For example, Rectangle, Draw_line and _No1 are all legal identifiers, while NO.1 and 1st are illegal identifiers.

3. Literal Constants

Literal constants are directly represented by symbols in programs, which include numbers, characters, alphabetic strings, and Boolean literals. They are to be covered in the next section.

4. Operators

Operators are symbols used to realize operations, such as +, –, *, /, and ... Details of operators are to be covered in the second section of this chapter and the following chapters.

5. Separators

Separators are used to detach lexical tokens or program bodies. C++ has the following separators:

() {} , : ;

These separators stand for no actual operation and are only used to construct programs. More details will be covered later.

6. Blanks

A program body is divided into lexical tokens and blanks during its lexical analysis in the compiling phase. Blank is the general name for space, tab (generated by pressing TAB), line break (generated by pressing ENTER), or comment.

Blanks are used to identify the starting and ending positions of lexical marks. But for this function, all the other blanks are omitted. Thus you do not need to write programs strictly line by line: anywhere blanks are left, a new line can be made. For example, the following three ways perform, in effect, the same function:

```
    int i;
and,
    int i;
and
    int

    i

    ;
```

However, it is strongly recommended to write programs with clearness and readability. This is because programs not only need to be executed by machines, but also need to be revised and maintained by programmers.

Comments in a program are used to explain and interpret the program to improve its readability. When the compiling system compiles the source program, it first strips the comments. Thus comments have no effect on the realization of a program's functions. In addition, since they are stripped by the compiler before code generation, they will not increase the size of the final executable program. Comments, if used properly, can make a program more readable.

There are two ways to add comments in C++. One follows the C language, using "/*" and "*/" to enclose comments just as follows:

```
/* This is
a comment.
*/
int i; /* i is an integer */
```

Here all the symbols between "/*" and "*/" are to be recognized as comments.

The other way uses "//" to delimit a single-line comment. Starting from "//" and ending until the finishing point of that line, all the characters in between are viewed as comments. For example,

```
// This is a comment.
int i; // i is an integer
```

2.2 Basic Data Types and Expressions

Data are the objects programs process. They can be classified according to their characteristics. For example, in mathematics there are concepts like integers, real numbers, etc.; in daily life we need character strings to denote a person's names and addresses; the answers of some questions can only be "yes" or "no" (i.e., "true" or "false" in logic). Different types of data have different processing methods. For example, both integers and real numbers can participate in arithmetical operations, while real numbers differ from integers in that they have to retain a certain part of decimal fractions; character strings can be concatenated; logical data can participate in logical operations such as "and", "or", "non-", etc.

We write programs to solve practical questions in the objective world. Therefore, high-level languages provide us with a wealth of data types and operations. C++ data types are divided into two categories: basic data types and user-defined data types. Basic data types are predefined within the C++ compiler system. We will first introduce the basic data type in this section.

2.2.1 Basic Data Types

Basic C++ data types are shown in Table 2.1.

We can see from Table 2.1 that basic C++ data types include *bool* (Boolean type), *char* (character type), *int* (integer type), *float* (floating-point type, representing real numbers), and *double* (double-precision floating-point type, or double-precision type). Apart from *bool* these data types can be classified into two main categories: integer and floating-point. *char* is an integer type essentially. It is a one-length integer, so usually we use the ASCII code to store characters. Keywords *signed*, *unsigned*, *short*, and *long* are called qualifiers.

When *short* is used to qualify *int*, *short int* denotes short integers, occupying 2 bytes. *int* can be omitted here, so the one listed in Table 2.1 is written as *short* instead of *short int*. *long* can be used to qualify *int* and *double*. When *long* qualifies *int*, *long int* denotes long integers, occupying 4 bytes. *int* here also can be omitted. From Table 2.1 we can see that *int* and *long* have the same length, so why do we need to provide two different data types in the syntax? This is because the number of bytes that *int* needs may not be the same in different systems, and we only listed the situation under the VC++6.0 compiler environment (also the situation in most compiler environments).

Tab. 2.1: Basic C++ Data Types.

Name	Length (bytes)	Range
bool	1	false, true
char(signed char)	1	$-128 \sim 127$
unsigned char	1	$0 \sim 255$
short(signed short)	2	$-32768 \sim 32767$
unsigned short	2	$0 \sim 65535$
int(signed int)	4	$-2147483648 \sim 2147483647$
unsigned int	4	$0 \sim 4294967295$
long(signed long)	4	$-2147483648 \sim 2147483647$
unsigned long	4	$0 \sim 4294967295$
float	4	$3.4 \times 10^{-38} \sim 3.4 \times 10^{38}$
double	8	$1.7 \times 10^{-308} \sim 1.7 \times 10^{308}$
long double	8	$1.7 \times 10^{-308} \sim 1.7 \times 10^{308}$

The numbers of bytes that *short* and *long* need are both fixed in any compiler system that supports standard C++. Therefore, if we want to write a program with good portability, we should declare the integer type as *short* or *long* instead of *int*.

signed and *unsigned* can be used to qualify *char* type and *int* type (including *long int*). *signed* indicates signed numbers, while *unsigned* indicates unsigned numbers. Signed integers are stored in computers in the two's complement form, and its most significant bit is the sign bit, where "0" denotes "positive" and "1" denotes "negative". Unsigned integers can only represent positive numbers, which are stored in the absolute form. Both *char* type and *int* type (including *long int*) in default (without qualification) are signed.

The value of *bool* (Boolean, also known as logical type) data can only be false or true. The number of bytes that the *bool* data needs may not be the same in different compiler systems. In the VC++6.0 compiler environment the *bool* type has only 1 byte.

Data that programs process can be divided into different types, while in each type the data can be constants or variables. We will detail all kinds of basic data types in the next section.

2.2.2 Constants

The value of a constant is immutable during the entire process of a program, i.e., a constant directly uses symbols (literals) to express its value. For example: *12, 3.5,* and *'A'* are all constants.

1. Integer Constants

Integer constants are integers in the form of literals. They include positive integers, negative integers, and zero. Integer constants can be represented in the decimal, octal, or hexadecimal form.

The general form of a decimal integer constant is the same as that in mathematics:

[±] several numbers from 0 to 9 ,

namely, a sign followed by several numbers from 0 to 9. Note that the numerical part cannot start with 0, and the positive sign in front of a positive number can be omitted.

The numerical part of an octal integer constant starts with 0, and its general form is:

[±] 0 several numbers from 0 to 7

The numerical part of a hexadecimal integer constant starts with 0x, and its general form is:

[±] 0x several numbers from 0 to 9 and/or letters from A to F (case insensitive)

Integer constants can use the suffix letter L (or l) to denote a long integer type, the suffix letter U (or u) to denote an unsigned type, or the suffix letters of both L and U (case insensitive) to denote an unsigned long integer type.

For example: *123, 0123*, and *-0x5af* are all legal constant forms.

2. Real Constants

Real constants are real numbers in the form of literals, and they have two representation forms: the general form and index form.

General form: for example: *12.5, -12.5* and so on.

Index form: for example, *0.345E+2* denotes 0.345×10^2 and *-34.4E-3* denotes -34.4×10^{-3}. Here the letter *E* is case insensitive. When using the index form to denote a real number, its integral part or the decimal fraction can be omitted, although they cannot be both omitted. For example: *.123E-1, 12.E 2*, and *1.E-3* are all correct forms, but *E-3* is wrong.

The default type of real constants is *double*, and the suffix F (or f) can convert a real constant into a float type. For example: *12.3f*.

3. Character Constants

A character constant is one character enclosed by single quotes, such as: *'a', 'D', '?'*, or *'$'*.

In addition, there are some characters that cannot be displayed or input by keyboard, such as ring, newline, tab, enter, etc. How does one write these characters into a program? C++ provides a set of escape sequences to represent these characters. The predefined escape sequences in C++ and their meanings are shown in Table 2.2.

Both general characters and nonprintable characters can be represented by octal or hexadecimal ASCII codes with the form as:

```
\nnn octal
\xnnn hexadecimal
```

nnn denotes a sequence of at most three octal or hexadecimal numbers.

Tab. 2.2: C++ Predefined Escape Characters.

Character constant form	ASCII code (hexadecimal)	Meaning
\a	07	Ring
\n	0A	Newline
\t	09	Horizontal tab
\v	0B	Vertical tab
\b	08	Backspace
\r	0D	Carriage Return
\\	5C	Character "\"
\"	22	Double quote
\'	27	Single quote

"CHINA" | C | H | I | N | A | \0 |

"a" | a | \0 |

'a' | a |

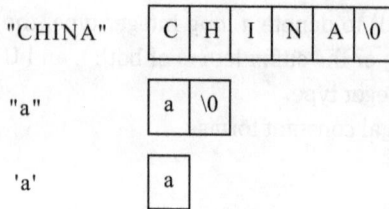

Fig. 2.1: Memory presentation of string and character.

For example, the hexadecimal ASCII code of 'a' is 61, so 'a' also can be written as '\x61.'

Since single quotes are the boundary of a character, a single quote itself needs to be represented using escape sequence '\'.'

Character data is stored in ASCII code in memory. Each character needs 1 byte, using the lowest 7 binary bits of the byte.

4. String Constants
String is short for string constants, using a pair of double quotes to enclose the character sequence. For example: *"abcd"*, *"China"*, and *"This is a string"*. are all string constants. Since double quotes are the boundary of characters, a double quote itself needs to be represented using the escape sequence. For example:

```
"Please enter \"Yes\" or \"No\""
```

means:

Please enter "Yes" or "No"

A string is different from a character. String is stored in memory as a sequence of characters in the order of the characters it owns. Each character takes up one byte, and at the end of the string '\0' should be added as an end mark. Figure 2.1 is an example. From the figure we can find out that string *"a"* and character 'a' are not the same.

5. Bool Constants
There are only two bool constants: false and true.

2.2.3 Variables

Variables have values that can change during the process of a program, and they need names to be identified.

1. Declaration and Definition of Variables
Just like constants, variables have various data types. We have to first declare the type and name of a variable before using it. Variables' names are also identifiers; thus to

name a variable, we should obey the rules of making up identifiers, which was introduced in the first section of this chapter. You can declare a number of variables with the same data type in one statement. The form of variable declaration statements is as below:

```
data type variable name 1, variable name 2, ..., variable name n;
```

For example, the following two statements declare two *int* variables and three *float* variables:

```
int num,total;
float v,r,h;
```

The declaration of a variable only tells the compiler the identifier-related information of the variable for the compiler to "know" the identifier, although it does not necessarily cause the allocation of memory. Defining a variable, on the other hand, means to allocate memory space for the variable to store data of the corresponding type. The variable's name is the name of its memory location. In C++ programs, defining a variable equals declaring the variable in most cases, and the definition is given when the variable is declared. The exception occurs when declaring external variables. We will introduce external variables in Chapter 5. We can initialize a variable while defining it, which is essentially initializing its memory location. For example:

```
int a=3;
double f=3.56;
char c='a';
```

There is another form of initialization when defining a variable, such as:

```
int a(3);
```

Note that although there are string constants in C++, there are no string variables. Then what type of variables should be used to store strings? In Chapter 6 we will introduce how to store strings using character arrays.

2. Storage Types of Variables

Besides data types, variables also have storage types. Storage types determine how to store variables:

auto storage type: a stack allocated memory space. It is a temporary storage, and the storage space can be overlapped by a number of variables multiple times.

register storage type: stored in general registers.

extern storage type: can be referred by all functions and procedures.

static storage type: stored at some fixed address in memory, and remains valid during the entire runtime.

For beginners, you can temporarily ignore storage types here. After studying the scope and visibility of variables in Chapter 5, you will get a deeper understanding of the storage types of variables.

2.2.4 Symbol Constants

Besides using literals to denote constants directly, we can also name a constant, which is called a symbol constant. Just like variables, symbol constants must be declared before they are used. The form of constant declaration statements is as follows:

```
const type of data constant name=constant value;
or:
type of data const constant name=constant value;
```

For example, we can declare a symbol constant to represent π:

```
const float pi=3.1415926;
```

Note that symbol constants must be initialized when they are declared and they cannot be changed during the process. For example, the following statement is wrong:

```
const float pi;
pi=3.1415926; //Wrong! Constants cannot be assigned.
```

Compared with using literals directly, giving a constant a meaningful name can improve the readability of the procedure. And if the procedure uses a literal constant (such as π = 3.14) several times, when the constant value needs to change (for example, π changes to 3.1416), multiple modifications may easily cause data inconsistency due to carelessness. By using symbol constants, since we only initialize a constant during its declaration, modifying it should be very easy and can thus avoid data inconsistency.

2.2.5 Operators and Expressions

Up to now, we have known the characteristics and representations of data types in C++. Then how does one process data? When handling a computation, normally we should list the formula and then calculate its value. Using C++ language to solve these problems has the same procedure. Expressions are the basic units for calculations in programs.

Expressions can be interpreted as formulas used for calculations, which are made up of operators (such as: + − * /), operands (can be constants, variables, etc.) and brackets. Implementing the operation of an expression, we can get the result of the expression. For example: $a+b$, x/y are all expressions.

Now we use a more strict language to define expression. It does not matter if you cannot fully understand it right now. Expressions are ubiquitous in programs and we will soon detail various types of expressions. You can gradually understand it in further studies.

An expression can be defined as follows:

- A constant or an identifier of a object is the simplest expression, and its value is the constant value or the value of the object.
- The value of an expression can take part in other operations, i.e., it can be used as operands for other operators, which forms a more complex expression.
- An expression inside a pair of brackets is still a expression, and its type and value are the same as the expression without brackets.

There are many operators in the C++ language, such as arithmetic operators, relational operators, logical operators, and so on. Some operators need two operands, and the form is as follows:

```
operand 1    operator    operand 2
```

Such operators are called binary operators. Some other operators only need one operand, and they are called unary operators.

Operators have precedence and associativity. When an expression contains more than one operator, the operation with the operator of higher precedence should be done first, and then the operations with the operators of lower precedence. If there are several operators of same precedence in an expression, the operation order depends on the operator's associativity. Associativity means the computation sequence where the operators on both sides of the operand have the same precedence. It can be from left to right or from right to left.

Now let us discuss the types of operators and expressions.

1. Arithmetic Operators and Arithmetic Expressions

Arithmetic operators in C++ include basic arithmetic operators, increments by one operator, and decrements by one operator. Expressions that are made up of arithmetic operators, operands, and brackets are called arithmetic expressions.

Basic arithmetic operators include: + (plus), − (minus or negative), * (multiply), / (divide), and % (modulus). "−" is a unitary operator when it represents a negative and is a dual operator in other cases. These basic arithmetic operators have the same meaning and precedence as their corresponding symbols in math. That is, multiplication and division have higher precedence compared with addition and subtraction, and operators associate left to right.

"%" is the modulus operator, can only be applied to integer operands. The result of the expression $a\%b$ is the remainder of a divided by b. The precedence of "%" is the same as "/".

Note that when "/" is used to divide two integers, its result is the integral part of the quotient, and the fractional part is automatically discarded. Therefore, the result of the expression 1/2 is 0.

In addition, ++ (increment) and -- (decrement) are two operators that are easy to use and often efficient in C++. They both are unitary operators and have two forms: preposition and postposition. For example: i++, --j, and so on. Both forms will add (subtract) 1 to the operand, and then rewrite the location of the operand in memory. For example, if the original value of the variable i is 1, then after computing the expression i++, the result of the expression is 2 and the value of i will also change to 2. If the original value of j is 2, then after computing the expression --j, the result of the expression is 1 and the value of j will change to 1. However, when the result of increment and decrement are used to continue participating in other operations, the preposition and postposition are totally different. For example, if the value of i is 1, the result of the following two statements are not the same:

```
cout<<i++;       // First output the value of i (which is 1), then do
                 // the increment, the value of i changes into 2
cout<<++i;       // First increase i to 2, then output the value of i
                 // (which is now 2)
```

2. Assignment Operators and Assignment Expressions

C++ provides several assignment operators, in which the simplest one is "=". Expressions with assignment operators are called assignment expressions. For example, n=n+5 is an assignment expression. An assignment expression assigns the value of the expression on the right side to the object on the left side. The type of the assignment expression is the same as the type of the object on the left side, and its result is the object's value after the assignment. The assignment operators associate from right to left. See the following assignment expressions:

a=5   Expression value is 5.
a=b=c=5   Expression value is 5; a, b, c are 5. The expression operates from
                    right to left: after c was updated to 5, the value of expression c=5
                    is 5, then b was updated to 5, and a was assigned to 5 at last.
a=5+(c=6)   Expression value is 11, a is 11, c is 6.
a=(b=4)+(c=6)   Expression value is 10, a is 10, b is 4, c is 6.
a=(b=10)/(c=2)   Expression value is 5, a is 5, b is 10, c is 2.

Besides "=", C++ also provides 10 kinds of compound assignment operators: +=, -=, *=, /=, %=, <<=, >>=, &=, ^=, and |=. The first five are compounded by assignment operators and arithmetic operators, while the rest are compounded by assignment operators and bitwise logical operators. We will talk about bitwise logical operators later. All the 10 kinds of compound assignment operators are binary operators, and they have the same precedence and associativity as "=". Now we give an example of compound assignment operators:

a+=3 equivalent to a=a+3

x*=y+8 equivalent to x=x*(y+8)

a+=a-=a*a equivalent to a=a+(a=a-a*a)

3. Comma Operation and Comma Expression

In C++, the comma is also an operator, and its form of use is as below:

expression 1, expression 2

Solve *expression 1* first, and then *expression 2*. The final result is the value of *expression 2*.

a=3*5,a*4   the final result is 60

4. Logical Operators and Logical Expressions

We often need to judge a situation or analyze complex conditions logically when we solve problems. C++ provides relational operators used for comparison and judgment, and logical operators used for logical analysis.

Relational operators are kinds of simple logical operators, and their precedences are as below:

< (less than) <= (less than or equal) > (greater than) >= (greater than or equal)   == (equal) != (not equal)

same precedence (high)   same precedence (low)

A relational expression connects two expressions using a relational operator. A relational expression is one of the simplest logical expressions. Its result type is *bool*, and the value can only be true or false.

For example: *a>b, c<=a+b, x+y==3* are all relational expressions. When *a* is greater than *b*, the value of expression *a>b* is true, and otherwise the value is false. When *c* is less than or equal to *a+b*, the value of expression *c<=a+b* is true, otherwise the value is false. When the value of *x+y* is 3, expression *x+y==3 is* true: be careful that there are two equals here, so do not mistake it as an assignment operator "=".

However, simple relation comparisons cannot meet the needs of programming, and we also need logical operators to connect simple relational expressions to form a more complex logical expression. The resulting type of logical expression is *bool*, and the value can only be true or false. The logical operators and their precedence in C++ are as below:

	! (non-)	&& (logical and)	|| (logical or)
Precedence order:	high	→	low

Tab. 2.3: Truth Table of Logical Operators.

a	B	!a	a&&b	a||b
True	True	false	true	true
True	False	false	false	true
False	True	true	false	true
False	False	true	false	false

"*!*" is an unitary operator, and its form of use is: *!* operand. A nonoperation reverses the operand: if the value of operand *a* is true, then the value of expression *!a* is false; if the value of operand *a* is false, then the value of expression *!a* is true.

"&&" and "//" are both binary operators. "&&"gets the logical *and* of the two operands, and the operation result is true only when both of the operands are true; otherwise the result will be false. "//"gets the logical *or* of the two operands, and the operation result will be false only when both of the operands are false; otherwise the result will be true.

The operation rule of logical operators can be explained through the truth table. Table 2.3 gives various logical operations on operand *a* and *b*, and the corresponding results.

For example, suppose there is a declaration as follows:

```
int a=5, b=3, x=10, y=20;
```

then the value of logical expression *(a>b)&&(x>y)* is false.

5. Conditional Operator and Conditional Expressions

The only ternary operator in C++ is the conditional operator "?", which can realize a simple selection. The form of the conditional expression is:

```
expression 1? expression 2: expression 3
```

expression 1 must be a bool-type expression. *expression 2* and *3* can be of any type, and the two types can be different. The result type of the conditional expression is the higher type of *expression 2* and *3* (we will explain this when we introduce type conversion).

The execution order of the conditional expression is: first estimate *expression 1*. If *expression 1* is true, then calculate *expression 2*, and the value of *expression 2* is the final result; if *expression 1* is false, then calculate *expression 3*, and the value of *expression 3* is the final result. Note that the precedence of the conditional operator is higher than assignment operators but lower than that of logical operators. The associativity acts from right to left.

Now let us have a look at an example of conditional expressions:

a) Let *a* and *b* be two integer variables, then the expression *(a<b)?a:b* is to get the smaller integer between the two

b) Let the variable *score* store the score of one student; now we need to determine whether it is greater than or equal to 60. If so, then output *"pass"*, otherwise output *"fail"*. The following statement can achieve this function:

```
cout<<(score>=60?"pass":"fail");
```

6. sizeof Operator

The **sizeof** operator is used to calculate the number of bytes a certain type of object occupies in memory. Its form of use is:

```
sizeof (type name)
```

or

```
sizeof (expression)
```

The result is the number of bytes occupied by the type specified by *"type name"*, or that occupied by the result type of *"expression"*. Note that this calculation process does not calculate the expression in the brackets.

7. Bitwise Operator

In the beginning of this chapter we mentioned that the C language has both the advantages of high-level languages and assembly languages. Bitwise operation embodies this advantage. Normally, the smallest data unit that high-level languages can deal with is bytes. But C is able to perform bitwise operations, and this advantage has now been fully inherited by C++. C++ provides 6 bitwise operators that can perform bitwise operations on integers.

a) Bitwise and(&)

The bitwise *and* operator applies the logical *and* operation on each corresponding bit of the two operands.

For example: compute *3 & 5*

$$
\begin{array}{r}
3: \quad 00000011 \\
5: (\&) \ 00000101 \\
\hline
3 \& 5: \quad 00000001
\end{array}
$$

By performing the bitwise *and* operation we can set designated bits in an operand to 0 (the other bits of the operand remain the same); or read out designated bits in an operand. See the following two examples:

1. The following statement sets the lowest bit of a char-type variable *a* to 0:

```
a = a & 0376;
```

2. Suppose there is *char c; int a;* The following statement reads out the lowest byte of *a*, and assigns it to *c*:

```
c = a & 0377;
```

b) Bitwise or(|)

The bitwise *or* operation applies the logical *or* operation on each corresponding bit of the two operands.

For example: compute *3 | 5*

$$
\begin{array}{ll}
3\text{:} & 0\,0\,0\,0\,0\,0\,1\,1 \\
5\text{: (|)} & 0\,0\,0\,0\,0\,1\,0\,1 \\
\hline
3\,|5\text{:} & 0\,0\,0\,0\,0\,1\,1\,1
\end{array}
$$

By performing the bitwise *or* operation we can set designated bits of an operand to 1 (the other bits of the operand remain the same). For example: set the lowest 8 bits of an int-type variable *a* to 1:

```
a = a | 0xff;
```

c) Bitwise xor(^)

The bitwise *xor* operation applies the *exclusive or* operation on each corresponding bit of the two operands. The rule of operation is: if two bits on the same bit position of the two operands are same, then the bit on that position of the result is 0; otherwise, it is 1.

For example: compute *071^052*

$$
\begin{array}{ll}
071\text{:} & 0\,0\,1\,1\,1\,0\,0\,1 \\
052\text{: (^)} & 0\,0\,1\,0\,1\,0\,1\,0 \\
\hline
071\text{^}052\text{:} & 0\,0\,0\,1\,0\,0\,1\,1
\end{array}
$$

By performing the bitwise *exclusive or* operation, we can flip designated bits of an operand. The result of (*bit* ^ *0*) is the original value of the bit. The result of (*bit* ^ *1*) is the opposite of the original value.

For example: if we want to flip the lowest four bits of 01111010, we can do the *xor* operation on it with 00001111:

$$
\begin{array}{ll}
& 0\,1\,1\,1\,1\,0\,1\,0 \\
(\text{^}) & 0\,0\,0\,0\,1\,1\,1\,1 \\
\hline
& 0\,1\,1\,1\,0\,1\,0\,1
\end{array}
$$

d) Bitwise complement(~)

Bitwise complement is a uniary operator, and it is used to flip each bit of a binary number. For example:

$$
\begin{array}{ll}
025\text{:} & 0000000000010101 \\
\text{~}025\text{:} & 1111111111101010
\end{array}
$$

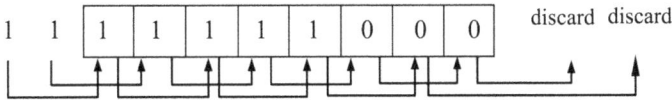

Fig. 2.2: The process of a>>2.

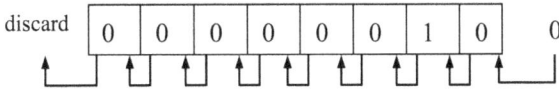

Fig. 2.3: The process of 2<<1.

e) Shift

In C++ there are two shift operators: the left shift operator (<<) and right shift operator (>>). Both of them are binary operators. The left operand of a shift operator is the number you want to perform the shift on, and the right operand gives the number of bits you want to shift.

Left shift shifts the binary value of the operand leftwards according to the designated number of bits. After the left shift, the vacated low bits will be filled with zero while the high bits that have been shifted out will be discarded.

Right shift shifts the binary value of a number rightwards according to the designated number of bits. After the right shift, the operator will discard the low bits that have been shifted out. If the number is an unsigned number, the operator will fill the vacated high bits with zero; if the number is a signed number, then the operator will fill the vacated high bits with zero or the sign bit depending on different systems. In VC++6.0, it fills the vacated bits with the sign bit.

Look at two examples:

1. If the value of a char-variable a is −8, then its complement code is 11111000. The value of expression $a>>2$ is −2. Figure 2.2 shows the process of this shift operation.
2. The value of expression 2<<1 is 4. Figure 2.3 shows the process.

Note that the result of a shift operation is the value of the expression ($a>>2$ and $2<<1$ in the above examples), while the value of the left operand of the shift operator (variable a and constant 2 in the above examples) will not change.

8. Operator Precedence

Table 2.4 lists the precedence and associativity of each operator in C++. Some of them have already been introduced, and others will be introduced in the following chapters.

9. Data type Conversions

We need type conversion when an operator in an expression has operands of different types. There are two kinds of type conversion: implicit conversion and explicit conversion.

Tab. 2.4: Operator Precedence.

Precedence	Operator	Associativity
1	[] () . -> postposition ++ postposition --	left → right
2	preposition ++ preposition -- sizeof & * +(positive sign) -(negative sign) ~ !	right → left
3	(cast)	right → left
4	.* ->*	left → right
5	* / %	left → right
6	+ -	left → right
7	<< >>	left → right
8	<> <= >=	left → right
9	== !=	left → right
10	&	left → right
11	^	left → right
12	|	left → right
13	&&	left → right
14	||	left → right
15	? :	right → left
16	= *= /= %= += -= <<= >>= &= ^= |=	right → left
17	,	left → right

a) Implicit conversion

Arithmetic operators, relational operators, logical operators, bitwise operators, and assignment operators are all binary operators, and the types of their two operands need to be the same. If the types of the operands involved in arithmetic operations or relational operations are not the same, the compiling system will convert them to a common type automatically (i.e., implicit conversion). The basic rule of conversion is to convert the lower data types into the higher data types. Here, a higher data type means greater data scope and higher precision. The order of basic data types (except for *bool*) is:

char short int unsigned long unsigned long float double

low ——————————————————————————————————→ high

Table 2.5 shows the rules of implicit conversion. This kind of conversion is safe because there is no loss of accuracy during the conversion.

The type of operands involved in the logical operations must be *bool*. If operands are of other types, the compiling system will convert them into the *bool* type automatically. The method is: convert nonzero data to *true* and zero to *false*.

The operands of bitwise operations must be integers. If the operands of a bitwise operation are different types of integers, the compiling system will do implicit conversions according to the rules in Table 2.5.

Tab. 2.5: Data Type Conversion.

Condition			Conversion
One *long-double-type* operand			Convert the other operand to long *double* type.
Does not meet the condition above, and there is one *double-type* operand			Convert the other operand to *double* type.
Does not meet the conditions above, and there is one *float-type* operand			Convert the other operand to *float* type.
Does not meet the conditions above (none of the two operands are *float-type*)	One *unsigned-long-type* operand		Convert the other operand to *unsigned long* type.
	One long-type operand, the other *unsigned int* type		Convert the other operand to *unsigned long* type.
	Does not meet the conditions above, and there is one *long-type* operand		Convert the other operand to long type.
	Does not meet the conditions above, and there is one *unsigned-int-type* operand		Convert the other operand to *unsigned int* type.
	Does not meet all the conditions above		Convert both operands to *int* type.

In assignment operations, the type of lvalue (value on the left side of the assignment operator) must be the same as the type of rvalue (value on the right side of the assignment operator). If not so, the compiling system will do implicit conversions. Note that this kind of implicit conversion does not follow the rules in Table 2.5, but always converts the type of rvalue to the type of lvalue before the assignment.

The following program shows the rules of data conversion:

```
float fVal;
double dVal;
int iVal;
unsigned long ulVal;
dVal = iVal * ulVal;   //convert iVal to unsigned long;
                       //the result of multiplication is converted to
                       //double.
dVal = ulVal + fVal;   //convert ulVal to float; the result of addition
                       //is converted to double.
```

b) Explicit Conversion

Explicit conversion converts the result type of an expression to another designated type. Before the emergence of standard C++, there are two syntax forms of explicit conversion:

```
type name (expression) //C++ cast notation
or
(type name) expression //C cast notation
```

Explicit conversion converts the result type of the *expression* to the type designated by *type name*. For example:

```
float Z = 7.56, fraction_part;
int whole_part;
whole_part = int(Z);              // when converting float type to int
                                  // type, it gets the integral part and
                                  // discards the decimal part
fraction_part = Z - (int)Z;       // subtract Z by its integral part and
                                  // get the decimal part
```

Cast operators in standard C++ include: static_cast, dynamic_cast, const_cast, and reinterpret_cast. Their syntax forms are:

```
const_cast<type identifier>(expression)
dynamic_cast<type identifier>(expression)
reinterpret_cast<type identifier>(expression)
static_cast<type identifier>(expression)
```

When using explicit conversion, note that:

- Cast is not safe. From the examples above we can find out that, when converting a higher data type to a lower data type, there is a loss of precision.
- Explicit conversion is temporary and one-time. For example, in the third row of the example above, cast operation *int(Z)* only takes out the value of *float*-type variable *Z*, converts it to *int* type temporarily and then assigns it to *whole_part*. At this time, the value of the memory unit that variable *Z* occupies does not really change. Therefore, when we use *Z* again, *Z* is still a *float*-type value.

2.2.6 Statement

Statements control the execution flow of a program, and executing a statement will cause corresponding results. C++ statements include the declaration statement, expression statement, case statement, loop statement, jump statement, compound statement, and label statement. For example, the declaration of a variable is achieved by a declaration statement; adding a semicolon (;) at the end of an expression can make it an expression statement; enclosing several statements with a pair of brackets can constitute a compound statement. We will introduce other statements in the following chapters.

Note that there are no assignment statements and function call statements in C++, and we have to use expressions to achieve assignment and function call. We have already introduced assignment expressions in Chapter 2.2.5, and we will introduce function calls in Chapter 3.

Adding a semicolon at the end of an assignment expression will make it a statement. For example:

```
a=a+3;
```

It is an expression statement, and it achieves the same function as an assignment statement.

The difference between an expression and expression statement is: an expression can be a part of another compound expression and continue to participate in operations, while a statement does not have this function.

2.3 Data Input and Output

2.3.1 I/O Stream

In C++, the movement of data from one object to another is abstracted as a "stream". One should establish a stream before using it, and delete it after use. To get data out from a stream is called an extract operation, and to put data into a stream is called an insert operation. I/O stream is used to achieve data input and output, and *cin* and *cout* are predefined stream-type objects. *cin* deals with standard inputs, i.e., input from terminal. *cout* deals with standard outputs, i.e., output directed to terminal.

2.3.2 Predefined Input and Output Operator

"<<" is the predefined input operator. Using it on the stream-type object *cout* can achieve most general screen outputs. The format is:

```
cout<< expression<< expression...
```

You can use successive output operators in one output statement to output several data items. You can write any compound expression after the output operator, and the compiling system will calculate its value and deliver it to the output operator automatically. For example:

```
cout<<''Hello!\n'';
```

It outputs the character string *"Hello!"* to the screen and then jumps to a new line.

```
cout<<''a+b=''<<a+b;
```

It outputs the character string "*a+b=*" and the result of *a+b* successively to the screen.

The most general keyboard input is to use the input operator on stream-type object *cin*. The format is:

```
cin>>expression >>expression...
```

In an input statement, one can write several input operators contiguously, each followed by an expression that stores the input variable. For example:

```
int a,b;
cin>>a>>b;
```

To input two int-type numbers from the keyboard, we can use space to separate the two numbers. If one enters:

```
5 6↵
```

Then the value of variable *a* is 5 and the value of variable *b* is 6.

2.3.3 Simple I/O Format Control

When using *cin* and *cout* for data input and output, computers can process any type of data according to the default format automatically. But this is not enough. We often need special formats. There are many ways to set a format, and we will detail them in Chapter 11. In this section we only introduce the simplest format control.

A C++ I/O-stream library provides some operators that can be directly embedded into the input/output statements to achieve I/O format control. To use these operators, we should first include an *iomanip* head file at the beginning of the source program. The commonly used I/O-stream library operators are listed in Table 2.6.

For example, if you want to output a floating number 3.1415 to the screen and jump to a new line, you can set the field width to five characters and keep two significant digits after the decimal point. The output statement would be:

```
cout<<setw(5)<<setprecision(3)<<3.1415<<endl;
```

Tab. 2.6: Commonly Used I/O-stream Library Operators.

Operator Name	Meaning
Dec	Use decimal system to represent data
Hex	Use hexadecimal system to represent data
Oct	Use octal system to represent data
Ws	Extract blank characters
Endl	Insert line break and flush the stream
Ends	Insert the null character
setprecision (int)	Set decimal digits of a floating number (include decimal point)
setw (int)	Set field width

2.4 The Fundamental Control Structures of Algorithms

After studying data types, expressions, assignment statements, and data input/output, we can write programs that can achieve simple functions. However, the programs we can write now are only statement sequences of an ordered execution. In fact, the objective world is not that simple, and the ways to solve problems usually cannot be described clearly using this kind of ordered steps.

For example: the following piecewise function calculates the value of y when entering a value of x.

$$y = \begin{cases} -1 & (x < 0) \\ 0 & (x = 0) \\ 1 & (x > 0) \end{cases}$$

It is not hard to calculate this problem manually, while the question is how to use programming languages to describe this calculation clearly and instruct the computer to do the calculation. Apparently, we cannot describe it using an ordered statement sequence. We must pass judgment be selective here: we need to use selective control structures.

See another simple example: count the average height of an arbitrary crowd. This is a simple calculation that even primary school students can do. But when the statistical data amount is very large, we have to use computers. The only advantage of a computer is its high calculation speed, since we have to describe the calculation method accurately for it. The major part of this algorithm is the accumulation, although to repeat the same action many times using ordered statements is clearly inappropriate (and impossible when there are large amounts of data). In this case we need a loop control structure.

There are three types of basic control structures: the sequential structure, case structure, and loop structure. The simplest one is the sequential structure, which we have already studied. Here we will introduce the case structure and loop structure. First of all, we will introduce program flow charts. A flow chart is used to describe an algorithm. Compared with natural language, a flow chart is simple, intuitive, and accurate. The symbols used in flow charts are listed in Figure 2.4.

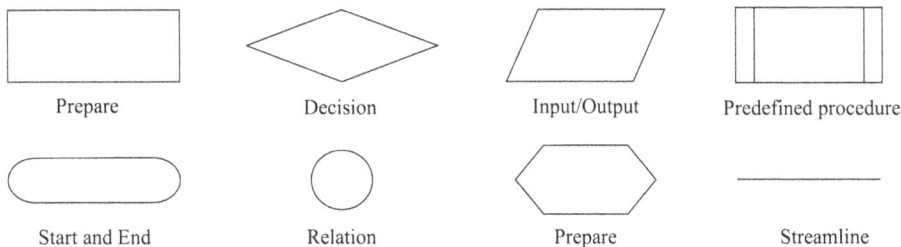

| Prepare | Decision | Input/Output | Predefined procedure |

| Start and End | Relation | Prepare | Streamline |

Fig. 2.4: Standard symbols in flow charts.

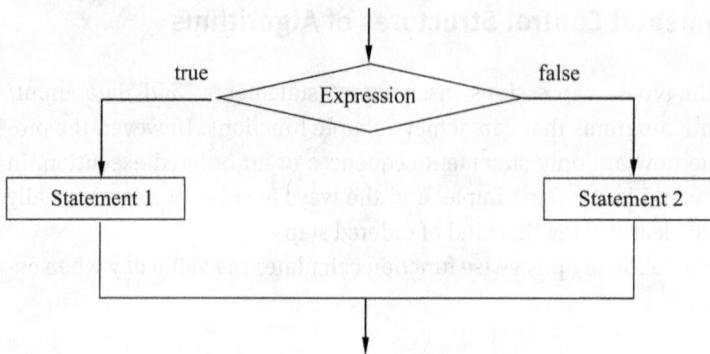

Fig. 2.5: Flow chart of statement *if else.*

2.4.1 Achieving Case Structure Using *if* Statement

if statements are designed to achieve case structure. Their syntax form is:

```
if (expression) statement 1
else statement 2
```

The execution order is: firstly evaluate the *expression*; if the *expression* is true, execute *statement 1*; otherwise execute *statement 2*. The flow chart of an *if* statement is shown in Figure 2.5.

Here *Statement 1* and *2* can also be several statements enclosed in brackets (known as a compound statement).

For example:

```
if (x>y) cout<<x;
else cout<<y;
```

The above statements output the larger number between *x* and *y*.

Statement 2 can be empty. When *statement 2* is empty, we can ignore *else*, and the syntax form becomes as the following:

```
if (expression) statement
```

For example:

```
if (x>y) cout<<x;
```

Example 2.2: Input a certain year and determine whether it is a leap year.
Analysis: a leap year is divisible by 4 but indivisible by 100, or is divisible by 400. Therefore, we can first store the value of the input year into the variable *year*, and then evaluate the expression *((year % 4 == 0 && year % 100 != 0) || (year % 400 == 0))*. If the expression is *true*, then the input year is a leap year; otherwise it is not.

Source code:

```
//2_2.cpp
#include <iostream>
using namespace std;
int main()
{
    int year;
    bool IsLeapYear;

    cout << "Enter the year: ";
    cin >> year;
    IsLeapYear = ((year % 4 == 0 && year % 100 != 0) ||
                  (year % 400 == 0));

    if (IsLeapYear)
        cout << year << " is a leap year" << endl;
    else
        cout << year << " is not a leap year" << endl;
}
```

The result (the underlined part is the input content, the rest is output content. All the examples afterwards are the same) is:

```
Enter the year: 2000
2000 is a leap year
```

2.4.2 Multiple Selection Structure

There are many problems that cannot be solved by only one simple selection, and they need multiple judgments and selections. There are several methods to achieve multiple selection structures:

1. Nested *if* Statement
Syntax form:

```
if (expression 1)
    if (expression 2) statement 1
    else expression 2
else
    if (expression 3) statement 3
    else statement 4
```

Attention: *statement 1, 2, 3*, and *4* can be a compound statement; the *if* of each hierarchy has to match with an *else*. If you want to omit one *else*, you must use {} to enclose the *if* statement of that hierarchy to force the correct hierarchy relation.

Example 2.3: Compare two numbers.

Analysis: compare two numbers x and y; there are three resulting possibilities: $x=y$, $x>y$, and $x<y$. Therefore, we need a multiple selection structure. We choose the nested *if else* statement here.

Source code:

```
//2_3.cpp
#include<iostream>
using namespace std;
int main()
{
    int x,y;
    cout<<"Enter x and y:";
    cin>>x>>y;
    if (x!=y)
        if (x>y)
            cout<<"x>y"<<endl;
        else
            cout<<"x<y"<<endl;
    else
        cout<<"x=y"<<endl;
}
```

Result 1:

```
Enter x and y:5 8
x<y
```

Result 2:

```
Enter x and y:8 8
x=y
```

Result 3:

```
Enter x and y:12 8
x>y
```

2. *if…else if* Statement

If all the nested *if* statements are in a branch *else*, we can use the statement *if…else if*. The syntax form is:

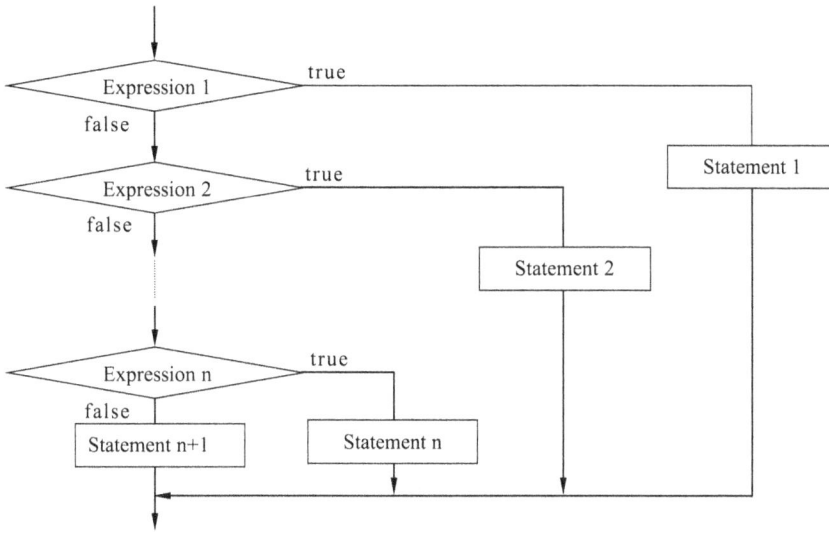

Fig. 2.6: Flow chart of statement *if... else if.*

```
if (expression 1) statement 1
else if (expression 2) statement 2
else if (expression 3) statement 3
        . . .
else statement n
```

Statement 1, 2, 3, ... n can be a compound statement. The execution order of the statement *if... else if* is shown in Figure 2.6.

3. *switch* Statement

In some problems, though there need to be multiple selections, each judgment evaluates the same expression, and thus it is not necessary to calculate the value of the expression in each nested *if* statement. The *switch* statement is designed to solve this problem in C++. The syntax form is:

```
switch (expression)
    { case constant expression 1: statement 1
        case constant expression 2: statement 2
            ⋮
        case constant expression n: statement n
        default : statement n+1
    }
```

The execution order of a *switch* statement is: first calculate the value of the *expression* in a *switch* statement; then find the first case labeled by a *constant expression* that matches the value of the *expression*, use the case as an entry label, and start execution. If no case matches the value of the *expression*, then execute from *"default:"*.

You should pay attention to the following issues when using *switch* statements:

– The expression in *switch* statements can be int-type, character-type, or enumeration-type.
– The value of each *constant expression* must be different, although their sequence order does not affect the execution result.
– There can be several statements in each *case*, and you do not need to use {}.
– Each *case* is only an entry label, and it cannot decide the endpoint of the execution. So you need to add a *break* statement at the end of a *case* branch to exit early from the whole *switch* structure; otherwise execution will fall through to the next statement when the code of that *case* branch is done.
– When several branches need to do the same action, they can use the same group of statements.

Example 2.4: Enter an integer between 0~6, convert it into the corresponding day of week, and then output it.

Analysis: In this example, the number entered decides the output information, because numbers 0~6 represent seven conditions: "Sunday", "Monday".... Thus we need to use a multiple selection structure. Since it is judging the day of the week, a *switch* statement is most appropriate.

Source code:

```cpp
//2_4.cpp
#include <iostream>
using namespace std;
int main()
{
    int day;

    cin >> day;
    switch (day)
    {
    case 0: cout << "Sunday" << endl;
            break;
    case 1: cout << "Monday" << endl;
            break;
    case 2: cout << "Tuesday" << endl;
            break;
    case 3: cout << "Wednesday" << endl;
            break;
```

```
        case 4: cout << "Thursday" << endl;
                break;
        case 5: cout << "Friday" << endl;
                break;
        case 6: cout << "Saturday" << endl;
                break;
        default: cout << "Day out of range Sunday .. Saturday" << endl;
                break;
    }
}
```

Running sample:

```
2
Tuesday
```

2.4.3 Loop Structure

There are three kinds of loop control structures in C++:

1. *while* statement
Syntax form:

```
while (expression) statement
```

Execution order: first evaluate the *expression* (loop condition); if it is true, execute the loop body (*statement*) and re-evaluate the *expression*; continue the cycle until *expression* becomes false. When using while statement, generally there should be statements in the loop body that can change the value of expression, i.e., the loop condition, otherwise it will be an infinite loop (dead loop).

Figure 2.7 is the flow chart of a *while* statement.

When using *while* statement, generally there should be statements in the loop body that can change the value of *expression*, i.e., the loop condition, otherwise it will be an infinite loop (dead loop).

Example 2.5: Calculate the sum of numbers 1~10.

Analysis: we need to use an accumulation algorithm here. An accumulation process is a loop process, and it can be achieved by a *while* statement.

Source code:

```
//2_5.cpp
#include<iostream>
using namespace std;
```

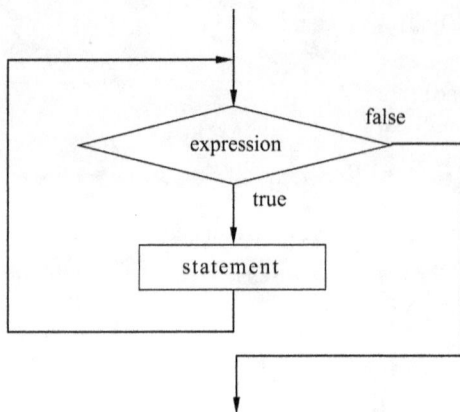

Fig. 2.7: Flow chart of statement *while*.

```
int main()
{
    int i(1), sum(0);
    while(i<=10)
    {
        sum+=i;
        i++;
    }
    cout<<"sum="<<sum<<endl;
}
```

Result:

```
sum=55
```

2. *do-while* Statement
Syntax form:

```
do statement
while (expression)
```

The execution order is: execute loop body *statement* first, and then evaluate the *expression* (loop condition). If the *expression* is *true*, continue the execution-evaluation cycle; otherwise end the loop. Figure 2.8 is the flow chart of a *do-while* statement.

Like in *while* statements, generally there should be statements in the loop body that can change the value of *expression*; otherwise it will be a dead loop.

Example 2.6: Enter an integer and output in the reverse order of each digit of the integer.
Analysis: output each digit of an integer the reversed order is to first output the ones

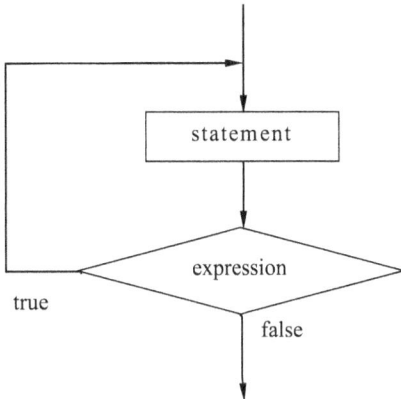

Fig. 2.8: Flow chart of *do-while* statement.

of the integer, and then its tens, its hundreds.... We can divide the integer by 10 continuously until the quotient is 0. This is a loop process, and no matter which integer it is, we have to output at least one digit (even if it is 0). Therefore, we can use a *do-while* loop statement: first execute the loop body and then evaluate the loop condition.

Source code:

```
//2_6.cpp
#include <iostream>
using namespace std;
int main()
{
    int n, right_digit, newnum = 0;
    cout << "Enter the number: ";
    cin >> n;

    cout << "The number in reverse order is ";
    do
    {
        right_digit = n % 10;
        cout << right_digit;
        n /= 10;
    }
    while (n != 0);
    cout<<endl;
}
```

Result:

```
Enter the number: 365
The number in reversed digit order is 563
```

Both the *do-while* statement and *while* statement achieve the loop structure, while the difference between the two is: the *while* statement first evaluates the expression, and executes the loop body only if the expression is *true*; the *do-while* statement first executes the loop body and then evaluates the expression, and the loop body is always executed at least once. Example 2.7 achieves the same function as Example 2.5, using a *do-while* statement.

Example 2.7: Use a *do-while* statement to calculate the sum of numbers 1~10.

```
//2_7.cpp
#include<iostream>
using namespace std;
int main()
{
    int i(1), sum(0);
    do {
        sum+=i;
        i++;
    } while(i<=10);
        cout<<"sum="<<sum<<endl;
}
```

Result:

```
sum=55
```

We can see that the result is the same as in Example 2.5. Most of the time, if the loop conditions and the loop bodies of the *while* loop and the *do-while* loop are both the same, the results of the two loops are the same. This is because in most cases, the loop condition at the beginning of the loop is *true*, so whether or not one first considers the loop condition does not affect the result. But if the loop condition at the beginning of the loop is *false*, the *do-while* loop will at least execute loop body once, while the *while* loop will not execute the loop body at all. Now we make a little change in Example 2.5 and 2.7: integer *i* now is to be input from the keyboard. Please analyze the results of the two programs below in both conditions, where variable i is greater than 10 and not.

Program 1:

```
#include<iostream>
using namespace std;
int main()
{
int i, sum(0);
cin>>i;
```

Program 2:

```
#include<iostream>
using namespace std;
int main()
{
int i, sum(0);
cin>>i;
```

```
while(i<=10)                          do {
   {                                     sum+=i;
   sum+=i;                               i++;
   i++;                                  } while(i<=10);
   }                                     cout<<''sum=''<<sum<<endl;
   cout<<''sum=''<<sum<<endl;          }
}
```

3. *for* Statement

The use of *for* statements is the most flexible. They can be used when the number of loops is either certain or not. The syntax form of a *for* statement is as below:

```
for (expression 1; expression 2; expression 3)
statement
```

Figure 2.9 is the flow chart of a *for* statement.

We can see from Figure 2.9 that the execution flow of a *for* statement is: first calculate the value of *expression 1*, and then evaluate *expression 2* (loop condition). If *expression 2* is true, execute the statements in the loop body once; otherwise quit the loop. After each execution of the loop body, calculate *expression 3* and then re-evaluate *expression 2* to decide whether to continue the execution or not.

Some important points about *for* statements:

– *Expression 1, 2,* and *3* can be omitted, but you cannot omit the semicolons between them. If you omit the three expressions, the statement form becomes:

```
for (;;) statement //equals to while (true) statement
```

This will become a dead cycle.

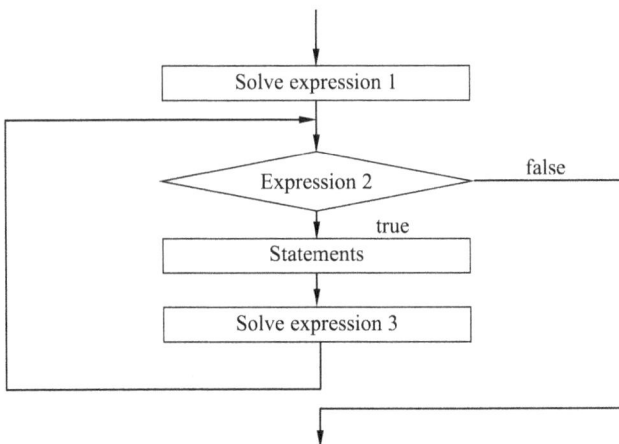

Fig. 2.9: Execution flow of a *for* statement.

- *Expression 2* is the loop condition, so omitting it will cause a dead cycle.
- *Expression 1* is often used to initialize the loop condition. It can also be an expression that is independent of the loop variable. If you omit expression 1 or if it is independent of the loop condition, you must initialize the loop condition before the *for* statement. See the following three program segments:

Program segment 1:

```
for (i=1;i<=100;i++) sum=sum+i;      //initialize the loop condition
                                     //in expression 1
```

Program segment 2:

```
i=1; //initialize the loop condition before for statement
for ( ; i<=100 ; i++) sum=sum+i;      //omit expression 1
```

Program segment 3:

```
i=1; //initialize the loop condition before for statement
for (sum=0 ; i<=100 ; i++) sum=sum+i; //expression 1 is independent
                                      //of the loop condition
```

- *Expression 1* and *expression 3* can be simple expressions or comma expressions. For example:

```
for (i=0,j=100; i<=j; i++,j--) k=i+j;
```

- *Expression 3* is often used to change the loop condition. If *expression 3* is omitted or independent of the loop condition, there should be other statements in the loop body that can change the loop condition to make sure that the cycle ends normally, such as:

```
for (sum=0,i=1; i<=100; ) //omit expression 3
{ sum=sum+i;
    i++;                   //change the loop condition in the loop body
}
```

- If there only exists *expression 2*, and *expression* 1 and 3 are omitted, the *for* statement becomes the same as the *while* statement. For example, the program segments below are the same:

```
for (; i<=100;)              while (i<=100)
{ sum=sum+i;                 { sum=sum+i;
    i++;                         i++;
}                            }
```

A *for* statement is a highly functional loop statement, including all the functions of *while* statements. Besides giving the loop condition, it also can do initialization, increase the loop variable automatically, and so on. *for* statements can solve all loop problems in programming.

Example 2.8: Enter an integer and calculate all its factors.

Analysis: we can use the enumeration method to get all the factors of integer n: consider integers $1\sim n$, any number that can divide n exactly is a factor of n. It is a loop with known cycle times, so we can use a *for* statement.

Source code:

```
//2_8.cpp
#include <iostream>
using namespace std;
int main()
{
    int n, k;

    cout << "Enter a positive integer: ";
    cin >> n;
    cout << "Number " << n << " Factors ";

    for (k=1; k <= n; k++)
        if (n % k == 0)
            cout << k << " ";
        cout << endl;
}
```

Result 1:

```
Enter a positive integer: 36
Number 36 Factors 1 2 3 4 6 9 12 18 36
```

Result 2:

```
Enter a positive integer: 7
Number 7 Factors 1 7
```

2.4.4 Nestings of Loop Structure and Case Structure

1. Nested Case Structure

As already stated, we can achieve multiple selections using nested case structures.

2. Nested Loop Structure

We can construct a multiple loop structure by including one loop structure in the loop body of another loop structure. The three kinds of loop statements, *while, do-while,* and *for,* can nest each other. For example, in the following program a *do-while* loop is nested in a *for* loop:

```cpp
#include<iostream>
using namespace std;
int main()
{
    int i(1),a(0);
    for(;i<=5;i++)
    {
        do{
            i++;
            a++;
        }while(i<3);
        i++;
    }
    cout<<a<<'',''<<i<<endl;
}
```

Example 2.9: Write a program that can output the following pattern:

```
    *
   ***
  *****
 *******
  *****
   ***
    *
```

Source code:

```cpp
//2_9.cpp
#include<iostream>
using namespace std;
int main()
{ int i,j,n=4;
    for(i=1;i<=n;i++)          //output the first 4 rows of pattern
    { for(j=1;j<=30;j++)
        cout<<' ';             //set the 30 columns on the left of the
                               //pattern as empty
    for(j=1; j<=8-2*i ;j++)
        cout<<' ';
    for(j=1; j<=2*i-1 ;j++)
        cout<<'*';
    cout<<endl;
    }
```

```
for(i=1;i<=n-1;i++)          //output the last 3 rows of pattern
{ for(j=1;j<=30;j++)
    cout<<' ';               //set the 30 columns on the left of the
                             //pattern as empty
  for(j=1; j<=7-2*i ;j++)
    cout<<'*';
  cout<<endl;
}
}
```

3. Mutual Nesting between Loop Structure and Case Structure

Loop structure and case structure can also nest each other to implement complex algorithms. Any branch of a case structure can nest a whole loop structure, and the loop body of a loop structure can nest a whole case structure. For example, the following program is for finding the numbers between 100 and 200 that cannot be divided exactly by 3. In the example, an *if* statement is nested in the loop body of a *for* statement:

```
#include<iostream>
using namespace std;
int main()
{
    int n;
    for(n=100; n<=200; n++)
    {
        if (n%3!=0)
        cout<<n;
    }
}
```

Example 2.10: Read a series of integers, and count the number of positive integers (stored in variable *i*) and the number of negative integers (stored in variable *j*). If the input integer is 0 then end the program.

Analysis: we need to read a series of integers, while the number of integers is uncertain. We have to make a decision after each reading of a number: if the number input is not 0, we process the number and continue reading; otherwise we finish the work. Therefore, the *while*-loop is the most appropriate structure to use, and the loop control condition should be n!=0. Because we have to count the number of positive integers and negative integers respectively, we need to nest a case structure inside the loop body.

Source code:

```
//2_10.cpp
#include<iostream>
```

```
using namespace std;
int main()
{ int i=0, j=0, n;
  cout<<" Please enter a series of numbers(enter 0 to end): \n";
  cin>>n;
  while( n!=0 )
  { if(n>0) i+=1;
    if(n<0) j+=1;
    cin>>n ;
  }
  cout<<"the number of positive integers: "<<i<<"the number of
        negative integers: "<<j<<endl;
}
```

Result:

```
Please enter a series of numbers(enter 0 to end):
2 3 -19 54 -67 8 3 0
the number of positive integers: 5 the number of negative integers: 2
```

2.4.5 Other Control Statements

1. *break* Statement

break statements are used inside *switch* statements or a loop body to provide an immediate exit from the *switch* statement or the loop body. Execution will then continue from the next statement of the *switch* statement or the loop structure. *break* statements should not be used elsewhere.

2. *continue* Statement

continue statements can be used inside a loop body to end this loop, and then start the next loop if the loop condition is satisfied.

3. *goto* Statement

The syntax form of a *goto* statement is:

```
goto statement label
```

Statement labels are used to label a statement. They are placed at the front of the statement, and are separated from the statement by a colon (:).

goto statements are used to make the execution flow jump to the statement specified by the *statement label*. The use of a *goto* statement will destroy the structure of a program, and we should avoid using it.

2.5 User-Defined Data Type

C++ not only has abundant built-in basic data types, but also allows users to define data types themselves. User-defined data types include: the enumeration type, structure type, union type, array type, class type, and so on. We will introduce the enumeration type, structure type, and union type in this section, and the rest will be introduced in the following chapters.

2.5.1 *typedef* Declaration

When writing a program, besides built-in data type names and user-defined data type names, we can also create new names for a known data type. In this way, we can give a known type a specific name based on different applications, thus to improve the readability of the program. Also, creating a shorter name for an existed long type name can make the program more concise. *typedef* is used to declare an identifier as another name of a data type, and the identifier can then be used as the data type name.

The syntax form of *typedef* declaration is:

```
typedef known type name name list of new type names;
```

There can be several identifiers in the *name list of new type names*, which are separated by commas. In this way, we can give several names to a known data type in one *typedef* statement.

For example:

```
typedef double area,volume;
typedef int natural;
natural i1,i2;
area a;
volume v;
```

2.5.2 Enumeration Type – enum

Readers must have experienced this kind of situation when solving problems: win, lose, tie, and cancel are the only four results of a game; there are only red, yellow, blue, white, and black balls in a bag; there are only seven days in one week, etc. The data variables above all have limited possible values. Though we can use int-type or char-type to represent them, validity checks on data values would become troublesome. For example, if we use integers from 0 to 6 to represent the seven days in one week, then if the variable value is 8, it is invalid. Enumeration type in C++ is designed to solve this problem.

We can construct an enumeration type by listing all the possible values of a variable. The declaration form of an enumeration type is:

```
enum enumeration type name {list of variable values};
```

For example:

```
enum weekday {sun,mon,tue,wed,thu,fri,sat};
```

Notes on using an enumeration type:

- Enumeration elements should be treated as constants, and they cannot be assigned. For example, the following statement is illegal:

  ```
  sun=0;//sun is an enumeration element, illegal statement
  ```

- Enumeration elements have default values which are: 0, 1, 2, ... For example, the value of *sun* in the example above is 0, and *mon* is 1, *tue* is 2, ..., *sat* is 6.
- One can also specify the value of enumeration elements, such as:

  ```
  enum weekday {sun=7,mon=1,tue,wed,thu,fri,sat};
  ```

  The statement defines sun as 7 and mon as 1. The following unspecified elements will in turn have values greater by 1 than their previous, thus tue will be 2, ..., sat will be 6.

- Enumeration values can be used in relational calculations directly.
- Integer values cannot be assigned to enumeration variables directly. If the assignment is needed, we should perform a cast first.

Example 2.11: There are four possible results in one game: win, lose, tie, and cancel. Write a program to output these four situations.
Analysis: because there are only four possible results in a game, we can declare an enumeration variable and use it to store the results of the game.

Source code:

```
//2_11.cpp
#include <iostream>
using namespace std;
enum game_result {WIN, LOSE, TIE, CANCEL};
int main()
{
    game_result result;                 //when declaring the variable,
                                         //you can omit keyword enum
    enum game_result omit = CANCEL;      //you also can write enum before
                                         //type name
    int count;
```

```
    for (count = WIN ; count <= CANCEL ; count++)
    {
        result = (game_result)count;
        if (result == omit)
        {
            cout << "The game was cancelled\n";
        }
        else
        {
            cout << "The game was played ";
            if (result == WIN)
                cout << "and we won!";
            if (result == LOSE)
                cout << "and we lost.";
            cout << "\n";
        }
    }

}
```

Result:

```
The game was played and we won!
The game was played and we lost.
The game was played
The game was cancelled
```

Notice:

```
game_result result;
enum game_result omit = CANCEL;
```

The above two statements are both right. After declaring an enumeration type, we do not need to write the keyword *enum* before the type name when declaring a variable.

2.5.3 Structure

We have learned basic data types and the enumeration type (a collection of integers) so far, while in many cases we need to combine different data types together. For example, consider the student number, name, age, and score of one student. Although they are of different data types, they are closely related in that they belong to one person. In this case, we need to declare a structure type for this group of information. Structure type is a collection of different types of data, and its declaration form is as below:

```
struct struct name
{
    data type identifier 1 member name 1;
    data type identifier 2 member name 2;

    :

    data type identifier n member name n;
};
```

For example:

```
struct student       //structure of student information
{
    int num;         //student number
    char name[20];   //name, character array, used to store a string,
                     //the details are introduced in Chapter 6
    char sex;        //sex
    int age;         //age
    float score;     //score
    char addr[30];   //address, character array, used to store a string,
                     //the details are introduced in Chapter 6
};
```

It declares a structure of student information.

To use structure-type data, only declaring the structure type is not enough, since we also have to declare the structure variables. The syntax form of structure variable declaration is:

```
struct name struct variable name;
```

Notice:
-   Structure variable declaration is after the structure type declaration, while they can also be done at the same time.
-   You can use the *sizeof* operation to calculate how many bytes the structure variable occupies in memory.
    ```
    sizeof(type name or variable name)
    ```
-   You can initiate a structure variable while declaring it.

The form of referencing a member of a structure is:

```
struct variable name.member name
```

Example 2.12: The initialization and use of a structure variable.

```cpp
//2_12.cpp
#include <iostream>
#include <iomanip>
using namespace std;
struct student          //structure of student information
{
    int num;            //student number
    char name[20];      //name
    char sex;           //sex
    int age             //age
}stu={97001,"Lin Lin",'F',19};

int main()
{
    cout<<setw(7)<<stu.num<<setw(20)<<stu.name<<setw(3)<<stu.sex
        <<setw(3)<<stu.age;
}
```

Result:

```
97001 Lin Lin F 19
```

The same type of data can also construct a structure. The structure *animal* in Example 2.13 is made up of two int-type members.

Example 2.13: There are three animals and all of them have two attributes: weight and height. Now we need to assign their weights and heights, and then output their weights.
Analysis: these three animals all have a weight and height attribute; therefore we can declare a structure that includes the two attribute members (weight and height).

Source code:

```cpp
//2_13.cpp
#include <iostream>
using namespace std;
struct animal
{
    int weight;
    int feet;
};
```

```
int main()
{
    animal dog1, dog2, chicken;

    dog1.weight = 15;
    dog2.weight = 37;
    chicken.weight = 3;

    dog1.feet = 4;
    dog2.feet = 4;
    chicken.feet = 2;

    cout << "The weight of dog1 is " << dog1.weight << "\n";
    cout << "The weight of dog2 is " << dog2.weight << "\n";
    cout << "The weight of chicken is "<< chicken.weight << "\n";
}
```

Result:

```
The weight of dog1 is 15
The weight of dog2 is 37
The weight of chicken is 3
```

2.5.4 Union

Sometimes several different types of data need to share the same storage area. In this case we can declare a union type. The syntax form of a union type declaration is:

```
union union type name
{
    data type identifier 1 member name 1;
    data type identifier 2 member name 2;

        ⋮

    data type identifier n member name n;
};
```

Syntax form of union-type variable declaration:

```
union type name union-type variable name;
```

Syntax form of referencing a member of a union-type variable:

```
Union-type variable name.member name
```

uarea   c_data   s_data   l_data

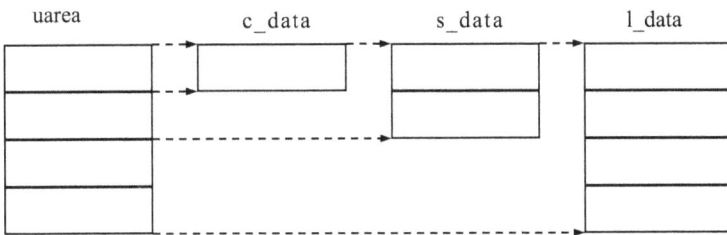

Fig. 2.10: Storage structure of a variable of union type *uarea*.

For example, the following is a declaration of a union type:

```
union uarea
{ char c_data;
    short s_data;
    long l_data;
};
```

Figure 2.10 is the storage structure of a variable of union type *uarea*.

A union type may have no name when it is declared, and at this time it is called an unnamed union. Unnamed unions do not have names; they only declare a collection of members that have the same memory address. We can access these members by their member names directly.

For example, declare an unnamed union:

```
union
{ int i;
    float f;
};
```

We can use it in a program like this:

```
i=10;
f=2.2;
```

An unnamed union is usually used as a nested member in a structure body, see Example 2.14.

Example 2.14: A structure that can describe fighters, bombers, or transport planes.

```
//2_14.cpp
#include <iostream>
using namespace std;
struct aircraft
{
    int wingspan;                       //wingspread
    int passengers;                     //passenger
```

```
    union //Unnamed union used as a nested member in the structure body
    {
        float fuel_load;                    //fuel carried by fighters
        float bomb_load;                    //bombs carried by bombers
        int pallets;                        //pallets of transport planes
    };
} fighter, bomber, transport;

int main()
{
    fighter.wingspan = 40;
    fighter.passengers = 1;
    fighter.fuel_load = 12000.0;

    bomber.wingspan = 90;
    bomber.passengers = 12;
    bomber.bomb_load = 14000.0;

    transport.wingspan = 106;
    transport.passengers = 4;
    transport.pallets = 42;

    transport.fuel_load = 18000.0;
    fighter.pallets = 4;

    cout << "The fighter carries "<< fighter.pallets << " pallets.\n";
    cout << "The bomber bomb load is " << bomber.bomb_load << "\n";
}
```

Result:

```
The fighter carries 4 pallets.
The bomber bomb load is 14000
```

2.6 Summary

C++ is evolved from C. Dennis Ritchie from Bell Labs created the C language on the basis of the B language in 1972. It has many advantages: concision and flexibility, plenty of operators and data structures, structured control statements, high execution efficiency of procedures, and having both the advantages of a high-level language and an assembly language.

C++, a general-purpose programming language, was created by Dr. Bjame Strous-trup from AT&T Bell labs in 1980. C++ was developed to support the object-oriented program designs based on the C language. C++ has two main features: one is that it is fully compatible with C; the other is that it supports object-oriented methods.

Data is the processing object in programs, which can be classified by its charac-teristics. Data types in C++ can be divided into basic types and user-defined types. Basic types are predefined in the C++ compiling system, including the bool type, char (character) type, int (integral) type, float type (represent real numbers), and double type (double precision floating point type, or double precision type). Apart from the bool type, these basic types can be classified into two categories: integer type and float type. Here char type is an integer type essentially: it is an integer whose length is 1 byte, and is usually used to store the ASCII code of characters. C++ language does not only have abundant predefined basic types, but also allows user-defined types. User-defined types include enumeration type, structure type, union type, array type, class type, and so on. We introduced enumeration type, structure type, and union type in this chapter. Class type is the core of C++ object-oriented program design, and it is the main content of the following chapters. The other user-defined data types will also be introduced in the following chapters. We introduced the basic methods of data input/output in this chapter.

Program design includes data structure design and algorithm design. An algo-rithm is made up of a sequence of control structures. Sequential, case, and loop struc-tures are the basic control structures in program design and they are the basis of con-structing complex algorithms.

Exercises

2.1 What are the main characteristics and advantages of C++?

2.2 Which of the following identifiers are legal?

```
Program, -page, _lock, test2, 3in1, @mail, A_B_C_D
```

2.3 What is the effect of each statement in Example 2.1?

```
#include <iostream>
using namespace std;
int main()
{
cout<<"Hello!\n";
cout<<"Welcome to c++!\n";
}
```

2.4 What is the advantage of using the keyword *const* instead of using a *#define* statement?

2.5 Please write a statement in C++ that declares a constant PI with the value of 3.1415; and then declare a float variable *a*, and assign the value of PI to *a*.

2.6 What is the value of BLUE in the following enumeration type?

```
enum COLOR { WHITE, BLACK = 100, RED, BLUE, GREEN = 300 };
```

2.7 What is the use of comments? Which comment forms does C++ have? What are their differences?

2.8 What is an expression? Is *x=5+7* an expression? What is its value?

2.9 What are the values of the following expressions?
a) 201 / 4
b) 201 % 4
c) 201 / 4.0

2.10 What is the value of variables *a*, *b*, and *c* after executing the following statements?

```
a = 30;
b = a++;
c = ++a;
```

2.11 Can we initialize several variables in a *for* statement? How to achieve this?

2.12 What is the value of *n* after executing the following statements?

```
int n;
for (n = 0; n < 100; n++);
```

2.13 Write a *for* statement: the loop condition is that n is between 100 and 200, and step length is 2; then use a *while* and *do...while* statement to do the same loop.

2.14 What is the difference between statements *if (x = 3)* and *if (x = = 3)*?

2.15 What is a scope? What is a local variable? What is a global variable? How does one use a global variable?

2.16 Given two variables *x* and *y*, write a simple *if* statement to assign the smaller value of the two variables to the variable that has the greater value.

2.17 Correct the errors in the following program. What is the result after your correction?

```
#include <iostream>
using namespace std;
int main()
    int i
    int j;
    i = 10;                            /* assign i */
    j = 20;                            /* assign j */
    cout << ``i + j = << i + j;        /* output the result */
    return 0;
}
```

2.18 Write a program to prompt users to enter a number and then show the number on the screen.

2.19 Which data types does C++ have? List the range of each data type. Write a program to show the number of bytes every data type occupies in the computer you are using.

2.20 Write a program to output the ASCII code of characters that are between 32 and 127.

2.21 Run the following program and observe the output. Is it the same as you think?

```
#include <iostream>
using namespace std;
int main()
{
unsigned int x;
unsigned int y = 100;
unsigned int z = 50;
x= y - z;
cout << ``Difference is: `` << x;
x = z - y;
cout << ``\nNow difference is: `` << x <<endl;
}
```

2.22 Run the following program, observe the output, and figure the difference between *i*++ and ++*i*.

```
#include <iostream>
using namespace std;
int main()
```

```
{
    int myAge = 39;                                    //initialize two integers
    int yourAge = 39;
    cout << ``I am: `` << myAge << `` years old.\n'';
    cout << ``You are: `` << yourAge << `` years old\n'';
        myAge++;                                        //postfix increment
        ++yourAge;                                      //prefix increment
    cout << ``One year passes...\n'';
    cout << ``I am: `` << myAge << `` years old.\n'';
    cout << ``You are: `` << yourAge << `` years old\n'';
    cout << ``Another year passes\n'';
    cout << ``I am: `` << myAge++ << `` years old.\n'';
    cout << ``You are: `` << ++yourAge << `` years old\n'';
    cout << ``Let's print it again.\n'';
    cout << ``I am: `` << myAge << `` years old.\n'';
    cout << ``You are: `` << yourAge << `` years old\n'';
}
```

2.23 What is a constant? What is a variable?

2.24 Which storage types do variables have?

2.25 Write down the values of the following expressions:
a) $2 < 3$ && $6 < 9$
b) $!(4 < 7)$
c) $!(3 > 5) \,||\, (6 < 2)$

2.26 If a = 1, b = 2, c = 3, then what are the results of the following expressions?
a) a | b − c
b) a ^ b & − c
c) a & b | c
d) a | b & c

2.27 If a = 1, then what are the results of the following expressions?
a) ! a | a
b) ~ a | a
c) a ^ a
d) a >> 2

2.28 Write a program to achieve this function: ask the user "Is it raining now?" and prompt the user to enter Y or N. If the user enters Y, then display "It is raining now."; if N is entered, then display "It is not raining now."; otherwise, continue asking "Is it raining now?"

2.29 Write a program that asks the user "What score did you get? (0~100)." Once an input is received, judge and output its rank. The rules are as below:

$$
\text{Rank} = \begin{cases}
A & 90 \leq \text{score} \leq 100 \\
B & 80 \leq \text{score} < 90 \\
C & 60 \leq \text{score} < 80 \\
D & 0 \leq \text{score} < 60
\end{cases}
$$

2.30 Implement a simple menu program: when executing, display "Menu: A(dd) D(elete) S(ort) Q(uit), Select one:" to prompt users to enter a letter. Here A represents add, D represents delete, S represents sort, and Q represents quit. When the user enters A, D, or S, display "Data has been added/deleted/sorted." correspondingly; when the input is Q, end the program.
1. Use an *if...else* statement to judge the inputs and use *break* and *continue* to control the flow.
2. Use a *switch* statement.

2.31 Use the enumeration method to find out all the prime numbers between 1 and 100 and display them. Use a *while, do-while*, and *for* loop statement respectively.

2.32 Compare the different usages between a *break* statement and *continue* statement.

2.33 Declare a structure type that represents time. It can show year, month, day, hours, minutes, and seconds. Prompt the user to enter the value of year, month, day, hours, minutes, seconds, and then display them.

2.34 Define an integer variable in a program and assign it a value between 1 and 100. Prompt the user to guess the value, compare the two values, and show the comparing result to the user. Continue the guess until the user gives the right answer. Use a *while* and *do-while* loop statement respectively.

2.35 Declare an enumeration type *weekday* that includes seven elements (from *Sunday* to *Saturday*). Declare a variable of the *weekday* type and assign it a value. Then declare an *int-type* variable. See if you can assign the *int-type* variable the value of the *weekday*-type variable.

2.36 There are several balls of colors red, yellow, blue, white, and black in the pocket. Picking three balls of different colors each time, how many possibilities are there?

2.37 Output the multiplication table.

3 Functions

C++ inherits all the C syntax, including the definition and usage of functions. In process-oriented programming (also known as structured programming), function is the basic unit of module division, and an abstract of the problem-solving process. Function is also important in object-oriented programming, in which it is an abstract of functionalities.

To develop or debug a complex system, engineers will usually divide it into several subsystems, and then develop or debug based on these subsystems. Subprograms in high-level program languages are used to realize this kind of module division. In C and C++, subprograms are embodied as functions. We usually abstract functions from independent and frequently used functionality modules. Once a function is written, we can reuse it only knowing its functions and usage, without needing to know its specific implementation. In this way code is reused, development efficiency and program reliability are improved, and collaboration, modification, and maintenance can be realized more easily.

3.1 Definition and Use of Function

A C++ program consists of one main function and several subfunctions. A program is executed starting from its main function. The main function may call subfunctions, and subfunctions may in turn call other subfunctions.

The function that calls other functions is named a **"calling function"**, and the function called by others is named a **"called function"**. A function may call another function and also be called by another. Thus it can be a calling function in one occasion and a called function in another.

3.1.1 Definition of Function

1. Syntax form of function definition

```
Type identifier Function name (Formal Parameter list)
{
    Statements
}
```

2. Type of function and return value
The type identifier defines the type of the function, and also the type of the return value of the function. The return value of the function is the result that the function returns to its calling function, which is given by a *return* statement, such as "*return 0*".

https://doi.org/10.1515/9783110471977-003

The function without a return value has a type identifier of *void*, and there need not be a *return* statement in the function.

3. Formal parameters

Here is the form of a formal parameter list:

```
type 1 name 1, type 2 name2, ..., type n name n
```

type1, type2, ..., *type n* are type identifiers that represent the types of formal parameters, and *name1, name2, ...*, *name n* are the names of formal parameters. Formal parameters are used to realize the connection between the called function and the calling function. We often let the data that needs to process, factors that affect the function's behavior, or the processing results of the function be the function's formal parameters. Functions without formal parameters should have *void* on the position of the parameter list.

The *main* function can also have formal parameters and a return value. The formal parameters of the *main* function are also called command line parameters, which are initialized by the operating system when starting the program. The return value of the *main* function is returned to the operating system. The types and number of formal parameters of the *main* function have a special format. Refer to the experiment instructions in *<Student's Book>* to write programs with command line parameters.

A function is only a piece of text before it has been called, and its formal parameters at the time are just symbols, indicating what type of data should appear at the position of the formal parameter. A function starts execution when it is called, and at that time, the calling function assigns the actual parameters to the formal parameters. This is similar to the definition of a function in mathematics:

$$f(x) = x^2 + x + 1$$

The function f will not be calculated until its argument has been assigned a value.

3.1.2 Function Calls

1. Form of function calls

Before calling a function we first need to declare the **function prototype**. The declaration can be in the calling function or before all the functions, with the following form:

```
Type identifier Function name(Formal parameter list with type
    declarations);
```

If a function prototype is declared before all the functions, it is effective in the whole program file. That is, we can call the corresponding function anywhere in the file according to the prototype. If a function prototype is declared inside a calling function, it is only effective in this calling function.

After declaring the function prototype, we can make a function call with the following form:

```
Function name(Actual parameter list)
```

The actual parameter list should provide parameters that accurately match the formal parameters in number and in types. A function call can be used as a statement, where the return value of the function is not needed; a function call can also appear in an expression, where an explicit return value of the function is needed.

Similar to the declaration and definition of variable, declaring a function only tells the compiler its relevant information (function name, parameters, return type, etc.) without generating any codes, while defining a function mainly gives the function code in addition to its relevant information.

Example 3.1: Writing a function to calculate the nth power of x.

```cpp
//3_1.cpp
#include <iostream>
using namespace std;
double power (double x, int n);
int main()
{
    cout << "5 to the power 2 is " << power(5,2) << endl;
    //Function call is counted as an expression in the output statement.
}
double power (double x, int n)
{
    double val = 1.0;
    while (n--)
    val *= x;
    return(val);
}
```

Running result:

```
5 to the power 2 is 25
```

Example 3.2: Enter an 8-bit binary number, convert it to its decimal form, and then output the result.

Analysis: To convert a binary number to its decimal form, we need to multiply every bit of the binary number with the corresponding weight, and then add them up. For example: $00001101_2 = 0(2^7)+0(2^6)+0(2^5)+0(2^4)+1(2^3)+1(2^2)+0(2^1)+1(2^0) = 13_{10}$. So when the input is 1101, the output should be 13.

Here we make a function call on the function *power* in Example 3.1 to calculate 2^n.

Source code:

```
//3_2.cpp
#include <iostream>
using namespace std;
double power (double x, int n);

int main()
{
    int i;
    int value = 0;
    char ch;

    cout << "Enter an 8 bit binary number ";
    for (i = 7; i >= 0; i--)
    {
        cin >> ch;
        if (ch == '1')
            value += int(power(2,i));
    }
    cout <<"Decimal value is "<<value<<endl;
}

double power (double x, int n)
{
    double val = 1.0;

    while (n--)
        val *= x;
    return(val);
}
```

Running result:

```
Enter an 8 bit binary number 01101001
Decimal value is 105
```

Example 3.3: Write a program to compute the value of π using the following formula.

$$\pi = 16 \arctan\left(\frac{1}{5}\right) - 4\arctan\left(\frac{1}{239}\right)$$

Use the following series to calculate the arctangent of a number:

Continue accumulating until the absolute value of one item in the series is less than 10^{-15}. The type of π and x are both double.

$$\arctan(x) = x - \frac{x^3}{3} + \frac{x^5}{5} - \frac{x^7}{7} + \cdots$$

Source code:

```
//3_3.cpp
#include<iostream>
using namespace std;
int main()
{
  double a, b;
  double arctan(double x) ;
  a=16.0*arctan(1/5.0) ;
  b=4.0*arctan(1/239.0) ;
 //Note: Since the division of integers is to be rounded off, the
 //value of 1/5 and 1/239 are both 0.
  cout<<"PI="<<a-b<<endl;
}
double arctan(double x)
{
  int i;
  double r, e, f, sqr;
  sqr=x*x;
  r=0;
  e=x;
  i=1;
  while(e/i>1e-15)
  {
    f=e/i;
    r=(i%4==1)? r+f : r-f ;
    e=e*sqr;
    i+=2;
  }
  return r ;
}
```

Running result:

```
PI=3.14159
```

Example 3.4: Find the number m between 11 and 999 where m, m^2, and m^3 are all palindromes, and then output m.

Palindromes are numbers that have symmetrical number digits. For example: 121, 676, and 94249 are all palindromes. One instance that satisfies this subject's requirement is: $m = 11$, $m^2 = 121$, $m^3 = 1331$.

Analysis: To check whether a number is a palindrome or not, we can get every digit of the number by continuously dividing it by 10 and obtaining the remainders. After getting all the digits, we reverse the digit order to get a new number, and compare the new number with the original one. The original number is a palindrome if and only if it is the same as the new number.

Source code:

```
//3_4.cpp
#include <iostream>
using namespace std;
int main()
{
  bool symm(long n);
  long m;
  for(m=11; m<1000; m++)
      if (symm(m)&&symm(m*m)&&symm(m*m*m))
          cout<<"m="<<m<<"  m*m="<<m*m<<"  m*m*m="<<m*m*m<<endl;
}

bool symm(long n)
{
  long i, m;
  i=n ; m=0 ;
  while(i)
  {
    m=m*10+i%10;
    i=i/10 ;
  }
  return ( m==n );
}
```

Running result:

```
m=11  m*m=121  m*m*m=1331
m=101  m*m=10201  m*m*m=1030301
m=111  m*m=12321  m*m*m=1367631
```

Example 3.5: Compute the value of the following formula and output the result.

$$k = \begin{cases} \sqrt{\sin^2(r) + \sin^2(s)} & \text{when} \quad r^2 \leq s^2 \\ \frac{1}{2}\sin(r \times s) & \text{when} \quad r^2 > s^2 \end{cases}$$

Here the values of r and s are input from the keyboard. The approximate value of $\sin x$ is calculated using following formula:

$$\sin x = \frac{x}{1!} - \frac{x^3}{3!} + \frac{x^5}{5!} - \frac{x^7}{7!} + \cdots = \sum_{n=1}^{\infty}(-1)^{n-1}\frac{x^{2n-1}}{(2n-1)!}$$

The precision of the calculation is 10^{-6}. Stop accumulating when the absolute value of one item is less than the precision, and the accumulated value is the approximate value of $\sin x$.

Source code:

```cpp
//3_5.cpp
#include <iostream>
#include<cmath>
          //Header file cmath has declaration of mathematic functions
using namespace std;
int main()
{
  double k,r,s;
  double tsin(double x);
  cout<<"r=";
  cin>>r;
  cout<<"s=";
  cin>>s;
  if (r*r<=s*s)
    k=sqrt(tsin(r)*tsin(r)+tsin(s)*tsin(s)) ;
  else
    k=tsin(r*s)/2;
  cout<<k<<endl;
}

double tsin(double x)
{
  double p=0.000001,g=0,t=x;
  int n=1;
  do {
    g=g+t;
    n++;
```

```
    t=-t*x*x/(2*n-1)/(2*n-2);
    }while(fabs(t)>=p);
    return g;
}
```

Running result:

```
r=5
s=8
1.37781
```

Example 3.6: Game of casting dice.

Game rules: Dice has six faces – counting by the points, they are 1, 2, 3, 4, 5, and 6. The player inputs an unsigned integer, which is used as the seed to generate a random number at the beginning of the program.

In each turn the dice is casted twice, and we can get the total number of points. In the first turn, if the total number of points is 7 or 11, the player wins and the game is over; if the point total is 2, 3, or 12, the player loses and the game is over; otherwise the player records the point total as his point. In the following turns, if the point total is equal to the player's point, the player wins and the game is over; if the point total is 7, the player loses and the game is over; otherwise, it goes on to the next round.

The function *rolldice* is used to simulate rolling the dice, getting the point total, and outputting it.

Note: The system function *int rand(void)* generates a pseudorandom number. The pseudorandom number is not really random. When we call this function continuously in a program in the hope that it will generate a sequence of random numbers, we may discover that it will generate the same sequence each time we run the program. This sequence is called a pseudorandom number sequence. It is because *rand* needs an initial number called "seed", and different seeds will generate different sequences. Thus, if we give the program a different seed in each run, continuously calling *rand* will generate a different random number sequence. If the seed is not set, *rand* will use the default value 1 as the seed. Note that the method for setting the seed is somewhat special: it is not through the parameters of *rand*, but by calling another function *void srand(unsigned int seed)* to set the seed before calling *rand*, and the parameter *seed* in the function *srand* is the seed of *rand*.

Source code:

```
//3_6.cpp
#include <iostream>
#include <cstdlib>
using namespace std;
int rolldice(void);
int main()
```

```
{
  int gamestatus,sum,mypoint;
  unsigned seed;
  cout<<"Please enter an unsigned integer:";
  cin>>seed;       //Input the seed for the random number
  srand(seed);     //Pass the seed to rand()
  sum=rolldice(); //The first round, roll the dice and get the
                   //point total
  switch(sum)
  {
    case 7:        //Win if the point total is 7 or 11, status=1
    case 11:
          gamestatus=1;
           break;
    case 2:        //Lose if the total point is 2, 3 or 12, status=2
    case 3:
    case 12:
          gamestatus=2;
          break;
    default:       //Otherwise, continue the game, record the player's
                   //point, and set status=0
          gamestatus=0;
          mypoint=sum ;
          cout<<"point is "<<mypoint<<endl;
    break;
  }
  while (gamestatus==0) //Go to the next round if status = 0
  {
    sum=rolldice();
    if(sum==mypoint) //Win if the point total is equal to the
                      //player's point, set status=1
      gamestatus=1 ;
    else
      if ( sum==7 ) //Lose if the point total is 7, set status=2
        gamestatus=2;
  }
//When the status is not 0, the loop above ends, and the following
//code outputs the result
  if( gamestatus==1 )
    cout<<"player wins\n";
  else
    cout<<"player loses\n";
}
```

```
int rolldice(void)
{ //Roll the dice, get the total point, and output it
  int die1,die2,worksum;
  die1=1+rand()%6;
  die2=1+rand()%6;
  worksum=die1+die2;
  cout<<"player rolled "<<die1<<'+'<<die2<<'='<<worksum<<endl;
  return worksum;
}
```

Running result 1:

```
Please enter an unsigned integer:8
player rolled 5 + 1 = 6
point is 6
player rolled 6 + 6 = 12
player rolled 6 + 4 = 10
player rolled 6 + 6 = 12
player rolled 6 + 6 = 12
player rolled 3 + 2 = 5
player rolled 2 + 2 = 4
player rolled 3 + 4 = 7
player loses
```

Running result 2:

```
Please enter an unsigned integer:23
player rolled 6 + 3 = 9
point is 9
player rolled 5 + 4 = 9
player wins
```

2. Procedure of calling a function

The compiler compiles a C++ program and outputs a piece of executable code, which is then stored as a file suffixed with *exe* in the external storage. When the program is started, the computer first loads the executable code from the external storage into the code area of the memory, and then executes the code from the entry address (the beginning of the *main* function). During the execution, the computer will stop executing the current function when a function call occurs. It will then save the address of the next instruction (return address is used as the entry point of execution when returned from the called function), save the execution scene, jump to the entry address of the called function, and execute the called function. When meeting a *return* statement or reaching the end of the called function, the computer will restore the scene previously

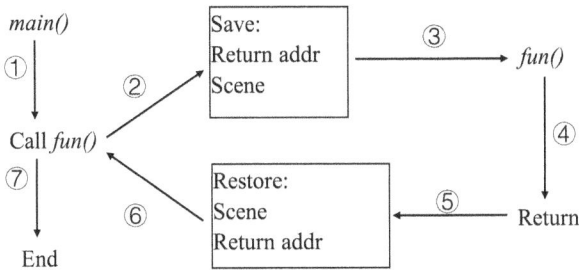

Fig. 3.1: Procedure of function call and function return.

stored, jump back to the return address, and continue the execution. Figure 3.1 shows the procedure of calling a function and returning from the call. The labels in the figure indicate the order of execution.

3. Nested function call

A nested call is allowed in a function. For example, function A calls function B, then function B calls function C, and this forms a nested call.

Example 3.7: Input two integers and compute the sum of their squares.
Analysis: Although the problem is easy, we design two functions to show how a nested call works: The function named *fun1* is used to compute the sum of squares, and the function named *fun2* is used to compute the square of an integer. The main function calls *fun1*, and *fun1* calls *fun2*.

Source code:

```
//3_7.cpp
#include <iostream>
using namespace std;
int main()
{
    int a,b;
    int fun1(int x,int y);
    cin>>a>>b;
    cout<<"Sum of squares of a and b:"<<fun1(a,b)<<endl;
}

int fun1(int x,int y)
{
    int fun2(int m);
    return (fun2(x)+fun2(y));
}
```

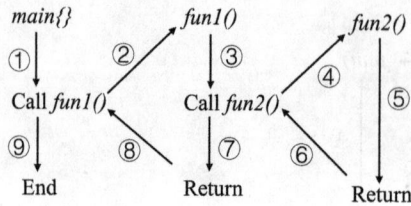

Fig. 3.2: The order of function calls in Example 3.7.

```
int fun2(int m)
{
    return (m*m);
}
```

Running result:

```
3 4
Sum of squares of a and b:25
```

Figure 3.2 shows the order of function calls in Example 3.7. The labels in the figure indicate the executing order.

4. Recursive call

A function can call itself directly or indirectly. This kind of function call is called a recursive call.

Calling oneself directly means that the body of a function contains a function call to itself, for example:

```
void fun1(void)
{
    ...
    fun1(); //A function call in fun1 to itself
    ...
}
```

And here is another example of a function indirectly calling itself:

```
void fun1(void)
{
    ...
    fun2();
    ...
}
void fun2(void)
{
```

```
...
     fun1();
...
}
```

Here *fun1* calls *fun2* and *fun2* in turn calls *fun1*. These two calls constitute an indirect recursive call.

The essence of recursion is that it decomposes the original problem into a new problem, which may use the solution of the original problem. Continue the decomposition according to this principle, and each new problem emerged is a simplified subset of the original problem. The ultimately decomposed problem should be one whose solution is already known. The procedure above is a finite recursive call. Only a finite recursive call makes sense; an infinite recursive call will not get any results and it makes no sense.

The procedure of a recursive call consists of two parts:

First stage: Recurrence. Decompose the original problem continuously into new subproblems until we reach a known situation, at which point the recurrence ends.

For example, to calculate 5!, we can make a decomposition as follows:

$$5! = 5 \times 4! \rightarrow 4! = 4 \times 3! \rightarrow 3! = 3 \times 2! \rightarrow 2! = 2 \times 1! \rightarrow 1! = 1 \times 0! \rightarrow 0! = 1$$

Unknown ──→ Known

Second stage: Regression. Starting from the known situation, use the result of the decomposed problem to solve the previous (more complex) problem. Repeat this process regressively according to the reversed order of the recurrence stage, until we reach the start of the recurrence. The regression then ends and the whole recursion finishes.

The regression procedure of calculating 5! is:

$$5! = 5 \times 4! = 120 \leftarrow 4! = 4 \times 3! = 24 \leftarrow 3! = 3 \times 2! = 6 \leftarrow 2! = 2 \times 1! = 2 \leftarrow 1! = 1 \times 0! = 1 \leftarrow 0! = 1$$

Unknown ←── Known

Example 3.8: Compute $n!$.

Analysis: The formula for calculating $n!$ is:

$$n! = \begin{cases} 1 & (n = 0) \\ n(n-1)! & (n > 0) \end{cases}$$

This formula is recursive, since it calculates a factorial by using another factorial. Thus the program uses a recursive call. The ending condition of the recursion is n=0.

Source code:

```
//3_8.cpp
#include <iostream>
using namespace std;
```

```
long fac(int n)
{
    long f;
    if (n<0) cout<<"n<0,data error!"<<endl;
    else if (n==0) f=1;
    else f=fac(n-1)*n;
    return(f);
}

int main()
{
    long fac(int n);
    int n;
    long y;
    cout<<"Enter a positive integer:";
    cin>>n;
    y=fac(n);
    cout<<n<<"!="<<y<<endl;
}
```

Running result:

```
Enter a positive integer:8
8!=40320
```

Example 3.9: Calculate the number of possible combinations (i.e., the combinatorial number) of selecting k person(s) out of n person(s) to form a committee.

Analysis: The combinatorial number of selecting k person(s) out of n person(s)

= The combinatorial number of selecting k person(s) out of $n - 1$ person(s)

+ The combinatorial number of selecting $k - 1$ person(s) out of $n - 1$ person(s)

Since the formula is recursive, it is easy to write a recursive function to implement the calculation. The ending condition of the recursion is n==k||k==0, at which time the combinatorial number is 1. Then the regression may start.

Source code:

```
//3_9.cpp
#include<iostream>
using namespace std;
int main()
{
    int n,k;
    int comm(int n, int k);
```

```
    cin>>n>>k;
    cout<<comm(n,k) <<endl;
}
int comm(int n, int k)
{
    if ( k>n )
        return 0;
    else if( n==k||k==0 )
        return 1;
    else
        return comm(n-1,k)+comm(n-1,k-1);
}
```

Running result:

```
18 5
8568
```

Example 3.10: Hanoi Tower Game.

There are three pillars A, B, and C. N plates of different sizes have been piled on pillar A, with larger plates being under smaller plates, as shown in Figure 3.3. The procedure of the game is to move the plates from pillar A to pillar C. The player can use pillar B during the game, though he can only move one plate at a time, and larger plates should always be under smaller plates during the movement.

Analysis: We could compress the procedure of moving n plates from pillar A to pillar C into three steps:

1. Move $n - 1$ plates from pillar A to pillar B;
2. Move the last plate on pillar A to pillar C;
3. Move $n - 1$ plates from pillar B to pillar C;

Actually, the three steps contain two kinds of operations:

1. Moving multiple plates from one pillar to another. This is a recursive operation.
2. Moving one plate from one pillar to another.

The following program uses two functions to implement the two kinds of operations above – function *hanoi* for the first operation and function *move* for the second.

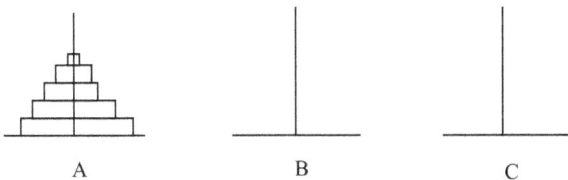

A   B   C   **Fig. 3.3:** Hanoi Tower Game.

Source code:

```
//3_10.cpp
#include <iostream>
using namespace std;
void move(char getone,char putone)
{
    cout<< getone <<"-->"<<putone<<endl;
}
void hanoi(int n,char one,char two,char three)
{
    void move(char getone,char putone);
    if (n==1) move (one,three);
    else
    {
        hanoi (n-1,one,three,two);
        move(one,three);
        hanoi(n-1,two,one,three);
    }
}

int main()
{
    void hanoi(int n,char one,char two,char three);
    int m;
    cout<<"Enter the number of discs:";
    cin>>m;
    cout<<"the steps to moving "<<m<<" discs:"<<endl;
    hanoi(m,'A','B','C');
}
```

Running result:

```
Enter the number of discs:3
the steps to moving 3 discs:
A-->C
A-->B
C-->B
A-->C
B-->A
B-->C
A-->C
```

3.1.3 Passing Parameters Between Functions

Before a function is called, the formal parameters of this function neither take up any real memory space nor have real values. When a function call is made, the computer allocates memory for the formal parameters and assigns the actual parameters to the formal parameters. An actual parameter could be a constant, variable, or expression, and should match the type of the corresponding formal parameter (the parameter in the same position in its parameter list). Passing parameters between functions is the process of assigning formal parameters according to actual parameters. C++ has two ways to pass parameters: Call-by-Value and Call-by-Reference.

1. Call-by-Value
The procedure of Call-by-Value consists of two steps: allocating memory space for a formal parameter, and using the actual parameter to initialize the formal parameter (assigning the actual parameter to the formal parameter). This procedure just passes the value of the actual parameter to the formal parameter. The formal parameter does not have any relation to the actual parameter once it has been initialized, and any change of the formal parameters afterwards cannot affect the actual parameter.

Example 3.11: Swap and output two integers.

```
//3_11.cpp
#include<iostream>
using namespace std;
void Swap(int a, int b);

int main()
{
    int x(5), y(10);
    cout<<"x="<<x<<" y="<<y<<endl;
    Swap(x,y);
    cout<<"x="<<x<<" y="<<y<<endl;
}

void Swap(int a, int b)
{
    int t;
    t=a;
    a=b;
    b=t;
}
```

Execute the function call in the main function:

Swap(x,y)

Inside the function Swap:

t=a;   a=b;   b=t;

Returned to the main function:

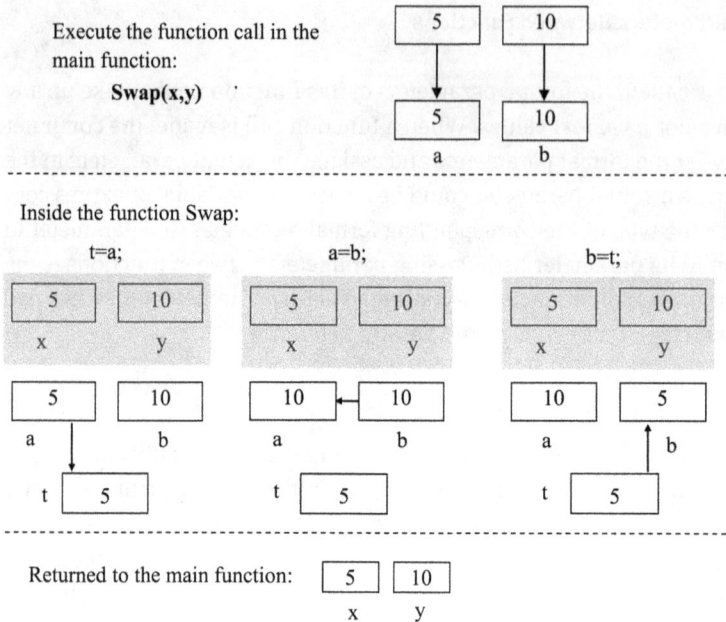

Fig. 3.4: The status of variables when the program in Example 3.11 is running.

Running result:

```
x=5  y=10
x=5  y=10
```

Analysis: From the running result we can see that the values of variable *x* and *y* have not been swapped. It's because in the function call above we use Call-by-Value to pass parameters, only where the values of the actual parameters are passed to the formal parameters. Thus the change of the formal parameters afterwards will not affect the actual parameters. Figure 3.4 shows the status of the variables when the program is running.

2. Call-by-Reference

We have seen that passing parameters through Call-by-Value is unidirectional. So how can changes made in the called function on formal parameters affect the actual parameters in the calling function? We can use Call-by-Reference to achieve this.

Reference is a special type of variable; it can be viewed as an alias of another variable. Accessing the reference of a variable is the same as accessing the variable itself. Here is an example:

```
int i,j;
int &ri=i;    //Make an int type reference of ri, initialize it to an
              //alias of i
j=10;
ri=j;         //Same as i=j;
```

The following rules must be followed when using references:
-   A reference must be initialized to refer to an existing object when it is declared.
-   Once a reference is initialized, it cannot be changed to refer to other objects.

The rules above indicate that a reference should be fixed to refer to an object in its whole life, from its definition to its end.

Formal parameters can also be references. When a formal parameter is a reference, the situation is a bit different: the formal parameter of the reference type is not initialized during its type declaration, and it is only when the function is called that the computer allocates memory space for the formal parameter and initializes it to the actual parameter. In this way, the formal parameter of the reference type becomes an alias of the actual parameter, and every operation on the formal parameter directly affects the actual parameters.

The function call that uses references as formal parameters is called Call-by-Reference.

Example 3.12: Rewrite the program of Example 3.11, using Call-by-Reference to make the two integers swap correctly.

```
//3_12.cpp
#include<iostream>
using namespace std;
void Swap(int& a, int& b);
int main()
{
    int x(5), y(10);
    cout<<"x="<<x<<" y="<<y<<endl;
    Swap(x,y);
    cout<<"x="<<x<<" y="<<y<<endl;
}

void Swap(int& a, int& b)
{
    int t;
    t=a;
    a=b;
    b=t;
}
```

Execute the function call in the
main function:

Swap(x,y);

Inside the function Swap:

t=a;   a=b;   b=t;

Returned to the main function:

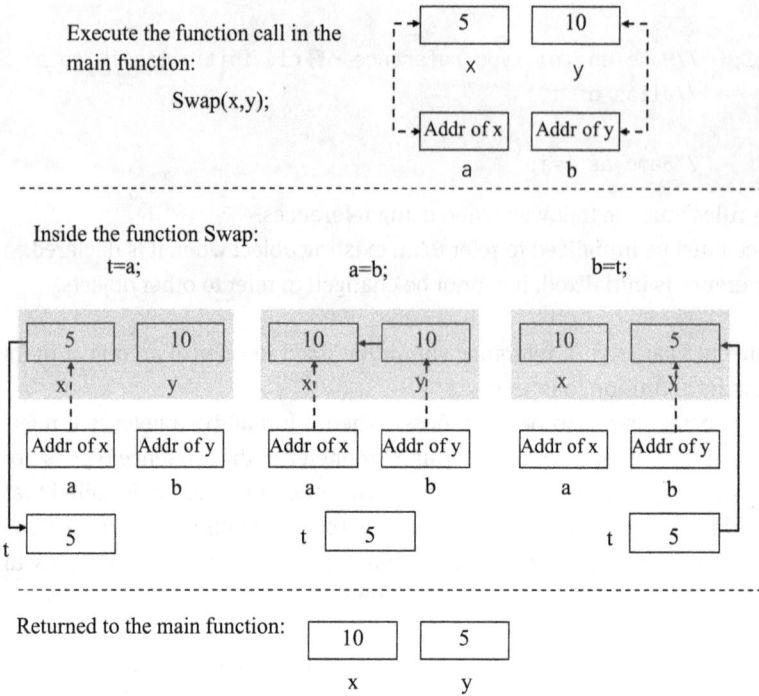

Fig. 3.5: The status of variables when the program in Example 3.12 is running.

Running result:

```
x=5 y=10
x=10 y=5
```

Analysis: We can see from the running result that the swap is successful when the program uses Call-by-Reference to pass parameters. The only difference between Call-by-Value and Call-by-Reference lies in the declaration of the formal parameters, while the function call statements in the calling function are the same. Figure 3.5 shows the status of variables when the program is running.

Example 3.13: An example of Call-by-Reference.

```
//3_13.cpp
#include <iostream>
#include <iomanip>
using namespace std;
void fiddle(int in1, int &in2);
int main()
{
    int count = 7, index = 12;'
```

```
    cout << "The values are ";
    cout<<setw(5)<<count;
    cout<<setw(5)<<index<<endl;
    fiddle(count, index);
    cout << "The values are ";
    cout<<setw(5)<<count;
    cout<<setw(5)<<index<<endl;
}

void fiddle(int in1, int &in2)
{
    in1 = in1 + 100;
    in2 = in2 + 100;
    cout << "The values are ";
    cout<<setw(5)<<in1;
    cout<<setw(5)<<in2<<endl;
}
```

Running result:

```
The values are    7  12
The values are  107 112
The values are    7 112
```

Analysis: The first parameter *in1* of function *fiddle* has type *int*, and is assigned the value of the actual parameter *count* when the function is called. The second parameter *in2* is a reference, and is initialized by the actual parameter *index* to an alias of *index*. Thus, the change on *in1* in the called function has no effect on the actual parameter *count*, while the change on *in2* in the called function is in fact the change on the variable *index* in the *main* function. When returned back to the *main* function, the value of *count* has not been changed, while the value of *index* has been changed.

3.2 Inline Functions

At the beginning of this chapter, we mentioned that using functions helps developers to reuse codes, improve the development efficiency and the reliability of the program, and facilitate the collaboration and modification of the program. But function calls can also reduce the execution efficiency of programs. When a function call is made, the computer needs to save the execution scene and return address before jumping to the entry address of the called function and starting execution; when returned from the called function, the computer needs to restore the scene and return address previously saved before continuing the execution. These procedures take time and memory space.

For some simple, small, but frequently used functions, we can use inline functions. An inline function does not cause control transfer when it is called, but makes itself embedded in every place it is called during the compilation. In this way, the cost of passing parameters and control transfers can be saved.

Inline functions use the keyword "inline" in the function definition. The form is like this:

```
inline Type identifier Function name (Parameters) { Function body; }
```

There are several points that require our attention when using inline functions:
- Generally, loop statements and *switch* statements should not appear in an inline function.
- Inline functions must be defined before their first call.
- Inline functions do not support abnormal interface statements. (Abnormal interface statements will be discussed in Chapter 12)

Generally, inline functions should be simple functions, with simple structures and few statements. Defining a complex function as an inline function may lead to code bloat and also increase the cost. In this case, most compilers will automatically convert the inline function into a common function before processing. What kind of functions should be counted as complex? The answer depends on compilers. Generally, functions that have loop statements cannot be processed as inline functions.

Therefore, the keyword *inline* is just a request. The compiler does not promise that every function with the keyword *inline* will be processed as an inline function. Moreover, functions without the *inline* keyword can possibly be compiled as inline functions.

Example 3.14: An example of an inline function.

```cpp
//3_14.cpp
#include<iostream>
using namespace std;
inline double CalArea(double radius) //Inline function, to calculate
                                     //the area of a circle
{
    return 3.14*radius*radius;
}

int main()
{
    double r(3.0);                   //r is the radius of the circle
    double area;
    area=CalArea(r);
```

```
/*Call inline function to calculate the area of the circle. This
will be replaced by the body of function CalArea during the
compiling.*/
cout<<area<<endl;
}
```

Running result:

```
28.26
```

3.3 Default Formal Parameters in Functions

Functions can declare default values of formal parameters in its definition. In such cases, if the actual parameter is provided when the function is called, the formal parameter will be initialized by the actual parameter; otherwise it will use its default value. For example:

```
int add(int x=5,int y=6) //Declare the default parameters
{ return x+y;
}
int main()
{ add(10,20); //Use actual parameters to initialize parameters,
                //calculate 10+20
    add(10); //Parameter x is initialized by actual parameter 10,
                //parameter y is initialized by its default parameter 5,
                //calculate 10+6
    add();   //Parameter x and y are all initialized by their
                //default parameters, calculate 5+6
}
```

Default parameters must be declared from right to left. Formal parameters without default values should not appear at the right side of any formal parameter that has a default value. This is because formal parameters are initialized by the actual parameters from left to right. For example:

```
int add(int x,int y=5,int z=6); //Correct
int add(int x=1,int y=5,int z); //Wrong
int add(int x=1,int y,int z=6); //Wrong
```

Default values should also be provided in the function prototype. For example:

```
int add(int x=5,int y=6);//Default value is provided in the function
                            //prototype
```

```
int main()
{ add();
}
int add(int x,int y)
{ return x+y;
}
```

Within the same scope, the declaration of default values for formal parameters should be uniform; but in different scopes, declarations of default values for formal parameters can be different. Here scope refers to the area enclosed by the braces that embodies the function prototype. More details about scope will be discussed in Chapter 5. For example:

```
int add(int x=1,int y=2);
int main()
{ int add(int x=3,int y=4);
      add(); //Use the local default parameter(calculate 3+4)
}
void fun(void)
{ ...
      add(); //Use the global default parameter(calculate 1+2)
}
```

Example 3.15: An example of a function using default parameters.
The function of the program is to calculate the volume of cuboids. The subfunction *get_volume* is used to calculate the volume, which has three parameters: *length*, *width*, and *height*. The parameters *width* and *height* have default values. The main function calls *get_volume* using different parameters. Analyze the running result of the program.

```
//3_15.cpp
#include <iostream>
#include <iomanip>
using namespace std;
int get_volume(int length, int width = 2, int height = 3);
int main()
{
    int x = 10, y = 12, z = 15;
    cout << "Some box data is " ;
    cout << get_volume(x, y, z) << endl;
    cout << "Some box data is " ;
    cout << get_volume(x, y) << endl;
```

```
        cout << "Some box data is " ;
        cout << get_volume(x) << endl;
        cout << "Some box data is ";
        cout << get_volume(x, 7) << endl;
        cout << "Some box data is ";
        cout << get_volume(5, 5, 5) << endl;
    }

    int get_volume(int length, int width, int height)
    {
        cout<<setw(5)<<length<<setw(5)<<width<<setw(5)<<height<<' ';
        return length * width * height;
    }
```

Running result:

```
Some box data is 10 12 15 1800
Some box data is 10 12  3   360
Some box data is 10  2  3    60
Some box data is 10  7  3   210
Some box data is  5  5  5   125
```

Since the first parameter of the function *get_volume* has no default value, every function call on *get_volume* must provide the first actual parameter to initialize the formal parameter *length*. The parameters *width* and *height* have default values. So all three formal parameters will be initialized by actual parameters if the function call provides three actual parameters; the last formal parameter *height* will use the default value if the function call provides two actual parameters; the last two formal parameters *width* and *height* will use the default values if the function call only provides one actual parameter.

When overloading functions that have default values, we should avoid ambiguity. For example, the following two function prototypes will cause ambiguity in that they cannot be recognized as different overloaded forms by the compiler:

```
    void fun(int length, int width = 2, int height = 3);
    void fun(int length);
```

In other words, when the function *fun* is called in the following form, the compiler is unable to decide which overloaded function should be executed:

```
    fun(1);
```

The compiler will count this as a compiling error.

3.4 Function Overloading

In programs, a function name is essentially the name of an operation. With the help of names similar to natural languages, we can write programs that are easy to understand and modify. Here comes a problem: how to reflect the tiny differences in natural languages using programming languages? Usually, a word in a natural language can have different meanings in different contexts. This is called polysemy, which in programming language is called "overloading". For example: in a natural language, *play the piano, play chess and play basketball* all use the same verb "*play*", while the actions that *play* indicates in the three contexts are quite different. We can understand these phrases, since we have learned how to play different objects in our life. So nobody would say "Please play the piano just as you would play chess, or play the chess just as you would play basketball". Is it possible for a computer to have the same ability? This is up to the programs we write. C++ provides the support for function overloading, which enables us to give different functions the same name. The compiler will choose an appropriate function to execute according to the context (number and types of parameters).

Function overloading means that two or more functions share the same name, albeit with differences in the number or in the types of their formal parameters. The compiler will automatically choose a function that best fits the calling context according to the number and the types of formal parameters.

Without function overloading, for the same operation on different data types, we need to define several functions with different names. For example, when defining the addition function, we need different function names for the addition of integers and the addition of float numbers:

```
int iadd(int x, int y);
float fadd(float x, float y);
```

It is quite inconvenient when making function calls.

C++ allows functions with similar functionalities to use the same name within the same scope, which allows for overloading. It is easy to use and remember. For example:

1. `int add(int x, int y);`
    `float add(float x, float y);` } Different types of parameters

2. `int add(int x,int y);`
    `int add(int x,int y,int z);` } Different number of parameters

Notes:
– The formal parameters of overloaded functions must have differences in the number or in the types of parameters, or in both. Compiler will choose the appropriate function according to the number and the types of parameters when there is a function call. If functions of the same name have the same number of parame-

ters and the same types of parameters (no matter what their return types are), the compiler will count it as a compiling error (function redefinition). For example:

1.
```
int add(int x,int y);
int add(int a,int b); //Error: compiler doesn't discriminate
                      //functions by their parameter names
```

2.
```
int add(int x,int y);
void add(int x,int y); //Error: compiler doesn't discriminate
                       //functions by their return types
```

- Do not set functions of different functionalities with the same name, in case any misunderstanding or confusion of the calling result may occur.

```
int add(int x,int y) { return x+y; }
float add(float x,float y) { return x-y; }
```

Here, let us see an example of function overloading.

Example 3.16: An example of function overloading.
Write three overloaded functions with the same name *add*, and make them implement the following operations respectively – the addition of two integers, the addition of two real numbers, and the addition of two complex numbers.

Source code:
```
//3_16.cpp
#include<iostream>
using namespace std;
struct complex
{
    double real;
    double imaginary;
};

int main()
{
    int m, n;
    double x, y;
    complex c1, c2, c3;
    int add(int m, int n);
    double add(double x, double y);
    complex add(complex c1, complex c2);

    cout<<"Enter two integer: ";
    cin>>m>>n;
    cout<<"integer "<<m<<'+'<<n<<"="<<add(m,n)<<endl;
```

```
    cout<<"Enter two real number: ";
    cin>>x>>y;
    cout<<"real number "<<x<<'+'<<y<<"= "<<add(x,y)<<endl;

    cout<<"Enter the first complex number: ";
    cin>>c1.real>>c1.imaginary;
    cout<<"Enter the second complex number: ";
    cin>>c2.real>>c2.imaginary;
    c3=add(c1,c2);
    cout<<"complex number ("<<c1.real<<','<<c1.imaginary<<")+("
    <<c2.real<<','<<c2.imaginary<<")= ("<<c3.real<<','<<
        c3.imaginary<<")\n";
}
int add(int m, int n)
{ return m+n; }

double add(double x, double y)
{ return x+y; }

complex add(complex c1, complex c2)
{
    complex c;
    c.real=c1.real+c2.real;
    c.imaginary=c1.imaginary+c2.imaginary;
    return c;
}
```

Running result:

```
Enter two integer: 3 5
integer 3 + 5 = 8
Enter two real number: 2.3 5.8
real number 2.3 + 5.8 = 8.1
Enter the first complex number: 12.3 45.6
Enter the second complex number: 56.7 67.8
complex number (12.3,45.6)+(56.7,67.8)= (69,113.4)
```

3.5 Using C++ System Functions

C++ not only allows us to design functions ourselves, but also provides hundreds of functions in the C++ system library (system functions) for us to use. For example: the function to calculate square root (*sqrt*), the function to calculate absolute value (*abs*), etc.

We know that program must declare the function prototype before calling the function. The prototypes of system functions have all been provided by the C++ system library, which sorts and stores them in several header files. Programmers only need to embed the related header files into the code using the *include* instruction, and then they can use the system functions. For example, if you want to use mathematic functions, you should include the header file *cmath*.

Example 3.17: An example of using C++ system functions.
Input an angle value from the keyboard, and calculate its sine, cosine, and tangent values.

Analysis: The C++ system library provides the functions to calculate the sine, cosine, and tangent of an angle: *sin()*, *cos()* and *tan()*, and these function prototypes are contained in the header file *cmath*.

Source code:

```
//3_18.cpp
#include<iostream>
#include<cmath>
using namespace std;
const double pi(3.14159265);
int main()
{
    double a,b;
    cin>>a;
    b=a*pi/180;
    cout<<"sin("<<a<<")="<<sin(b)<<endl;
    cout<<"cos("<<a<<")="<<cos(b)<<endl;
    cout<<"tan("<<a<<")="<<tan(b)<<endl;
}
```

Running result:

```
30
sin(30)=0.5
cos(30)=0.866025
tan(30)=0.57735
```

Making full use of system functions can greatly reduce the work of programming and improve the execution efficiency and reliability of the program. When using system functions, we should pay attention to two points:

1. Be familiar with the system functions provided by your C++ development environment. Different compilers may provide different system functions. Even compilers

from the same company, if they are in different versions, may provide different system functions. So programmers must consult the manual of the system library or the online help of the compiler, to check out the functionality, parameters, return value, and usage of system functions.

2. Make clear which header file contains the declaration of the system function you want to use. This can also be found in the manual of the system library or in the online help.

For example, the way to find the category list of the system functions of VC++6.0 from MSDN Library Visual Studio 6.0 is: First select "Visual C++ Documentation" in "Activity Subset"; then go through the following path: Visual C++ Documentation → Using Visual C++ → Visual C++ Programmer's Guide → Run-Time Library Reference → Run-Time Routines by Category → Run-Time Routines by Category, as shown in Figure 3.6.

The helping system lists the functions in the following groups:

- Argument access
- Floating-point support
- Buffer manipulation
- Input and output
- Byte classification

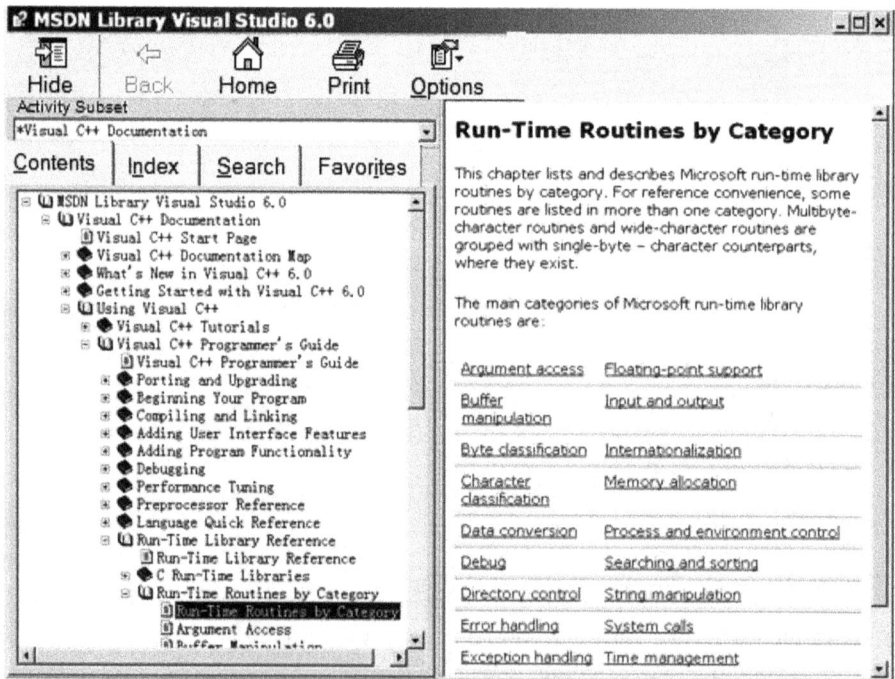

Fig. 3.6: MSDN Library in Visual Studio 6.0.

- Internationalization
- Character classification
- Memory allocation
- Data conversion
- Process and environment control
- Debugging
- Searching and sorting
- Directory control
- String manipulation
- Error handling
- System calls
- Exception handling
- Time management
- File handling

3.6 Summary

In object-oriented programming, the function is the basic unit of functionality abstraction.

A complex system usually needs to be divided into several subsystems, which then are developed and debugged separately. Subprograms are embodied as functions in C++. The functionality abstraction of objects is also implemented through functions. Functions can be reused once completed. We can use a function only knowing its behavior and usage, without the need to know its implementation. In this way, codes can be reused, the development efficiency and the reliability of the program can be improved, and collaboration, modification, and maintenance can be realized more easily.

A C++ program may consist of a main function and several subfunctions. The main function is the entry point of the program execution. The main function may call subfunctions, and subfunctions may call other subfunctions.

Function overloading allows functions with similar operations to share the same name. It is easy to use and can make the code more readable. The overloaded functions are discriminated by their formal parameters, and functions with the same name must have differences in the number of parameters or in the types of parameters, or in both.

In addition, the C++ system library provides hundreds of functions for programmers to use. The declarations of system function prototypes have all been provided in the C++ system library, which sorts and stores them in different header files. Programmers need to use *include* instruction to embed the related header files into their code, and then they can use the system functions.

Exercises

3.1 What is a function in C++? What is a calling function, and what is a called function? What is the relationship between them? How does one make a function call?

3.2 Look at the running result of the following program. Is there any difference from what you presumed ? Think over the usage of references.

Source code:

```
#include <iostream>
using namespace std;
int main()
{
    int intOne;
    int &rSomeRef = intOne;

    intOne = 5;
    cout << "intOne:\t" << intOne << endl;
    cout << "rSomeRef:\t" << rSomeRef << endl;
    cout << "&intOne:\t" << &intOne << endl;
    cout << "&rSomeRef:\t" << &rSomeRef << endl;

    int intTwo = 8;
    rSomeRef = intTwo; //not what you think!
    cout << "\nintOne:\t" << intOne << endl;
    cout << "intTwo:\t" << intTwo << endl;
    cout << "rSomeRef:\t" << rSomeRef << endl;
    cout << "&intOne:\t" << &intOne << endl;
    cout << "&intTwo:\t" << &intTwo << endl;
    cout << "&rSomeRef:\t" << &rSomeRef << endl;
}
```

3.3 Compare Call-by-Value and Call-by-Reference, and list their similarities and differences.

3.4 What is an inline function? What are its characteristics?

3.5 Must the following three names be the same: the formal parameter name in the function prototype, the formal parameter name in the function definition, and the actual parameter name in the function call?

3.6 How does one differentiate overloaded functions?

3.7 Write a function that contains two *unsigned short int* parameters. When the second parameter is nonzero, it returns the result of the first parameter dividing by the second parameter, and the result is of the *short int* type; otherwise, it returns –1. Realize input and output in the main function.

3.8 Write a function to convert Fahrenheit degrees to Celsius degrees. The formula is: C = (F – 32) * 5/9. In the main function, prompt users to input a Celsius degree, convert it into the corresponding Fahrenheit degree, and output the result.

3.9 Write a function to judge whether a number is prime or not. Realize input and output in the main function.

3.10 Write a function to get the greatest common divisor and the least common multiple of two integers.

3.11 What is a nested call? What is a recursive call?

3.12 Input an integer n in the main function, and write a function to calculate $1 + 2 + \cdots + n$ in a recursive way.

3.13 Write a recursive function Power(int x, int y) to calculate the y-th power of x. Realize input and output in the main function.

3.14 Write a function to calculate Fibonacci numbers in a recursive way. The formula is:
$$\text{fib}(n) = \text{fib}(n-1) + \text{fib}(n-2), \quad n > 2; \quad \text{fib}(1) = \text{fib}(2) = 1$$
Observe the procedure of making a recursive call.

3.15 Write a function to calculate the n-th Legendre Polynomial in a recursive way. Realize input and output in the main function. The recursion formula of the n-th Legendre Polynomial is:

$$p_n(x) = \begin{cases} 1 & (n = 0) \\ x & (n = 1) \\ ((2n - 1) \times x \times p_{n-1}(x) - (n - 1) \times p_{n-2}(x))/n & (n > 1) \end{cases}$$

4 Class and Object

Everything in the real world we are familiar with is an object. Objects can not only be visible, as houses, cars, airplanes, animals and plants, but also be invisible, as a plan. Objects can be a simple unit, like a person; and they can also be a combination of several objects; for example, there are multiple departments in a company, and each department has several staff members. A class can be formed based on the common attributes abstracted from similar objects. These are the concepts and methods we are familiar with in the real world. The aim of programming is to describe and solve problems in the real world, so the first step is to describe objects and classes faithfully in programs. C++, an object-oriented programming language, supports this kind of abstraction. A class in C++ is formed by the encapsulation of abstracted data and functions.

In this chapter, we will first introduce the main features of object-oriented design: abstraction, encapsulation, inheritance, and polymorphism. We then focus on the core concept of object-oriented design – **class**, which includes how to define and implement a class, and how to use classes to solve problems.

4.1 Basic Features of Object-Oriented Design

4.1.1 Abstraction

As a fundamental way to understand problems, abstraction is not new to us. Abstraction in the object-oriented method is a procedure in which specific issues (objects) are summarized and abstracted into the common attributes of a class of objects; it also includes the procedure of describing these attributes. The procedure of abstraction is also a procedure of analyzing and understanding problems. In the development of object-oriented software, we should first know the essence and the description of the problem; and then find the specific procedure to solve it. Generally, the abstraction of a problem should include two aspects: **abstraction of data and abstraction of behavior** (or abstraction of function, abstraction of code). The former describes the attributes or states of a class of objects, i.e., the characteristics used to distinguish this class of objects from other classes; the latter describes the common behavior or functional characteristics of a class of objects.

Let us see two simple examples: first we implement a simple clock program on a computer. From the analyses of the clock we can see that we need three integers to store time, which represent the hour, minute, and second respectively. This is an abstraction of the data that a clock possesses. In addition, a clock needs some simple functions, such as time display and time setup. This is an abstraction of the behavior of the clock. Using variables and functions in C++, we can describe the abstracted attributes of a clock like this:

https://doi.org/10.1515/9783110471977-004

Abstraction of data:

```
int Hour, int Minute, int Second
```

Abstraction of function:

```
ShowTime(), SetTime()
```

The second example concerns the abstraction of human beings. Based on the generalization and abstraction of human beings, we extract the common characteristics and have abstract descriptions as below:

Common attributes: name, sex, and age, which form the data abstraction of human beings. Using C++ variables to represent them, they can be:

```
char *name; char *sex; int age;
```

Common function: biological behaviors like eating and walking, and social behaviors like working and studying. They make up the function abstraction of human beings. We can also use C++ functions to represent them:

```
Eat(); Walk(); Work(); Study();
```

If we need to develop the personnel management software for a company, the common human characteristics mentioned above may not be enough, and we also need to concern wages, working age, department, operational capability, subordination, and so on.

From these two examples we can see that, focusing on different aspects of the same object can lead to different abstraction results. Even for the same problem, different requirements of problem solving may lead to different abstraction results.

4.1.2 Encapsulation

Encapsulation means combining abstracted data and behaviors (or functions) together to form an organic whole. In other words, encapsulation means to combine data and the functions operating on the data together to form a "class", and the data and the functions are both members of the class. For example, based on abstraction, we can encapsulate the data and the functions of a clock to make a class of that clock. According to C++ grammar, the class *Clock* can be defined as below:

```
class Clock                                    //class keyword, class name
{                                              //boundary
public:                                        //exterior interface
    void SetTime(int NewH, int NewM, int New S); //function, code
                                               //member
    void ShowTime();                           //function, code member
```

```
    private:                            //specific access permission
        int Hour,Minute,Second;         //attribute, data member
    };                                  //boundary
```

Here we defined a class *Clock* – its function members and data members describe the abstraction result of a clock. {} limits the boundary of that class. Keywords *public* and *private* are used to specify different access permissions of the members, which will be further discussed in 4.2.2. The two functions declared as *public* are the external interfaces of the class; the outside world can only communicate with the class *Clock* though these two interfaces. The three integers declared as *private* are the private data of this class, and they cannot be accessed directly by the outside.

We can see that encapsulation makes some members the external interfaces between the class and the outside, while hiding other members. Through encapsulation we can properly control the access permissions of class members, minimize the interactions between different classes, improve data security, and simplify the coding work.

By encapsulating data and code into a reusable program module, we can use the module efficiently while writing a program. Since we can use an encapsulated module only through its external interfaces and by some specific access rules, we need to not know its implementation details.

4.1.3 Inheritance

Knowledge acquisition is a long process, and for some questions there may have already been in-depth studies. How do we use these research results? And, if we get a better understanding of the problem at a later stage of the program design, how do we integrate the new understandings into what we have already done? If we start from scratch over and over again, how can we improve the productivity of the software industry?

Inheritance is designed to solve these problems. Only by using inheritance can we make progress based on existing achievements and avoid duplicating analyses and developments. C++ offers the inheritance mechanism of class, which allows programmers to make more specified, more detailed descriptions for a class while keeping the original attributes of the class. This hierarchy structure can effectively reflect the developing process of human understanding. Chapter 7 will discuss the inheritance of class.

4.1.4 Polymorphism

Polymorphism in object-oriented design is a direct simulation of human ways of thinking. Take 'play ball' for example: the word 'play' is a piece of abstracted information with multiple meanings. We can say play basketball, play volleyball, and play bad-minton, where 'play' indicates participating in some kind of sport, while the rules and actual movements in each case are totally different. In fact, this is an abstraction of multiple sports behaviors. In programming it is the same, and the overloaded function Chapter 3 introduces is a way to achieve polymorphism.

Generally speaking, polymorphism means that a program can deal with multiple types of objects. In C++, this polymorphism falls into forced polymorphism, overloading polymorphism, type parameter polymorphism, and inclusion polymorphism.

Forced polymorphism is realized by converting one type of data into another type of data, a type conversion (explicit or implicit) introduced before. Overloading means to give the same name different meanings. We have already introduced function overloading in Chapter 3, and operator overloading will be covered in Chapter 8. These two kinds of polymorphism belong to special polymorphisms, which are only superficial polymorphisms.

Inclusion polymorphism and type parameter polymorphism are general polymorphisms, which are real polymorphisms. C++ uses virtual functions to realize inclusion polymorphism. Virtual functions are the essence of polymorphism, and will be discussed in Chapter 8. Templates in C++ are used to achieve type parameter polymorphism, which includes function templates and class templates, and we will discuss them in Chapter 9.

4.2 Class and Object

Class is the key point of the object-oriented design method. We can use class to achieve the encapsulation of data.

In procedure-oriented structured programming design, program modules are implemented through functions. Functions encapsulate logically correlated codes and data to achieve a specific usage. **In object-oriented programming design, program modules are implemented through classes.** Classes encapsulate logically correlated functions and data, and they are the abstract description of the problem. Thus, compared with functions, classes have a higher degree of integration, and are more suitable for developments of large and complex projects.

Section 4.1 introduced the concept of class from the perspectives of abstraction and encapsulation. It is helpful for the beginner to understand class in another simpler way. Let's first take a look at basic data types, such as *int, double, bool*, and so on. When defining a variable of a basic data type, what happens exactly? Let's see the following statements:

```
int i;
bool b;
```

Obviously these statements define how variable *i* is used to store *int* data and variable *b* is used to store *bool* data. But that's not all that a variable definition indicates. Another important indication may usually be ignored, and that is the restriction of operations on the defined variable. For example, we can do arithmetic and comparison operations on *i*; while we can do logical and comparison operations on *b*. This shows that each data type includes not only the data attributes but also the operations on the data.

No matter what kind of program language it is, the amount of its basic data types is limited. The basic data types that C++ provides also cannot describe all the objects in the real world. So C++ supports a user-defined data type, class. In fact, because class is a user-defined data type, we can theoretically define infinite new classes. In this way, we can use the basic data type *int* to describe integers, and use user-defined class to describe objects like 'clock,' 'car,' 'geometric figure,' and 'people.' Just as a basic data type includes data and operation, when defining a class we have to describe its data and operations. This is what was introduced in Section 4.1, that through data abstraction and function abstraction of objects in the real world, we can get the data members and function members of a class.

After defining a class, we can define the variable of the class, and this variable is called the object (or instance) of the class. A definition of a variable of a class is called an instantiation of the class.

4.2.1 Definition of Class

Let's take the clock for example again. Class *Clock* is defined as below:

```
class Clock
{
public:
    void SetTime(int NewH, int NewM, int NewS);
    void ShowTime();
private:
    int Hour,Minute,Second;
};
```

Here the data and behavior of the clock are encapsulated as the **data member** and **function member** of Class *Clock*. The grammar of defining a class is as follows:

```
class class-name
{
    public:
            exterior interface
    protected:
            protected member
```

```
        private:
                private member
   };
```

Public, *protected*, and *private* respectively denote different access permissions for different members, which will be detailed in Section 4.2.2. Note that we can just define the function prototype inside the class, and the implement of the function (the function body) can be defined outside the class definition:

```
void Clock::SetTime(int NewH, int NewM, int NewS)
{
    Hour=NewH;
    Minute=NewM;
    Second=NewS;
}

void Clock::ShowTime()
{
    cout<<Hour<<":"<<Minute<<":"<<Second<<endl;
}
```

We can see that unlike common functions, the names of the member functions of a class need to be restricted by the name of the class, such as *'Clock::ShowTime.'*

4.2.2 Access Control to Class Members

Class members include data members describing the attributes of the problem and function members describing the behaviors of the problem, which are two indivisible aspects. In order to understand access control to class members, let's see the clock example again. Any clock records time and has a panel, a knob, or a button. As discussed in Section 4.1, we can abstract all these common attributes of clocks into a *Clock* class. In normal use, users can only look up time through the panel and adjust time using the knob or button. A mender can take the clock apart, while others had better not try. In this way, the panel, the knob, and the button are the only ways for us to touch and use a clock. Thus we can design them as the external interfaces of the *Clock* class. The time recorded by the clock is the private member of the class, which users can only access through the external interfaces.

The access control to class members is realized by setting the access control attributes of class members. There are three kinds of access control attributes: **public, private, and protected.**

Public members define the external interfaces of the class. Public members are declared by the keyword *public*. We can only access public members outside the

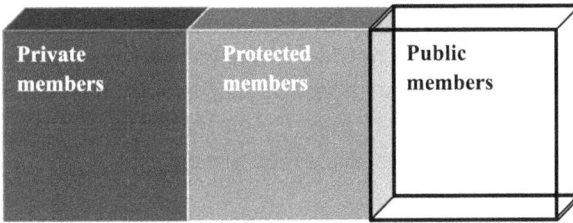

Fig. 4.1: Access restriction of class members.

class. For the class *Clock*, we can only use the public function members *SetTime()* and *ShowTime()* to adjust or display time.

Class members defined after the keyword *private* are private members of the class. If the private members immediately follow the class name, then keyword *private* can be omitted. **Private members can only be accessed by the member functions of the class, and any access to private members from outside of the class is illegal.** Thus, private members are completely hidden in the class, which protect the security of data. *Hour, Minute,* and *Second* in class *Clock* are all private members.

Protected members are much like private members; the differences lie in their effects on newly generated classes during the inheritance procedure. Chapter 7 will discussed this issue in detail.

Figure 4.1 describes the access control attributes of class members visually: set the members needed to be hidden to private, make them an inaccessible black box from the outside; set interfaces provided for the outside to public, and then they are transparent to the outside; protected members are like a cage, which offer some special access attributes for derived classes.

Now imagine, if a clock can neither tell the time nor adjust the time, would you like to buy it? You may say: 'what use is it!' This is like a class out of any external interface – it cannot be used. So remember, designing a class is for usage, and we must design necessary external interfaces for its use.

In the definition of a class, members with different access attributes can appear in any order. The keywords to denote access attributes can also appear at any time. But each member can only have one access attribute. For example, the follow definition of class *Clock* is also right:

```
class Clock
{
public:
    void SetTime(int NewH, int NewM, int NewS);
private:
    int Hour,Minute,Second;
public:
    void ShowTime();
};
```

Generally we put public members in the front when writing a class definition. This is easy to read, because public members are what need to be known when the outside needs to access the class. In general, all the data members of a class should be declared as private, and thus the internal data structure won't affect the outside of the class, and the mutual influences between program modules can be minimized.

4.2.3 Member Function of Class

Function members of a class describe the behaviors of the class, such as the function members *SetTime()* and *ShowTime()* of class *Clock*. Member functions implement the program algorithm and are the methods used to process the encapsulated data.

1. Declaration and Implementation of Member Functions
The function prototype should be defined in the class body. A function prototype describes the parameter list and the return type of the function. The implementation of the function is written outside the class body. Different from ordinary functions, a member function should specify its class name when it is implemented. The implementation form is:

```
Return Type _ Class Name::Member Function Name (parameters)
{
      Function body
}
```

2. Member Function with Default Formal Parameters
In Chapter 3 we introduced functions with default parameters. Member functions can also have default formal parameters, and its calling rules are the same as those of ordinary functions. Sometimes default formal parameters can bring great convenience. For example, class *Clock*'s member function *SetTime()* can have default parameters as below:

```
void Clock::SetTime(int NewH=0, int NewM=0, int NewS=0)
{
      Hour=NewH;
      Minute=NewM;
      Second=NewS;
}
```

If this member function is called without actual parameters, the clock time will be set to 0 AM according to the default values.

3. Inline Member Function

We know that calling a function costs some memory resources and CPU time to pass parameters, to return value, and to record the calling state in order to correctly return and run after the call finished. If a member function needs to be called frequently, and the function code is simple, such a function can also be defined as an inline function. Like the ordinary inline function introduced in Section 3, the function body of an inline member function will be inserted into wherever it is called at the compiling time. By doing this, the cost of function call is reduced and the execution efficiency is improved, while the code length after the compiling is increased. So we should carefully weigh the pros and cons, and only define fairly simple member functions as inline functions.

Two ways can be used to define an inline function: implicit definition and explicit definition.

Implicit definition puts the function body directly into the class body. For example, to define the member function *ShowTime()* of class *Clock* as an inline function, we can write:

```
class Clock
{
public:
    void SetTime(int NewH, int NewM, int NewS);
    void ShowTime()
{ cout<<Hour<<":"<<Minute<<":"<<Second<<endl;}
private:
    int Hour,Minute,Second;
};
```

To keep the definition simple, we commonly use the keyword *inline* to define a function explicitly. That is to say, we put the keyword *inline* before the function's return type in the function definition, and don't include the body of *ShowTime()* in the definition of class:

```
inline void Clock::ShowTime()
{
    cout<<Hour<<":"<<Minute<<":"<<Second<<endl;
}
```

It is the same as the implicit declaration mentioned above.

4.2.4 Object

Class is an abstraction mechanism; it describes the common attributes and behaviors of a type of problem. In C++, an object of a class is a specific entity (or instance) of the class. For instance, take all the employees in a company as a class, and then each employee is a specific instance, i.e., an object.

In Chapter 2 we introduced basic data types and user-defined types. In fact, each data type is an abstraction of a class of data, and every variable defined in a program is an instance of its data type. If we treat class as a user-defined type, then the object of a class can be treated as a variable of this type. For this reason, sometimes both ordinary variables and objects of a class are called objects in this book.

Defining an object is the same as defining an ordinary variable – they both use the following form:

```
Class name object name;
```

For example:

```
Clock myClock;
```

It defines an object of class *Clock*, called *myClock*.

After defining a class and its objects, we can access the public members of the objects. For instance, set and display the time of object *myClock*. We use operator '.' to achieve this accession, and the general form is:

```
Object name.public member_function_name(parameter_list)
```

For example, to access the function member *ShowTime()* of *myClock*, which is an object of class *Clock*, we use:

```
myClock.ShowTime()
```

Only public members of a class can be accessed from outside, while inside the class, every member can be accessed directly by its name. This provides an effective control over the accessing range.

4.2.5 Program Instance

Example 4.1: Complete implementation of class clock.

```cpp
//4_1.cpp
#include<iostream>
using namespace std;
class Clock                              //definition of class Clock
{
public: //exterior interface, public function member
    void SetTime(int NewH=0, int NewM=0, int NewS=0);
    void ShowTime();
private:                                 //private data member
    int Hour,Minute,Second;
};
```

```
//implementation of function member of class Clock
void Clock::SetTime(int NewH, int NewM, int NewS)
{
    Hour=NewH;
    Minute=NewM;
    Second=NewS;
}

inline void Clock::ShowTime()
{
    cout<<Hour<<":"<<Minute<<":"<<Second<<endl;
}
//main function
int main()    -
{
    Clock myClock;                          //define object myClock
    cout<<"First time set and output:"<<endl;
    myClock.SetTime();                      //set time to default value
    myClock.ShowTime();                     //show time
    cout<<"Second time set and output:"<<endl;
    myClock.SetTime(8,30,30);               //set time to 8:30:30
    myClock.ShowTime();                     //show time
}
```

Analysis: This program can be divided into three comparatively independent parts: the first is the definition of class *Clock*; the second is the implementation of the function members of class *Clock*; the third is the main function. From earlier discussions we know that defining a class and its function members is only a description of the problem with high abstraction and encapsulation. To solve the problem, we also need messages passing between instances, or objects, of the class. Here the main function is to define the object and pass the messages.

Beware that the member function *SetTime* is a function with default parameters, and it has three default parameters. The function *ShowTime* is an explicitly defined inline member function, because it has only a few statements. In the main function, we first declare an object *myClock* of class *Clock*, and then use this object to call its member function. The first call sets the time to its default value and outputs it. The second call sets the time to 8:30:30 and outputs it. The running result of the program is:

```
First time set and output:
0:0:0
Second time set and output:
8:30:30
```

4.3 Constructor and Destructor

The relation between class and object is like the relation between basic types and their variables, i.e., general and special. An object differs from other objects mainly in two ways: the first is its name, which is the external difference; the second is the values of its data attributes, which is the internal difference. Just like how we can initialize a basic-type variable when defining it, we can also initialize the data members of an object when defining the object. Setting values to data members of an object while defining the object is called the initialization of that object. After the use of a specific object is finished, we usually need to do some cleaning. In C++, there are two special function members used to do this work, called **constructors** and **destructors**.

4.3.1 Class Constructors

To understand the constructor of a class, first we have to understand the procedure of creating an object. To this end let's see how a variable of a basic type is initialized. When a program is running, every variable of it takes up some memory space. Initializing a variable during its definition means to set an initial value to the memory space when it is allocated. This kind of initialization seems simple in C++ source code, but in fact, to achieve this initialization the compiler needs to generalize some codes automatically according to the variable type.

The procedure of creating an object is similar: during the execution of a program, when it comes to the declaration statement of an object, the program will apply for some memory space from the operating system to store the new object. We hope that the program would fill the initial values for data members of the object when allocating them with memory space, just like what it does to common variables. Unfortunately, compared with common variables, a class object is too complex, and the compiler has no idea how to generalize codes to achieve the initialization. So programmers have to write codes manually to do this initialization. If a programmer hasn't written his initialization code but rashly gives some initial value to an object during its definition, he won't have the object initialized and probably will get a compiler syntax error. That's why none of the objects in the former examples of this book have been initialized.

Despite this, the compiler system of C++ still does lots of work for us on the problem of object initialization. C++ strictly defines the interface form of an initializing program, and has a set of automatic calling mechanisms. Here the initializing program is called a constructor.

A constructor constructs an object with specific values when creating this object, and initializes it to a specific state. The constructor is also a member function of a class, and besides the common characters of member functions, the constructor has some special attributes: the constructor shares the same name with the class and has no return value and the constructor is usually declared as a public function. Once a class has a constructor, the compiler will automatically insert the calling code on the constructor at the place where the new object is defined. So we often say the "constructor is automatically called where the object is defined".

If a class has no constructor, the compiler will automatically generate a default constructor – with no parameters and doing nothing. If a class has defined a constructor (whether with parameters or not), the compiler will not generate any other constructor.

In the *Clock* class example, there is no function that has the same name as the class, i.e., there is no constructor. Thus the compiler will generate a default constructor for the class, while the constructor does nothing. So why do we need a constructor that does nothing? That's because calling the constructor of an object during its creation is a necessary behavior in a C++ program. If the programmer defines a proper constructor, an object of class *Clock* will receive an initial time value during its creation. Now we modify class *Clock* as follows:

```
class Clock
{
public:
    Clock (int NewH, int NewM, int NewS);       //constructor
    void SetTime(int NewH, int NewM, int NewS);
    void ShowTime();
private:
    int Hour,Minute,Second;
};
```

Implementation of constructor:

```
Clock::Clock(int NewH, int NewM, int NewS)
{
    Hour= NewH;
    Minute= NewM;
    Second= NewS;
}
```

Let's see what the constructor does when creating the object:

```
int main()
{
    Clock c (0,0,0);
    c.ShowTime();
    c.SetTime(8,30,30);
}
```

When creating object *c*, the constructor is called implicitly and the actual parameters will be used as the initial values.

Because in class *Clock* there has already been a constructor, the compiler system won't generate a default constructor. The user-defined constructor here has formal parameters, so initial values of the parameters should be given, which are used as formal parameters when calling the constructor during the creation of an object. If we define an object in the main function as follows:

```
Clock c2;
```

There will be a syntax error when compiling the program, because we do not provide the actual parameters.

As a member function of a class, a constructor can access all data members of the class directly; it can be an inline function, have the parameter list and default parameter values, and be overloaded. With these characters, we can choose the proper form of constructor according to the different needs of problems, to initialize an object to a specific state. Let's see the following example in which an overloaded constructor is called:

```
class Clock
{
public:
    Clock (int NewH, int NewM, int NewS); //constructor
    Clock()                               //constructor
    { Hour=0; Minute=0; Second=0; }
    void SetTime(int NewH, int NewM, int NewS);
    void ShowTime();
private:
    int Hour,Minute,Second;
};
//omit implementations of other functions
int main()
{
    Clock c1 (0,0,0);        //call constructor with parameters
    Clock c2;                //call constructor without parameters
    //......
}
```

The above example shows cases of constructors with and without parameter forms. A constructor without parameters is also called a default form constructor.

Also note that the memory space an object occupies is only used to store member data, and there is no copy of member functions in every object.

4.3.2 The Copy Constructor

Many of us have used a copy machine: when we need a copy of a file, we fetch white paper and use a copy machine to get a copy exactly the same as the original. There are lots of examples of making a copy in our real world. Since the object-oriented programming design aims to faithfully reflect problems in the real world, C++ needs the ability of copying an object.

There are two ways to generate a copy of an object. The first one is to build a new object and set each data member of the new object exactly to the values from the old object. This method works but is a little fussy. Why don't we make a class that has the ability of automatically copying an object of its own? That's what a copy constructor does.

A copy constructor is a special constructor. It has all the features of common constructors, while **its formal parameter is a reference to an object of the class.** It is used to initialize a new object of the same class by the existing object specified by the formal parameter.

Programmers can define a specific copy constructor as needed, to achieve the copying of data members of objects in the same class. If the programmer hasn't defined a copy constructor for a class, the system will automatically generate a default copy constructer when needed. This default copy constructor copies the value of every data member to the new object, or we can say it clones the old object to get a new one. The new object and the old one have exactly the same data members.

Here is the common way to define and implement a copy constructor:

```
class class_name
{
public:
    class_name(parameters_list);          //constructor
    class_name(class_name &object_name);  //copy constructor
    ...
};
Class_name::class_name(class_name & object_name);
//implementation of copy construction
{ function body
}
```

Let's see an example of a copy constructor: locate a point on the screen according to the coordinates x and y. Class *Point* is defined as follows:

```
class Point
{
public:
    Point(int xx=0, int yy=0) {X=xx;Y=yy;} //constructor
```

```
        Point(Point &p);                        //copy constructor
        int GetX() {return X;}
        int GetY() {return Y;}
    private:
        int X,Y;
    };
```

Inline constructor and copy constructor are declared inside the class body. The copy constructor is implemented as follows:

```
    Point::Point(Point &p)
    {
        X=p.X;
        Y=p.Y;
        cout<<"call the copy constructor"<<endl;
    }
```

Common constructors are called when the objects are created, while copy constructor would be called in any of the following three situations:

1. **When using an object to initialize another object of the same class.** For example:

```
    int main()
    { Point A(1,2);
        Point B(A);        //using object A to initialize object B,
                           //copy constructor is called
        cout<<B.GetX()<<endl;
        return 0;
    }
```

2. **When calling the function and passing parameters, if the formal parameter of a function is an object of a class.** For example:

```
    void f(Point p)
    { cout<<p.GetX()<<endl;
    }
    int main()
    { Point A(1,2);
        f(A); //parameter is an object, when calling the function, copy
              //constructor is called
    }
```

3. **When the function is finished and is going to return to its caller, if the return value of a function is an object of a class.** For example:

```
    Point g()
    { Point A(1,2);
```

```
        return A; //return value is an object, when returning the value,
                  //copy constructor is called
}
int main()
{
    Point B;
    B=g();
}
```

In the example above, why is the copy constructor called when returning the function value? On the surface, function *g* seems to return *A* to the main function. But *A* is a local object of *g()* and will disappear when function *g* terminates, and thus *A* can't exist after the process returns to the main function (this will be further discussed in Chapter 5). So in this situation, the compiler will generate a temporary unnamed object in the main function, whose lifetime is only in the statement of the function call, i.e., statement '*B* = *g()*.' When executing statement '*return A;*,' actually the copy constructor is called to copy the value of *A* as a temporary object. After function *g* terminates, object *A* disappears while the temporary object exists in statement '*B* = *g()*.' After computing the statement, this temporary object will also disappear.

Example 4.2: Complete program for *point* class.
In the main function, there are three sections that demonstrate three situations of calling a copy constructor, respectively.

```
//4_2.cpp
#include <iostream>
using namespace std;
class Point                              //Definition of class Point
{
public:                                  //external interface
    Point(int xx=0, int yy=0) {X=xx;Y=yy;} //constructor
    Point(Point &p);                     //copy constructor
    int GetX() {return X;}
    int GetY() {return Y;}
private:                                  //private data
    int X,Y;
};
//implementations of member functions
Point::Point(Point &p)
{
    X=p.X;
    Y=p.Y;
```

```
        cout<<"copy constructor is called"<<endl;
    }
    //a function with an object of class Point as parameter
    void fun1(Point p)
    { cout<<p.GetX()<<endl;
    }
    //a function with an object of class Point as return value
    Point fun2()
    {
        Point A(1,2);
        return A;
    }
    //main function
    int main()
    {
        Point A(4,5);                          //first object A
        Point B(A); //situation one, use A to initialize B. First time to
                    //call copy constructor
        cout<<B.GetX()<<endl;
        fun1(B); //situation two, use object B as the formal parameter of
                 //fun1. Second time to call copy constructor
        B=fun2(); //situation three, the return value of the function is
                  //an object. Call copy constructor when returning to
                  //the main function
        cout<<B.GetX()<<endl;
    }
```

Running result:

```
copy constructor is called
4
copy constructor is called
4
copy constructor is called
1
```

Readers may wonder at how the copy constructor and default copy constructor in the example above do the same job: they both pass values in the old object directly to the new object. Then why do we need to write our own copy constructor in this situation? Yes, if things always go like this, we don't have to write a copy constructer particularly; just using the default copy constructer is enough. However, remember that when using copy machines we sometimes only want to copy part of a page, in which case we can use white paper to cover the unneeded part before the copying. There are many other situations, such as when we want to copy with zooming in or out, etc. Things are similar in object copying in programs, where we can copy an object according to our needs. Readers can try to modify the above example code to make the copy constructor construct a new point with a certain amount offset from the old point. Besides, when some of the data members are of pointer types, default copy constructer can only do shallow copying, which causes security problems. To achieve the correct copy, i.e., deep copy, we must write our own copy constructor. Details about pointer types and issues of deep copy will be introduced in Chapter 6. Examples in Chapter 9 will show more about deep copy.

4.3.3 Class Destructor

Besides a good start, we also need a good finish. Programming also needs to consider the round-off work. In C++, when an object disappears, we often need to take care of the mop-up.

Will an object disappear? Sure! Like every living thing in the world, objects in programs have their own lifetime. We already know that an object is created when it is defined, and when the object will disappear involves the issues of the object's lifetime, which will be discussed in Chapter 5. Here we only consider one situation: if a local object is defined inside a function, then it will disappear when the function terminates.

What should be done when an object is going to disappear? The most classical situation is: when constructing an object, some resources are allocated by the constructor, such as dynamically allocating some memory space. When the object disappears, these resources have to be released. This is reflected in Examples 7.10 in Chapter 7, in some examples in Chapter 9, and is detailed in Section 7.7.4 "Running Result and Analysis". Dynamic memory allocation is detailed in Chapter 6. In this chapter, we just make a simple introduction of using destructors to do the round-off work.

Basically, a destructor does almost exactly the opposite of what a constructor does. **A destructor does some** round-off **work before the object disappears.** A destructor is called automatically when the lifetime of the object ends. After calling the destructor, the object disappears and the corresponding memory space is released.

Like a constructor, a destructor is often a public member function. Its name is composed by the class name with the prefix '~'. The destructor has no return value. Differently from constructors, destructors don't accept any parameter, while it can be a virtual function (Chapter 8 will introduce virtual functions). If not declared explicitly, the system will also generate a default destructor, which does nothing.

For example, we add an empty inline destructor to class *Clock*, which has the same function as the default destructor that the system generates.

```
class Clock
{
public:
    Clock();                              //constructor
    void SetTime(int NewH, int NewM, int NewS);
    void ShowTime();
    ~Clock(){}
private:
    int Hour,Minute,Second;
};
```

Generally speaking, if we want the program to do some work automatically before the object disappears (without manually calling a function), we can write the work into the destructor.

4.3.4 Program Instance

Example 4.3: Budget for rebuilding a pool with *Circle* class.

We need to build a circle aisle and a circle fence around a pool shown in Figure 4.2. Fencing costs 35$/m and an aisle costs 20$/m². The width of the aisle is 3 meters, and the radius of the pool will be input from the keyboard. Write a program to compute and output the costs of the aisle and the fence.

The pool and the fence can be viewed as two concentric circles. The circumference of the larger circle is the length of the fence, the area of the circular ring is the area of the aisle, and the area of the circular ring is the difference between the larger circle's area and the smaller circle's area. We can define a class *Circle* to describe this problem: the radius of the circle is a private data member, and the function of class *Circle* is to compute the girth and the area of the circle. We use two objects to represent the fence and pool, and then we can get the area of the aisle and the girth of the fence. Given the unit prices, we can get the budget of the whole project. Let's see the implementation of the program:

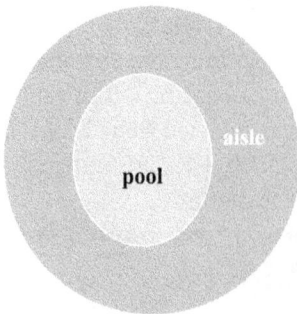

Fig. 4.2: The pool.

```cpp
//4_3.cpp
#include <iostream>
using namespace std;
const float PI = (float)3.14159; //give value of p
const float FencePrice = 35.;    //unit price of the fence
const float ConcretePrice = 20.; //unit price of the concrete for the
                                 //aisle
class Circle               //define Circle and data & function member
{
public:                    //external interface
    Circle(float r);            //constructor
    float Circumference();  //compute the circumference of the circle
    float Area();               //compute the area of the circle
private:                    //private data member
    float radius;
};
//Implementation of class
Circle::Circle(float r) { radius=r; } //constructor initializes data
                                      //member radius
float Circle::Circumference() //compute the circumference of the
                              //circle
{
    return 2 * PI * radius;
}
float Circle::Area()        //compute the area of the circle
{
    return PI * radius * radius;
}
//main function
void main ()
{
    float radius;
    float FenceCost, ConcreteCost;
    cout << "Enter the radius of the pool: "; //ask user to enter the
                                              //radius value
    cin >> radius;
    Circle Pool(radius);    //define objects of Circle
    Circle PoolRim(radius + 3);
    //compute the cost of fence and output it
    FenceCost = PoolRim.Circumference() * FencePrice;
    cout << "Fencing Cost is ¥" << FenceCost << endl;
    //compute the cost of aisle and output it
```

```
    ConcreteCost = (PoolRim.Area() - Pool.Area())*ConcretePrice;
    cout << "Concrete Cost is $" << ConcreteCost << endl;
}
```

Running result:

```
Enter the radius of the pool: 10
Fencing Cost is $2858.85
Concrete Cost is $4335.39
```

When running the main function, we first define three variables of type *float*. After reading the radius of the pool, we create an object *Pool* using the constructor to initialize its data member with the input value. Then we create the second object *PoolRim* to represent the fence. The two objects call their function members respectively, and then the problem is solved.

4.4 Combination of Classes

Lots of problems in the real world are too complicated to imagine, but complex problems can be divided into simpler subproblems. By gradual division, we can finally describe and solve the problem. Actually this method of division and combination has been widely used in industry for a long time. For example, an important part of television is the kinescope, and many TV factories choose to buy kinescopes from special kinescope producers instead of producing kinescopes themselves. At the same time, a kinescope producer may sell kinescopes to many TV factories. Through this specialization and cooperation, productivity is largely improved. Now an important way to improve the productivity of software is to achieve the industrial production of software.

In object-oriented programming design, we can divide and abstract a complex object into a combination of simpler objects, and combine it using component objects that are easy to understand and implement.

4.4.1 Combination

We have always used the method of combination to build a class, so let's see the class *Circle* below:

```
class Circle              //define class Circle, its data and functions
{
public:                   //external interface
    Circle(float r);      //constructors
    float Circumference(); //compute circumference
    float Area();         //computer area
```

```
private:                    //private data members
    float radius;
};
```

As we can see, class *Circle* includes data of type *float*. We are used to using basic types of C++ as the components of a class. In fact, the data member of a class can be either of basic type or of user-defined type, or a class object. So we can use the method of combination, using existed class objects to build new class. These combined classes, compared with integrated classes, are easier to design and implement.

The combination of classes describes the situations where a class object is embedded in another class as a data member. The relationship between the two classes is that of including and being included. For example, we use a class to describe the computer system. First we can divide it into hardware and software. Hardware includes CPU, memory, and I/O devices; software includes system software and application software. Each of these components can be further divided. Described from the view of class, this is a combination of classes. Figure 4.3 shows their relationships. We can describe a complex problem using the method of combination, which conforms to the logic of stepwise refinement.

When defining an object, if there are embedded object members in this class, then each embedded object is to be created first automatically, because the component object is a part of the complex object. Thus, when creating an object, both the basic type members and the embedded object members should be initialized. It is important to understand the order of calling these objects' constructors.

The general form of the constructor of a combined class is:

```
Class_name::class_name(parameter_list):embedded_object1
    (parameter_list), embedded_object2(parameter_list), ...
{ initialization of class}
```

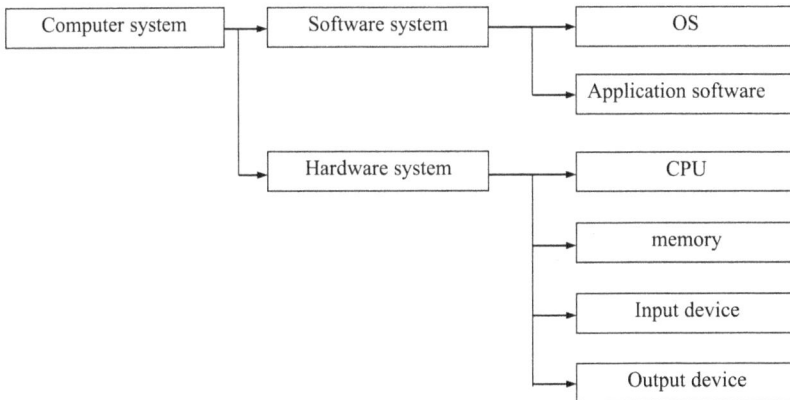

Fig. 4.3: Combination relationships in the class of a computer system.

Here, 'embedded_object1(parameter_list),embedded_object2(parameter_list),...' is called the initialization list, which is used to initialize embedded objects.

Data members of basic types can also be initialized like this, and using an initialization list is more efficient than using assignment statements. For example, the constructor of class *Circle* can also be written like this:

```
Circle::Circle(float r): radius(r)\{\}
```

When creating an object of a combined class, not only its own constructor will be called, but also the constructors of its embedded objects will be called. The calling order is:
1. Call the constructors of the embedded objects according to their definition order in the class.
2. Call the constructor of the combined class.

When defining an object of a combined class, if there is no initial value given for the object, then the default constructor (with no parameter) will be called, and the default constructors of the embedded objects will be called together. **The calling order of destructors is exactly the opposite as that of constructors.**

How does one write a copy constructor for a combined class? If the programmer has not written a copy constructor, the compiler system will generate a default copy constructor when needed. If this default copy constructor is called when creating an object, then the compiler will automatically call the copy constructors of the embedded objects.

If we want to write a copy constructor for a combined class, we also need to pass parameters for the copy constructors of the embedded objects. For example, suppose object *b* of class *B* is embedded in class *C*. Then the copy constructor of class *C* will be like this:

```
C::C(C &c1):b(c1.b)
{...}
```

Now let's see an example.

Example 4.4: Combination of class with *Line* class.
We design a *Line* class to represent a line, and use a *Point* class mentioned in the last section to represent a point. This problem can be solved using combined classes: the *Line* class includes two objects of the *Point* class, *p1* and *p2*, as its data members. Class *Line* has the function of computing its length, which is implemented in its constructor. The source code is as follows:

```
//4_4.cpp
#include <iostream>
#include <cmath>
using namespace std;
```

```
class Point                       //definition of class Point
{
public:
    Point(int xx=0, int yy=0) {X=xx;Y=yy;}
    Point(Point &p);
    int GetX() {return X;}
    int GetY() {return Y;}
private:
    int X,Y;
};
Point::Point(Point &p)        //implementation of copy constructor
{
    X=p.X;
    Y=p.Y;
    cout<<"Copy constructor of Point is called"<<endl;
}
//combination of class
class Line                        //definition of class Line
{
public:                           //external interface
    Line (Point xp1, Point xp2);
    Line (Line &);
    double GetLen(){return len;}
private:                          //private data members
    Point p1,p2;                  //objects p1 p2 of class Point
    double len;
};
//constructor of combine class
Line:: Line (Point xp1, Point xp2)
:p1(xp1),p2(xp2)
{
    cout<<"Constructor of Line is called"<<endl;
    double x=double(p1.GetX()-p2.GetX());
    double y=double(p1.GetY()-p2.GetY());
    len=sqrt(x*x+y*y);
}

//Copy constructor of combine class
Line:: Line (Line &L): p1(L.p1), p2(L.p2)
{
    cout<<"Copy constructor of Line is called"<<endl;
    len=Seg.len;
}
```

```
//main function
int main()
{
    Point myp1(1,1),myp2(4,5); //create object of class Point
    Line line(myp1,myp2);      //create object of class Line
    Line line2(line);          //create a new object using copy
                               //constructor
    cout<<"The length of the line is:";
    cout<<line.GetLen()<<endl;
    cout<<"The length of the line2 is:";
    cout<<line2.GetLen()<<endl;
}
```

Running result is:

```
Copy constructor of Point is called
Copy constructor of Point is called
Copy constructor of Point is called
Copy constructor of Point is called
Constructor of Line is called
Copy constructor of Point is called
Copy constructor of Point is called
Copy constructor of Line is called
The length of the line is:5
The length of the line2 is:5
```

When calling the main function, two objects of class *Point* are created first, and then the object line of class *Line* is created. After that, the second object *line2* of class *Line* is created using a copy constructor. Lastly the distance between the two points is output. During the running of the program, the copy constructor of class *Point* is called six times, all of which are called before the constructor of class *Line* is executed. The six calls on the copy constructor of class *Point* happen respectively when: two objects of class *Line* are created, embedded objects are initialized, and *line2* is created using a copy constructor. The distance between the two points is computed inside the constructor of class *Line*, and is stored in the private data member *len* which can only be accessed by the public member function *GetLen()*.

4.4.2 Forward Declaration

We know that in C++ a class should be defined before being used. But when we deal with some complex problems, considering the combination of classes, we may come to a situation where two classes reference each other, which is also called circular dependency. For example:

```
class A                 //definition of class A
{
public:                 //external interface
    void f(B b);        //member function with object b of class B
                        //as parameter, which cause compile error,
                        //because 'B' is an unknown symbol.
    };
class B                 //definition of class B
{
public:                 //external interface
    void g(A a);        //function member with object a of class A
                        //as parameter
};
```

Here the parameter of the public member function *f* of class *A* is an object of class *B*, while the parameter of the public member function *g* of class *B* is an object of class *A*. Because a class must be defined before it is used, no matter the definition of which class is put at the front, it will cause a compiling error. One way to solve this problem is to use forward declaration. Forward declaration means telling the name of an undefined class to the compiler before the class is used, so the compiler knows that it is a class name. When this name is used in the program, the compiler won't consider it as an error, and the complete definition of the class can be put elsewhere in the program. By adding forward declaration to the program we talked above, the problem will be solved:

```
class B;                //Forward declaration
class A                 //definition of class A
{
public:                 //external interface
    void f(B b);        //member function with object b of class B
                        //as parameter
    };
class B                 //definition of class B
{
public:                 //external interface
    void g(A a);        //function member with object a of class A
                        //as parameter
};
```

Forward declaration can help in some situations, but it is not omnipotent. It is important to know that even if forward declaration is used, we can't define an object of this class or use an object of this class in an inline function before we provide a complete definition of the class. Let's see the code below:

```
class Fred;              //forward declaration
class Barney {
   Fred x;               //error: missing definition of class Fred
};
class Fred {
   Barney y;
};
```

For this program, the compiler will report an error. It is because the forward declaration of class *Fred* only tells that Fred is a name of a class, while there is no complete definition of class *Fred*. So we can't define an object of class *Fred* as a data member of class *Barney*. So for two classes it is illegal to mutually make an object of one class be a data member of the other.

Let's see another program:

```
class Fred;      //forward declaration

class Barney {
public:
  void method()
  {
     x->yabbaDabbaDo(); //error : object of class Fred is used before
                        //it is defined
  }
private:
   Fred* x;      //correct, after forward declaration, we can declare
                //pointer to object of class Fred
};
class Fred {
public:
   void yabbaDabbaDo();
private:
   Barney* y;
};
```

The compiler will report an error because the inline function in class *Barney* uses an object of class *Fred* pointed by x, while class *Fred* hasn't been completely defined. To solve this problem, we can change the definition order of the two classes, or change function *method()* to noinline and provide the definition of the function after the complete definition of class Fred is given.

Remember that when using forward declaration, only the symbol declared can be used, and any detail of the class can't be used.

4.5 UML

In previous sections we have learned the concepts of class and object in OOD in C++. In this section, we will introduce a diagram representation to describe these concepts more visually, to facilitate easier communication among people.

Nowadays there are many widely-used object-oriented modeling languages. In the last two versions of this book, we used Coad/Yourdon notation, and in the third version we use UML (Unified Modeling Language). UML was first adopted and popularized by the OMG (Object Management Group) in 1997. Now it has become the representative standardized language and is widely used. UML includes all the diagram symbols that we need.

UML language is a large and complex system modeling language. The aim of the language is to solve the problem of visual modeling for the whole development process of OO software. Complete descriptions of UML are far beyond the range of this book, and this section only introduces the part of UML language that is directly related to this book. With this study, readers can selectively understand the characteristics of UML language, use simple UML diagrams to describe the key concepts in this book such as class and object in C++, and lay a solid foundation for learning and developing software in the future. Actually the content introduced here is one of the most basic parts of UML. If readers want to know more about UML, please refer to related websites and books.

4.5.1 Brief Introduction of UML

UML language is a typical OO modeling language, rather than being a programming language. In UML, concepts are represented by symbols, and relations between concepts are represented by lines.

OO modeling language can be traced back to the 1970s. In the 1980s, lots of OO programming languages came out, marking the maturity of the OO Method. In the mid-1990s, many OO analysis and design methods came out, which introduced various identifiers independent of languages. Among them, the Coad/Yourdon method was one of the earliest OO analysis and design methods. These methods were easy to understand and suited beginners that study OO technique. Booch was the one of the earliest advocates of OO method. He put forward the concept of OO software engineering, which is a good way to design and build systems. Rumbaugh, etc. presented an object-modeling technique (OMT) that uses the OO concept. The OOSE method introduced by Jacobson is suitable for supporting business engineering and demand analysis.

Among various modeling languages, users can hardly distinguish the characteristics of different languages, so they cannot find a language that suits their application characteristics. Besides, although different languages are similar in many aspects, their representation forms vary a lot, which greatly hinder the communications between users. Thus it was objectively necessary to find a unified modeling language. In October 1994, Grady Booch and Jim Rumbaugh began to work on this. They first unified Booch and OMT methods together, and published the public version of this modeling language in October 1995, calling it UM 0.8 (Unified Method). By the end of 1995, the founder of OOSE, Ivar Jacobson, joined them. With the efforts of Booch, Rumbaugh, and Jacobson, the new version was published in June 1996, named UML 0.9, and UM was renamed UML (Unified Modeling Language). On 11/17/1997, OMG accepted UML 1.1 as an OO-based unified modeling language. In June 2003, OMG accepted the 2.0 version of UML.

The important content of UML is different kinds of diagrams, which are used to represent the static structure and dynamic behavior of software models, and the organization and management of modules. This book mainly uses diagrams in UML to represent classes, objects, and their relationships in software, using the basic class diagram that belongs to Static Structure Diagrams.

4.5.2 UML Class Diagrams

A class diagram is a diagram that is composed of class and related static relationships. A class diagram shows the static structure of a software model, the inner structure of the class, and the relationships between this class and other classes. UML also defines an object diagram, and a static object diagram is an instance of a specific object diagram, which shows an instance of a specific state of a real software system. Class diagrams can contain objects, and a class diagram containing only objects without any class is an object diagram. We can consider object diagrams as a specific instance of class diagrams. The use of object diagrams is very limited, so in versions above UML1.5 it is explicitly pointed out that tools software is not required to implement this kind of diagram.

Using class diagrams, we can describe all the OO concepts introduced in this book, such as class, template class, and the relationships among them. Class diagram is composed of diagram symbols that describe a class or object, and diagram symbols that describe their relationships. Now we detail diagram symbols.

1. Class and Object

The basic thing to do in a class diagram is to describe class graphically, to represent the name, data member, and function member of a class, and the access control attributes of each class member.

In UML language, we use a rectangle that is divided into three parts vertically to represent a class. The class name is written in the top section, data members (data, called attributes in UML) are in the middle section, and function members (behavior, called operation in UML) are in the bottom section. Surely it can be seen as three rect-

Clock
- Hour : int - Minute : int - Second : int
+ ShowTime() : void + SetTime(NewH : int = 0, NewM : int = 0, NewS : int = 0) : void

(a)

Clock

(b)

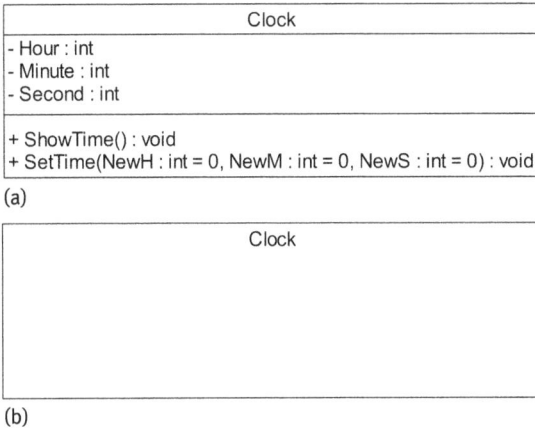

Fig. 4.4: Two ways to represent class *Clock* from Example 4.1; (a) Complete representation of class *Clock*, (b) Simple representation of class *Clock*.

angles, which represent the name, attributes, and operations of a class respectively, folded vertically. Besides the name section, the other two parts are optional, i.e., attributes and operations of a class can be hidden, and simply a rectangle with a class name in it can represent a class.

Let's take class *Clock* in Example 4.1 for example, to see the representation of a class. Readers can refer to the source code in Example 4.1.

Figure 4.4 demonstrates different ways of representing class in UML. Figure 4.4a gives a complete representation of a class with visible explanations of data and behavior. Figure 4.4b is a representation that hides data and behavior. Obviously, Figure 4.4b is simple but has little information. Different representation methods are used in different situations according to the aim of drawing the figure. If we want to describe the members of the class and their access control attributes in detail, we should use the method shown in Figure 4.4a; if we care only about relations among classes and not the things inside the class (for example, in the beginning of designing a program when we need to mark out classes), we should use the method shown in Figure 4.4b.

Now let's see how to represent data and function members in the complete representation of a class.

Depending on the level of detail of a diagram, each data member can include its access control attribute, name, type, default value, and restrictions. The simplest situation is to only include the member name, while the other parts are all optional. The grammar of representing a data member in UML is:

```
[access control attribute] name [multiplicity] [: type]
    [=default value] [{restrictions}]
```

At least the name of the data member must be given, while others are optional. Here,

Access control attribute: can be public, private, or protected, corresponding to '+', '−', and '#' respectively in UML.

Name: string to identify the data member.

Multiplicity: multiplicity of attributes in the following [].

Type: type of data member. It can be a basic type, such as integer, floating, Boolean, etc., and can also be user-defined type or a class.

Default value: initial value assigned to this member.

Restriction: an explanation of restriction to this data member, such as '{read only}' means that this member is read only.

In Figure 4.4a class Clock, data member Hour is described as:

```
- Hour : int
```

Access control attribute '−' means that it is a private member, its name is 'Hour', its type is 'int', and there is no default value or restriction.

In the following example, we represent a public data member called size, with type Area, and a default value of (100,100).

```
+size: Area = (100,100)
```

Each function member can include its access control attribute, name, parameter list, return type, and restriction. The simplest situation is to only include its name, since other parts are optional, according to the level of detail of the diagram. The grammar of representing a function member in UML is:

```
[Access control attribute] name [(parameter list)] [: return type]
    [{restriction}]
```

Access control attribute: can be public, private, or protected, corresponding to '+', '−', and '#' respectively in UML.

Name: string to identify the function member.

Parameter list: includes parameters separated by comma. The syntax form to represent the parameter list is '[direction] name: type=default value.' Note that this form is different from that in cpp files. The direction tells whether the parameter is used to represent in, out, or inout.

Return type: type of the return value. It can be basic type, user-defined type, class, or a pointer of the above types.

Restriction: an explanation of restriction to this function member.

In Figure 4.4a class *Clock*, function member *SetTime* is described as:

```
+ SetTime(NewH: int =0, NewM: int =0, NewS: int =0) : void
```

myClock : Clock
- Hour : int
- Minute : int
- Second : int

myClock : Clock

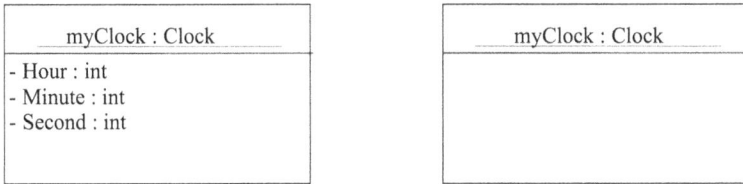

Fig. 4.5: Different representations of the object *myClock*.

Access control attribute '+' tells that it is a public member. Its name is *'SetTime,'* its parameter list is in the bracket, the return type is *'void,'* and there are no restrictions.

In UML language, when using a rectangle to represent an object, the name of the object should be underlined. The whole name of the object is written in the top section of the rectangle, which is composed of the class name and object name that are separated by a colon. The syntax form is *'object_name:class_name'*, while in some situations the object name or the class name can be omitted. Data members and their values are written in the bottom section, and data members are optional.

We take the class *Clock* as an example:

Figure 4.5 shows different ways to represent an object in UML. The left figure gives a complete representation of an object with data. The right figure only gives the name of the object. The principle of choosing which way to represent an object is the same as that of choosing representations of a class.

2. Diagram Symbols for Relationships

We have introduced the diagram representations of class and object in UML, although with these diagram symbols only, we still can't describe relationships between class and class, object and object, and class and object in a large system. For example, there can be inheritance relationships or calling relationships between classes, etc.

UML uses lines with specific symbols or dashed lines to represent relationships. Let's see how to use these symbols to describe the relationships this book has mentioned, such as calling, combination of classes, inheritance, etc.

a) Dependency

Dependency between classes or between objects indicates that changes of one thing may affect another thing that uses it, while it is not true for the opposite. When a class uses another class as a parameter of its function member, we use the dependency relationship. Generally, calling and friends (will be discussed in Chapter 5) between classes, and instantiation of class all belong to this kind of relationship. Simple, original dependency is sufficient in most of the situations when dependency relationship is needed. But to demonstrate the nuance of different dependency meanings, UML also defined some stereotypes for dependency. The most commonly used stereotype is 'use.' When we need to represent the uses of relationship between two classes, we use the stereotype <<use>>. Other stereotypes will not be detailed here, and some stereotypes will be used in latter chapters, which will be discussed then.

Fig. 4.6: Dependency.

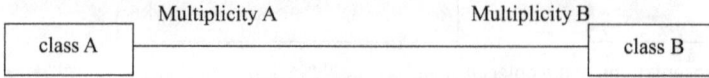

Fig. 4.7: Representation of association in UML.

Figure 4.6 shows how to represent dependency between classes. UML uses a dashed line pointing to the thing depended on to represent dependency between classes. In Figure 4.6, class *A* is the source and class *B* is the destination, meaning that class *A* uses class *B*, or class *A* depends on class *B*.

b) Relationship – Association

Association is used to represent the interaction relationship between objects from different classes. In UML, a line segment is used to represent association between two classes (or the same class). Generally there are multiplicities at both ends of the line segment. Multiplicity is the most important characteristic of association. Multiplicity in one end of a line segment means: each object on the other end of the line segment should have interaction with a certain number of objects of the class on this end. Figure 4.7 shows how to represent association in UML.

In Figure 4.7, 'Multiplicity A' decides how many objects in class A will have interaction with each object in class B, and it is the same meaning for 'Multiplicity B.' The symbol forms of multiplicity and their meanings are list in Table 4.1.

c) Inclusion Relation – Aggregation and Composition

Inclusion relation between classes or objects is described by two concepts in UML: aggregation and composition, which belong to a special kind of association. Aggregation in UML means that the relation between classes is that of whole and part, and 'include,' 'compose,' and 'divided into ... parts' are all aggregations. A line segment having two end points is an example of aggregation. Aggregation can be further divided into shared aggregation and composition aggregation (abbreviated as composi-

Tab. 4.1: Symbol and Meaning of Multiplicity.

Symbol	Meaning
*	Any amount of objects (includes 0)
1	One object exactly
n	N object exactly
0..1	0 or 1 object (means that association is optional)
$n..m$	N objects at least, m objects at most (n, m are integers)
2, 4	Discrete association (for example 2 or 4)

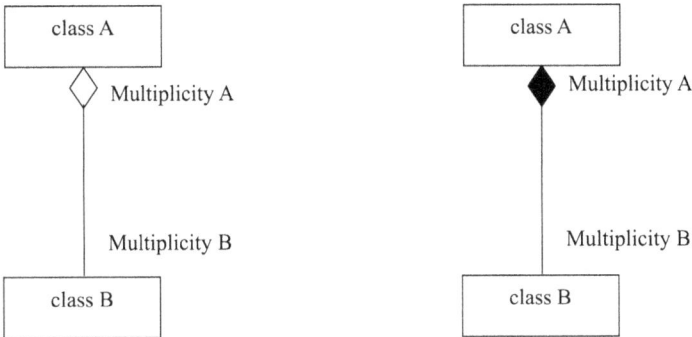

Fig. 4.8: Aggregation and composition.

tion). For example, a team has lots of members, while each member can be a member of another team, i.e., a part can join multiple wholes, which is called shared aggregation. Another example is that the whole owns each part, and if the whole disappears, each part disappears too, which is called composition. Composition is a simple form of aggregation, but it has stronger ownership relation: the whole owns every part, and if the whole disappears, each part disappears too. For example, a view window is composed of a title, outline, and display area. In UML, aggregation is represented by a hollow lozenge, and composition is represented by a solid lozenge.

Figure 4.8 shows how to represent aggregation and composition between classes.

Example 4.5: Use UML to represent relations between class *Line* and class *Point* in Example 4.4.

Data members of class *Line* include two objects of class *Point*, p1 and p2, so the multiplicity is 2. The objects of class *Point* are parts of class *Line*, so aggregation should be used to describe the relation. Besides, the constructor of class *Line* uses two objects of class *Point*, p1 and p2, so we can use dependency to describe this relationship clearly. Figure 4.9 uses UML to represent these relations between class *Line* and class *Point*.

d) Inheritance Relation – Generalization

The inheritance relation between classes (which will be discussed in Chapter 7) is called generalization in UML. UML uses a line with a triangle to represent this relation. An angle of the triangle points to the parent class, and the line on the opposite side points to the child class. Figure 4.10 shows this generalization relation. Child *class 1* illustrates single inheritance and child *class 2* illustrates multiple inheritance.

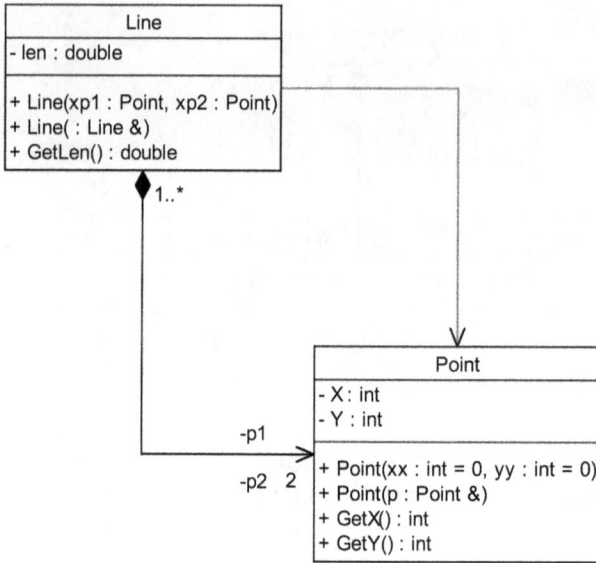

Fig. 4.9: Relations between class *Line* and class *Point*.

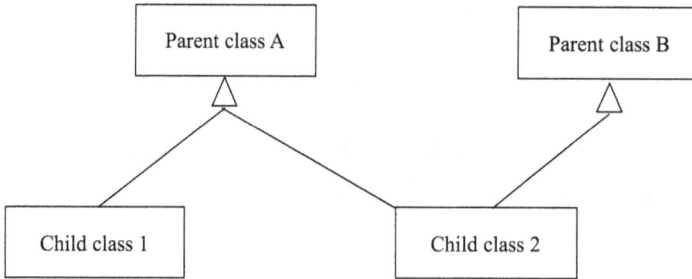

Fig. 4.10: Generalization relation.

3. Comments

To represent classes, objects, and relations among them in a more lively fashion, UML uses some auxiliary symbols besides the basic symbols introduced above. Here we introduce comments.

Comments in UML are an important kind of symbol, and can exist independently. Comments are attached on elements or on element sets for description or annotation. By commenting, we can add information like description and comment on the model. In UML, comments are represented as rectangles with angled folds and are linked to other elements of UML using a dashed line.

Example 4.6: Description of class *Line* and class *Point* with comments (see Figure 4.11).

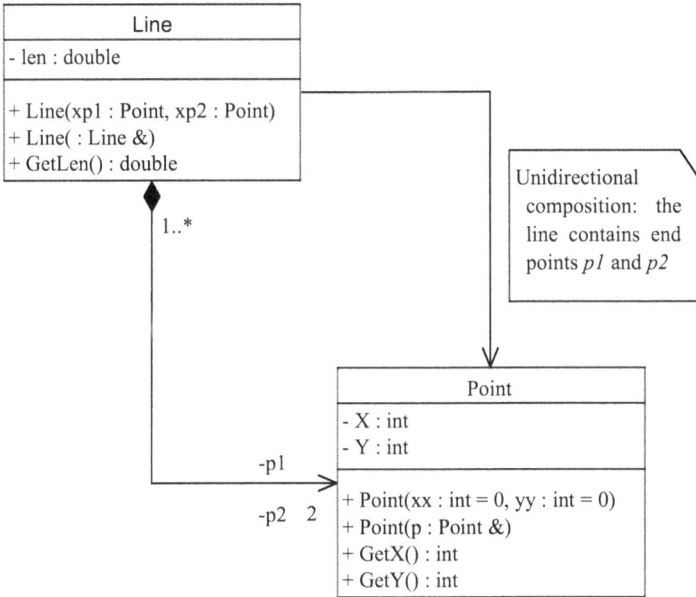

Fig. 4.11: Relation between class *Line* and class *Point* with comments.

4.6 Program Instance – Personnel Information Management Program

In this section, we take the personnel information management of a small company for example, to see how to design a class and its member functions.

4.6.1 Design of Class

A small company needs to store the ID, grade, and payment of each employee, and display all the information. According to these needs, we design a class *employee*. In this class, besides defining a constructor and destructor, we also have to uniformly define operations on personnel information. Data members in the class *employee* include ID, grade, and payment, and function members in class *employee* include getting ID, computing and getting the grade, and setting and getting payment. The constructor is used to set initial values for ID, grade, and payment. The class diagram is shown in Figure 4.12.

employee
individualEmpNo : int
grade : int
accumPay : float
+ employee()
+ ~employee()
+ IncreaseEmpNo(: int) : void
+ promote(: int) : void
+ SetaccumPay(: float) : void
+ GetindividualEmpNo() : int
+ Getgrade() : int
+ GetaccumPay() : float

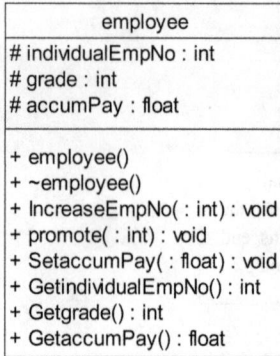

Fig. 4.12: UML diagram for class *employee*.

4.6.2 Source Code and Description

Example 4.7: Personnel information management.
The whole program is divided into two independent documents: employee.h includes declaration and definition of classes, and 4_5.cpp is the main function file.

```
//employee.h
class employee
{
protected:
    int individualEmpNo;          //id
    int grade;                    //grade
    float accumPay;               //payment
public:
    employee();                   //constructor
    ~employee();                  //destructor
    void IncreaseEmpNo (int);     //increasing id function
    void promote(int);            //promoting function
    void SetaccumPay (float);     //setting payment function
    int GetindividualEmpNo();     //getting id function
    int Getgrade();               //getting grade function
    float GetaccumPay();          //getting payment function
};

employee::employee()
{ individualEmpNo=1000;           //max id of employee now is 1000
    grade=1;                      //initial grade is 1
    accumPay=0.0;                 //initial payment is 0
}

employee::~employee() {}          //destructor is empty
```

```cpp
void employee::IncreaseEmpNo (int steps)
{ individualEmpNo+=steps;}        //increase id by steps

void employee::promote(int increment)
{ grade+=increment;}              //promote grade by increment

void employee::SetaccumPay (float pa)
{ accumPay=pa;}                   //set payment

int employee::GetindividualEmpNo()
{ return individualEmpNo;}        //get member id
int employee::Getgrade()
{ return grade;}                  //get grade

float employee::GetaccumPay()
{ return accumPay;}               //get payment

//4_5.cpp
#include<iostream>
#include"employee.h"
using namespace std;
int main()
{
    employee m1;
    employee t1;
    employee sm1;
    employee s1;

    cout<<"Please input payment of next employee:";
    float pa;
    cin>> pa;
    m1.IncreaseEmpNo(0);          //set m1's id to current id
    m1.promote(3);                //m1 promoted by 3 grades
    m1.SetaccumPay (pa);          //set payment of m1

    cout<<" Please input payment of next employee:";
    cin>>pa;
    t1.IncreaseEmpNo(1);          //set t1's id to current id plus 1
    t1.promote(2);                //t1 promoted by 2 grades
    t1.SetaccumPay (pa);          //set payment of t1

    cout<<" Please input payment of next employee:";
```

```
cin>> pa;
sm1.IncreaseEmpNo(2);              //set sm1's id to current id plus 2
sm1.promote(2);                    //sm1 promoted by 2 grades
sm1.SetaccumPay (pa);              //set grade of sm1

cout<<" Please input payment of next employee:";
cin >>pa;
s1.IncreaseEmpNo(3);               //set s1's id to current id plus 3
s1.SetaccumPay (pa);               //set payment of s1

//display information of m1
cout<<"ID"<<m1.GetindividualEmpNo()
 <<" grade is "<<m1.Getgrade()<<",
    payment is "<<m1.GetaccumPay()<<endl;

//display information of t1
cout<<"ID"<<t1.GetindividualEmpNo()
 <<" grade is "<<t1.Getgrade()<<",
    payment is"<<t1.GetaccumPay()<<endl;

//display information of sm1
cout<<"ID"<<sm1.GetindividualEmpNo()
 <<" grade is"<<sm1.Getgrade()<<",
    payment is"<<sm1.GetaccumPay()<<endl;

//display information of s1
cout<<"ID"<<s1.GetindividualEmpNo()
 <<" grade is"<<s1.Getgrade()<<",
    payment is"<<s1.GetaccumPay()<<endl;
}
```

4.6.3 Running Result and Analyses

Running result:

```
Please input payment of next employee: 8000
Please input payment of next employee: 4000
Please input payment of next employee: 7000
Please input payment of next employee: 1600
ID 1000 grade is 4, payment is 8000
ID 1001 grade is 3, payment is 4000
ID 1002 grade is 3, payment is 7000
ID 1003 grade is 1, payment is 1600
```

In the above program, we extract common parts of an employee's information, using class *employee* to abstract them to data members *individualEmpNo*, *grade*, and *accumPay*, then we write operating functions according to each data member to achieve access to private data members. In function *main()*, we built four objects of class *employee* and applied the same operation on them, such as setting ID, grade, and payment, and displaying this information.

4.7 Summary

Object-oriented programming uses abstraction, encapsulation, inheritance, and polymorphism to maximize the reusability and scalability of codes, to improve the productivity of software, and to control the cost of development and maintenance of software. Class is the core of OO programming. Using class, we can realize the encapsulation and hiding of data; using the inheritance and the derivation of class, we can make abstract descriptions of problems in depth.

Class is an encapsulation of function and data, which are related logically, and it is an abstract description of a problem. In fact, class belongs to the user-defined type. Different from basic data types, class includes operations on the data.

Access control attributes control access to the class members, by which we achieve data hiding. An object is an instance of class. An object is unique compared with other objects of the same class in that it has its own attributes– data members. Setting values to data members when defining an object is called initializing the object. After the use of an object is finished, some cleaning work must be done. Constructors and destructors in C++ are used to do the initialization and the cleaning work. Copy constructors are a special constructor that use an existing object to initialize a new object.

Exercises

4.1 Explain the use of public and private. What are the differences between public member and private member?

4.2 What is the use of keyword protection?

4.3 What are the uses of constructors and destructors?

4.4 Can data members be public? Can function members be private?

4.5 Class *A* has a data member *int a*. If we define two objects of class *A*, *A1*, and *A2*, can the values of *a* in the two objects be different?

4.6 What is a copy constructor? When is it called?

4.7 What is the difference between a copy constructor and operator =?

4.8 Define a class *Dog*, which includes attributes like age and weight, and functions to operate on the attributes. Implement and test this class.

4.9 Design and test a class *Rectangle* whose attributes are coordinates of the left bottom point and the right top point. This class should be able to compute the area of the rectangle.

4.10 Design a class *'employee'* for personnel management. Considering the generality, we only abstract attributes that everyone has: ID, sex, birth date, and PIN. Here, birth date should be declared as an embedded object of class *'Date.'* Use member functions to realize input and display data. A constructor, destructor, copy constructor, inline member function, function with default values, and combination of classes must be used.

4.11 Define a class *Rectangle* with attributes length and width, and use a function member to compute area.

4.12 Define a class data type that can deal with char, integer, and float data types. Give its constructor.

4.13 Define a class *Circle* with data member radius, and use function member *GetArea()* to compute area. Create an object of *Circle* to test the code.

4.14 Define a class *tree* with data member *age*, function member *grow(int years)* which increases *ages* by *years*, and *age()* to display the value of *ages*.

4.15 Draw an UML diagram of class *Circle* according to its source code in Example 4.3.

4.16 Draw UML diagrams to represent the inheritance relations among class *ZRF*, class *SSH*, and class *Person* according to the following code:

```
class Person
{
  public:
     Person(const Person& right);
     ~Person();
  private:
     char Name;
     int Age;
};

class ZRF : protected Person
{
};

class SSH : private Person
{
};
```

4.17 In a course selection system of a college, there are two classes: class *CourseSchedule* and class *Course*. The relations between the two classes are: the parameters of the member functions of class *CourseSchedule*, *add* and *remove*, are objects of class *Course*. Please use UML to represent this dependency explicitly.

4.18 For a department personnel information system, we need to build a model for the relation between *Department* and *Teacher*. The relation can be described as: each *Teacher* belongs to 0 or multiple *Departments*, while each *Department* includes at least one *Teacher*. Please draw a UML diagram according to the above relation.

5 Data Sharing and Protecting

An important characteristic of C++ is that it is a language in which it is suitable to write large complex programs and enables data sharing and protection mechanisms. In this chapter we will introduce the concept of scope, visibility, and the lifetime of identifiers, as well as the sharing and protection mechanism of class members. At last we will introduce the multifile structure and compilation preprocessing directives, that is, how to use several source files to organize large programs.

5.1 Scope and Visibility of Identifiers

Scope concerns the effective range of an identifier, while visibility concerns whether an identifier can be referenced. We know that a variable declared in a function can only be effective in this function, which is due to the restriction of the scope and visibility of variables. Scope and visibility are interrelated but different.

5.1.1 Scope

Scope is the region where an identifier is effective in the program body. The scopes of identifiers in C++ include function prototype scope, block scope (also termed local scope), class scope, and file scope.

Function Prototype Scope
Function prototype scope is the smallest scope in a C++ program. In Chapter 3 we introduced how there must be a type specification of formal parameters in the function prototype. Function prototype scope is the effective area of formal parameters during the declaration of function prototype. The following is an example of a declaration of a function.

```
double Area(double radius);
```

The effective area of identifier *radius* is between the two brackets of *Area*'s parameter list, and you cannot reference this identifier in other places of the program. Therefore, the scope of identifier *radius* is called the function prototype scope. Since formal parameter type is the only factor that works in the formal parameter list of a function prototype, omitting the identifier will not affect the compiling and running results. Considering the readability of the program, we usually give each formal parameter an identifier while declaring a function prototype.

https://doi.org/10.1515/9783110471977-005

Block Scope

To understand block scope, let us first look at an example:

```
void fun(int a)
{ int b(a);
    cin>>b;
    if(b>0)
    {
        int c;
        ... ...
    }
}
```

c's scope

b's scope

Here, variable *b* is declared inside function *fun()*, and is initialized by the value of *a*. Then variable *c* is declared inside the *if* statement. Both *b* and *c* have block scopes, though they belong to different block scopes. A block is a section of program that is enclosed in a pair of brackets. In this example, the function body itself is a block; the branch body after the *if* statement is a smaller block – the two blocks have an inclusive relationship. Identifiers declared in a block have a scope starting from the declaration and ending at the end bracket of the block. Therefore, the scope of variable *b* is from its declaration to the end of the block it is in (i.e., the whole function body), and the scope of variable *c* is from its declaration to the end of the block it is in (i.e., the branch body). **A variable that has a local scope is also called a local variable.**

Class Scope

A class can be viewed as a collection of named members, and member *M* of class *X* has a class scope. The access method of *M* is:

If there is no declaration of local scope identifiers of the same name in *X*'s member functions, then we can access member *M* inside this function. That is, *M* works in all these kinds of functions. The use of class encapsulation is to limit the scope of data.

Access *M* through the expression *x.M* or *x::M*, which is the most basic method to access object members in a program.

Access *M* through the expression *prt->M*, where *prt* is a pointer that points to an object of class *X*. More details about pointers are in Chapter 6.

Other special access methods and the scope rules of classes and their objects in C++ will be discussed in the following chapters.

File Scope

Declarations that appear in none of the scopes talked above have file scopes. The scope of this kind of identifier starts from the declaration point and ends at the end of the

file. The global variables declared in Example 5.1 have file scope, and they are effective
in the whole file.

Example 5.1: Examples of scope and visibility.

```
//5_1.cpp
#include <iostream>
using namespace std;
int i;                              //global variable, file scope
int main()
{
    i=5;                            //initialize i of the file scope
    {                               //subblock 1
     int i;                         //local variable, local scope
     i=7;
     cout<<"i="<<i<<endl;           //output 7
    }
    cout<<"i="<<i<<endl;            //output 5
}
```

In this example, variable i declared before the main function has file scope, and its
effective area is the whole source file. We initialize i to 5 at the beginning of the main
function, then declare a variable of the same name in block 1 and initialize it to 7. The
first output result is 7, because the variable with local scope covers the variable with file
scope – that is, the variable with file scope becomes invisible (this is the visibility issue,
which we will discuss later). When the program finishes executing block 1 and starts
the second output, the output is the value of the variable with file scope, which is 5.
   A variable with file scope is also called a global variable.

5.1.2 Visibility

Now, let us have a look at the effective area of a variable from the perspective of an identifier reference – that is, the visibility of the identifier. When a program executes to one
point, the identifier that can be referenced is the identifier that is visible at this point.
To understand visibility, we first look at the relationship between different scopes. File
scope is the largest scope, followed by class scope and local scope. Figure 5.1 describes
the general relationship between scopes. Visibility represents what you can see when
you "look" from inner scope to outer scope. Therefore, visibility and scope are closely
interrelated.
   The general rules of scope visibility are:
–   You must first declare an identifier before referencing it.
–   You cannot declare identifiers of the same name in the same scope.

File scope

Class scope

Local scope

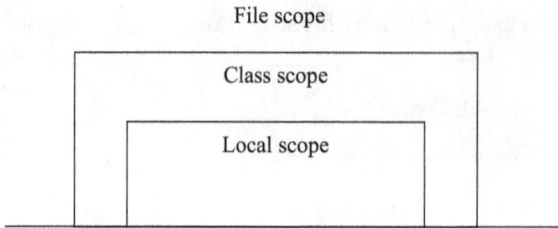

Fig. 5.1: Relationships of scopes.

- If identifiers of the same name are declared in different scopes that do not include each other, these identifiers will not affect each other.
- If identifiers of the same name are declared in two or more scopes with inclusion relations, the outer identifiers are invisible from inner scopes.

Look at Example 5.1 again. This is an example of file scope including a local scope. You can reference the variable with file scope outside block 1, which means that it is visible. When the program execution enters block 1, it can only reference variables of the same name with local scope, while variables of the same name with file scope are hidden.

Rules of scope and visibility do not only apply to simple variables, but also apply to user-defined data types and objects of classes.

5.2 Lifetime of Object

Each object (including simple variable) has a birth time and disappearing time. The period from birth to end is the object's lifetime. During the lifetime, the object will remain in its state (the value of data member) and the variable will retain its value, until they have been updated. In this section, we will use objects to represent both class objects and general variables. The lifetime of an object can be divided into static lifetime and dynamic lifetime.

5.2.1 Static Lifetime

If the lifetime of an object is the same as the running period of the program, then it has a static lifetime. All the objects with file scope have a static lifetime. If we want to declare an object with local scope inside the function to have a static lifetime, we have to use the keyword **static.** For example, the variable i declared in the following statement is a variable that has a static lifetime, which is also called a static variable:

```
static int i;
```

We will discuss static members in Section 5.3.

5.2.2 Dynamic Lifetime

Besides the two situations discussed above, all the other objects have a dynamic lifetime. Objects declared to have a dynamic lifetime in local scope are customarily called
local lifetime objects. Dynamic lifetimes start from the declaration point and end at
the ending part of the identifier's scope.

Example 5.2: Lifetime and visibility of variables.

```cpp
//5_2.cpp
#include<iostream>
using namespace std;
int i=1;          //i is a global variable with static lifetime
int main()
{ static int a;   //a is a static local variable that has static
                  //lifetime, locally visible
  int b=-10;      //b, c are local variables that have dynamic
                  //lifetime
  int c=0;
  void other(void);
  cout<<"---MAIN---\n";
  cout<<" i: "<<i<<" a: "<<a<<" b: "<<b<<" c: "<<c<<endl;
  c=c+8; other();
  cout<<"---MAIN---\n";
  cout<<" i: "<<i<<" a: "<<a<<" b: "<<b<<" c: "<<c<<endl;
  i=i+10; other(); }
void other(void)
{
  static int a=2;
  static int b;
//a,b are static local variables that have global lifetime, locally
//visible, and only initialized when the function is executed for
//the first time.
  int c=10;       //c is a local variable that has dynamic lifetime,
                  //should be initialized every time the function is
                  //executed.
  a=a+2; i=i+32; c=c+5;
  cout<<"---OTHER---\n";
  cout<<" i: "<<i<<" a: "<<a<<" b: "<<b<<" c: "<<c<<endl;
  b=a;
}
```

Result:

```
---MAIN---
  i: 1 a: 0 b: -10 c: 0
---OTHER---
  i: 33 a: 4 b: 0 c: 15
---MAIN---
  i: 33 a: 0 b: -10 c: 8
---OTHER---
  i: 75 a: 6 b: 4 c: 15
```

Example 5.3: A clock program that has static and dynamic lifetime objects.
We still use class *Clock* as an example here. In this example, we declare objects that have function prototype scope, local scope, class scope, and file scope separately, and discuss their visibility and lifetime.

```cpp
//5_3.cpp
#include<iostream>
using namespace std;
class Clock                         //class clock definition
{
public:                             //external interface
    Clock();
    void SetTime(int NewH, int NewM, int NewS);
            //all the three parameters have function prototype scope
    void ShowTime();
    ~Clock(){}
private:                            //private data member
    int Hour,Minute,Second;
};
//realize class Clock member function
Clock::Clock()                      //constructor
{
    Hour=0;
    Minute=0;
    Second=0;
}
void Clock::SetTime(int NewH, int NewM, int NewS)
{
    Hour=NewH;
    Minute=NewM;
    Second=NewS;
}
```

```
void Clock::ShowTime()
{
    cout<<Hour<<":"<<Minute<<":"<<Second<<endl;
}
Clock globClock; //declare object globClock, which has static
                 //lifetime, file scope
                 //use default constructor to initialize it to 0:0:0
int main()                          //main function
{
    cout<<"First time output:"<<endl;
    //quote object globClock that has file scope
    globClock.ShowTime();           //the member function of object has
                                    //class scope
                                    //display 0:0:0
    globClock.SetTime(8,30,30);     //set the time to 8:30:30
    Clock myClock(globClock);       //declare object myClock that has
                                    //local scope
                                    //call copy constructor, initialize
                                    //it by globClock
    cout<<"Second time output:"<<endl;
    myClock.ShowTime();             //reference object myClock that has
                                    //local scope
                                    //output 8:30:30

}
```

Result:

```
First time output:
0:0:0
First time output:
8:30:30
```

This program includes variables and objects of all kinds of scopes: in the definition of class *Clock*, the three parameters of function member *SetTime* have function prototype scope; object *myClock* has local scope; data members and function members of class *Clock* have class scope; and object *globClock* has file scope. These variables, objects, and public members are all visible in the main function. As for lifetime, apart from object *globClock* with file scope having a static lifetime, which is the same as the running period of the program, all the others have a dynamic lifetime.

5.3 Static Members of Class

The basic unit of program modules in structured program design is function. Therefore, memory data sharing between modules is achieved through the data sharing between functions, including, parameter passing and global variables.

Object-oriented program design method concerns both data sharing and data protection. It encapsulates data and functions operating the data together, to construct more integrated modules. The data members of a class can be accessed by any function of the same class. Thus, on the one hand data sharing is achieved between functions within a class; on the other hand this kind of data sharing is restricted – we can set appropriate access control attributes to limit the data sharing within the class scope, and class data members are still hidden from the outside of the class, thus to achieve both sharing and hiding.

Yet, this is not all of data sharing. Data sharing is also needed between objects.

Static members are designed to solve the problem of data sharing between different objects of the same class. For example, we can abstract the common attributes of all the employees of a company, and design the following *employee* class:

```
class employee
{
private:
    int EmpNo;
    int ID;
    char *name;    //use character pointer to point to the first
                   //address of the character string, the details are
                   //in Chapter 6

    ......
    //omit other data members and functions
}
```

If we need to count the total number of employees, where do we store this data? If you use a variable outside the class to store the total number, then you cannot hide this data. If you add a data member in the class to store the total number, then every object should store a copy of this data, which not only is redundant but also may cause data inconsistency. Since this data should be shared among all the objects in the class *employee*, the best way is to let all the objects of the class have the same data member that stores the total number, which is the static data member we will introduce next.

5.3.1 Static Data Member

When we say that "all the objects in a class have the same attribute", we mean that the number, the name, and the data type of the attribute of each object are the same, while the attribute value of each object can be different. This kind of attribute is called "instance attribute" in the object-oriented method, and is represented by a nonstatic data member of class in C++ programs. For example, the *EmpNo*, *ID*, and *name* of class *employee* in the example above are all instance attributes represented by nonstatic data members. Nonstatic data members have a copy in every object of the class, by which an object differs from other objects of the same class.

There is a concept called "class attribute" in the object-oriented method. If there is an attribute that belongs to the whole class and does not belong to any specific object, then we can use the keyword **static** to declare it a static member. A static member has only one copy in a class, and it is protected and used by all the objects of this class, to achieve data sharing among different objects of the same class. Class attribute is a data item that describes the common characteristic of all the objects of one class. Its attribute value is the same to all object instances. In short, if we compare a "class" to a factory, and objects to the products made by the factory, then static members would be stored in the factory and belong to the factory, and they would not belong to each product.

A static data member has a static lifetime. Because static data does not belong to any object, we can only access it through a class name, and the general way is "**class name::identifier.**" We only do a referential declaration of a static data member in the definition of its class, while the definitional declaration must be done using the class name qualification at someplace in the file scope, and the initialization can also be done during the definitional declaration. UML language underlines the data member to represent a static data member. We can find out the usage of static data members in the following example.

Example 5.4: Class *Point* with static data members.
This program is modified from the class *Point* in Chapter 4. It brings in a static data member *countP* to count the object number of class *Point*. The UML diagram of class *Point* that includes static data member *countP* is as shown in Figure 5.2:

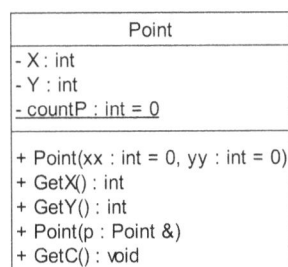

Point
- X : int - Y : int - <u>countP : int = 0</u>
+ Point(xx : int = 0, yy : int = 0) + GetX() : int + GetY() : int + Point(p : Point &) + GetC() : void

Fig. 5.2: UML diagram of class *Point* that includes static data member.

```
//5_4.cpp
#include <iostream>
using namespace std;
```

```
class Point                     //definition of class Point
{
public:                         //external interface
    Point(int xx=0, int yy=0) {X=xx; Y=yy; countP++; } //constructor
    Point(Point &p);            //copy constructor
    ~Point(){ countP--; }
    int GetX() {return X;}
    int GetY() {return Y;}
    void GetC() {cout<<" Object id="<<countP<<endl;} //output static
                                //data member
private:                        //private data members
    int X,Y;
    static int countP;          //referential declaration of static data
                                //member, used to record the number of points
};
Point::Point(Point &p)
{
    X=p.X;
    Y=p.Y;
    countP++; //accumulate countP in constructor, all the objects
              //maintain the same countP
}
int Point::countP=0;            //definitional declaration and initialization
                                //of static data member, qualified with class
                                //name
int main()                      //the main function
{
    Point A(4,5);               //define object A, its constructor will make
                                //countP add 1
    cout<<"Point A,"<<A.GetX()<<","<<A.GetY();
    A.GetC();                   //output the number of objects
    Point B(A);                 //define object B, its constructor will make
                                //countP add 1
    cout<<"Point B,"<<B.GetX()<<","<<B.GetY();
    B.GetC();                   //output the number of objects
}
```

In the example above, data member *countP* in class *Point* is declared static, and used to count the number of objects in class *Point*; every time a new object is defined, the value of *countP* increases by 1. The definition and initialization of static data member *countP* are done outside the class. Pay attention to the reference method when initializing the static data member. First, it uses the class name to qualify the data member; next, although this static data member is private, it can be initialized directly. Except for this special occasion, in other places, such as in the main function, no direct access is allowed. The value of *countP* is calculated in the constructor: when object *A* is created, the constructor with default parameters is called; when object *B* is created, the copy constructor is called. These two constructors access the same static member *countP*. Also, the output of calling function *GetC* through object *A* and *B* respectively is the values of the same *countP* at different times. In this way, we can achieve data sharing between *A* and *B* directly.

The result of the program:

```
Point A,4,5 Object id=1
Point B,4,5 Object id=2
```

Furthermore, we usually access static data members through noninline functions, because the compiler will make sure that it has initialized the static data members before calling any noninline functions. However, when using inline functions to call static members from another compiling unit, it is possible that the static member has not been initialized yet; therefore this kind of calling is unsafe.

5.3.2 Static Function Member

In Example 5.3, function *GetC()* is devoted to output static member *countP*. We can only output *countP* by calling function *GetC()* through one object of class *Point*. Before declaring all the objects, the value of *countP* is its initial value 0. How can we output this initial value? It is obvious that we cannot call *GetC()* through an object since there has been no object declared yet. Because *countP* belongs to the whole class instead of any object, we hope to access *countP* without going through objects. Now let us try to rewrite the main function of Example 5.3 as follows:

```
int main()
{
    Point::GetC();   //call the function directly through class name
                     //to output the initial value of the number of
                     //objects
    Point A(4,5);
    cout<<"Point A,"<<A.GetX()<<","<<A.GetY();
    A.GetC();
    Point B(A);
    cout<<"Point B,"<<B.GetX()<<","<<B.GetY();
    B.GetC();
}
```

Unfortunately, there are errors during the compiling: we must call general function members through object names.

Still, there are methods that can help us achieve our expectations above, that is, static member functions. The so-called static member function is a function member declared by the keyword *static*. Just like a static data member, a static member function belongs to the whole class, is owned by all the objects of the same class, and is shared by all these objects.

As a member function, the access attribute of a static data member is controlled strictly by class. For a public static member function, we can call it through the class name or object name. A general nonstatic member function can only be called through the object name.

Static member functions can access static data and function members of this class directly. To access nonstatic data members, they first have to get the object name through parameter passing, and then access the nonstatic data member through the object name. Let's have a look at the following program segment:

```
class A
{
    public:
        static void f(A a);
    private:
        int x;
};
void A::f(A a)
{
    cout<<x;              //wrong reference of x
    cout<<a.x;            //correct
}
```

We can find out that it is inconvenient for static function members to access nonstatic members. Generally, a static function member is primarily used to access static data members in the same class, and to maintain the data shared among objects.

In UML language, a static function member is represented by adding the <<static>> stereotype to function members.

Example 5.5: Class *Point* with static data and static function members.
In Example 5.4, we use the static private data member *countP* to count the number of objects in the *Point* class; now we use a static function member to access *countP* in this example. The UML diagram of the *Point* class that has the added static function member is as shown in Figure 5.3:

```
//5_5.cpp
#include <iostream>
using namespace std;
class Point                              //define class Point
```

Point
- X : int
- Y : int
- countP : int = 0
+ Point(xx : int = 0, yy : int = 0)
+ GetX() : int
+ GetY() : int
+ Point(p : Point &)
<<static>> + GetC() : void

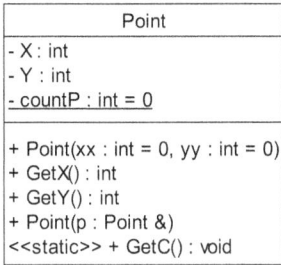

Fig. 5.3: UML diagram that includes static function member.

```cpp
{
public:                                 //external interface
    Point(int xx=0, int yy=0) {X=xx;Y=yy;countP++;} //constructor
    Point(Point &p);                    //copy constructor
    ~Point(){ countP--; }
    int GetX() {return X;}
    int GetY() {return Y;}
    static void GetC() {cout<<" Object id="<<countP<<endl;}
    //static function member
private:                                //private data member
    int X,Y;
    static int countP;                  //referential declaration of
                                        //static data member
};
Point::Point(Point &p)
{
    X=p.X;
    Y=p.Y;
    countP++;
}
int Point::countP=0;                    //definitional declaration of
                                        //static data member
//initialization, use class name limitation
int main()                              //main function
{
    Point A(4,5);                       //define object A
    cout<<"Point A,"<<A.GetX()<<","<<A.GetY();
    A.GetC();                           //output the number of object,
                                        //object name reference
    Point B(A);                         //define object B
    cout<<"Point B,"<<B.GetX()<<","<<B.GetY();
    Point::GetC();                      //output the number of objects,
                                        //class name reference
}
```

Compared with Example 5.4, we only change *GetC()* to a static member function in the definition of the class. Then, we can use both class name and object name to call *GetC()* in the main function.

The result of this program is the same as the one in Example 5.4. Compared with Example 5.4, the advantage of a static function member is that it is object-independent, so we can access the static data directly.

Pay attention to that while using a static data member: if you want to access the static data member through a nonstatic function, you should use a noninline function, and the definition of this noninline function should be in the same source file as the initialization of the static member. Why should we do so? It is because that static data member should be initialized before being accessed, and the compiler can only make sure to initialize static data members of class before calling any nonstatic function defined in the same source file. We will introduce a multifile structure in Section 5.6, and we will see that one project can be made up of several source files. The definition of class, the initialization of static data members, and the definition of member functions can be in different source files. In this case, using a nonstatic inline member function to access a static data member will cause unexpected errors.

5.4 Friend of Class

The encapsulation of data and the function operating the data to form a class can achieve both data sharing and data hiding, which is obviously a great advantage of object-oriented program design. But encapsulation is not omnipotent. Now, consider a simple example of the *Point* class that we are familiar with, in which each object represents a "point". If we want to calculate the distance between two arbitrary points, how do we design this function?

If we design the distance calculator function as a general function outside the class, we cannot reflect the relation between the function and "point", and functions outside the class cannot refer to the coordinates of the "point" (private member) directly, which makes the calculation inconvenient.

Then what about designing the calculator function as a member function of class *Point*? It is not hard to implement from a grammatical point of view, but it is hard to understand. This is because that distance is a relation between two points, and it does not belong to any point, nor to the whole class. In other words, to design the function whether as a nonstatic member or as a static member, it will always affect the readability of the program.

We once used a combination of classes in Chapter 4, where two objects of class *Point* combine to form a class *Line* (line segment), and class *Line* has the function of calculating the length of a line segment. However, class *Line* is an abstract of a line segment. If the problem we are facing is there are lots of points, and the distance between any two arbitrary points needs to be calculated frequently, then it has to create an object of *line* every time we calculate the distance. This is inconvenient and affects the program's readability.

Therefore, we need a function outside class *Point* that has a special relationship with class *Point*.

Have a look at the following program segment:

```
class A
{
    public:
            void Display() {cout<<x<<endl;}
            int Getx() {return x; }
            //omit other members
    private:
            int x;
}
class B
{
     public:
            void Set(int i);
            void Display();
     private:
            A a;
};
```

This is a case of class combination, where the object of class *A* is embedded in class *B*, but the member function of *B* cannot access *A*'s private member *x* directly. From the view of data security, this is the safest option – the embedded components are equal to a black box. But it is inconvenient to use. For example, realizing the member function *Set()* of *B* by the following writing will cause compiling errors:

```
void B::Set(int i)
{ a.x=i; }
```

Since the objects of *A* are embedded in *B*, can we let *B*'s functions access the private data of *A* directly?

C++ provides syntax support for the needs above, in the form of friends.

A friend provides a data sharing mechanism among member functions of different classes or of different objects, and among member functions of a class and general functions. Or, more generally, a friend enables a class to actively declare which classes or functions are its friends, to give them permission to access this class. In other words, a general function or a member function of a class can access data that is encapsulated in another class through the relation of friend. A friend destroys the hiding and encapsulation of data to a certain extent. However, in order to share data and to improve the efficiency and readability of a program, this kind of small damage is necessary in many cases. The key point is to find a balance between sharing and encapsulation.

We can use the keyword *friend* to declare a function or a class as a friend in a class. If a friend is a general function or a member function of a class, then it is called a friend function; if a friend is a class, then it is called a friend class, and all the member functions of the friend class will become friend functions automatically.

5.4.1 Friend Function

Friend function is a nonmember function modified by the keyword *friend* in the class. A friend function can be a general function or a member function of another class. Although it is not the member function of this class, it can access the private and protected members of the class through object names. A friend function is represented by adding the <<friend>> stereotype before the member function in UML language. Have a look at the following example:

Example 5.6: Use friend function to calculate the distance between two points.
We used class *Line* composed by the combination of two objects of class *Point* to calculate the length of the line segment when introducing the class combination. In this example, we will use a friend function to achieve a more general functionality: calculate the distance between two arbitrary points. We still use *Point* to describe the points on the screen, and use a general function *fDist* to calculate the distance between two points. During the calculation, this function needs to access the private data members *X* and *Y* of class *Point*, so we declare *fDist* as a friend function of class *Point*. The UML diagram of class *Point* is as shown in Figure 5.4:

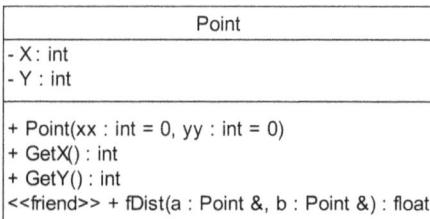

Point
- X : int
- Y : int
+ Point(xx : int = 0, yy : int = 0)
+ GetX() : int
+ GetY() : int
<<friend>> + fDist(a : Point &, b : Point &) : float

Fig. 5.4: UML diagram of class *Point* that includes a friend function member.

```
//5_6.cpp
#include <iostream>
#include <cmath>
using namespace std;
class Point                          //define class Point
{
public:                              //external interface
```

```
    Point(int xx=0, int yy=0) {X=xx;Y=yy;}
    int GetX() {return X;}
    int GetY() {return Y;}
    friend float fDist(Point &a, Point &b);
                                        //friend function declaration
private:                                //private data member
    int X,Y;
};
float fDist(Point &p1, Point &p2)       //implement friend function
{ double x=double(p1.X-p2.X);           //access private data member
                                        //through object

  double y=double(p1.Y-p2.Y);
  return float(sqrt(x*x+y*y));
}
int main()                              //main function
{
    Point myp1(1,1),myp2(4,5);          //define object of class Point
    cout<<"The distance is:";
    cout<<fDist(myp1,myp2)<<endl;        //calculate the distance between
                                        //two points

}
```

Result:

```
  The distance is: 5
```

We only declare the prototype of a friend function in the definition of class *Point*, while the definition of friend function *fDist* is outside the class. We can find out that the friend function accesses the private members X and Y of class *Point* through object names, which is the key point of friend relation. To calculate the distance between two points, we can use a friend to make the program more readable. Of course, if you want to represent a line segment, class *Line* is a better choice. This means that although from the grammatical prospective there are many methods to solve one problem, we should choose a method that can describe the essentials of the problem more directly, and this kind of program will be more readable.

A friend function can be either a general function or a member function of a class. Using the method of a friend member function is almost the same as that of a friend general function, while we need to access the friend member function through the corresponding class or object name.

5.4.2 Friend Class

Like with the friend function, one class can declare another class as its friend class. If class A is the friend class of class B, then all the member functions of class A are friend functions of class B, and they can access class B's private and protected members. The syntax form of a friend class declaration is:

```
class B
{
    ... ...                   //member declaration of class B
    friend class A;           //declare A as B's friend class
    ... ...
};
```

Declaring a friend class is a method to correlate classes and achieve data sharing among classes. UML language uses the <<friend>> stereotype to represent friendship between two classes. Now, modify the program segment at the beginning of this section into the following form: class B is the friend class of class A, and then the member functions of B can access the private member x of A directly. Figure 5.5 shows how to use UML diagram to describe the friendship between class A and class B:

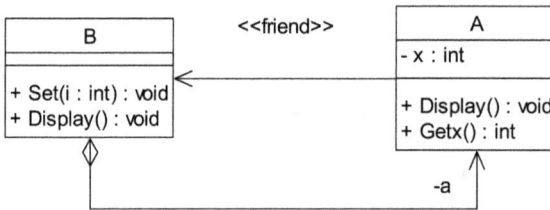

Fig. 5.5: UML diagram of the friendship between class A and class B.

```
class A
{
    public:
            void Display() {cout<<x<<endl;}
            int Getx() {return x; }
        friend class B; //class B is class A's friend class
    //omit other members
        private:
            int x;
}
class B
{
```

```
    public:
        void Set(int i);
        void Display();
    private:
        A a;
};
void B::Set(int i)
{
a. x=i; //B is A's friend, so B's member function can access private
        //members of class A's objects
}
//omit other functions' implementations
```

We will use a friend class to implement the matrix operation in the next chapter.

There are some points you have to pay attention to, regarding friends: firstly, **friendship is not transitive**. Suppose class B is class A's friend and class C is class B's friend, if there is no declaration, then class C and class A do not have any friendship, and they cannot share data. Secondly, a **friendship relation is unidirectional**. If class B is declared as a friend of class A, then member functions of class B can access the private and protected data of class A, while member functions of class A cannot access the private and protected data of class B. Thirdly, **friendship cannot be inherited**. If class B is class A's friend, the derived class of class B will not become class A's friend automatically. For example, someone may trust you, but he may not trust your children.

5.5 Protection of Shared Data

Although hiding data can ensure the safety of data, different kinds of data sharing may damage the safety of data to certain extents. Therefore, for data that needs both sharing and protection from being unchanged, we should declare it as constant. Because a constant is unchangeable during the program execution, the data can be protected effectively. We have introduced the simple data type of constants in Chapter 2. The object can also be modified by *const* when we declare it, and we call it a constant object. We will introduce the constant reference, constant object, and constant member of an object. Constant arrays and constant pointers will be introduced in the next chapter.

5.5.1 Constant Reference

If we use *const* to modify a reference when we declare it, the declared reference is a constant reference. **The object referenced by a constant reference cannot be up-**

dated. If we use a constant reference as a formal parameter, changes on the actual parameter will not happen. The declaration form of a constant reference is:

```
const type identifier &reference name;
```

Example 5.7: Constant reference as formal parameter.

```
//5_7.cpp
#include<iostream>
using namespace std;
void display(const double& r);
int main()
{
    double d(9.5);
    display(d);
}
void display(const double& r)
//Use constant reference as a formal parameter, cannot update the
//object referenced by r in the function, so it will not damage the
//corresponding actual parameter
{ cout<<r<<endl; }
```

5.5.2 Constant Object

A constant object is an object that the value of its data member cannot be changed during the whole lifetime of the object. That is to say, **constant objects must be initialized, but cannot be updated**. The syntax form of declaring a constant object is:

```
class name const object name;
```

For example:

```
class A
{
    public:
        A(int i,int j) {x=i; y=j;}
                ...
    private:
        int x,y;
};
A const a(3,4); //a is a constant object, and cannot be updated
```

Similar to the constant of a basic data type, the value of a constant object cannot be changed. C++ provides reliable protection for constants of basic data types. If the following statements appear in a program, there will be errors. That is to say, syntax checking ensures that the constant will not be assigned again.

```
int const n=10;
n=20;
```

How can syntax ensure that the value of a constant object will not be changed? There are two ways to change the value of an object data member: one is to access public data members through the object name from outside the class, in which case syntax will restrict any reassignment; the other is to change the value of the data member in the member function of the same class, but you cannot predict and count which member function will change the value, so the syntax can only prescribe that the general member functions cannot be called through constant objects. But then what's the use of the constant object? It does not have any external interfaces to use. Do not worry. We can use constant member functions specially defined for constant objects, which will be introduced in the next section.

5.5.3 Class Members Modified by *const*

1. Constant Member Function

Functions modified by keyword *const* are called constant member functions, and their declaration form is as below:

```
Type identifier function name (parameter list) const;
```

Notes:
a) *const* is a part of the function type, so the definition of the function should also have the keyword *const*.
b) A constant member function cannot update the data members of object, and it cannot call member functions without the *const* modification in this class. (This ensures that the values of data members will not change in the constant member function.)
c) If you declare an object a constant object, then it can only call its constant member function, and cannot call other member functions. (This is the protection mechanism of constant objects from a grammatical point of view in C++, and constant member functions are the only external interfaces of constant objects.)
d) The keyword *const* can be used to differentiate overloading functions. For example, if you declare like this in the class:

```
void print();
void print() const;
```

This is an effective overloading of *print*.

R
- R1 : int
- R2 : int
+ R(r1 : int, r2 : int)
+ print() : void
<<const>> + print() : void

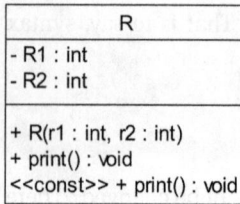

Fig. 5.6: UML diagram of class R that includes constant member function.

Constant member function is represented by adding <<const>> stereotype before member function in UML language.

Example 5.8: Example of constant member function.
The example declares a constant member function in class *R*, and the UML diagram is as below,

```
//5_8.cpp
#include<iostream>
using namespace std;
class R
{
public:
    R(int r1, int r2){R1=r1;R2=r2;}
    void print();
    void print() const;
private:
    int R1,R2;
};

void R::print()
{
    cout<<R1<<":"<<R2<<endl;
}
void R::print() const
{
    cout<<R1<<";"<<R2<<endl;
}
int main()
{
    R a(5,4);
    a.print();          //call void print()
    const R b(20,52);
    b.print();          //call void print() const
}
```

Analysis: Two functions of the same name *print* are declared in class *R*, and one of them is a constant function. In the main function, two objects – *a* and *b* are declared, and object *b* is a constant object. Then we call functions that are not modified by *const* through object *a*, and call constant functions modified by *const* through object *b*.

2. Constant Data Member

Just like general data, data members of class can also be constants or constant references. A data member declared by *const* is called a constant data member. If a constant data member is declared in a class, then it cannot be assigned values in any function. A constructor can only initialize this kind of data member using the initialization list. A constant data member is represented by adding *const* type before the data member type in UML language. Please have a look at the following example:

Example 5.9: An example of a constant data member.
In this example, a constant data function is declared in class *A*, which is presented in the following UML diagram (Figure 5.7):

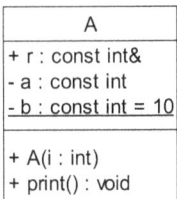

A
+ r : const int&
- a : const int
- b : const int = 10
+ A(i : int)
+ print() : void

Fig. 5.7: UML diagram of class A with constant data members.

```
//5_9.cpp
#include<iostream>
using namespace std;
class A
{
public:
    A(int i);
    void print();
    const int& r;
private:
    const int a;
    static const int b; //static constant data member
};
const int A::b=10; //declare and initialize static constant data
                   //member outside the class
A::A(int i):a(i),r(a) /* constant data member can only be initialized
                       through the initialization list */
```

```
    {
    }
    void A::print()
    {
        cout<<a<<":"<<b<<":"<<r<<endl;
    }
    int main()
    {
    /* create object a and b, and use the initial values of 100 and 0 to
    call constructor respectively, constant data member is initialized
    through the initialization list of constructor*/
        A a1(100),a2(0);
        a1.print();
        a2.print();
    }
```

Result:

```
100:10:100
0:10:0
```

5.6 Multifile Structure and Compilation Preprocessing Directives

5.6.1 General Organization Structure of C++ Program

Up to now, we have studied many complete C++ source program examples and analyzed their structures. These programs are basically made up of three parts: the definition of class, the implementation of class members, and the main function. Since the examples we have studied are relatively small, those three parts are written in the same file. Large projects often need several source program files, where each source program file is called a compiling unit. In this case, C++ syntax requires that the definition of a class must appear in all the compiling units that use this class. A good and usual way is to write the definition of the class in a header file, and each compiling unit that uses this class should include this header file. Usually, a project can be divided into at least three files: the class definition file (*.h file), class implementation file (*.cpp file), and class application file (*.cpp, main function file). For more complex programs, each class has its own definition and implementation files. By using this kind of organization structure, different files can be written and compiled separately, and then be linked together. This kind of structure can also make full use of the benefits of class encapsulation – when debugging and modifying, we only need to modify the definition and implementation of one class and keep other classes unmodified.

Now we divide the program in Example 5.5 using the above method, and rewrite the program as below:

Example 5.10: A class *Point* that has static data and function members and a multifile structure.

```
//File 1, definition of class, point.h
#include <iostream>
using namespace std;
class Point                          //definition of class
{
public:                              //external interface
    Point(int xx=0, int yy=0) {X=xx;Y=yy;countP++;}
    Point(Point &p);
    ~Point(){ countP--; }
    int GetX() {return X;}
    int GetY() {return Y;}
    static void GetC() {cout<<" Object id="<<countP<<endl;}
                                     //static function member
private:                             //private data member
    int X,Y;
    static int countP;               //static data member
};

//file 2, implementation of class, point.cpp
#include "point.h"
nt Point::countP=0;                  //initialize static data member
                                     //through the class name
Point::Point(Point &p)               //copy constructor
{
    X=p.X;
    Y=p.Y;
    countP++;
}

//file 3, main function, 5_10.cpp
#include "point.h"
int main()
{
    Point A(4,5);
    cout<<"Point A,"<<A.GetX()<<","<<A.GetY();
    A.GetC();                        //use object name to call static
                                     //function member
```

```
        Point B(A);
        cout<<"Point B,"<<B.GetX()<<","<<B.GetY();
        Point::GetC();                          //use class name to call static
                                                //function member

    }
```

Let's analyze the structure of the whole program. It is made up of three separate source files, whose relationship as well as the process of compiling and linking are illustrated in Figure 5.8.

We can see that the two *.cpp* files in the multifile structure both have added a new *include* statement. When we do input/output operations, we need to use the statement *#include <iostream>* to include the standard header file *iostream* provided by the system in the source program. Here, we also need to use the statement *#include "point.h"* to include the user-defined header file. The *#include* instruction in C++ is used to embed the specified source file into the current file at the position of the *#include* instruction; the embedded file can be either an *.h* file or a *.cpp* file.

There are two forms for writing an *include* instruction. The form "*#include <file name>*" indicates for the compiler to search the file that needs to be embedded in the standard way, and that the file to be embedded is located in the subdirectory *include* of the C++ system directory. This form is usually used to embed standard files provided by the system, such as standard header file *iostream*. The other form is "*#include "file name""*, which indicates for the compiler to first search the file that needs to be embedded under the current directory; if the file cannot be found, the compiler will use the standard searching method. This form is usually used if the files are written by the user, such as the class definition file *point.h* in this example.

#include is a compilation preprocessing directive, which will be detailed later.

We can see from Figure 5.8 that compiling the two *.cpp* files respectively can generate their own object files suffixed with *.obj*, which are then linked together to generate

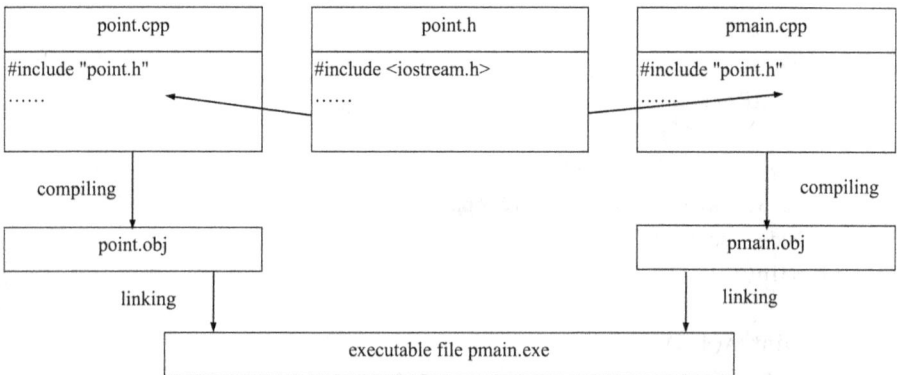

Fig. 5.8: C++ multi-file organization structure.

an executable file suffixed with *.exe*. If we only modify the implementation part of a class member function, then we only need to recompile the file *point.cpp* and reapply the linking, while all the other files can remain unchanged. If the program is large and has a lot of statements, then this method can greatly improve the efficiency.

This kind of multifile organization structure is achieved by different methods in different environments. We usually use a project to manage multiple files under Windows, while we use the *make* tool to do it under Unix. While developing a program, we also need to study the programming environment

While using a multifile structure, we have to pay attention to the specificity of inline functions. Like the definition of class, an inline function needs to provide a uniform complete implementation in each compiling unit that calls it. A good and usual way is to write the implementation of an inline function in a header file, and include this header file in each compiling unit that calls the inline function.

5.6.2 External Variable and External Function

1. External Variable

If we want a variable to be used by other files than the source file that defines it, we can declare it as an external variable by using the keyword *extern* in its declaration.

An external variable has file scope, and is defined outside any function. When declaring an external variable, we can give its definition, or just refer to an external variable that is declared elsewhere. Let's see the following example:

```
//source file 1
int i = 3;                              //define variable i
void next( void );                      //declare function prototype
int main()
{
    i++;
    next();
}
void next( void )
{
    i++;
    other();
}

//source file 2
extern int i; //declare an external variable i which is defined in
              //another file
 void other( void )
```

```
{
    i++;
}
```

Although *i* is defined in source file 1, because it is declared as an external variable in source file 2, we can still use it. The external variable is a global variable shared by several source files.

The declaration of an external variable can be a definitional declaration, i.e., defining the variable (allocate memory and initialize it) while declaring it, or a referential declaration (referring to a variable defined elsewhere). For example, the source file 1 above defines variable *i* while declaring it (i.e., a definitional declaration), while the declaration of *i* in source file 2 is only a referential declaration.

External variables can be declared at many places using *extern*, while they can be defined and initialized only once.

When declaring a file scope variable, its default state can be shared by different compiling units (source program files), as long as the compiling unit uses *extern* to declare this variable. However, if we use *static* to declare a variable in a file scope, then the effective area of this variable is limited to the compiling unit that defines it, and it cannot be accessed by other compiling units.

2. External Function

All of the functions declared outside all the classes (i.e., non-member functions) have file scopes. If there is no special declaration, this kind of functions can be called in different compiling units, as long as you declare the function prototype before calling it. Of course, you can also use *extern* while declaring a function prototype or defining a function, which works the same as the default state without the *extern* modification.

If you use the keyword *static* to declare a function prototype or to define a function, it will limit the function scope to the current compiling unit. In this case, the compiler will require the current compiling unit to include the definition of the function, and the definition of this function is only visible in the current compiling unit. Then you cannot call this function in other compiling units.

5.6.3 Standard C++ Library and Namespace

In C, system functions and some macrodefinitions are placed inside the runtime library. The C++ library retains most of the C language system functions, and it also adds some predefined templates and classes. A standard C++ class library is a flexible and scalable collection of reusable software modules. Standard C++ classes and components are classified into six types logically:
- Input/output class
- Container class and ADT (abstract data type)

- Storage management class
- Algorithm
- Error handling
- Run-environment supporting

The declaration of predefined elements in the library is stored in different header files. To use these predefined elements, we should include the corresponding header files in our source files. The library and header files are a bit different in different compiling systems. For example, to use an I/O stream class in the VC++6.0 environment, the program should include the header file *iostream*.

To the readers that use a VC++ environment, in the early versions before VC++4.1, the library was called a runtime library, and header files were all named "*.h". The standard C++ library came into use since VC++4.2, and it meets the ANSI standard, enabling your program to be portable between different compiling systems and different platforms. New header files do not have ".h" as their name suffix anymore, while the C++ standard library still retains 18 C header files with ".h"-suffixed names.

You can use either header files of the old version ("*.h") or the new standard C++ library header files (with no filename suffix). The compiling system will determine which library to link automatically according to the name of the header file. But you must pay attention so that the two kinds of header files are not mixed in use. For example, if we have already included the header file *iostream*, then we cannot include *math.h*, and we should use the new header file *cmath*.

You can use predefined elements after including the corresponding header files. However, it is different when using standard C++ library, where you need to add the following statement to add the specified namespace to the current namespace:

```
using namespace std;
```

If we do not use the statement above, then we should use the namespace name "std::" to qualify the identifiers that belong to *std* namespace in use.

We will introduce the concept of namespace in Chapter 10.

5.6.4 Compilation Preprocessing

The compiler will first use the preprocessing program to preprocess the program text before compiling the source program. A preprocessing program provides a group of compilation preprocessing directives and preprocessing operators. Actually, preprocessing directives are not a part of C++; they are only used to extend the environment of C++ program design. Each preprocessing directive in a program occupies one separate line beginning with "#" and without a semicolon as the ending tag. Preprocessing directives can appear wherever they are needed.

1. #include Directive

The *#include* directive is also called a file inclusion directive. Its role is to embed another source file into the current source file. We usually use a *#include* directive to embed header files. There are two forms of file inclusion directives:

a) #include<file name>

Search the file that needs to be included using the standard method, and the file is under the *include* subdirectory of the C++ system directory.

b) #include"file name"

First search the file that needs to be included under the current directory; if the search fails, search the file using the standard method.

#include directives can be nested for use. Suppose there is a header file *myhead.h*. This header file can in turn have the following two *#include* directives:

```
\#include "file1.h"
\#include "file2.h"
```

2. #define and #undef Directives

We use *#define* to define symbolic constants in C. For example, the following preprocessing directive defines a symbolic constant *PI* to 3.14:

```
\#define PI 3.14
```

Although symbolic constants can be defined as above in C++, a better method is to use the *const* qualification in type declaration statements.

We can also use *#define* to define macros with parameters in C to achieve simple function calculations, which can improve the execution efficiency. However, this function is now replaced by inline functions in C++.

#undef is used to undefine macros defined by *#define*.

3. Conditional Compilation Directive

A conditional compilation directive instructs that some parts of a program can be compiled only when some conditions are satisfied. Therefore, we can use conditional compilation directives to make the same source file generate different object codes under different compiling conditions. For example, we can add some debugging statements during the program debugging to achieve tracing, and use conditional compilation directives to restrict the debug statements not to participate in the recompiling after the debugging. There are five forms of frequently used conditional compilation statements:

a) Form 1

```
#if constant expression
   Program segment    //compile the program segment when constant
                      //expression is not 0
   #endif
```

b) Form 2

```
#if constant expression
   Program segment 1 //compile the program segment when constant
                     //expression is not 0
#else
   Program segment 2 //compile the program segment when constant
                     //expression is 0
#endif
```

c) Form 3

```
#if constant expression 1
   Program segment 1 //compile the program segment when constant
                     //expression 1 is not 0
#elif constant expression 2
   Program segment 2 //compile the program segment when constant
                     //expression 1 is 0 //and constant expression 2
                     //is not 0
      ⋮
#elif constant expression n
   Program segment n //compile the program segment when constant
                     //expression 1, ... ,constant expression n-1 are
                     //all 0 and constant expression n is not 0
#else
      constant expression n+1 //compile under other cases
#endif
```

d) Form 4

```
#ifdef identifier
      Program segment 1
#else
      Program segment 2
#endif
```

If "identifier" is defined by *#defined*, and has not been undefined by *undef*, then compile program segment 1; else compile program segment 2. If there is no program segment 2, then omit *#else*:

```
#ifdef identifier
        Program segment 1
#endif
```

e) Form 5

```
#ifndef identifier
        Program segment 1
#else
        Program segment 2
#endif
```

If "identifier" has not been defined, then compile program segment 1; else compile program segment 2. If there is no program segment 2, then omit *#else*:

```
#ifndef identifier
        Program segment 1
#endif
```

4. Operator *defined*

defined is a preprocessing operator, not a directive. So we should not use it beginning with #. The *defined* operator is used like this:

```
defined(identifier)
```

If "identifier" has been defined by *#define*, and has not been undefined by *#undef*, then the expression above is not 0, else the value of the expression above is 0. The following two expressions are equal in effects:

```
#ifndef MYHEAD_H
        #define MYHEAD_H
        ...
#endif

#if !defined(MYHEAD_H)
        #define MYHEAD_H
        ...
#endif
```

Since the *#include* directive can be nested, we should avoid including one header file many times in a program design; otherwise it will cause the redefinitions of variables and classes. For example, suppose a project has the following four source files:

```
//main.cpp
#include "file1.h"
#include "file2.h"
int main()
{
    ...
}

//file1.h
#include "head.h"
    ...

//file2.h
#include "head.h"
    ...

//head.h
    ...
class Point
{
    ...
}
    ...
```

Because of the nested use of the *#include* directive, header file *head.h* has been included twice, and then the system will indicate errors during the compiling and redefinition of class *Point*. How does one avoid this error? We need to use conditional compilation directives in the header files that may have been included multiple times. We can use an exclusive identifier to mark whether a file has been compiled or not: if it has already been compiled, then this program segment should have been included repeatedly, and the compiler will not recompile the repeated part any more. Thus, "head.h"can be rewritten as:

```
//head.h
#ifndef HEAD_H
  #define HEAD_H
    ...
  class Point
  {
      ...
  }
```

. . .

```
#endif
```

In this header file, the compiler first needs to judge whether the identifier HEAD_H has been defined or not. If it has not been defined, then the header file should not have been compiled yet, and the compiler will macrodefine the identifier HEAD_H and compile the following program segment. The defined identifier marks that the file has been compiled; if the identifier has already been defined, then the file should have been compiled and the compiler will not recompile the following program segment anymore. In this way, we can avoid the redefinition of class *Point*.

5.7 Example – Personnel Information Management Program

We have used a personnel information management program for a small company in Chapter 4 as an example to explain the design and use of classes and member functions. In this section we will do the following improvements for Example 4.5 from the last chapter:

1. We have introduced static data members in Section 5.2.1 and 5.3.1 In this example we will use the property that a static data member has a static lifetime to process a data member – the number of employees. This new functionality is: add a static data member in class *employee* to store the currently maximum employee number, and the currently maximum number will increase automatically when adding a new employee. Through this, we can avoid the problem of frequently calling the member function *IncreaseEmpNo (int steps)*.
2. We have introduced the general structure of C++ programs in Section 5.6.1. Here we will adjust the program structure based on Example 4.5 in the last chapter: we will divide the definition part and implementation part of class *employee* into two files.

The class design in this example is almost the same as the one in Example 4.5. Expect that we add a static data member *static int employeeNo* in the base class *employee* to store the currently maximum employee number; we also delete the member function

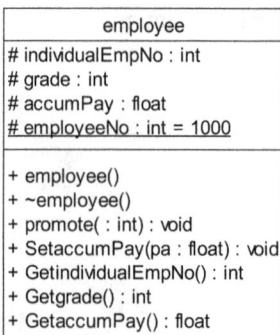

employee
individualEmpNo : int
grade : int
accumPay : float
employeeNo : int = 1000
+ employee()
+ ~employee()
+ promote(: int) : void
+ SetaccumPay(pa : float) : void
+ GetindividualEmpNo() : int
+ Getgrade() : int
+ GetaccumPay() : float

Fig. 5.9: UML diagram of personnel information management program.

IncreaseEmpNo (int steps), whose functionality is achieved by the constructor. The UML diagram of this class design is as shown in Figure 5.9.

Example 5.11: Personnel information management program.
The whole program is divided into three files: class definition header file *employee.h*, class implementation file *employee.cpp*, and main function file *5_11.cpp*. We should link *5_11.cpp* and *employee.cpp* together after compiling. If we use the VC++ environment, we should put *5_11.cpp* and *employee.cpp* in the same project.

```cpp
//employee.h
class employee
{
protected:
    int individualEmpNo;           //individual number
    int grade;                     //grade
    float accumPay;                //monthly pay
    static int employeeNo;         //currently maximum employee number
public:
    employee();                    //constructor
    ~employee();                   //destructor
    void promote(int);             //promotion function
    void SetaccumPay (float pa);   //setting monthly pay function
    int GetindividualEmpNo ();     //getting number function
    int Getgrade();                //getting grade function
    float GetaccumPay();           //getting monthly pay function
};

//employee.cpp
#include<iostream>
#include"employee.h"
using namespace std;
int employee::employeeNo=1000;    //basic value of employee number is
                                  //1000

employee::employee()
{individualEmpNo=employeeNo++;    //the newly added employee number is
                                  //the currently maximum number plus 1
    grade=1;                      //initial value of grade is 1
    accumPay=0.0; }               //initial value of monthly pay is 0

employee::~employee() {}
void employee::promote(int increment)
{ grade+=increment;}              //promotion, the level promoted is
                                  //indicated by the increment
```

```
void employee::SetaccumPay (float pa)
{ accumPay=pa;}                         //set monthly pay

int employee::GetindividualEmpNo()
{ return individualEmpNo;}              //get member number

int employee::Getgrade()
{ return grade;}                        //get grade

float employee::GetaccumPay()
{ return accumPay;}                     //get monthly pay

//5_11.cpp
#include<iostream>
#include"employee.h"
using namespace std;
int main()
{
    employee m1;
    employee t1;
    employee sm1;
    employee s1;
    cout<<"Please enter an employee's monthly pay:";
    float pa;
    cin>> pa;
    m1.promote(3);                      //promote m1 by 3 levels
    m1. SetaccumPay (pa);               //set monthly pay of m1

    cout<<" Please enter an employee's monthly pay:";
    cin>>pa;
    t1.promote(2);                      //promote t1 by 2 levels
    t1. SetaccumPay (pa);               //set monthly pay of t1

    cout<<" Please enter an employee's monthly pay:";
    cin>> pa;
    sm1.promote(2);                     //promote s1 by 2 levels
    sm1. SetaccumPay (pa);              //set monthly pay of sm1

    cout<<" Please enter an employee's monthly pay:";
    cin >>pa;
    s1. SetaccumPay (pa);               //set monthly pay of s1
```

```
//display information of m1
cout<<"number:"<<m1.GetindividualEmpNo()
 <<"level:"<<m1.Getgrade()<<", this month's pay:
    "<<m1.GetaccumPay()<<endl;

//display information of t1
cout<< number:"<<t1.GetindividualEmpNo()
 <<" level:"<<t1.Getgrade()<<", this month's pay:
    "<<t1.GetaccumPay()<<endl;

//display information of sm1
cout<<" number:"<<sm1.GetindividualEmpNo()
 <<" level:"<<sm1.Getgrade()<<", this month's pay:
    "<<sm1.GetaccumPay()<<endl;

//display information of s1
cout<<" number:"<<s1.GetindividualEmpNo()
 <<" level:"<<s1.Getgrade()<<", this month's pay:
    "<<s1.GetaccumPay()<<endl;
}
```

Result:

```
Please enter an employee's monthly pay: 8000
Please enter an employee's monthly pay: 4000
Please enter an employee's monthly pay: 7000
Please enter an employee's monthly pay: 1600
Number:1000 level:4, this month's pay: 8000
Number:1001 level:3, this month's pay: 4000
Number:1002 level:3, this month's pay: 7000
Number:1003 level:1, this month's pay: 1600
```

We can find out that the result of this example is the same as the result of Example 4.5. However, the use of a static data member in the *employee* class makes all the objects of the class share this static data. Through this, the employee number can be generated automatically by a constructor every time an object is created.

Also, we have introduced conditional compilation directives in Section 5.6.2. Through the use of conditional compilation directives, we can avoid the compiling error of repeatedly including the *employee* class. Readers can refer to Section 5.6.2 to add conditional compilation directives into *employee.h*.

5.8 Summary

Data sharing and data protection mechanisms are very important features in C++. They include scope, visibility and lifetime of identifiers, achieving data sharing and operation sharing between different objects of a same class by using static members of the class, and using constant members to set the protection attributes of members.

A multifile structure helps to write several source files to organize a large program. Also, by using preprocessor directives, we can do necessary preprocessing work for source programs, thus avoiding many unnecessary troubles and errors.

Exercises

5.1 What is scope? What kinds of scopes are there in C++?

5.2 What is visibility? What are the general rules of visibility?

5.3 What is the result of running the following program? Run it and see if it is the same as you think.

```
#include <iostream>
using namespace std;
void myFunction();
int x = 5, y = 7;
int main()
{
    cout << "x from main: " << x << "\n";
    cout << "y from main: " << y << "\n\n";
    myFunction();
    cout << "Back from myFunction!\n\n";
    cout << "x from main: " << x << "\n";
    cout << "y from main: " << y << "\n";
}
void myFunction()
{
    int y = 10;
    cout << "x from myFunction: " << x << "\n";
    cout << "y from myFunction: " << y << "\n\n";
}
```

5.4 Suppose there are two independent classes – *Engine* and *Fuel*, how does one make the members of *Fuel* access the private and protected members of *Engine*?

5.5 What is a static data member? What are its characteristics?

5.6 What is a static function member? What are its characteristics?

5.7 Define a class *Cat*: it has static data member *HowManyCats* that counts the number of cats; static member function *GetHowMany()* that can access *HowManyCats*. Design a program to test this class, and learn the use of the static data member and static member function.

5.8 What is a friend function? What is a friend class?

5.9 If class *A* is a friend of class *B*, class *B* is a friend of class *C*, and class *D* is a derived class of class *A*, then is class *B* a friend of class *A*? Is class *C* a friend of class *A*? Is class *D* a friend of class *B*?

5.10 Can static member variables be private? Declare a private static integral member variable.

5.11 Define a global variable *n* and main function *main()* in one file, and then define a function *fn1()* in another file. Assign *n* in *main()*, then call *fn1()* and reassign *n* in *fn1()*. Display the final value of *n*.

5.12 Define a static variable *n* in function *fn1()*, and so that *fn1()* adds *n* by 1. Call *fn1()* 10 times in the main function, and then display *n*.

5.13 Define classes *X, Y, Z*, and function *h(X*)*: class *X* has a private member *i*; member function *g(X*)* of *Y* is a friend function of *X*, which adds 1 to the member *i* of *X*; class *Z* is a friend class of class *X*, and its member function *f(X*)* adds 5 to *i*; function *h(X*)* is a friend function of *X*, which adds 10 to *i*. Define and implement the three classes in one file, and implement function *main()* in another file.

5.14 Define class *Boat* and class *Car*, both of which have an attribute *weight*. Define their friend function *totalWeight()*, and calculate the sum of their weights.

6 Arrays, Pointers, and Strings

After studying the concepts and applications of basic control structures, functions, and classes of C++, many problems can be described and solved. However, for large scales of data, especially when they are mutually correlated or are similar and correlated data, how to present and organize them efficiently remains a problem. The array type in C++ provides an effective way to organize objects of the same type.

An important characteristic, which C++ inherits from C, is that we can directly use an address to access memory, and the pointer variable is an important data type for realizing this feature. Using pointers, we can conveniently process large amounts of data continuously stored in memory, achieve massive data sharing between functions at a comparatively low cost, and easily realize dynamic memory allocations.

Using character arrays to make up the deficiency of string variables is an effective method inherited from C. However, from the object-oriented and security perspectives, strings represented by character arrays have deficiencies. Therefore, the standard class library of C++ provides the *string* class, which is a good example of expanding data types based on the class library.

In this chapter, we will introduce the array type, pointer type, dynamic memory allocation, and how to store and process string data.

6.1 Arrays

To understand the function of an array, please consider this problem: how does one store and process a series of n integers in a program? If n is small, for example, n is 3, we can easily declare three variables of the *int* type. If n is 10,000, then we need to declare 10,000 variables of *int* type to represent these 10,000 numbers by *int* variables. How can we process these 10,000 variables? It is not hard to imagine the complexity and difficulty. The array is designed to solve this kind of problems, which is used to store and process massive data sets of the same type.

An array is a data structure consisting of a group of ordered objects. The objects that make up an array are called array elements. Array elements are denoted by array name and one or more subscripts (each is enclosed with a pair of square brackets). Elements of an array have the same type. An array can be made up of elements of any type except for the *void* type. The relationship between array elements and an array is very similar to that between numbers and vectors or matrices in mathematics.

If for an array, we need to denote each of its elements by the array name and n subscripts, then this array is called an n-dimensional array. If we name a one-dimensional array by *ARRAY*, and it has $N + 1$ elements, then these elements can be denoted as *ARRAY[0], ARRAY[1], ..., ARRAY[N]*. This array can store N+1 data elements sequentially, so $N + 1$ is the size of the array *ARRAY*. Besides, the lower bound and the upper bound of the element's subscript in this example are 0 and N respectively.

https://doi.org/10.1515/9783110471977-006

6.1.1 Declaration and Use of Arrays

1. Declaration of Arrays

An array is a user-defined data type, and needs to be declared before being used. The declaration of an array should consist of the following parts:

a) Define the array's name;
b) Define the types of its elements;
c) Define the structure of the array (such as the dimension of the array, the size of each dimension, and so on)

The common form for declaring an array type is as follows,

```
Data type Identifier[Constant expression 1]
    [ Constant expression 1]...;
```

The type of elements in an array is specified by "Data type". This data type can be either basic types such as *int, float,* or user-defined types such as structure and class.

The array name is specified as the "Identifier". The **array name is a constant, which represents the starting address of array elements in memory.**

Expressions like "Constant Expression 1", "Constant Expression 2", etc. are called subscript expressions. They must be of the *unsigned int* type. The subscripts of an array are used to limit the number of elements in an array, and also to specify the element order and the position of each element in the array. In C, an n-dimensional array is actually a one-dimensional array, each of whose elements is an $(n - 1)$-dimensional array. Thus, in C an n-dimensional array is declared as the array name plus n subscript expressions, where the value of each subscript expression denotes the size of each dimension (note that this is not the upper bound of the subscript in that dimension). The number of array elements can be calculated by multiplying the values of all subscript expressions from the array declaration. For example,

```
int b[10];
```

indicates that b is an array of the *int* type, and it has 10 elements: *b[0]...b[9]*. It can be used to store an integer array of 10 elements.

```
int a[5][3];
```

indicates that a is a two-dimensional array of the *int* type. The size of its first dimension is 5 (subscripts from 0 to 4), and the size of its second dimension is 3 (subscripts from 0 to 2). Thus the total number of a's elements is 15. It can be used to store a table of *int* type, which has five rows and three columns. It is worth noticing that the starting value of array subscripts is 0. For the array a declared above, the first element is *a[0][0]*, and the last element is *a[4][2]*. In other words, the subscript of every dimension starts from 0.

2. Use of Arrays

When using an array, we can operate its elements respectively. Array elements are denoted by subscripts. To a declared array, we can reference its elements like this:

```
Array name[Subscript expression 1][ Subscript expression 2] ...;
```

Here the amount of subscript expressions depends on the dimensions of the array. For an N-dimensional array, each of its elements has to be denoted by N subscript expressions.

Each element of an array equals a variable of the corresponding type. We can use array elements wherever the variable of this type is permitted to use. For example, we can use each element of an integer array like an integer variable. Similarly, each element of an array of a class type can be used as a common object of that class. Note that:

a) Subscript expression of array element can be any legal arithmetic expressions as long as the value of the expression is an integer.

b) The subscript value of one dimension of an array element cannot exceed the upper and lower bounds of that dimension of the array originally declared. Otherwise, the "The array bound is out of range" error may occur when running.

Example 6.1: Declaration and Use of Arrays.

```cpp
//6_1.cpp
#include <iostream>
using namespace std;
int main()
{
    int A[10],B[10];
    int i;
    for(i=0;i<10;i++)
    {
        A[i]=i*2-1;
        B[10-i-1]=A[i];
    }
    for(i=0;i<10;i++)
    {
        cout<<"A["<<i<<"]="<<A[i];
        cout<<" B["<<i<<"]="<<B[i]<<endl;
    }
}
```

In this program, we declare two one-dimensional arrays A and B with 10 elements each. We use the *for* loop to assign values to their elements. When referring to the elements of B, we use arithmetic expressions as subscripts. After running the program,

−1, 1, 3, . . . , 17 are assigned to elements of A: *A[0]*, *A[1]*, ..., *A[9]* respectively. Then B's elements are just A's elements in reversed order.

If we rewrite the two loop control statements *for (i=0; i<10; i++)* to *for (i=1; i<=10; i++)*, it won't produce any error in the compiling and linking processes. But in the running process, instead of getting correct results, we may encounter unexpected errors, and the process may even affect the normal operations of other programs. This is a typical "The array bound is out of range" error.

6.1.2 Storage and Initialization of Arrays

1. Storage of Arrays
Array elements are stored orderly and continuously in memory. They occupy a group of consecutive storage locations in memory. Elements that are logically adjacent are also physically adjacent. The array name represents the starting memory address of array elements. The elements of a one-dimensional array are simply stored orderly and continuously according to their subscripts. Elements of a multidimensional array are also stored orderly and continuously, and the rule of the storage order is very important.

The issue of the storage order of array elements is related to what kind of order we operate the array elements when processing the array as an entity. Many operations in C++ are related to the storage order of array elements, such as array initialization and data transfer between program units.

A one-dimensional array can be viewed as a column vector in mathematics, and each element is continuously stored in memory according to their subscripts. For example, the following array declaration statement

```
int ay[5];
```

declares a one-dimensional array of *int* type with five elements. This array can be viewed as a column vector [ay[0], ay[1], ay[2], ay[3], and ay[4]]^T. The storage order of array elements in memory is demonstrated in Figure 6.1.

A two-dimensional array can be viewed as a matrix in mathematics; the first subscript of each array element is called the row subscript of the element, and the second subscript is called the column subscript. For example, the array declaration statement

```
int M[2][3]
```

declares a two-dimensional array, which equals a matrix with two rows and three columns

$$M = \begin{bmatrix} M(1, 1) & M(1, 2) & M(1, 3) \\ M(2, 1) & M(2, 2) & M(2, 3) \end{bmatrix}$$

Ay[0]	Ay[1]	Ay[2]	Ay[3]	Ay[4]

Fig. 6.1: Storage structure of a one-dimensional array.

M[0][0]	M[0][1]	M[0][2]	M[1][0]	M[1][1]	M[1][2]

First row   Second row

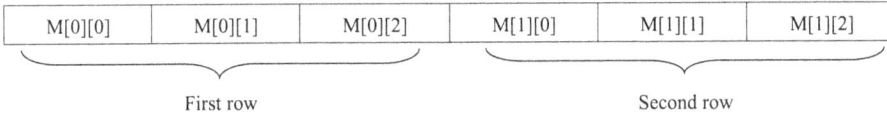

Fig. 6.2: Storage structure of a two-dimensional array.

However, in C++, the subscript of each dimension of an array element starts from 0. So in the program, the array above is represented as

$$M = \begin{bmatrix} M[0][0] & M[0][1] & M[0][2] \\ M[1][0] & M[1][1] & M[1][2] \end{bmatrix}$$

Element *M[1][0]*, with 1 as its row subscript and 0 as its column subscript, denotes the first element of the second row of the matrix. A two-dimensional array is stored by rows in memory. That is, the first row is stored first, and then the second row, and so on. The elements of each row are stored according to their column subscripts. This storage method is also called row-major storage. The storage order of the two-dimensional array *M* in memory is demonstrated in Figure 6.2.

For an *n*-dimensional array, we use a similar method to orderly store the array elements. We can view the subscripts of the *n* dimensions as a counter, where the later subscript is the lower order digit, and every digit ranges between the lower bound and the upper bound of the corresponding dimension. When the count of some digit exceeds the related upper bound, a carry is made to the previous digit, and the current and lower digits all recount from their respective lower bounds. We can discover that the subscript of the first dimension varies slowest, and the subscript of the last dimension varies quickest. It is noticeable that for each dimension, the lower bound is 0 and the upper bound is the value of the subscript expression in the array declaration minus 1. For example, the following array declaration statement

```
int M[2][3][4];
```

declares a three-dimensional array, and the storage order of elements is indicated in Figure 6.3.

In general, arrays with three or more dimensions are rarely used, and the most frequently used is a one-dimensional array.

M[0][0][0]	M[0][0][1]	M[0][0][2]	M[0][0][3]	M[0][1][0]	M[0][1][1]
M[0][1][2]	M[0][1][3]	M[0][2][0]	M[0][2][1]	M[0][2][2]	M[0][2][3]
M[1][0][0]	M[1][0][1]	M[1][0][2]	M[1][0][3]	M[1][1][0]	M[1][1][1]
M[1][1][2]	M[1][1][3]	M[1][2][0]	M[1][2][1]	M[1][2][2]	M[1][2][3]

Fig. 6.3: Storage structure of a three-dimensional array.

2. Initialization of Array

The initialization of an array is to assign values to part or all of the array elements when declaring an array. To the array of basic types, the initialization assigns values to array elements; to an object array, every element is a class object, so the initialization needs to call the constructor of the object. We will introduce object arrays later in detail.

When declaring an array, we can initialize the array elements. For example,

```
int a[3]={1,1,1};
```

indicates that we declare an array of *int* type which has three elements, and values of *a[0], a[1], a[3]* are all 1. If we list all the initial values of array elements during the array declaration, then we need not explicitly give the number of elements. The statement below is completely equivalent to the statement above.

```
int a[]={1,1,1};
```

We can also only initialize part of the array elements during an array declaration. For example, when declaring a *float* type array with five elements, we can assign the first three elements 1.0, 2.0, and 3.0 respectively, and it can be written as

```
float fa[5]={1.0, 2.0, 3.0};
```

Here, the number of array elements must be specified, and it is unnecessary to give any explanation for the last two elements. Note that we can only initialize all the elements or the first several elements of an array, and we cannot initialize array elements selectively.

The initialization of a multidimensional array follows the same rule as a one-dimensional array. Moreover, if we give initial values to all the elements, the subscript of the first dimension doesn't need to be declared explicitly. For example,

```
int a[2][3]={1, 0, 0, 0, 1, 0};
```

equals to

```
int a[][3]={1, 0, 0, 0, 1, 0};
```

Elements of a multidimensional array can be grouped according to the subscript of the first dimension, and we can use braces to enclose each group. For a two-dimensional array, we can use braces to enclose the members of the same row into a group. The statement below is completely equivalent to the statement above:

```
int a[2][3]={{1, 0, 0}, {0, 1, 0}};
```

The writing form of grouping by braces is easy to recognize and understand.

6.1.3 Using Arrays as Function Parameters

Array elements and array names can be used as parameters of functions to achieve data passing and data sharing between functions.

We can use an array element as an actual parameter when calling a function, which is completely equivalent to using a variable (or object) of the same type as an actual parameter.

If we use an array name as a parameter of a function, then the actual parameter and the formal parameter should be both the array name and both be of the same type. Differently from common variables, **when we use an array name to pass data, we are actually passing the starting address of the array.** The starting address of the formal parameter array is the same as that of the actual parameter array, and the following elements of the formal and the actual parameter arrays correspondingly share the same addresses. Thus, the number of elements of the actual parameter array should not be less than that of the formal parameter array. It is noticeable that if we change the values of the formal parameter array elements in the called function, the corresponding values of the actual parameter array elements in the calling function will also be changed.

Example 6.2: Using array name as function parameter.
The program below first initializes a matrix and outputs each element of the matrix in the main function; then, a subfunction is called to sum up the elements in each row and save the result as the first element of each row. At last, the main function outputs the sum of elements in each row.

```
//6_2.cpp
#include <iostream>
using namespace std;
void RowSum(int A[][4], int nrow)
        //Compute the sum of elements in each row of the two dimensional
        //array A; nrow is the number of rows
{
    for (int i = 0; i < nrow; i++)
    {
        for(int j = 1; j < 4; j++)
          A[i][0] += A[i][j];
    }
}
int main()                              //main function
{
    int Table[3][4] = {{1,2,3,4},{2,3,4,5},{3,4,5,6}};
                                //declare and initialize an array
    for (int i = 0; i < 3; i++)  //Output array elements
```

```
        {
            for (int j = 0; j < 4; j++)
             cout << Table[i][j] << " ";
            cout << endl;
        }
        RowSum(Table,3);                    //Call the subfunction to compute the
                                            //sum of elements of each row
        for (i = 0; i < 3; i++)       //Output the results
        {
          cout << "Sum of row " << i << " is " <<Table[i][0]<< endl;
        }
    }
```

The result of the program is:

```
1 2 3 4
2 3 4 5
3 4 5 6
Sum of row 0 is 10
Sum of row 1 is 14
Sum of row 2 is 18
```

Analyzing the output result of the program carefully, we can find that before calling the subfunction, *Table[i][0]* is 1, 2, and 3 respectively; after calling, *Table[i][0]* changes to 10, 14, and 18 respectively. That is to say, the operation on formal parameter array elements in subfunction directly affects the corresponding actual parameter array elements in the function.

6.1.4 Object Arrays

The type of array elements not only can be basic data types, but also can be user-defined types. For example, if we want to store and process the information of all employees of a corporation, we can construct an object array for an employee class. The elements of an object array are objects that have data members as well as function members. Therefore, compared with arrays of basic data types, object arrays have some special characteristics.

The form for declaring a one-dimensional object array is:

```
Class name Array name[Subscript expression];
```

Like arrays of basic data types, we can only refer to single array elements when using object arrays. Each array element is an object by which we can access its public members. The general form of accessing a public name of an object array element is

```
Array name[Subscript].Member name
```

In Chapter 4, we introduced the process of using a constructor to initialize an object. The process of initializing an object array is in fact the process of calling a constructor to initialize every element object. If we assign initial values to each array element when declaring an array, the constructor that has matching formal parameters will be called in the initialization process of the array. For example,

```
Location A[2]={Location(1, 2), Location(3, 4)};
```

When the above statement is executed, the constructor with formal parameters will be called twice to initialize A[0] and A[1], respectively. If we do not assign initial values to array elements, the default constructor will be called. For example,

```
Location A[2]={Location(1, 2)};
```

When the above statement is executed, the constructor with formal parameters will first be called to initialize A[0], and then the default constructor will be called to initialize A[1].

If we need to construct an object array of a class, we must fully consider the need of the initialization of array elements while designing the constructor of the class: when we need to assign the same initial values to all the element objects, we should define a constructor with default formal parameters; when we need to assign different initial values of the element objects, we should define a constructor with formal parameters (without default values).

When the element object of an array is to be deleted, the system will call the destructor of the class to do the round-off work.

Example 6.3: Application examples of object arrays.

```
//Point.h
#if !defined(_POINT_H)
#define _POINT_H
class Point
{
   public:
       Point();
       Point(int xx,int yy);
       ~Point();
       void Move(int x,int y);
       int GetX() {return X;}
       int GetY() {return Y;}
   private:
       int X,Y;
};
#endif
```

```
//Point.cpp
#include<iostream>
#include "Point.h"
using namespace std;
Point::Point()
{ X=Y=0;
    cout<<"Default Constructor called."<<endl;
}
Point::Point(int xx,int yy)
{ X=xx;
  Y=yy;
    cout<< "Constructor called."<<endl;
}
Point::~Point()
{
    cout<<"Destructor called."<<endl;
}
void Point::Move(int x,int y)
{
    X=x;
    Y=y;
}


//6-3.cpp
#include<iostream>
#include "Point.h"
using namespace std;
int main()
{
    cout<<"Entering main..."<<endl;
    Point A[2];
    for(int i=0;i<2;i++)
        A[i].Move(i+10,i+20);
    cout<<"Exiting main..."<<endl;
}
```

The result of the actual run is:

```
Entering main. . .
Default Constructor called.
Default Constructor called.
```

```
Exiting main. . .
Destructor called.
Destructor called.
```

6.1.5 Program Examples

Example 6.4: Using *Point* class to realize linear fit of points.

1. Simple Analysis

A linear fit of points is the most common way to process experimental data in general. Let us consider a problem of fitting a line by N data points. The linear model is

$$y(x) = y(x; a, b) = ax + b$$

This problem is called linear regression. Suppose that variable y varies along with the independent variable x. Given n observed data (x_i, y_i), we want to use a line to fit these points. Here, a and b are the slope and intercept of the line, which are called regression coefficients.

In order to determine the regression coefficients, we generally use the least square method, that is, to minimize the expression below:

$$Q = \sum_{i=0}^{n-1} [y_i - (ax_i + b)]^2 \tag{6.1}$$

According to the extremum principle, a and b satisfy the equations below,

$$\frac{\partial Q}{\partial a} = 2 \sum_{i=0}^{n-1} [y_i - (ax_i + b)](-x_i) = 0 \tag{6.2}$$

$$\frac{\partial Q}{\partial b} = 2 \sum_{i=0}^{n-1} [y_i - (ax_i + b)](-1) = 0 \tag{6.3}$$

Then we get,

$$a = \frac{L_{xy}}{L_{xx}} = \frac{\sum_{i=0}^{n-1}(x_i - \bar{x})(y_i - \bar{y})}{\sum_{i=0}^{n-1}(x_i - \bar{x})^2} \tag{6.4}$$

$$b = \bar{y} - a\bar{x} \tag{6.5}$$

$$\bar{x} = \sum_{i=0}^{n-1} x_i/n, \qquad \bar{y} = \sum_{i=0}^{n-1} y_i/n \tag{6.6}$$

Finally, we can have the linear equation $y(x)=ax+b$.

For any group of data, we can always use this method to fit a line. However, some data points may be far from the line while some data points may be very close to the

Point
- X : float
- Y : float
+ Point(xx : float = 0, yy : float = 0)
+ GetX() : float
+ GetY() : float
<<friend>> + linefit(l_point : Point [], n_point : int) : float

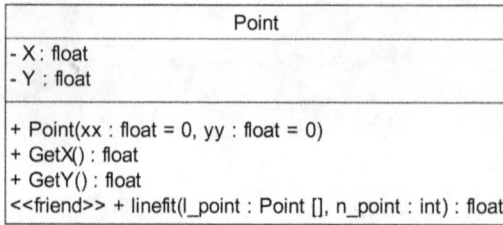

Fig. 6.4: *Point* class used for linear regression.

line. Here we need a criterion. Correlation coefficient is the general criterion of the linearity degree of the line that is fitted, which can be used to judge the degree of the linear correlation of a group of data. It is defined as,

$$r = \frac{L_{xy}}{\sqrt{L_{xx}L_{yy}}} \tag{6.7}$$

Here, the definition of L_{xy} and L_{xx} can be seen in formula (6.4), whereas L_{yy} is defined as,

$$L_{yy} = \sum_{i=0}^{n-1} (y_u - \bar{y})^2 \tag{6.8}$$

The closer the absolute value of r is to 1, the better the linear relation of the data is. When the data has an accurate linear relation, $r=1$. If the correlation coefficient is close to 0, it denotes that the linear relation of the data is bad or that the data has no linear relation at all. Therefore, after linear fitting, we usually need to compute the correlation coefficient to measure the linearity degree of the line.

In the program of this example, we use the *Point* class given by Chapter 4 as the base, and use an object array of class *Point* to store points. In order to do the fitting computation, we add a friend function. The computation results are a, b, and r. r is used to measure the degree of approximation.

The relationship between a class and its friend function can be represented by the UML stereotype, as shown in Figure 6.4.

2. Program Source Code

The whole program is divided into two files. One is header file *point.h* for the *Pointer* class, and the other one is file *6_4.cpp*, which contains the main function of the program.

```
//point.h
class Point                         //Definition of Point class
{
public:                             //external interface
    Point(float xx=0, float yy=0) {X=xx;Y=yy;}
    float GetX() {return X;}
```

```
    float GetY() {return Y;}
    friend float linefit(Point l_point[], int n_point);
                                    //friend function
    //variable of int type is the number of points
private:                            //private data members
    float X,Y;
};
//End of point.h


//6_4.cpp
#include<iostream>
#include<cmath>
#include "point.h"
using namespace std;
float linefit(Point l_point[], int n_point) //friend function body
{
    float av_x,av_y;                //declare variables
    float L_xx,L_yy,L_xy;
    //The initialization of variables
    av_x=0;                         //The average value of X
    av_y=0;                         //The average value of Y
    L_xx=0;                         //Lxx
    L_yy=0;                         //Lyy
    L_xy=0;                         //Lxy
    for(int i=0;i<n_point;i++)      //Compute the average value of X, Y
    {
     av_x+=l_point[i].X/n_point;
     av_y+=l_point[i].Y/n_point;
    }
    for(i=0;i<n_point;i++)          //Compute Lxx, Lyy and Lxy
    {
     L_xx+=(l_point[i].X-av_x)*(l_point[i].X-av_x);
     L_yy+=(l_point[i].Y-av_y)*(l_point[i].Y-av_y);
     L_xy+=(l_point[i].X-av_x)*(l_point[i].Y-av_y);
    }
    cout<<"This line can be fitted by y=ax+b."<<endl;
    cout<<"a="<<L_xy/L_xx;          //Output regression coefficient a
    cout<<" b="<<av_y-L_xy*av_x/L_xx<<endl;
                                    //Output regression coefficient b
    return float(L_xy/sqrt(L_xx*L_yy));
                                    //Return correlation coefficient r

}
```

```
int main()
{
    Point l_p[10]={Point(6,10),Point(14,20),Point(26,30),
    Point(33,40),Point(46,50),Point(54,60),Point(67,70),
    Point(75,80),Point(84,90),Point(100,100)};
                                //Initialize the data points
    float r=linefit(l_p,10);    //Do linear regression computation
    cout<<"Line coefficient r="<<r<<endl;
                                //Output correlation coefficient
}
```

3. The Result
The result of the program is

```
This line can be fitted by y=ax+b.
a=0.97223 b=5.90237
Line coefficient r=0.998193
```

4. Analysis and Explanation
The main function of this program first declares an object array of *Point* class to store the points to be fitted. We initialize the array during its declaration, and this initialization is completed by calling the constructor of the *Point* class one by one. Then *linefit*, the friend function of the *Point* class, is called to do the linear regression computation. Finally, we output the regression coefficients *a*, *b*, and linear coefficient *r*.

In the above program, we use an object array of the *Point* class to organize the data points and use a friend function to access the encapsulated data directly. If we don't use a friend function when we want to access the private data members *X* and *Y* during the process of linear fitting, we can only use the external interfaces of the class, *GetX()* and *GetY()*. Every access to the private data members then needs an extra function call, which takes up more memory and CPU. Therefore, using a friend function in this program will improve the efficiency of the program significantly.

However, the limitation of this program is that the number of data points is fixed, which is decided by the size of the object array. In the following chapters, we will modify this program to adapt to the case of any number of data pairs.

6.2 Pointers

A pointer is an important data type in C++, which is inherited from C. It provides a relatively direct method for operating addresses. Using pointers correctly can organize and represent complex data structures flexibly and effectively. Dynamic memory allocation and memory management depend on pointers, too. On the other hand, pointers are a main difficulty of C++. In order to understand pointers, we should first study the concept of memory addresses.

6.2.1 Access Method of Memory Space

The memory of a computer is divided into many storage locations that are numbered by certain rules. The number of a storage location is its address. The basic unit of address coding is the byte, and each byte is composed of 8 bits. In other words, each byte is a basic memory location and has an address. Computers use this way to accurately locate storage locations to manage the reading and writing of memory data. Figure 6.5 is a simplified block diagram of a memory structure.

How can C++ program access data using memory locations? One way is using the name of the variable; the other way is using the address of the memory location. Variables declared by a program will occupy some memory space. For example, a *short*-type variable occupies 2 bytes, and a *long*-type variable occupies 4 bytes. The memory space of variables with static life periods has been allocated before a program starts, while the memory space of variables with dynamic life periods will not be allocated until the running program meets the related variable declaration statements. When the memory space of a variable has been allocated, its name becomes the name of the corresponding memory space. During the whole life period of the variable, we can use this name to access the memory space, which is represented in the program as using the variable name to access the content of variable. However, when it is inconvenient to use the variable name or there isn't any variable name to use, we need to access the memory location by its address. For example, when we pass massive data between different functions, if we only pass the addresses of variables instead of the values of variables, the system overhead can be reduced and efficiency can be improved. For dy-

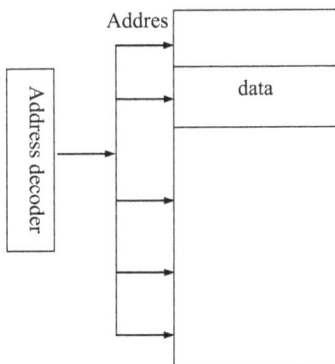

Fig. 6.5: Storage structure diagram.

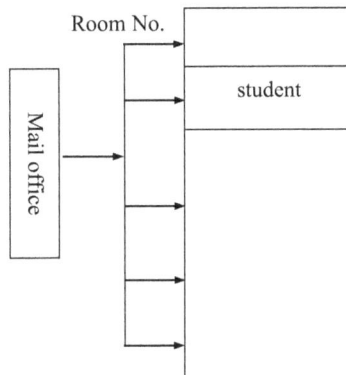

Fig. 6.6: Apartment structure diagram.

namic allocated memory locations (introduced in Section 6.3), there will be no names and we can only access them by their addresses.

The access management of memory locations is analogous to the management of student apartments, which is shown in Figure 6.6. Suppose that each student lives in one room separately. Each student equals the content of a variable, each room equals a storage location, and each room number equals a storage address. If we know the name of a student, we can use this name to visit the student, which equals using the variable name to access data. If we know the room number, we can also visit the student, which equals accessing data via address.

C++ has a data type specialized for storing memory addresses, which is called a pointer.

6.2.2 Declaration of Pointer Variables

A pointer is also a kind of data type, and variables of the pointer type are called pointer variables. **A pointer variable is used to store a memory address.**

Accessing a variable by its name is direct, while accessing a variable by a pointer is indirect. Suppose that you want to find a student and don't know where he lives, though you know that his address can be found at Room 201. When you walk into Room 201, you see a note "Please come to 302 to find me". Then you go to Room 302 specified in the note and find the student. Here, Room 201 equals a pointer variable, and the word in the note is the content that the pointer variable stores. The student that lives in Room 302 equals the content of the variable that the pointer points to.

Pointer should be declared before being used. The grammatical form of declaring a pointer is

```
Data type *identifier;
```

Here '*' represents that the statement declares a variable of pointer type. "Data type" can be any type that refers to the type of the object (a variable and an object of a class) that the pointer points to. This illustrates what type of data can be stored in the memory location that the pointer points to, and we call it the type of the pointer. The default type of all pointers is the *unsigned long int* type. For example, statement

```
int *i_pointer;
```

declares a pointer variable of *int* type. This pointer has a name of *i_pointer* and is only used to store the address of an *int*-type variable.

Readers may have this question: why should we specify the type of the object a pointer points to when declaring a pointer variable? To understand this point, we should first consider what information we declare when declaring a variable in a program. Maybe we only know that we declare the memory space that the variable needs. But this is only one aspect. Another important aspect is that the variable declaration limits the operations and related rules that we can perform on the variable. For example, the following statement

```
short i;
```

means that *i* is a variable of the *short* type. This not only means that the variable needs to occupy a memory space of 2 bytes, but also provides that *i* can participate in arithmetic operations, relational operations, etc., under the corresponding operational rules.

Operations of pointers will be introduced later, and you will see that the operational rules of a pointer variable are closely related to the object type the pointer points to. Therefore, there is no isolated "address" type in C++. When declaring a pointer, we must specify clearly of what type of data it is used to store the address.

Pointers can point to various types, including basic types, arrays (array elements), functions, objects, and even pointers.

6.2.3 Operations Related to Addresses – '*' and '&'

C++ provides two operations related to addresses – '*' and '&'. '*' is called an indirection operator (also called a dereferencing operator), and is used to access the variable that a pointer points to. It is a unary operator. For example, *i_pointer* denotes the value of the *int* type data that *i_pointer* points to. '&' is called an address-of operator, which is also a unary operator. It can be used to get the address of an object. For example, we can get the address of the storage location of variable *i* by using &*i*.

Note that both '*' and '&', when appearing in declaration statements and in execution statements, have different meanings. Also, when acting as unary operators and as binary operators, both '*' and '&' have different meanings. When the unary operator '*' appears in a declaration statement and is before the name of the declared variable, it indicates a pointer. For example,

```
int *p; //declare that p is a pointer of int type
```

When '*' appears as a unary operator in an execution statement or in the initial expression of a declaration statement, it means for it to access the content of the object that a pointer points to. For example,

```
cout<<*p; //output the content of the object that pointer p points to
```

When '&' appears in a variable declaration statement and is on the left side of the declared variable, it indicates a reference. For example,

```
int &rf; //declare a reference rf of int type
```

When '&' appears as a unary operator on the right side of an equal sign when initializing a variable or in an executing statement, it means for it to access the address of the object. For example,

```
int a, b;
int *pa, *pb=&b;
pa=&a;
```

More details of assignment of pointers will be discussed in the next section.

6.2.4 Assignment of Pointers

When declaring a pointer, we can only get a pointer variable, which is used to store the address, while the pointer variable has no definite, but instead, a random, value. In other words, we are not sure which memory address is stored by the pointer variable after the declaration, and the random memory address that the pointer points to may store important data or program code. If it is accessed rashly, data destruction or system malfunction may occur. Therefore, after declaring a pointer, we must assign it a value before using it. Like variables of other types, there are two ways to assign an initial value to a pointer:

1. Initialize the pointer when declaring it. The grammatical form is,

```
Storage type Data type *Pointer name=initial address;
```

2. Use an assignment statement after the declaration of the pointer. The grammatical form of the assignment statement is,

```
Pointer name= address;
```

If we use the address of an object as the initial value of a pointer, or assign the address of an object to a pointer variable in an assignment statement, then this object must be declared before the assignment of the pointer, and the object's type must be consistent with the type of the pointer. An assigned pointer can be used to initialize another pointer. That is to say, multiple pointers can point to the same address.

To variables of basic types, array elements, structure members, or objects of classes, we can use the address-of operator & to get their addresses. For example, we can use &*i* to get the address of variable *i* of the *int* type.

The starting address of an array is its name. For example,

```
int a[10];            //declare an array of int type
int *i_pointer=a;     //declare and initialize a pointer of int type
```

The first statement declares an array *a* of 10 *int*-type elements, and the second statement declares a pointer *i_pointer* of *int* type and uses the starting address of the array *a* to initialize the pointer.

Let us review the knowledge of pointers by the following example.

Example 6.5: Declaration, assignment, and use of pointers.

```
//6_5.cpp
#include<iostream>
using namespace std;
int main()
{
    int *i_pointer;      //declare pointer i_pointer of int type
    int i;               //declare variable i of int type
    i_pointer=&i;        //assign the address of i to i_pointer
    i=10;                //initialize the variable of int type
    cout<<"Output int i="<<i<<endl; //Output the value of the int-type
                         //variable
    cout<<"Output int pointer i="<<*i_pointer<<endl;
    //Output the content of the address that the pointer of int type
    //points to
}
```

The result of the program is:

```
Output int i=10
Output int pointer i=10
```

Let us analyze the running process of the program. In the program, it first declares a pointer *i_pointer* of *int* type; then it declares an *int* type variable *i* and uses an address-of operator to get the address of *i*. Next it assigns this address to the pointer *i_pointer* and assigns 10 to *i*. The states of related variables at this time can be simply described in Figure 6.7. Here, we suppose the memory addresses of *i* and *i_pointer* are 3000 and 2000 respectively.

The content of variable *i* is 10, and *i_pointer* stores the address of variable *i*, which is 3000. The value of &*i* is *i*'s address 3000. *i_pointer* is 10, which is the value of vari-

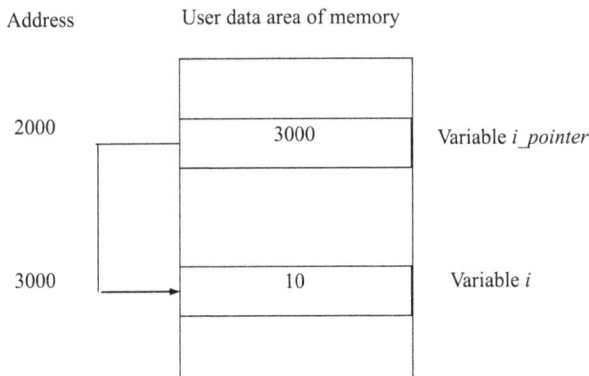

Fig. 6.7: States of related variables.

able *i* pointed by *i_pointer*. Here, both the value of *i* and **i_pointer* are 10. The former is a direct access, and the latter is an indirect access by the pointer.

i_pointer appears twice in the program, though its meanings are different. In the pointer declaration statement, '' before the identifier indicates that the declared identifier is a pointer; in the output statement, '*' is the pointer operator that leads an indirect access to the variable that the pointer points to.

Several points should be noted about the type of pointer.

1. We can declare **a pointer to a const**. In this case, we cannot change the value of the object through the pointer, although the value of the pointer itself can be changed to point to other objects. For example,

```
const char *name1= "John";
                        //name1 is a pointer which points to a const
char s[]="abc";
name1=s;                //correct, the value of name1 can be changed
*name1='1';
    //compiling error, the value of the object that name1 points to
    //cannot be changed through name1
```

Using a pointer that points to a constant can avoid the const from being changed accidentally. If we use a general pointer to store the address of a constant, the compiler cannot ensure that the object pointed by the pointer remains unchanged, and errors may occur during the running time. The following program segment is an example.

```
char *name1 = "John";
    //name1 is a general pointer, but it stores the starting address
    //of a string constant
*name1='A';
    //compilation succeeds, but error in running. The content of the
    //string constant cannot be changed.
```

Here, we try to change characters of the string constant "John" through pointer *name1*. Because *name1* is a general pointer, the compiler is unaware of this error. But it goes wrong when running the program. So in this situation, we should declare *name1* as a pointer that points to a string constant.

2. We can declare **a constant of the pointer type**, and the value of the pointer cannot be changed during the execution of the program. For example,

```
char *const name2 = "John";
name2="abc";
    //error, name2 is a pointer constant, and its value cannot be
    //changed
```

3. In general, the value of a pointer can only be assigned to pointers of the same type. But there is a special kind of **pointers that belong to the *void* type**. Such a pointer

can store the address of an object of any type. That is to say, pointers of any type can be assigned to a pointer variable of *void* type. Through type casting, we can access data of any type using a *void*-type pointer. *Void*-type pointers can also point to any function except for the class member function.

Example 6.6: Using *void*-type pointers.

```
void vobject;       //Wrong, cannot declare a variable of void type
void *pv;           //Right, can declare a pointer of void type
int *pint; int i;
int main()          //Functions of void type have no return value
{
    pv = &i;        //Pointer of void type points to int variable
    pint = (int *)pv; //type cast
    //assign the value of the pointer of void type to the pointer of
    //int type
}
```

6.2.5 Pointer Operations

A pointer is a data type. Like other data types, pointer variables can participate in some operations, including arithmetic operations, relational operations, and assignment operations. The assignment operation of pointers has been introduced before. In this section, we will introduce arithmetic operations and relational operations of pointers.

Pointers can perform simple addition and subtraction operations with integers. But the operational rule is special. It has been discussed that when declaring a pointer variable, we must specify the type of the object it points to. Here, we will see that the results of addition and subtraction operations of a pointer are closely related to the type of the pointer. If we have pointer *p1* and integer *n1*, then *p1+n1* denotes the address of the *n1*-th object after the current object that *p1* points to; *p1-n1* denotes the address of the *n1*-th object before the current object that *p1* points to. "pointer++" or "pointer−" denotes the address of the next or previous object of the current object that pointer points to. Figure 6.8 gives a simple diagram of the addition and subtraction operations of pointers.

Generally, arithmetic operations of pointers are associated with the use of arrays – for we can only get continuous operable memory space when using arrays. If we perform arithmetic operations on a pointer that points to an individual variable and then access the data through the result pointer, we may destroy the data or code of that address. Therefore, when doing arithmetic operations of pointers, we must ensure that the result pointer points to an address that has been allocated in the program.

Relational operations of pointer variables refer to relational operations between pointers of the same type. If two pointers of the same type have the same value, it

short *pa   long *pb

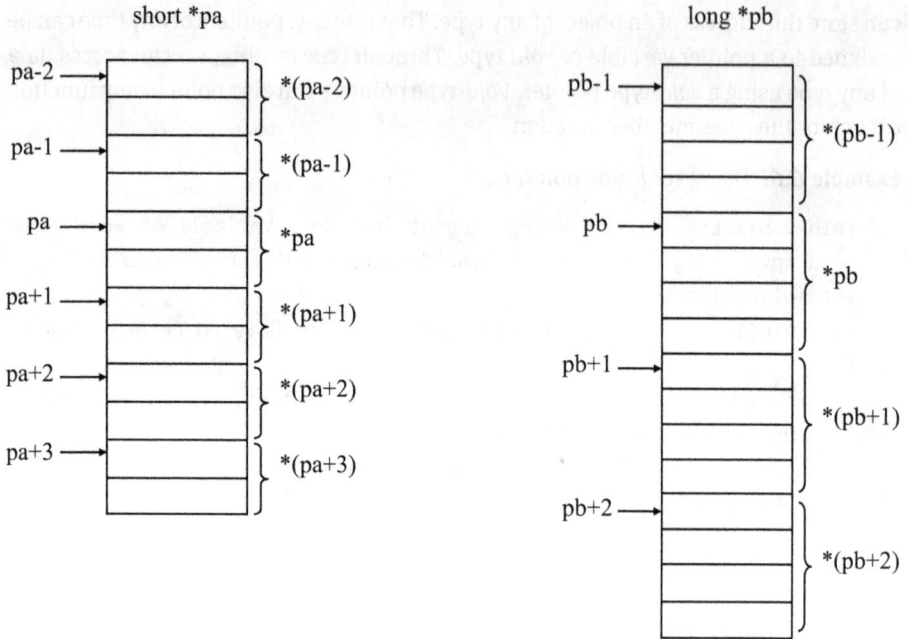

Fig. 6.8: Arithmetic operations of pointers.

means that the two pointers point to the same address. It is meaningless to do relational operations between pointers of different types or between pointers and nonzero integers. But pointer variables can be compared with the integer 0. This is a special mark of a pointer operation, which we will use in later examples.

The method of assigning pointers has been detailed in the last section. Here we stress that the value assigned to pointers must be address constants (e.g., array name) or address variables and they cannot be nonzero integers. If we assign 0 to a pointer variable, it denotes that this pointer is a null pointer that doesn't point to any address. For example,

```
int *p;    //declare a pointer p of int type
p=0;       //set p as null pointer which doesn't point to any address
```

Why do we need to set a pointer as a null pointer using the method above? This is because sometimes when declaring a pointer, there is no definite address value that can be assigned to it. Only when the program runs to a point does it assign an address value to this pointer. During the period from the birth of the pointer to the time it has a definite value, its value is random. If we wrongly use this random value as an address to access some memory location, it will lead to unexpected error. Therefore, in this situation we should first set the pointer as a null pointer.

6.2.6 Using Pointers to Process Array Elements

The addition and subtraction characteristics of pointers make them especially suitable for processing the same type of data that is stored in a continuous memory space. An array is a set of same-type variables that have some ordinal relation; array elements are stored continuously physically; and the array name is the starting address of the array. We can use pointers to do convenient and quick operations on arrays and array elements. For example,

```
int array[5];
```

declares a one-dimensional array that stores five *int*-type elements. The array name *array* is the starting address of the array (the address of its first element). That is, *array* is the same as &*array[0]*. Five integers in the array are stored orderly, so we can access array elements by using the array name and some simple arithmetic operations. The array element whose subscript is *i* is *(array name+i)*. For example, *array* is *array[0]*, and *(array+3)* is *array[3]*.

Example 6.7: Suppose there is an array *a* of the *int* type, which has 10 elements. Use three methods to output all the elements.
Program 1: Using array name and subscripts

```cpp
//6_7_1.cpp
#include <iostream>
using namespace std;
int main()
{
    int a[10]={1,2,3,4,5,6,7,8,9,0};
    int i;
    for(i=0; i<10; i++)
     cout<<a[i]<<" ";
    cout<<endl;
}
```

Program 2: Using array name and pointer operations

```cpp
//6_7_2.cpp
#include <iostream>
using namespace std;
int main()
{
    int a[10]={1,2,3,4,5,6,7,8,9,0};
    int i;
    for(i=0; i<10; i++)
     cout<<*(a+i)<< " ";
```

```
    cout<<endl;
}
```

Program 3: Using pointer variables

```
//6_7_3.cpp
#include <iostream>
using namespace std;
int main()
{
    int a[10]={1,2,3,4,5,6,7,8,9,0};
    int *p;
    for(p=a; p<(a+10); p++)
        cout<<*p<<" ";
    cout<<endl;
}
```

The running results of the above programs are the same. And the result is:

```
1 2 3 4 5 6 7 8 9 0
```

This example is very simple, and readers can analyze the running results themselves. Think carefully about the relationships and differences between the array name, subscripts of array elements, and pointers that point to array elements.

6.2.7 Pointer Arrays

If each element of an array is a pointer variable, then this array is a pointer array. Each element of a pointer array must be pointers of the same type.

The grammatical form of declaring a one-dimensional pointer array is:

```
Type name T *Array name[Subscript expression];
```

The subscript expression denotes the number of array elements. The type name specifies the type of every pointer element. The array name is the name of the pointer array, and is also the starting address of this array. For example,

```
int *p_i[3];
```

declares a pointer array p_i of int type. It has three elements, each of which is a pointer pointing to data of the int type.

Because each element of a pointer array is a pointer, which cannot be used before assignment, thus after declaring a pointer array, it is necessary to assign an initial value to each pointer element.

Example 6.8: Using pointer arrays to output identity matrix.
An identity matrix is a matrix whose elements in the principal diagonal are all 1, and elements in other positions are all 0. The following example concerns an identity matrix of three rows and three columns.

```
//6_8.cpp
#include <iostream>
using namespace std;
int main()
{
    int line1[]={1,0,0}; //declare array, the first row of the matrix
    int line2[]={0,1,0}; //declare array, the second row of the matrix
    int line3[]={0,0,1}; //declare array, the third row of the matrix

    int *p_line[3];       //declare a pointer array of int type
    p_line[0]=line1;      //initialize elements of pointer array
    p_line[1]=line2;
    p_line[2]=line3;

    cout<<"Matrix test:"<<endl; //Output the identity matrix
    for(int i=0;i<3;i++) //loop through all the elements of pointer
                         //array
    {
     for(int j=0;j<3;j++) //loop through all the elements in each row
                          //of the matrix
     { cout<<p_line[i][j]<<" "; }
     cout<<endl;
    }
}
```

The program declares a pointer array of the *int* type that has three elements. Each pointer element points to one row in the matrix using the assign statements. Each row of the matrix is stored by an array. By referencing elements of the pointer array, we can access the *int*-type arrays used to store the matrix data. The output of the program is:

```
Matrix test:
1,0,0
0,1,0
0,0,1
```

The two-dimensional array is stored in memory in the row-major way, according to the order of the first dimension. To understand a two-dimensional array, we can parse it according to the structure of a one-dimensional array . The array name is its starting address. The number of elements of a pointer array is the number of rows, and each element is a pointer that points to a row in the two-dimensional array. For example, declaring a two-dimensional *int*-type array:

```
int array2[2][3]={{11,12,13},{21,22,23}};
```

We can understand it as:

```
         ┌─ array2[0] —— array[00]  array[01]  array[02]
array2   │
         └─ array2[1] —— array[10]  array[11]  array[12]
```

This two-dimensional array has two rows and three columns. It equals a one-dimensional pointer *int*-type array. The number of elements of the pointer array is the number of rows of the two-dimensional array. Two elements of the pointer array, *array2[0]* and *array2[1]*, denote the starting addresses of the first and second row of the two-dimensional array respectively. Each row of the two-dimensional array equals a one-dimensional *int*-type array, which has three elements.

The following program processes a two-dimensional array through this method.

Example 6.9: An example of a two-dimensional array.

```
//6_9.cpp
#include <iostream>
using namespace std;
int main()
{
    int array2[2][3]={{11,12,13},{21,22,23}};
    //declare a two-dimensional array of int type
    for(int i=0;i<2;i++)
      {
      cout<<*(array2+i)<<endl;
//output the starting address of row i of the two-dimensional array
        for(int j=0;j<3;j++)
            { cout<<*(*(array2+i)+j)<<" "; }
//output elements of row i one by one
        cout<<endl;
      }
}
```

A possible running result of the program is

```
0X0065FDE0
11,12,13
0X0065FDEC
21,22,23
```

The program first outputs a memory address that stores the first row of the array *array2*. Similarly, the second address stores the second row of *array2*. We can access elements of the two-dimensional array through addresses pointed to array elements. The form is as follows:

```
*(*(array2+i)+j)
```

This is the element of row *i* and column *j* of *array2*, corresponding to *array2[i][j]*, which is denoted by the subscript. Note that the addresses output by the program may be totally different each time we run the program, which is related to the memory allocation status of the system during the running process.

For a multidimensional array, we can understand it as a multidimensional pointer array whose dimension is one less. If you are interested in this topic, try to analyze a three-dimensional array as an exercise.

6.2.8 Using Pointers as Function Parameters

When we need to transfer a large amount of data between different functions, the cost of calling functions during the program execution will be large. In this case, if the data that needs transferring is stored continuously in memory, we can only pass the starting address of the data rather than passing data values, which will decrease cost and increase efficiency. The grammar of C++ provides support for this functionality: parameters of functions can not only be variables of basic types, object names, array names, or function names, but also be pointers. If we use pointers as formal parameters, the corresponding actual parameters will be transferred to the formal parameters when the function is called. That is, the actual and formal parameter pointer variables point to the same memory address. In this way, we can change data through formal parameter pointers in the subfunction, which also affect the data values that the actual parameter pointers point to.

Pointers in C++ are inherited from C. In C, there are three functions for using pointers as formal parameters of functions: first, it can make actual parameter pointers and formal parameter pointers point to the same memory space to realize bidirectional parameter passing. That is, we can process the data of the calling function in the called function directly and return the processing result to the calling function. This use has been realized in C++ by references, which has been detailed in the introduction of using references as function parameters in Chapter 3; secondly, it can decrease the cost of data transfer when calling functions. This use can also be realized by reference in C++ sometimes, while in some cases pointers are still needed; the third use is to pass the starting address of the function code by the pointer which points to it. This will be introduced later.

When designing a program, using pointers and using references as formal parameters can achieve the same thing, so we can use references that can make the program more readable.

Example 6.10: Read in three floating point numbers and output the integral part and the decimal part of the number respectively.

The program is made up of a main function and a subfunction, which is used to decompose the floating point numbers. After decomposing the floating point numbers in the subfunction, the integral part and decimal part will be returned to the main function to be output. It is imaginable that if we use *int-* and *float-*type variables directly, changes made on the formal parameters in the subfuction cannot be transferred to the main function. We use pointers as parameters of the function, and the source code is as follows:

```
//6_10.cpp
#include <iostream>
using namespace std;
void splitfloat(float x, int *intpart, float *fracpart)
                //formal parameters intpart and fracpart are pointers
{
    *intpart=int(x);         //get the integral part of x
    *fracpart=x-*intpart;    //get the decimal part of x
}

int main()
{
    int i,n;
    float x,f;
    cout<<"Enter 3 float point numbers:"<<endl;
    for(i=0;i<3;i++)
    {
     cin>>x;
     splitfloat(x,&n,&f);    //Use variable addresses as actual
                             //parameters
     cout<<"Integer Part="<<n<<" Fraction Part="<<f<<endl;
    }
}
```

The *splitfloat* function in the program uses two pointer variables as parameters. The main function uses the addresses of variables as actual parameters when calling *splitfloat*. When we unite the formal and actual parameters together, the value of *intpart* in the subfunction is the address of the *int-*type variable *n* in the main function. Thus, changes made on **inpart* in the subfunction can affect the value of the variable *n* in the main function directly. *Fracpart* and the floating point number *f* have a similar relationship.

The running result of the program is:

```
Enter 3 float point numbers:
4.7
Integer Part=4 Fraction Part=0.7
8.913
Integer Part=8 Fraction Part=0.913
-4.7518
Integer Part=-4 Fraction Part=-0.7518
```

In this program, using references as formal parameters can achieve the same result. Please try to modify the program in Example 6.10 and use references as the parameters of the function.

6.2.9 Pointer-Type Functions

Functions have return values after being called, except for *void*-type functions. Pointers can also be the return values of functions. When the return value of a function is a pointer, this function is a pointer-type function. The primary purpose of using a pointer as the return value of a function is to return large amounts of data from the called function to the calling function when the function call finishes. However, if the return value is not a pointer, the called function can only return a variable or an object when it finishes.

The general form of defining a pointer-type function is:

```
data type *function name (parameter list)
{
    function body
}
```

"Data type" denotes the type of the pointer that the function returns; "function name" and '*' identify a function of pointer type; and "parameter list" is the list of the formal parameters of the function.

6.2.10 Pointers that Point to Functions

Up to now, all the pointers that we have introduced are pointing to data, for example:

```
int *intpart;
float *fracpart;
```

During program execution, not only does data take up memory space, codes of the executive program are also loaded into memory and take up some memory space. Every function has a function name, and actually this function name denotes the starting address of the function code in memory. Thus, the common form of function calls, "function name (parameter list)", is essentially "the starting address of function code (parameter list)".

Function pointers are variables dedicated to storing the starting addresses of functions. In programs, we can use pointers that point to functions to call functions just like using function names. That is, once a function pointer points to a function, it plays the same role as the function name. The function name denotes the starting address of the function code, and it also contains information such as the type of the return value, and the number, the types, and the order of parameters. Therefore, when calling functions by function names, the compiling system can check whether actual and formal parameters match automatically. If we use the return values of functions to participate in other calculations, type consistency will be tested automatically.

When declaring a function pointer, we need to specify the return value and the formal parameter list of the function. Its general form is as follows

```
Data type (*function pointer name)(formal parameter list)
```

"Data type" denotes the type of the return value of the function that the function pointer points to. The content in the first parentheses specifies the name of a function pointer. "Formal parameter list" lists the formal parameters of the function that this function pointer points to.

The function pointer must be assigned to the starting address of an existed function before being used. The general form of assigning a function pointer is

```
Function pointer name=function name;
```

The function name on the right side of the equal sign must refer to a declared function that has the same return type and formal parameter list as the function pointer. After the assignment, we can reference the function that the pointer points to directly by the function pointer.

Please see the following example.

Example 6.11: An example of function pointers.

```
//6_11.cpp
#include <iostream>
using namespace std;
void print_stuff(float data_to_ignore);
void print_message(float list_this_data);
void print_float(float data_to_print);
void (*function_pointer)(float); //function pointer of void type

int main()                              //main function
```

```
{
    float pi = (float)3.14159;
    float two_pi = (float)2.0 * pi;
    print_stuff(pi);
    function_pointer = print_stuff;
                        //function pointer points to print_stuff
    function_pointer(pi); //function call by function pointer
    function_pointer = print_message;
                        //function pointer points to print_message
    function_pointer(two_pi); //function call by function pointer
    function_pointer(13.0); //function call by function pointer
    function_pointer = print_float;
                        //function pointer points to print_float
    function_pointer(pi); //function call by function pointer
    print_float(pi);
}

void print_stuff(float data_to_ignore)
{ cout<<"This is the print stuff function.\n"; }

void print_message(float list_this_data)
{ cout<<"The data to be listed is "<<list_this_data<<endl; }

void print_float(float data_to_print)
{ cout<<"The data to be printed is "<<data_to_print<<endl; }
```

The running result of the program is:

```
This is the print stuff function.
This is the print stuff function.
The data to be listed is 6.28318
The data to be listed is 13
The data to be printed is 3.14159
The data to be printed is 3.14159
```

The program in this example declares a function pointer of *void* type:

```
void (*function\_pointer)(float); //function pointer of void type
```

During the running process of the main function, we respectively make the pointer point to functions of *void* type *print_stuff*, *printa-message* and *print_float* by assignment statements, and then call these functions using the function pointer.

6.2.11 Object Pointers

1. General Concepts of Object Pointers

Like variables of basic data types, an object will take up some space in memory after the initialization. Therefore, we can access an object either by its name and or by its address. Although an object contains two types of members (data and functions), which is slightly different from general variables, the memory space the object occupies is used to store only data members, without the copies of function members. Object pointers are variables used to store object addresses, which follow the rules of general variable pointers. The general form of declaring object pointers is

```
Class name *object pointer name;
```

For example,

```
Point *p_Point; //declare an object pointer variable of Point class
                //p_Point
Point p1;       //declare the object of Point class p1
p_Point=&p1;    //assign the address of object p1 to p_Point and
                //make p_Point point to p1
```

Like accessing members of an object using the object's name, we can also access members of an object conveniently using the object pointer, whose syntax form is:

```
Object pointer name->member name
```

Example 6.12: Using pointers to access members of the *Point* class.

```
//6_12.cpp
#include <iostream>
using namespace std;
class Point                           //Definition of the class
{
public:                               //external interfaces
    Point(int xx=0, int yy=0) {X=xx;Y=yy;} //constructor
    int GetX() {return X;}            //inline function, return X
    int GetY() {return Y;}            //inline function, return Y
private:                              //private data
    int X,Y;
};

int main()                            //main function
{
    Point A(4,5);                     //declare and initialize object A
    Point *p1;                        //declare object pointer
```

```
    p1=&A;                          //assign the pointer the address of
                                    //object A
    cout<<p1->GetX()<<endl;         //Using pointer to access the
                                    //object's member
    cout<<A.GetX()<<endl;           //Using object name to access the
                                    //object's member
}
```

An object pointer must be assigned to a declared object before being used. We can access the public members of an object using an object pointer.

In Chapter 4, we used the following program segment as an example to introduce forward reference declaration:

```
class Fred;     //forward reference declaration
class Barney {
    Fred x;     //error: the definition of class Fred is not complete
};
class Fred {
    Barney y;
};
```

We already know that this program segment is wrong. But if it can be slightly modified as follows, the grammar will be correct.

```
class Fred;     //forward reference declaration
class Barney {
    Fred *x;
};
class Fred {
    Barney y;
};
```

Here, one is allowed to declare a pointer (not object) of class *Fred* in class *Barney*. Since the definition of *Fred* is after the definition of *Barney*, we can naturally declare an object of class *Barney* as a data member of class *Fred*. Therefore, this program is correct.

2. *this* pointer

The *this* pointer is a special pointer hidden in every member function (including the constructor and destructor) of a class, and is used to point to the object currently processed by the member function.

Let's first review the situation where we use the *Point* class array to solve the linear regression problem in the last section: in an array, there are many objects in the *Point* class, and we use array subscripts to identify them. In the initialization of each object, we need to call the constructor. The statements in a constructor body are:

```
X=xx;
Y=yy;
```

Each time the two statements are executed, the system needs to differentiate which object the assigned data member belongs to, and it uses the *this* pointer to achieve this. Each time the system executes the above two statements, it executes:

```
this->X=xx;
this->Y=yy;
```

The *this* pointer explicitly indicates which object the data member that the member function operates on belongs to. The actual process is as follows: when calling a member function by an object, the system first assigns the object address to the *this* pointer, and then calls the member function. When the member function operates on some data member, the *this* pointer is used implicitly.

In general program designs, we usually don't use the *this* pointer to reference object members. The *this* pointer is a pointer variable, so in a member function, we can use **this* to identify the object through which the function is being called.

3. Pointers to Nonstatic Members of a Class

Members of a class are variables, functions, objects, etc., so we can also store their addresses in pointer variables. In this way, we can make pointers point to members of objects and access these members using the pointers.

Pointers that point to members of objects should also be declared and assigned values before being used. So we should first specify which class the member pointed by the pointer belongs to during the declaration of the pointer. Note that using pointers we can only access public members. The syntax form of declaring a pointer that points to a class member is

```
type specifier class name::*pointer name;
        //declare a pointer which points to a public data member
type specifier (class name::*pointer name)(parameter list);
        //declare a pointer which points to a public function member
```

After declaring a pointer that points to a class member, we need to assign it the member of the class that the pointer is going to point to. The general syntax form of assigning a pointer that points to a data member is:

```
Pointer name=&class name::data member name;
```

For a common variable, we can use '**&**' operator to get its address. After assigning such an address to a pointer, we can access the variable by the pointer directly. However, things are a little complicated as to class members. The definition of a class only denotes the type and occupied memory size of each data member and their relative positions, while the specific memory addresses are not allocated for data members when defining the class. So the assignment introduced above only denotes which data member the pointer points to and it stores in the pointer the member's relative position in the class (offset from the starting address of the class), while we cannot access anything through such a pointer at the time.

Because classes are instantiated through objects, memory spaces will be allocated to objects when we declare the objects of classes. After declaring an object, we can access a data member of the object by combining the starting memory address of the object and the relative offset stored in the member pointer that points to the data member. When accessing data members, this combination can be realized by either of the following two syntax forms:

```
Object name.* class member pointer name
or: object pointer name-->*class member pointer name
```

Pointers that point to member functions of classes should be assigned values after their declarations through the following form.

```
Pointer name=class name::function member name;
```

The name of a common function denotes its starting address. By assigning the function's starting address to a pointer, we can call the function through this pointer. Although member functions of a class do not each have a copy of their object, grammatically, nonstatic member functions should be called through objects. Thus, after assigning a pointer to a member function through the form introduced above, rather than using the pointer to call the member function directly, we must first declare an object of the class and then use the function member pointer to call the member function using the statements below:

```
(object name.* class member pointer name)(parameter list)
or: (object pointer name-->*class member pointer name)(parameter list)
```

Note that the type of the return value and the parameter list of functions both must match during the declaration, as well as the assignment and the use of a member function pointer.

Example 6.13: Different ways to access public member functions of objects.

```
int main()        //main function
{
    Point A(4,5);  //declare object A
    Point *p1=&A;  //declare object pointer and initialize it
    int (Point::*p_GetX)()=Point::GetX;
                //declare member function pointer and initialize it

    cout<<(A.*p_GetX)()<<endl;
        //(1) use member function pointer to access member function
```

```
    cout<<(p1->GetX)()<<endl;
                     //(2)use object pointer to access member function
    cout<<A.GetX()<<endl;
                     //(3) use object name to access member function
}
```

The program in Example 6.13 only gives the main function part, and the definition of the class can be found in Example 6.12 in this section. In this example, it declares an object *A* of the *Point* class, and then accesses the member function *GetX* by the object name, the object pointer, and the function member pointer respectively. The results of the program are all the value of *A*'s private data member *X* 4. Please analyze the different uses of object pointers and member pointers.

4. Pointers to Static Members of a Class

Accessing static members of a class does not depend on specific objects, so we can use common pointers to point to and access static class members. Now, we make a few modifications on Example 5.4 in Chapter 5 and get two programs in Example 6.14 and Example 6.15, to explain how to use common pointer variables to access the static members of a class.

Example 6.14: Using pointers to access static data members of a class.

```
//6_14.cpp
#include <iostream>
using namespace std;
class Point                    //define the Point class
{
public:                        //external interface
    Point(int xx=0, int yy=0) {X=xx;Y=yy;countP++;} //constructor
    Point(Point &p);           //copy constructor
    int GetX() {return X;}
    int GetY() {return Y;}
    static int countP;         //referential declaration of static data
                               //member
private:                       //private data members
    int X,Y;
};
Point::Point(Point &p)
{
    X=p.X;
    Y=p.Y;
    countP++;
}
```

```
int Point::countP=0;          //definitional declaration of static data
                              //member


int main()                    //main function
{
    int *count=&Point::countP;
        //declare a pointer of int type that points to the static
        //member of the class
    Point A(4,5);             //declare object A
    cout<<"Point A,"<<A.GetX()<<","<<A.GetY();
    cout<<" Object id="<<*count<<endl;
                        //access static data member by pointer directly
    Point B(A);               //declare object B
    cout<<"Point B,"<<B.GetX()<<","<<B.GetY();
    cout<<" Object id="<<*count<<endl;
                        //access static data member by pointer directly
}
```

Example 6.15: Using pointers to access static function members of a class.

```
//6_15.cpp
#include <iostream>
using namespace std;
class Point              //define Point class
{
public:                  //external interface
    Point(int xx=0, int yy=0) {X=xx;Y=yy;countP++;} //constructor
    Point(Point &p);     //copy constructor
    int GetX() {return X;}
    int GetY() {return Y;}
    static void GetC() {cout<<" Object id="<<countP<<endl;}
                         //static function member
private:                 //private data members
    int X,Y;
    static int countP;   //referential declaration of static data
                         //member
};
Point::Point(Point &p)
{
    X=p.X;
    Y=p.Y;
    countP++;
}
```

```
int Point::countP=0;     //definition declaration of static data member
//initialization, use class name to restrict

int main()                    //main function
{
    void (*gc)()=Point::GetC; //declare a pointer that points to a
                              //static member function of the class
    Point A(4,5);               //declare object A
    cout<<"Point A,"<<A.GetX()<<","<<A.GetY();
    gc(); //output object number, access static function member by
          //pointer directly
    Point B(A);                 //declare object B
    cout<<"Point B,"<<B.GetX()<<","<<B.GetY();
    gc(); //output object number, access static function member by
          //pointer directly
}
```

6.3 Dynamic Memory Allocation

Although large amounts of data and objects can be managed effectively by arrays, in many cases we cannot know the exact number of elements in an array before the program runs. Take linear regression as an example: if the number of data pairs obtained by each experiment varies a lot, it would be a headache problem to determine the size of the object array of the *Point* class. If we declare the array too large, for example, declaring it with 200 elements while we only process 10 points, it would be very wasteful. If the array were declared too small, it would affect processing large amounts of data. In C++, the technique of dynamic memory allocation can ensure that the program applies for moderate memory according to actual needs during the execution, and the memory can be released after the use. This kind of storage locations applied for and released during runtime is called a heap object. The processes of applying for memory and releasing memory are called creating and deleting respectively.

6.3.1 *new* Operation and *delete* Operation

In C++, the program creates and deletes heap objects using two operators: *new* and *delete*.

The function of the *new* operator is to allocate dynamic memory, or to create heap objects dynamically. The grammar is

```
new type name T(initialization list);
```

This statement applies for memory space allocated to store *T*-type data, and uses values in the initialization list to initialize the data. If the application is successful, the *new* statement will return a *T*-type pointer to the starting address of the newly allocated memory space, and we can access the heap object using this pointer; if failed, the statement will return null pointer 0.

If the created heap object is a variable of a basic data type, the initialization of the variable is assigning values to the variable. For example,

```
int *point;
point = new int(2);
```

The second statement dynamically allocates the memory space used to store *int*-type data and stores the initial value 2 into this space, and then it assigns the starting address to the pointer *point* declared in the first statement.

If the created heap object is an object of a class, we need to call the constructor of the class according to the actual situations.

The *delete* operator is used to delete the heap object created by *new*, and release the memory space that the pointer points to. The format is

delete pointer name;

If the deleted heap object is an object of a class, the destructor of the class will be called. To an object created by *new*, we can only do the delete operation once using *delete*. Using *delete* to release the same memory space repeatedly will lead to runtime errors.

Example 6.16: Create objects dynamically.

```
//6_16.cpp
#include<iostream>
using namespace std;
class Point
{ public:
      Point()
      { X=Y=0; cout<<"Default Constructor called."<<endl; }
      Point(int xx,int yy)
      { X=xx; Y=yy; cout<< "Constructor called."<<endl; }
      ~Point()
      { cout<<"Destructor called."<<endl; }
      int GetX() {return X;}
      int GetY() {return Y;}
    void Move(int x,int y)
        { X=x; Y=y; }
  private:
      int X,Y;
};
```

```
int main()
{
    cout<<"Step One:"<<endl;
    Point *Ptr1=new Point;
        //create object dynamically and initial value is not given,
        //so default constructor is called.
    delete Ptr1; //delete object, call destructor automatically
    cout<<"Step Two:"<<endl;
    Ptr1=new Point(1,2);
        //create object dynamically and initial value is given, so
        //constructor with formal parameters is called
    delete Ptr1; //delete object, call destructor automatically
}
```

The running result of the program is as follows.

```
Step One:
Default Constructor called.
Destructor called.
Step Two:
Constructor called.
Destructor called.
```

Using the *new* operator can also create heap objects of the array type. In this case, we need to specify the array's structure. The syntax form of using the *new* operator to create a one-dimensional array is:

```
new type name T[Subscript expression];
```

The subscript expression denotes the number of array elements. Initial values of array elements cannot be assigned during the dynamic memory allocation of an array. Note that if the array is created by *new*, when it is deleted by *delete*, we should add "[]" before the pointer name.

Example 6.17: Create an object array dynamically.

```
//6_17.cpp
#include<iostream>
using namespace std;
class Point
{ //definition of the class is the same as in Example 6.16
    //......
};
```

```
int main()
{
    Point *Ptr=new Point[2];   //create object array
    Ptr[0].Move(5,10);         //access members of array elements by
                               //pointers
    Ptr[1].Move(15,20);        //access members of array elements by
                               //pointers
    cout<<"Deleting..."<<endl;
    delete[ ] Ptr;             //delete the whole object array
}
```

The result is as follows.

```
Default Constructor called.
Default Constructor called.
Deleting. . .
Destructor called.
Destructor called.
```

Here, we use dynamic memory allocation to realize dynamic creation of arrays. In this way the number of array elements can be determined according to the actual needs in runtime. But the processes of creating and deleting arrays are somewhat tedious. A better way is to encapsulate the creating and deleting processes to construct a dynamic array class. Example 6.18 is a simple demonstration of a dynamic array class. A more complete dynamic security array will be introduced in Chapter 9.

Example 6.18: A dynamic array class.
The dynamic array class *ArrayOfPoints* created in this example uses a relationship with the *Point* class. Its UML figure is as shown in Figure 6.9.

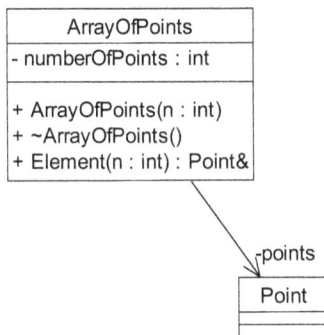

Fig. 6.9: Relationship between the *ArrayOfPoints* class and the *Point* class.

```
//6_18.cpp
#include<iostream>
using namespace std;
```

```
class Point
{ //definition of the class is the same as in Example 6.16
  //......
};

class ArrayOfPoints
{
   public:
     ArrayOfPoints(int n)
     { numberOfPoints=n; points=new Point[n]; }
     ~ArrayOfPoints()
     { cout<<"Deleting..."<<endl;
         numberOfPoints=0; delete[] points;
      }
     Point& Element(int n)
     { return points[n]; }
   private:
     Point *points;
     int numberOfPoints;
};

int main()
{
    int number;
    cout<<"Please enter the number of points:";
    cin>>number;
    ArrayOfPoints points(number);   //create object array
    points.Element(0).Move(5,10);   //access members of array elements
                                    //by pointers
    points.Element(1).Move(15,20);  //access members of array elements
                                    //by pointers
}
```

The result is as follows.

```
Please enter the number of points:2
Default Constructor called.
Default Constructor called.
Deleting. . .
Destructor called.
Destructor called.
```

In the *main()* function, we only create an object of the *ArrayOfPoints* class. The initialization parameter *number* of the object specifies the number of array elements. The processes of creating and deleting the object array are completed by the constructor and destructor of the *ArrayOfPoints* class respectively. Although through this way, we can make the *main()* function more compact, the access to array elements *("points.Element(0)")* seems verbose. If we want to access array elements using the subscript operator "[]" like in common arrays, we need to overload the subscript operator. This will be detailed in Chapter 9.

Using the *new* operator can also create multidimensional arrays, and the format is as follows.

```
new type name T[subscript expression 1][subscript expression 2]...;
```

"Subscript expression 1" can be any expression so long as its result is a positive integer, while other subscript expressions must be constant expressions whose results are positive integers. If the memory allocation is successful, the *new* operation will return a pointer that points to the starting address of the newly allocated memory space. Note that this pointer is not a *T*-type pointer, but rather a pointer to a *T*-type array. The number of array elements is the product of all subscript expressions besides the first subscript expression. For example,

```
float *fp;
fp = new float[10][25][10];
```

will result in an error. This is because that what the *new* operation generates is a pointer that points to a 25×10 two-dimensional array of float type, but *fp* is a pointer that points to a data variable of the *float* type. The correct form is

```
float (*cp)[25][10];
cp = new float[10][25][10];
```

The pointer *cp* can be used as a pointer or a three-dimensional array name. Please see the following program.

Example 6.19: Create a multidimensional array dynamically.

```
//6_19.cpp
#include<iostream>
using namespace std;
int main()
{
    float (*cp)[9][8];
    int i,j,k;
    cp = new float[8][9][8];
    for (i=0; i<8; i++)
        for (j=0; j<9; j++)
```

```
            for (k=0; k<8; k++)
                *(*(*(cp+i)+j)+k)=i*100+j*10+k; //Access array elements
                                                //by pointers
    for (i=0; i<8; i++)
    { for (j=0; j<9; j++)
        { for (k=0; k<8; k++)
            cout<<cp[i][j][k]<<" ";
            //Using pointer cp as array name, access array elements by
            //array name and subscripts
            cout<<endl;
        }
        cout<<endl;
    }
}
```

6.3.2 Dynamic Memory Allocation and Release Functions

Besides using *new* and *delete* operators to dynamically manage memory spaces, C++ also inherits the dynamic storage management functions from C. Here we make a simple introduction:

1. Dynamic memory allocation function
Prototype: void *malloc(size);
Parameter: *size* is the number of bytes to be allocated
Return value: return a pointer of *void* type if the allocation succeeds; otherwise return null pointer
Header files: <stdlib.h> and <malloc.h>

2. Dynamic memory release function
Prototype: void free(void *memblock);
Parameter: *memblock* is a pointer that points to the memory space to be deleted
Return value: none
Header files: <stdlib.h> and <malloc.h>

6.4 Deep Copy and Shallow Copy

Although we introduced copy constructors in Chapter 4, for most of the simple examples we have encountered before, there is no need to write copy constructors, because default copy constructors can realize the copy of data elements between objects. Therefore, readers may have questions on the necessity of writing copy constructors themselves. In fact, default copy constructors are not always appropriate, because they just realize shallow copy. The concept of shallow copy can be explained by the example below.

Example 6.20: Shallow copy of objects.
Here, we still use the *ArrayOfPoints* class to realize a dynamic array, and create two identical groups of points using the default copy constructor in the *main()* function to study the running result of the program.

```cpp
//6_20.cpp
#include<iostream>
using namespace std;
class Point
{ //definition of the class is the same as in Example 6.16
   //......
};

class ArrayOfPoints
{
   //definition of the class is the same as in Example 6.18
   //......
};

int main()
{
    int number;
    cout<<"Please enter the number of points:";
    cin>>number;
    ArrayOfPoints pointsArray1(number); //create object array
    pointsArray1.Element(0).Move(5,10);
                    //access members of array elements by pointers
    pointsArray1.Element(1).Move(15,20);
                    //access members of array elements by pointers
    ArrayOfPoints pointsArray2(pointsArray1);
                    //create an copy of the object array
    cout<<"Copy of pointsArray1:"<<endl;
    cout<<"Point_0 of array2: "
       <<pointsArray2.Element(0).GetX()
       <<", "<<pointsArray2.Element(0).GetY()<<endl;
    cout<<"Point_1 of array2: "
       <<pointsArray2.Element(1).GetX()
       <<", "<<pointsArray2.Element(1).GetY()<<endl;
```

```
        pointsArray1.Element(0).Move(25,30);
                    //access members of array elements by pointers
        pointsArray1.Element(1).Move(35,40);
                    //access members of array elements by pointers
        cout<<"After the moving of pointsArray1:"<<endl;
        cout<<"Point_0 of array2: "
            <<pointsArray2.Element(0).GetX()
            <<", "<<pointsArray2.Element(0).GetY()<<endl;
        cout<<"Point_1 of array2: "
            <<pointsArray2.Element(1).GetX()
            <<", "<<pointsArray2.Element(1).GetY()<<endl;
    }
```

The running result is as follows:

```
Please enter the number of points:2
Default Constructor called.
Default Constructor called.
Copy of pointsArray1:
Point_0 of array2: 5, 10
Point_1 of array2: 15, 20
After the moving of pointsArray1:
Point_0 of array2: 25, 30
Point_1 of array2: 35, 40
Deleting. . .
Destructor called.
Destructor called.
Deleting. . .
```

Then an exception occurs in the runtime, i.e., there is a running error. What is the reason? First, let us see the output above. In the program, *pointsArray2* is copied from *pointsArray1*, and their initial states are obviously the same. But when the first group of points in *pointsArray1* is moved by the *move* function, the second group of points in *pointsArray2* has the same movements. This means that there is some connection between the two groups of points, which is not expected. Maybe this is the root cause of errors in the program.

Here, we create the object *pointsArray2* by calling the default copy constructor to realize the direct copy of corresponding data items. This process is shown in Figure 6.10.

We can see from the figure that after the default copy constructor has simply copied the corresponding data items of the two objects, the member *points* of *pointArray1* and member *points* of *pointArray2* have the same value. That is, the two member pointers point to the same memory address. Although the copy has seemingly been com-

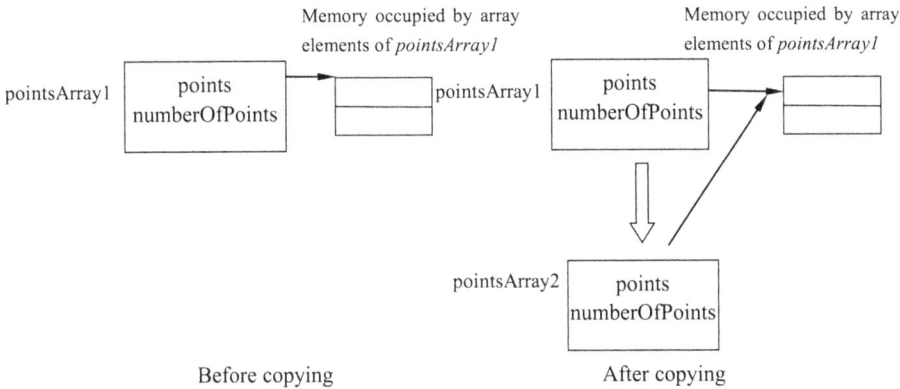

Fig. 6.10: Diagram of shallow copy.

pleted, it doesn't generate any real copy. Therefore, when the points in *pointsArray1* are moved, *pointsArray2* is also affected. This effect is "shallow copy".

There are greater drawbacks in shallow copy. Before the end of the program, destructors of *pointsArray1* and *pointsArray2* will be called automatically, and the memory space formerly allocated will be released. Since the two objects share the same memory space, the space will be released twice, which leads to running errors. The solution to this problem is writing copy constructors to realize "deep copy". Example 6.21 is a program to realize deep copy.

Example 6.21: Deep copy of objects.

```cpp
//6_21.cpp
#include<iostream>
using namespace std;
class Point
{ //definition of the class is the same as in Example 6.16
  //......
};
class ArrayOfPoints
{ public:
    ArrayOfPoints(ArrayOfPoints& pointsArray);
    //other members are the same as those of Example 6.18
};
ArrayOfPoints ::ArrayOfPoints(ArrayOfPoints& pointsArray)
{ numberOfPoints=pointsArray.numberOfPoints;
    points=new Point[numberOfPoints];
    for (int i=0; i<numberOfPoints; i++)
      points[i].Move(pointsArray.Element(i).GetX(),
          pointsArray.Element(i).GetY());
```

```
}
int main()
{
//The same as in Example 6.20
}
```

The result of the program is as follows.

```
Please enter the number of points:2
Default Constructor called.
Default Constructor called.
Default Constructor called.
Default Constructor called.
Copy of pointsArray1:
Point_0 of array2: 5, 10
Point_1 of array2: 15, 20
After the moving of pointsArray1:
Point_0 of array2: 5, 10
Point_1 of array2: 15, 20
Deleting. . .
Destructor called.
Destructor called.
Deleting. . .
Destructor called.
Destructor called.
```

We can see from the running result that deep copy is realized. Moving points in *pointsArray1* no longer affects points in *pointsArray2*, and releasing the memory space of *pointsArray1* and *pointsArray2* respectively will not result in errors. The process of deep copy is shown in Figure 6.11.

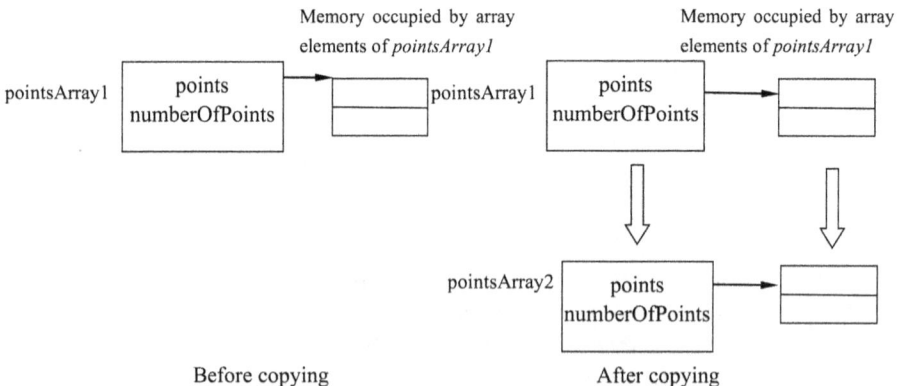

Fig. 6.11: Diagram of deep copy.

6.5 Strings

We introduced in Chapter 2 that a string constant is a character sequence enclosed in a pair of double quotes. For example, "abcd", "China", and "This is a string" are all string constants. In memory, string constants are stored according to the order of characters in the string, and each character occupies a byte; at the end '\0' is added as the ending tag.

However, like in C, a string variable is not a basic data type of C++. Then how does one store and process string variables? C uses character arrays to store strings, and C++ can still use this method. In addition, the standard C++ library predefines the string class. We will introduce these two methods in this section.

6.5.1 Using Character Arrays to Store and Process Strings

1. Declaration and Reference of Character Arrays

The method of declaring and referring character arrays is the same as for arrays of other types. We can explain this by the following example.

Example 6.22: Output a string.

```
//6_22.cpp
#include<iostream>
using namespace std;
int main()
{
    static char c[10]=
    {'I',' ','a','m',' ','a',' ','b','o','y'};
                        //declaration and initialization of one-
                        //dimensional character array
    int i;
    for(i=0;i<10;i++) //output elements in the character array one by
                        //one
        cout<<c[i];
    cout<<endl;
}
```

The result is:

```
I am a boy
```

Example 6.23: Output a diamond figure.

```
//6_23.cpp
#include<iostream>
```

```
using namespace std;
int main()
{
    /*declaration and initialization of a two-dimensional character
    array, elements that do not have initial values are all set to 0*/
    static char diamond[][5]={{' ',' ','*'},{' ',' ','*',' ',' ','*'},
        {'*',' ',' ',' ',' ','*'}, {' ',' ','*',' ',' ','*'}, {' ',' ',' ','*'}};
    int i,j;
    for (i=0;i<5;i++)
        //output elements of two-dimensional character array one by one
    {
        for(j=0;j<5 && diamond[i][j]!=0;j++)
            cout<<diamond[i][j];
        cout<<endl;
    }
}
```

The results are:

```
  *
 * *
*   *
 * *
  *
```

2. Using Character Arrays to Store Strings

In Example 6.22 and Example 6.23, we process array elements one by one, and characters in the array are independent. There is no '\0' at the end, so this doesn't comprise a C++ string. If we put '\0' at the end of a character array in its initialization, we will get a string of C++. Here we should note that the size of the array used to store a string must be no less than the length of the string (the number of characters) plus 1. When we initialize a character array, the form of initial values can be ASCII characters or character constants separated by commas, or a whole string constant ('\0' in the end is hidden). So the following statements are all correct:

```
static char str[8]={112,114,111,103,114,97,109,0};
static char str[8]={'p','r','o','g','r','a','m','\0'};
static char str[8]="program";
static char str[]="program";
```

If we use a character array to store a string, we can input and output characters one by one, or input and output the whole string at one time. For example:

```
char c[]="China";
cout<<c;
```

When inputting/outputting a whole string, we should note that:

1. Output characters don't contain '\0';
2. We use the character array name to specify the string to be output, and the outputting ends when meeting '\0';
3. When inputting multiple strings, we should separate them by spaces; when inputting a single string, there should not be spaces within it.

For example, there are statements in the program as follows:

```
static char str1[5],str2[5],str3[5];
cin>>str1>>str2>>str3;
```

If we input the following data in the runtime:

```
How are you?
```

The states of the variables in memory are as follows:

str1:	H	o	w	\0	
str2:	a	r	e	\0	
str3:	y	o	u	?	\0

If we modify the code to:

```
static char str[13];
cin>>str;
```

And input the following data in the runtime:

```
How are you?
```

The content of variable *str* in memory is:

str:	H	o	w	\0

Since the reading of inputs stops when meeting a space, we can only receive the first word.

We can use string-processing system functions to process strings, such as *strcat*(connect), *strcpy*(copy), *strcmp*(compare), *strlen*(get the length), *strlwr*(convert to lowercase), and *strupr*(covert to uppercase). We should include the header file *cstring* to the source program before using these functions. Readers can find instructions for these functions with the help of the compiling system.

6.5.2 The *string* Class

It is not convenient to use arrays to store strings and call system functions to process strings. Besides, the separation of data and functions processing the data doesn't conform to the requirements of object-oriented methods. Therefore, the C++ standard class library adds the concept of object-oriented string to C++, predefining the *string* class, which provides necessary operations to process strings. The header file *string* should be included when using the *string* class. The *string* class encapsulates attributes of strings and provides a series of functions to access these attributes. Data components of attributes or classes contain:
- Sequence of characters
- Size or length of the sequence of characters
- Types of characters
- Character traits
- Size of a character
- Allocator
- Iterators (we will introduce them in detail in Chapter 10)

The *string* class also has many functions related to string operations, including:
- Search
- Assign
- Concatenate
- Append

Here we introduce the constructors, and several common member functions and operations of the *string* class briefly. For simplicity, function prototypes are simplified and different from the forms in the header file. For more detailed information, reader can refer to the online help of the compiling system.

1. The Prototypes of the Constructors

```
string();        //default constructor, create a string of length 0
string(const string& rhs); //copy initialization constructor
string(const char *s);
    //use the string pointed by the pointer s to initialize the object
    //of the string class
string(const string& rhs, unsigned int pos, unsigned int n);
    //get n characters from the position pos in the string rhs to
    //initialize the object of the string class
    //Note: the position of first character in the string is 0
string(const char *s, unsigned int n);
```

```
//use the first n characters in the string pointed by the pointer s
//to initialize the object of the string class
string(unsigned int n, char c);
      //duplicate the character specified by the parameter c n times
      //to initialize the object of the string class
```

2. Brief Introduction of Common Member Functions

The *string* class has many member functions and each has multiple overloaded forms. Here we just list a small part of them. Readers can refer to online help for other functions and overloaded forms. In the following function explanations, we call the object that the member function belongs to, "this object", and the string in it, "this string".

```
string append (const char *s);
                    //add string s to the end of this string
string assign (const char *s);
                    //assign this object to the string pointed by s
int compare(const string& str) const;
/*compare this string and string str. When this string is smaller,
return a negative; when this string is greater, return a positive;
when the two strings equal, return 0.*/
```

Suppose we have two strings *s1* and *s2*; the rules of comparing them are as follows.
a) If the lengths of *s1* and *s2* are the same, and all characters in *s1* and *s2* are exactly the same, then *s1* equals to *s2*.
b) If the characters of *s1* and *s2* are not exactly the same, then compare the *ASCII* code of the first pair of characters that differ; the string with the smaller character is smaller.
c) If the length of *s1* (*n1*) is less than the length of *s2* (*n2*), and the first *n1* characters of the two strings are exactly the same, then *s1* is smaller than *s2*.

```
string& insert(unsigned int p0, const char *s);
//add the string pointed by s before the position p0 of this string
string substr(unsigned int pos, unsigned int n) const;
/*get a substr, get n characters from the position pos in this string
to construct a new object of the string class and return it*/
unsigned int find(const basic_string& str) const;
//find and return the position where str appears in this string for
//the first time
unsigned int length() const;
//return the length of the string (the number of characters)
void swap(string& str);
//swap this string with string str
```

Tab. 6.1: Operators of the *string* Class.

Operator	Example	Comments
+	s+t	Connect string *s* and *t* to construct a new string
=	s=t	Update *s* with *t*
+=	s+=t	Equals to *s* = *s* + *t*
==	s==t	Judge whether *s* is equal to *t*
!=	s!=t	Judge whether *s* is not equal to *t*
<	s<t	Judge whether *s* is less than *t*
<=	s<=t	Judge whether *s* is less than or equal to *t*
>	s>t	Judge whether *s* is greater than *t*
>=	s>=t	Judge whether *s* is greater than or equal to *t*
[]	s[i]	Access the character of subscript *i* in the string

3. Operators of the *string* class

Table 6.1 lists operators and their descriptions of the *string* class.

Let us see an example of the *string* class.

Example 6.24: An example of the *string* class.

```cpp
//6_24.cpp
#include <string>
#include <iostream>
using namespace std ;
void trueFalse(int x)
{
    cout << (x? "True": "False") << endl;
}
int main()
{
    string S1="DEF", S2="123";
    char CP1[]="ABC";
    char CP2[]="DEF";
    cout << "S1 is " << S1 << endl;
    cout << "S2 is " << S2 << endl;
    cout<<"length of S2:"<<S2.length()<<endl;
    cout << "CP1 is " << CP1 << endl;
    cout << "CP2 is " << CP2 << endl;
    cout << "S1<=CP1 returned ";
    trueFalse(S1<=CP1);
    cout << "CP2<=S1 returned ";
    trueFalse(CP2<=S1);
    S2+=S1;
    cout<<"S2=S2+S1:"<<S2<<endl;
```

```
        cout<<"length of S2:"<<S2.length()<<endl;
    }
```
The result is:
```
    S1 is DEF
    S2 is 123
    length of S2:3
    CP1 is ABC
    CP2 is DEF
    S1<=CP1 returned False
    CP2<=S1 returned True
    S2=S2+S1:123DEF
    length of S2:6
```
Please analyze the running result to understand the operations of strings.

6.6 Program Example – Personnel Information Management Program

In the previous two chapters, we take a personnel information management program for a small company as an example to explain the design and application of classes and member functions, the application of static data members, and the organization of program structure. In this section, we will further improve the personnel information management program on the basis of Example 5.11 in Chapter 5. In the previous two chapters, we turned aside the representation of names since we hadn't learned the concepts of arrays and strings. Now we can add a new data member in the *employee* class to denote the names of the staff, and complete the data members of the personnel information management program. Accordingly, we need to add member functions to operate this data member. We do not need to process the information of every person by duplicating statements in the main function. Instead, we can establish an information array for the staff, and do the same operation in a loop statement.

The design of the class in this example is to add a character array member *char name[20]* to store names of staffs in this company, and to add two member functions *SetName(char *)* and *char *GetName()* to set and get names. The UML class diagram is shown in Figure 6.12.

Example 6.25: Improvement of the personnel information management program. The whole program is divided into three files: *employee.h* is the header file of the class definition, *employee.cpp* is the file of class implementations, and *6_25.cpp* is the file of the main function. *6_25.cpp* and *employee.cpp* should be linked together after compiling. If we use the VC++ development environment, we should put *6_25.cpp* and *employee.cpp* in the same project.

employee
#name: char [20] #individualEmpNo: int #grade: int #eaccumPay: float
+ employee() + ~employee() + SetName(: char*) : void + promote(: int): void + SetaccumPay(pa : float): void + GetindividualEmpNo() : int

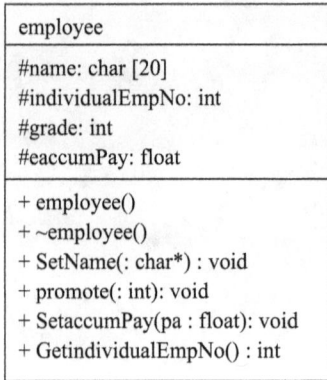

Fig. 6.12: UML diagram of personnel information management program in a small company.

```
//employee.h
class employee
{
protected:
    char name[20];              //Name
    int individualEmpNo;        //personnel number
    int grade;                  //grade
    float accumPay;             //monthly pay
    static int employeeNo;
                    //current maximum personnel number of this company
public:
    employee();                         //constructor
    ~employee();                        //destructor
    void SetName(char *);               //function for setting name
    char * GetName();                   //function for getting name
    void promote(int);                  //promotion function
    void SetaccumPay (float pa);        //function for setting monthly pay
    int GetindividualEmpNo();           //function for getting number
    int Getgrade();                     //function for getting grade
    float GetaccumPay();                //function for getting monthly pay
};
//employee.cpp
#include<iostream>
#include<cstring>                       //include the header file of string
                                        //operations
#include"employee.h"
using namespace std;
int employee::employeeNo=1000;  //the base of employee number is 1000
employee::employee()
```

```
{individualEmpNo=employeeNo++;
      //the number of newly input employee is the current maximum
      //number plus 1
   grade=1;                      //initial value of grade is 1
   accumPay=0.0; }               //initial value of monthly pay is 0

employee::~employee() {}

void employee::promote(int increment)
{ grade+=increment;}
            //promote, grades of promotion is specified by increment

void employee::SetName(char* names)
 strcpy(name,names);             //set name

char* employee::GetName()
 return name;                    //get employee name

void employee::SetaccumPay (float pa)
{ accumPay=pa;}                  //set monthly pay

int employee::GetindividualEmpNo()
{ return individualEmpNo;}       //get employee number

int employee::Getgrade()
{ return grade;}                 //get grade

float employee::GetaccumPay()
{ return accumPay;}              //get monthly pay

//6_25.cpp
#include<iostream>
#include"employee.h"
using namespace std;
int main()
{
    employee emp[4];
    char namestr[20];            //store the employee's name getting
                                 //from the input in namestr temporarily
    float pa;
    int grade, i;
    for (i=0; i<4; i++)
```

```
    {
        cout<<"Please input the name of next employee";
        cin>>namestr;
        emp[i].SetName(namestr);   //set name of employee emp[i]
        cout<<"Please input the monthly pay of the employee:";
        cin>> pa;
        emp[i]. SetaccumPay (pa); //set monthly pay of employee emp[i]
        cout<<"Please input promotion grades of the employee:";
        cin>>grade;
        emp[i].promote(grade);     //emp[i] promotes
    }

    //display information
    for (i=0; i<4; i++)
    {
        cout<< emp[i].GetName()<<"number"<< emp[i].GetindividualEmpNo()
        <<"grade is "<< emp[i].Getgrade()<<"grade, current month salary"
            << emp[i].GetaccumPay()<<endl;
    }
}
```

The result is:

```
Please input the name of next employee: Zhang
Please input the monthly pay of the employee: 8000
Please input promotion grades of the employee: 3
Please input the name of next employee: Wang
Please input the monthly pay of the employee: 4000
Please input promotion grades of the employee: 2
Please input the name of next employee: Li
Please input the monthly pay of the employee: 7000
Please input promotion grades of the employee: 2
Please input the name of next employee: Zhao
Please input the monthly pay of the employee: 1600
Please input promotion grades of the employee:0
Zhang number 1000 grade is 4 grade, current month salary 8000
Wang number 1001 grade is 3 grade, current month salary 4000
Li number 1002 grade is 3 grade, current month salary 7000
Zhao number 1003 grade is 1 grade, current month salary 1600
```

In the class *employee* of this example, we use the character array to store the "name" data member. In order to process the character array that stores the name, we use pointers to pass data. In the main function, we use a temporary array *namestr* to store the input name, and then pass the data to the corresponding objects using addresses. We get a name by returning the corresponding character pointer.

Similarly, we can process names using the standard *string* class introduced in Section 6.5. Please refer to the example above to design the program.

We can see from the running result of the program above that we need to input the monthly pay of each employee separately, and we cannot design specific algorithms to realize the monthly pay computation according to the actual situation of each employee. These functionalities will be realized through inheritance and the derivation of classes introduced in the next chapter.

6.7 Summary

This chapter introduces the method of organizing data by arrays and by pointers in C++. Arrays are the most common form of data organization. They are a set of several variables with certain ordinal relations. The variables that comprise the array are called array elements. All elements of the same array have the same data type. The data type here can be basic data types, or user-defined data types such as structure, class, and so on. If the data type of an array is a class, each element of the array is an object of this class, and we can call it an object array. The initialization of an object array is to call the constructor of the class repeatedly for every element. We can assign explicit initial values to array elements, where the system will call the corresponding constructors with formal parameters. If we don't assign initial values, the system will call default constructors in the initialization of the array. Similarly, when array elements need to be deleted, the system will call the destructor of the class.

A pointer is also a data type, and pointer-type variables are called pointer variables. Pointer variables are variables used to store addresses. Therefore, pointers provide a method of operating addresses directly.

Pointers can point to common variables, objects, and functions (including normal functions and member functions of objects). The process of using pointers consists of three steps – declaration, assignment, and reference. The initial value of the pointer is very important, so we must assign it and make it point to an existing data or function address before the pointer is used; otherwise, serious problems may occur in the runtime. The pointer is a difficult point in C++. We can organize and represent complex data structures flexibly and effectively by pointers.

This chapter also introduces dynamic memory allocation, which can manage memory dynamically.

Finally, using strings as examples, we explain the usage of a special kind of array – character array, and introduce some character processing functions and the *string* class provided by C++.

Exercises

6.1 How many elements does array *A[10][5][15]* have?

6.2 What are the first and last elements of array *A[20]*?

6.3 Use one statement to declare an array of the *int* type that has five elements, and initialize them with 1~5 one by one.

6.4 Suppose there is an array named *oneArray*; use one statement to calculate the number of its elements.

6.5 Declare a two-dimensional *int*-type array that has 5*3 elements using one statement, and initialize them with 1~15 one by one.

6.6 What are the uses of operators '*' and '&'?

6.7 What is a pointer? What is the difference between the address stored in the pointer and the content of this address?

6.8 Declare an *int*-type pointer, and allocate a memory space that contains 10 elements using the *new* statement.

6.9 What is the ending tag in string "Hello, world!"?

6.10 Declare an *int*-type array that has five elements, prompt the user to input the values of all the elements, and display them on the screen.

6.11 What is the difference between a reference and pointer? When can we use a pointer but cannot use a reference?

6.12 Declare the following pointers: pointer *pFloat* of the *float* type, pointer *pString* of the *char* type, and pointer *prec* of the *struct customer* type.

6.13 Given a pointer *fp* of the *float* type, write output statements to display the value of the variable pointed by *fp*.

6.14 Declare a pointer of the *double* type in the program, and display the number of bytes occupied by the pointer and the number of bytes occupied by the variable pointed by the pointer respectively.

6.15 What is the difference between *const int * p1* and *int * const p2*?

6.16 Declare a variable *a* of the *int* type, a pointer *p* of the *int* type, and a reference *r*. Change the value of *a* to 10 by *p*, and change the value of *a* to 5 by *r*.

6.17 What is the problem in the following program? Think about the problem that should be avoided when using pointers.

```
#include <iostream>
using namespace std;
int main()
{
    int *p;
    *pInt = 9;
    cout << "The value at p: " << *p;
}
```

6.18 What is the problem in the following program? Correct it and think about this problem that should be avoided when using pointers.

```
#include <iostream>
using namespace std;
int Fn1();
int main()
{
    int a = Fn1();
    cout << "the value of a is: " << a;
    return 0;
}

int Fn1()
{
    int * p = new int (5);
    return *p;
}
```

6.19 Declare a function pointer whose parameter is of the *int* type, and the return value is of the *long* type. Declare a member function pointer of class *A* whose parameter is of the *int* type, and the return value of the *long* type.

6.20 Realize a simple circle class named *SimpleCircle*. Its data member *int *itsRadius* is a pointer that points to the variable that stores its radius value. Design all operations on its data members, give the complete implementation of this class, and test it.

6.21 Write a function to count the number of characters in an English sentence and implement the input and output in the main function.

6.22 Write a function *int index(char *s, char *t)* to return the leftmost position where string *t* appears in string *s*. If there is no *t* matched in *s*, return −1.

6.23 Write a function *reverse(char *s)* to reverse the order of characters in string *s* using a recursive algorithm.

6.24 Suppose that the number of students is 8 (N = 8), prompt the user to input the examination scores of the N students, compute the average score, and display it.

6.25 Design a string class *MyString* which has a constructor, destructor, copy constructor, and overloaded operator +, =, += and []. Complete it to meet various needs. (Operator overloaded function is optional, and you can refer to Chapter 8.)

6.26 Write a function to transpose a 3×3 matrix, and input the data in the *main()* function.

6.27 Write a function to transpose a matrix. The number of rows and columns are input from the user in the program.

6.28 Define an *Employee* class that contains attributes such as *name, street address, city*, and *post code*, and functions such as *change_name()* and *display()*. Function *display()* displays *name, street address, city*, and *post code* using the *cout* statement, and function *change_name()* changes the name of the object. Implement and test this class.

7 Inheritance and Derivation

Programming mainly aims at describing and solving problems in the real world. *Class* in C++ effectively adopts human thinking methods of abstraction and classification. The relationship between an object and a class appropriately reflects the relationship between an individual and a group that has common features. A closer observation of the real world reveals that different things are not independent from each other, but instead they have complicated relationships. Inheritance is one such relationship. For example, children often resemble their parents, while clear distinctions exist between them. Both cars and bicycles belong to an abstract category: vehicles, but they differ from each other not only in appearance but also in performance.

Object-oriented programming provides the inheritance mechanism of class. It allows programmers to define more specific and detailed classes based on the characteristics of an existing class. We say that class *A* inherits from class *B* if *A* is a new class created on the basis of *B*. The advantages of inheritance are that codes can be reused and extended. The inheritance mechanism allows for the full utilization of existing researches and achievements. Also, after a software product has been developed, if new problems arise or we have better understandings of the original problem, the inheritance mechanism allows for efficient modifications or extensions of the existing software.

The process of deriving a new class from an existing class often includes three steps: accepting the existing class members, adjusting the existing class members, and adding new class members. This chapter is focused on this process of derivation. We will discuss the access controls of base class members, and the additions of constructor and destructor under different inheritance modes. We will then discuss the unique identification and visibility issues of class members under more complicated inheritances. In the last section of the chapter, two practical examples of inheritance will be given, respectively demonstrating how to solve a set of linear equations by the Gaussian pivoting elimination method and how to construct a personnel information management system for a small corporation.

7.1 Inheritance and Derivation of Class

7.1.1 Instances of Inheritance and Derivation

The inheritance and derivation hierarchy of classes is a reflection in program designs of the procedure that people use to classify, analyze, and understand problems. Things in the real world are mutually related and interacting. In the process of understanding problems, we classify them according to their common characteristics and differences for more efficient analysis and description. Figure 7.1 is an example of the classification of vehicles. The classification tree reflects the derivation relations of different vehicles.

https://doi.org/10.1515/9783110471977-007

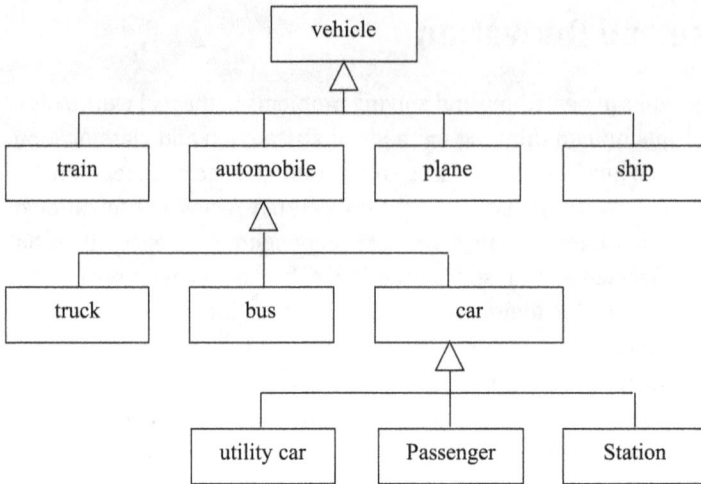

Fig. 7.1: UML hierarchy of vehicles.

The top layer of the tree has the highest degree of abstraction, representing the most universal and common concept. Each lower layer has all the features of its upper layer, while adding its own features. The lowest layer represents the most concrete concepts. In this hierarchy, from top to bottom it is a specification process, and from bottom to top it is a generalization process. The relationship between upper and lower layers can be seen as the relationship between base classes and derived classes.

Recall the examples of the personnel information management system in Chapters 4 to 6. The problem concerns a small corporation that has four groups of people: managers, part-time technicians, sales managers, and part-time salesmen. Our task is to store the name, ID number, rank, and the monthly salary of each staff, to calculate the total salary and to display all the information. Among these items, a staff ID should be generated at the time the staff information is created, which is the current maximum staff ID plus 1. The current maximum staff ID will be automatically increased by 1 each time we create a set of information for a staff member. These functionalities were realized in Chapter 6. In this chapter, we will implement specific promotion functions according to different groups of people. The calculation methods of the salaries are: a manager gets a fixed salary; a part-time technician gets a salary at an hourly rate; a part-time salesman gets a commission based on his sales; and a sales manager gets both a fixed salary and a commission.

We cannot describe the information of the four groups of people with one class since they have different processing methods (e.g., different ways of calculating their salaries). In this case, we can describe the four groups of people by four classes respectively. On the other hands, the four classes have many attributes in common, e.g., name, ID no., rank, and salary. There are also some member functions that each class has but are implemented in different ways, e.g., promotion function, salary calculating function, etc.

According to common sense, the simplest way to describe these four groups of people is to first describe the common characteristics of the entire staff, including the functions each staff member should have (e.g., calculating salary, although their calculating methods are different). When describing a specific group of the staff, we should firstly illustrate that they are staff members of this corporation, i.e., they share the common characteristics with all staff members; then we should describe the specific characteristics of this group (e.g., we should specify the commission rate for the salesmen and the hourly wage for part-time technicians), and provide the specific implementations in this group for functions of common uses (e.g., different methods for calculating salary for different people). Reflected in the object-oriented program design, this description method is the inheritance and derivation of classes. The uniform description of all the staff members forms a base class (or parent class), while the specific description of each group of people is implemented by a new class (called the child class) derived from the base class.

Inheritance preserves the attributes and behaviors of ancestors. The inheritance of a class means that the new class retains all the characteristics of the existing class. In other words, generating a new class from an existing class is the derivation of a class. The inheritance and derivation mechanism of classes enables programmers to make more specific modifications and extensions while keeping the characteristics of the original class. The new class includes the characteristics of the original class and its own new characteristics. The original class is called the **base class or parent class**. The newly generated class is called the **derived class or child class**. The derived class can also serve as a base class to generate new classes. This process forms a hierarchy of classes. The derivation of classes is a process of evolvement and development, i.e., to construct a new class from an existing class by extension, modification, and specialization. We can construct a family of objects that have common features through class derivation; hence the code can be reused. This inheritance and derivation mechanism greatly facilitates the development and modification of existing programs.

7.1.2 Definition of Derived Class

In C++, the syntax form of defining a derived class is

```
class Derived-Class Name: Inheritance Mode Base-Class Name 1,
    Inheritance Mode Base-Class Name 2, ...,
    Inheritance Mode Base-Class Name n
{
    Declaration of Derived Class Members,
};
```

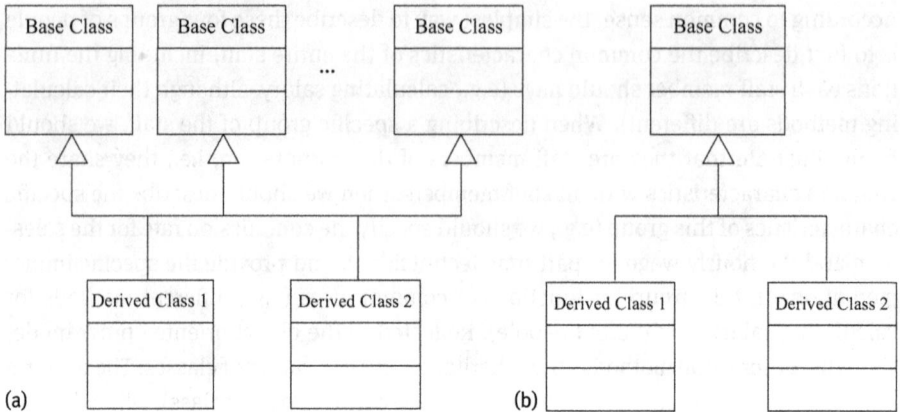

Fig. 7.2: UML of multiple inheritance and single inheritance. a: multiple inheritance, b: single inheritance.

For example, if base classes *Base 1* and *Base 2* have already been defined, the following statements define a derived class *Dr1*, which is derived from *Base 1* and *Base 2*.

```
class Dr1: public Base1, private Base2
{
public:
    Dr1();
    ~Dr1();
};
```

The base class names in the definition statement (e.g., *Base 1* and *Base 2*) are the names of existing classes, while the derived class name (e.g., *Dr1*) is the name of the newly generated class that inherits the characteristics of the existing classes. The case of a derived class having more than one base class is called multiple inheritance. In this case, the derived class has inherited characteristics from more than one existing class. The example illustrated above is an example of multiple inheritance. If a derived class has only one direct base class, then this case is called single inheritance. Single inheritance can be seen as the easiest case of multiple inheritance, and multiple inheritance can be seen as a combination of several cases of single inheritance. Multiple inheritance and single inheritance have many features in common. We will study the simpler single inheritance first.

In the process of derivation, the derived class can also serve as a base class to derive new classes; moreover, we can also derive many classes from one base class. That is to say, the characteristics of a derived class A, which is inherited from A's parent class, can in turn be inherited by a new class that is derived from class A; moreover, the characteristics of a parent class can be inherited by many child classes. In this way, a family of related classes is formed, which we sometimes call a 'class family.' In a class family, classes that derive a child class directly are named the **direct base classes** of the child class; the upper-layer base classes of the direct base class are named **the indirect base classes** of the derived class. For example, the class *Automobile* is derived from the class *Vehicle* and the class *Truck* is derived from the class *Automobile*, so the class *Automobile* is the direct base class of the class *Truck*, and the *Vehicle* class is the indirect base class of the *Truck* class.

In the definition of a derived class, besides specifying its base classes, the inheritance modes for each base class should also be specified. **Inheritance mode specifies how to access members inherited from a base class.** In the definition of a derived class, each inheritance mode only qualifies the base class that closely follows it. The key words of inheritance mode include: *public, protected,* and *private,* representing public inheritance, protected inheritance, and private inheritance respectively. If no inheritance mode is specified, the default mode is *private*. The inheritance mode indicates the access permissions of the members inherited from the base class through the members or objects of the derived class. We will discuss more details in the following section.

In the previous example, class *Base 1* is inherited publicly and class *Base 2* is inherited privately. Besides, the derived class declares its own constructor and destructor.

Derived class members refer to the newly added data and function members in the derived class that are not inherited from the base class. These new data and function members are the key elements by which the derived class differs from its base class, and they are the evidence of the development from the base class to the derived class. When we reuse and extend existing codes, we add new members in the derived class to gain new attributes and functions. This is the evolution and development of classes based on inheritance.

7.1.3 The Generation Process of Derived Classes

In C++ programming, a derived class is generated after the class has been declared and the member functions have been implemented. Once we have created the objects of a derived class, we can then use them to deal with actual problems. The process of generating a new derived class involves three steps: accepting base class members, modifying base class members, and adding new members. The main purpose of the inheritance and derivation mechanism is to reuse and extend code. Here, accepting base class members is code reusing, while modifying base class members and adding new members are code extending, which supplement each other. We will use the personnel information management system introduced in Section 7.1.1 as an example to illustrate these steps. The base class *employee* and the derived class *technician* are defined below. The function implementations of the classes are omitted temporarily, and the complete program of this example will be presented later in Section 7.7.

```
class employee
{
protected:
    char name[20];                //name
    int individualEmpNo;          //individual employee No.
    int grade;                    //grade
    float accumPay;               //monthly page
    static int employeeNo;        //the maximum employee number in the
                                  //company
public:
    employee();                   //constructor
    ~employee();                  //destructor
    void pay();                   //function to calculate monthly wage
    void promote(int);            //function to promote the grade
    void SetName(char *);         //function to set the name
    char * GetName();             //function to get the name
    int GetindividualEmpNo();     //function to get the employee number
    int Getgrade();               //function to get the grade
    float GetaccumPay();          //function to get the monthly wage
};

class technician:public employee //part-time technician
{
private:
    float hourlyRate;             //pay per hour
    int workHours;                //work hours in a month
public:
    technician();                 //constructor
    void SetworkHours(int wh);    //function to set the number of work
                                  //hours
    void pay();                   //function to calculate the pay
};
```

1. Accepting Base Class Members

The first step of class inheritance in C++ is to completely accept base class members. The derived class includes all the base class members except for the constructor and the destructor. The constructor and the destructor are not inherited in the process of derivation, which will be discussed in Section 7.3. Thus, the derived class *technician* inherits all the members from the base class *employee* except for the constructor and the destructor, including: *name, individualEmpNo, grade, accumPay, employeeNo, pay()*, *promote(int)*, *SetName(char *)*, *GetName()*, *GetindividualEmpNo()*, *Getgrade()*, and *GetaccumPay()*. These members will be reserved in the derived class after the inheritance.

2. Modifying Base Class Members

There are two aspects to modifying base class members: one is the change of access attributes of base class members, which mainly depends on the inheritance mode specified in the definition of the derived class, which will be discussed in Section 7.2; the other is the overriding of data or function members inherited from the base class. That is, declaring a data or function member in the derived class with the same name as a member inherited from the base class. If the derived class declares a new member *A with the same name as another member B inherited from its base class (if A and B are functions, then their argument lists should be the same; otherwise they should form a function overloading instead of the overriding here), then the new member A will cover the member B*, and we can access only *A* instead of *B* using the members or objects of the derived class. This case is called **homonymy cover.** Take the function *pay()* for example. The function *pay()* in the derived class *technician* covers the homonymous function inherited from the base class *employee.*

3. Adding New Members

The core of the inheritance and derivation mechanism is adding new members in the derived class, which ensures the development of the derived class. We can add appropriate data and function members in the derived class based on actual needs. In the previous example, new data members *hourlyRate* and *workHours* are added to the derived class *technician.*

Because constructors and destructors cannot be inherited from the base class in the class inheritance, to realize some special initialization and cleaning up work, new constructors and destructors should be added in the derived class. For example, we design the constructor *technician()* in the derived class *technician.*

This chapter is organized according to the three steps of derivation procedure described above. The first step in fact is finished once a derived class is defined and needs no intervention of programmers, hence we will not further discuss it. As for the second step, we mainly study the issues of access controls of the base class members under different inheritance modes. For the third step we focus on the addition of the constructor and destructor, because the methods and rules of adding other ordinary members in a derived class are the same as those when defining an ordinary class, to which readers can refer in Chapter 4. We will then discuss the issues of unique identification and access of class members under more complicated inheritance relationships. Finally, we will give instances of class inheritance as the review and summary of this chapter.

7.2 Access Control

The derived class inherits all the data members and function members from the base class except for the constructor and the destructor. However, the access attributes of these inherited members can be changed in the process of inheritance. The access attributes of inherited members are indicated by the inheritance mode specified in the definition of the derived class.

Base class members have three kinds of access attributes: public, protected, and private. Members of a base class can access any other members of the same class, while through objects of a base class we can only access the public members of that class.

There are three inheritance modes: public inheritance, protected inheritance, and private inheritance. Different inheritance modes result in different access attributes of the base class members in the derived class. There are two kinds of access situations: the first is new members in the derived class accessing members inherited from the base class; the second is accessing members inherited from the base class through objects of the derived class outside the derived class. We will discuss these different cases respectively.

7.2.1 Public Inheritance

If the inheritance mode is public, then in the derived class, the access attributes of the public and protected members inherited from the base class will not change, but the private members inherited from the base class cannot be directly accessed. That is to say, in public inheritance, the access attributes of public and protected members inherited from the base class will not change– they will remain public and protected members in the derived class and other members in the derived class can access them directly. Outside the class family, we can access public members inherited from the base class only through objects of the derived class. Neither the derived class members nor objects of the derived class can access private members of the base class **directly**.

Example 7.1: Public inheritance of the class *Point*.
The class *Point* has been mentioned many times in previous chapters. In this example, we will derive a new class *Rectangle* from the class *Point*. A rectangle is specified by a point, a width, and a length. The point of a rectangle has all the characteristics of the class *Point*, but a rectangle has its own features. This means that we should add new members while inheriting the class *Point*. The inheritance relations can be described in UML, as shown in Figure 7.3.

Let us start with the header file.

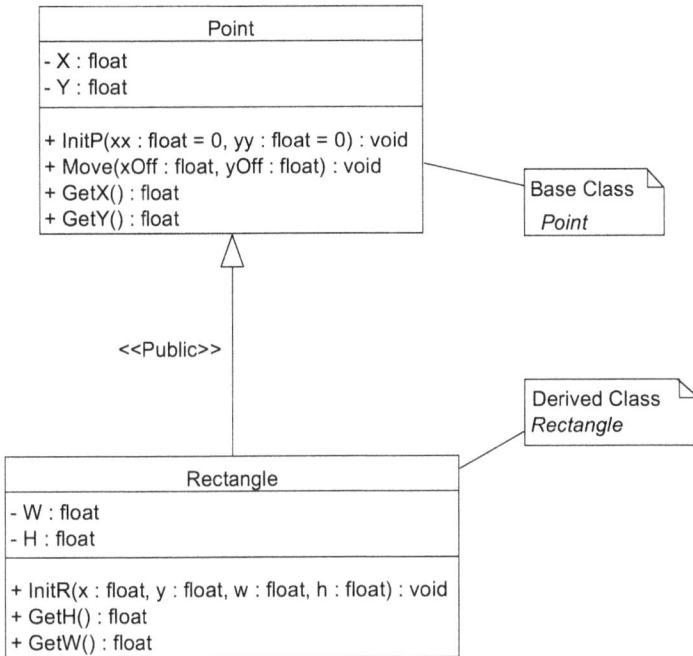

Fig. 7.3: UML of the inheritance relations between class *Point* and class *Rectangle*.

```
//Rectangle.h
class Point              //definition of the base class Point
{
public:                  //public member functions
    void InitP(float xx=0, float yy=0) {X=xx;Y=yy;}
    void Move(float xOff, float yOff) {X+=xOff;Y+=yOff;}
    float GetX() {return X;}
    float GetY() {return Y;}
private:                 //private member functions
    float X,Y;
};
class Rectangle: public Point
                         //definition of the derived class Rectangle
{
public:                  //new public member functions
    void InitR(float x, float y, float w, float h)
    {InitP(x,y);W=w;H=h;}
                         //call public member functions of the base class
    float GetH() {return H;}
    float GetW() {return W;}
```

```
private:                //new private data
    float W,H;
};
//End of Rectangle.h
```

Here, the base class *Point* is declared first. The derived class *Rectangle* inherits all the members that class *Point* has except the constructor and the destructor. So the members that the derived class has are the sum of the members inherited from the base class and the new members. The inheritance mode is public, thus public members inherited from the base class retain their access attributes in the derived class and are accessible by the member functions and objects of the derived class (e.g., the member function *InitR* in the derived class can call the member function *InitP* inherited from the base class directly). Private members of the base class (e.g., *X* and *Y* in the base class), on the other hand, are not accessible by the member functions and objects of the derived class. The original external interfaces of the base class (e.g., function *GetX()* and *GetY()* in the base class) now become a part of the external interfaces of the derived class. Obviously, the new members of the derived class can access each other.

The class *Rectangle* inherits all the members of class *Point*, thus realizing the reuse of code. Besides, by adding new members, the class *Rectangle* owns its new characteristics, and thus the code is extended.

The *main()* of the program is as follows:

```
//7_1.cpp
#include<iostream>
#include<cmath>
#include "rectangle.h"
using namespace std;
int main()
{
    Rectangle rect;              //declare an object of class Rectangle
    rect.InitR(2,3,20,10);       //set the arguments of the rectangle
    rect.Move(3,2);              //move the rectangle's position
    cout<<"The data of rect(X,Y,W,H):"<<endl;
    cout<<rect.GetX()<<","        //output the rectangle's arguments
        <<rect.GetY()<<","
        <<rect.GetW()<<","
        <<rect.GetH()<<endl;
}
//End of 7_1.cpp
```

An object *rect* of the derived class is created first in *main()*. The default constructor, which does nothing, is generated automatically by the system when the object is created. Then we call the public functions *InitR* and *Move* of the derived class and the public functions *GetX()* and *GetY()* inherited from the base class through the object of the derived class. In this example, we see under public inheritance, how to access public members inherited from the base class through member functions and objects of the derived class.

The running result of the program is:

```
The data of rect(X,Y,W,H):
5,5,20,10
```

7.2.2 Private Inheritance

If the inheritance mode is private, then after the inheritance, the public and protected members inherited from the base class will become private members of the derived class, and the private members inherited from the base class cannot be accessed directly in the derived class. That is to say, all the public and protected members of the base class will become private members after inheritance– they can be accessed directly by other derived class members, but cannot be accessed directly by objects of the derived class outside the class family. Neither derived class members nor objects of the derived class can access private members inherited from the base class.

Since after private inheritance, all the base class members become private or inaccessible members of the derived class, further derivations will result such that no member of the original base class will be accessible directly in newly derived classes. Therefore, after private inheritance, base class members will no longer play a role directly in further derived classes. In fact, private inheritance terminates further derivations of the original base class. Thus, private inheritance is less often used.

Example 7.2: Private inheritance of class *Point*.
The problem this example handles is the same as the one in Example 7.1, but this time we use a different inheritance mode during the inheritance. The following is the class definition in the program:

```
//rectangle.h
class Point                        //definition of the base class
{
public:
    void InitP(float xx=0, float yy=0) {X=xx;Y=yy;}
    void Move(float xOff, float yOff) {X+=xOff;Y+=yOff;}
    float GetX() {return X;}
    float GetY() {return Y;}
private:
    float X,Y;
};
```

```
    class Rectangle: private Point          //definition of the derived class
    {
    public:                                 //new external interfaces
        void InitR(float x, float y, float w, float h)
        {InitP(x,y);W=w;H=h;}
            //accessing public members inherited from the base class in the
            //function member of the derived class
        void Move(float xOff, float yOff) {Point::Move(xOff,yOff);}
        float GetX() {return Point::GetX();}
        float GetY() {return Point::GetY();}
        float GetH() {return H;}
        float GetW() {return W;}
    private:                                //new private data
        float W,H;
    };
    //End of rectangle.h
```

Similarly, the derived class *Rectangle* inherits the members of class *Point*. Therefore, the members of the derived class consist of the members inherited from the base class and the newly generated members in the derived class. The inheritance mode is private, which means that all the public and protected members in the base class become private members in the derived class and that private members of the base class (e.g., *X* and *Y* in the base class) cannot be accessed by the member functions and objects of the derived class. Members of the derived class can still access public and protected members inherited from the base class (for instance, we can call function *InitP* inherited from the base class in the member function *InitR* of the derived class), but members inherited from the base class cannot be accessed through objects of the derived class outside the derived class. The original external interfaces of the base class (for example, *GetX()* and *GetY()* in the base class) are encapsulated and hidden by the derived class. Of course, new members of the derived class can access each other freely.

Under private inheritance, in order to ensure that some external interfaces of the base class remain public in the derived class, we should declare members with the same name of the original external interfaces in the derived class. In the derived class *Rectangle*, we declare functions *Move*, *GetX*, and *GetY* again, using the access ability of the derived class to the members of the base class to copy their functionality into the derived class. The scope of the member functions redeclared in the derived class is smaller than that of the functions with the same name declared in the base class. So the function declared in the derived class will be called automatically when a function call with that name is made, according to the overlapping rule for functions with the same name. In program designs, this overlapping rule is a key method and is often used to modify original functions.

The *main()* in the following is identical to that in Example 7.1, but their executions are different.

```
//7_2.cpp
#include<iostream>
#include<cmath>
#include "rectangle.h"
using namespace std;
int main()
{
        Rectangle rect;        //declare an object of Rectangle
     rect.InitR(2,3,20,10);    //set the parameters of the rectangle
     rect.Move(3,2);           //move the rectangle
     cout<<"The data of rect(X,Y,W,H):"<<endl;
     cout<<rect.GetX()<<","     //output the parameters of the rectangle
            <<rect.GetY()<<","
            <<rect.GetW()<<","
            <<rect.GetH()<<endl;
}
//End of 7_2.cpp
```

The main difference between this *main()* function and that in Example 7.1 is that here all the functions that the object *rect* of the class *Rectangle* calls are public members declared by the derived class itself. Because this is a private inheritance, we cannot access any member inherited from the base class through the object *rect*. Compared with the public inheritance in Example 7.1, here we only modify the definition of the derived class, and the base class and the *main()* remain without change. Readers can see the advantage of encapsulation in object-oriented programming: while the external interfaces of the class *Rectangle* remain the same, modifications of the implementation of internal members will not influence other parts of the program. This is an example of code reusability and extendibility in object-oriented programming. The running result of this program is the same as that in the previous example.

7.2.3 Protected Inheritance

Under protected inheritance, public and protected members inherited from the base class will become protected members in the derived class, and the private members inherited from the base class are not accessible directly in the derived class. In this way, members in the derived class can access the public and protected members inherited from the base class directly, while they cannot be accessed through objects of the derived class outside the class family, as shown in Figure 7.4. Neither members nor

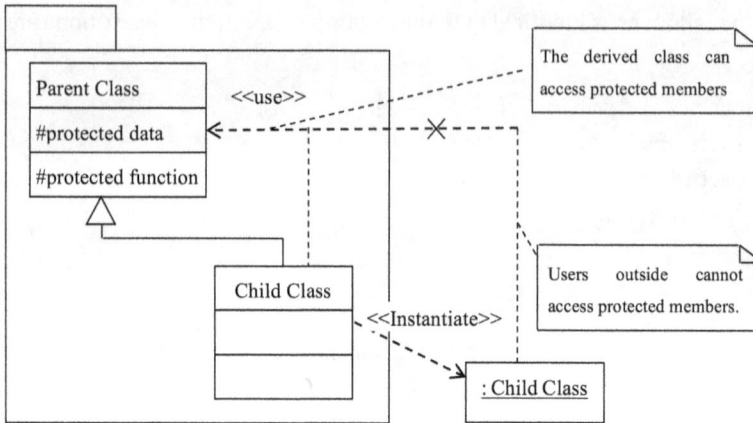

Fig. 7.4: UML of the access rules for protected class members.

objects of the derived class can directly access the private members inherited from the base class.

Comparing private inheritance with protected inheritance, we can see that all the access attributes of members in the directly derived class after inheritance are the same in the two cases. However, the difference appears when we use the derived class as a new base class to further derive classes. Suppose class *Rectangle* inherits class *Point* privately and class *Square* in turn inherits class *Rectangle*: then neither the members nor the objects of class *Square* can access members inherited indirectly from class *Point*. If class *Rectangle* inherits class *Point* in a protected way, then all the public and protected members in class *Point* will become protected members in class *Rectangle*. Public and protected members in class *Point* will become protected or private (depending on the inheritance mode between class *Rectangle* and class *Square*) in class *Square*. Therefore, members of class *Square* may access the members indirectly inherited from class *Point*.

From the access rules of inheritance, we can see the characteristics of protected members in a class. If class *Point* has protected members, then like private members, these protected members are not accessible through objects of class *Point*. If we derive a child class *Rectangle* from class *Point*, then for class *Rectangle*, protected members and public members have the same access attributes. In other words, protected members inherited from class *Point* can be accessed directly by the members of the derived class *Rectangle*, but can never be accessed by other external users (e.g., common functions in the program or other classes parallel to class *Point*). By using protected members properly, we can find a balance between data sharing and data hiding in complex layer relationships among classes, thus realizing the efficient reuse and extension of codes.

Example 7.3: Access protected members.
We will detail the above discussions through two simple examples. Suppose an arbitrary class *A* has a protected data member *x*; we will discuss the access attribute of *x*.
The definition of class *A* is:

```
class A
{
protected:              //protected data member
int x;
};
```

If *main()* is:

```
int main()
{
A a;
a.x=5;                  //Error!
}
```

An error will be detected in the compile time. The error is that the module establishing the object of class *A*, i.e., *main()*, tries to access the protected member of class *A*, which is not allowed because the access attribute of the protected member of class *A* is the same as that of the private members of class *A*. This illustrates that the protected members of class *A* are not accessible in the module establishing object *a* of class *A*. In this case, protected and private members are well hidden.

If we derive class *B* from class *A* publicly, then the protected and public members inherited from class *A* are accessible in class *B*. For example:

```
class A
{
protected:
    int x;
};
class B:public A    //public derivation
{
public:
    void function();
};
void B::function();
{
    x=5;
}
```

Protected members inherited from the base class are accessible using the member function *function* of the derived class B.

7.3 Type Compatible Rule

The type compatible rule refers to how an object of a publicly derived class can substitute an object of the base class wherever the latter one is needed. The derived class obtains all the members inherited from the base class except the constructor and the destructor through public inheritance. So, the publicly derived class can do whatever the base class can. The substitution referred in the **type compatible** rule includes the following situations:

- An object of a derived class can be assigned to an object of the base class.
- An object of a derived class can be used to initialize a reference of the base class.
- The address of an object of a derived class can be used to assign to a pointer of the base class.

After substitution, the object of the derived class can be used as an object of the base class. However, here only the members inherited from the base class can be used.

If class B is a base class and class D is a publicly derived class from class B, then class D owns all the members of class B except the constructor and the destructor. According to the type compatible rule, an object of the derived class D can substitute an object of the base class B wherever the latter one appears in the program. In the following program, $b1$ is an object of class B and $d1$ is an object of class D.

```
class B
{...}
class D:public B
{...}
B b1,*pb1;
D d1;
```

Here:

1. An object of the derived class can be assigned to an object of the base class, i.e., to assign the value of each member in the object of the derived class, which is inherited from the base class, to the corresponding member of an object of the base class:

   ```
   b1=d1;
   ```

2. An object of the derived class can also be used to initialize the reference of a base class object.

   ```
   B &bb=d1;
   ```

3. The address of an object of the derived class can be assigned to a pointer of the base class.

   ```
   pb1=&d1
   ```

Thanks to the type compatible rule, we can use the same functions to process objects of the base class and objects of the publicly derived class (because when a formal argument of a function is an object of the base class, the actual argument can be an object of the derived class). Since there is no need to design specific modules for every class, the program efficiency is greatly improved. This is another important feature of C++, i.e., polymorphism, which will be discussed in the next chapter. We can say that the type compatible rule is one of the important foundations of the polymorphism. In the following example, we use the same function to deal with objects in the same class family.

Example 7.4: Example of type compatible rule.
Class *B1* is publicly derived from the base class *B0*, and class *D1* is in turn publicly derived from class *B1*. The member function *display()* in base class *B0* is overridden in the derived classes. The derivation relations among these classes are as shown in Figure 7.5.

The program is:

```
//7_4.cpp
#include <iostream>
using namespace std;
class B0                       //define base class B0
{
public:
    void display(){cout<<"B0::display()"<<endl;}
                               //public member function
};
class B1: public B0       //define publicly derived class B1
{
public:
    void display(){cout<<"B1::display()"<<endl;}
                               //public member function
```

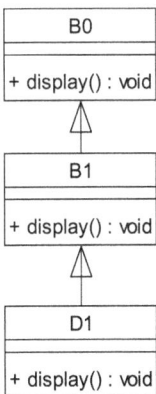

Fig. 7.5: UML of the derivation relations among the classes.

```
};
class D1: public B1        //define publicly derived class D1
{
public:
    void display(){cout<<"D1::display()"<<endl;}
                           //public member function
};
void fun(B0 *ptr)          //ordinary function
{                          //the argument is a pointer of the base class
    ptr->display();        //"object pointer -> member"
}

int main()                 //main()
{
    B0 b0;                 //declare an object of class B0
    B1 b1;                 //declare an object of class B1
    D1 d1;                 //declare an object of class D0
    B0 *p;                 //declare an pointer of class B0
    p=&b0;                 //pointer of B0 points to B0 object
    fun(p);
    p=&b1;                 //pointer of B0 points to B1 object
    fun(p);
    p=&d1;                 //pointer of B0 points to D1 object
    fun(p);
}
```

In the above example, by using the terms "object name. member name" or "object pointer->member name", we can access newly added homonymic members in the derived classes. According to the type compatible rule, we can assign the address of an object of the derived class to a pointer of base class *B0*, while only the members inherited from the base class can be accessed through this pointer.

In the program, we declare an ordinary function *fun* with a pointer of base class *B0* as its formal argument. Based on the type compatible rule that the address of an object of the publicly derived class can be assigned to a pointer of the base class, function *fun* can operate uniformly on the objects of this class family. In the execution of the program, the addresses of an object of the base class, an object of the derived class *B1*, and an object of the derived class *D1*, are respectively assigned to the base class pointer *p*. However, through pointer *p* we can only access members inherited from the base class. That is to say, although the pointer points to an object of the derived class *D1*, during the execution of the function *fun* we can only access the member function *display* inherited from the base class *B0* instead of the homonymic function declared in class *D1* through the pointer *p*. Thus, the three calls of function *fun* in *main()* have the same results: they all access the public member function declared in the base class. The execution results are as follows.

```
B0::display()
B0::display()
B0::display()
```

From this example, we can see that an object of the derived class can substitute an object of the base class according to the type compatible rule, but the object of the derived class only plays the role of the base class after the substitution. In the next chapter, we will learn another key feature of object-oriented programming: polymorphism. Through polymorphism, the base class and the derived class can give different responses to the same message, on the premise of the type compatible rule.

7.4 Constructor and Destructor of Derived Class

The purpose of inheritance is to develop. The derived class inherits the members of the base class, realizing code reuse. But code expansion is more important. Only by adding new members and functionalities can we make the derivation meaningful. In previous examples, we have studied the addition of ordinary members in derived class. In this section, we will focus on the constructor and the destructor of derived class. Since the constructor and the destructor of the base class cannot be inherited in the derivation, if we want to initialize the newly added members in the derived class, we have to add new constructor in the derived class. However, the constructor of the derived class can only initiate members newly added in the derived class, while the members inherited from the base class will still be initiated by the constructor of the base class. New destructors should also be added to the derived class to do the cleanup work of objects in the derived class.

7.4.1 Constructor

After defining a derived class, we need to create an object in the derived class in order to use the derived class. Objects must be initialized before being used. The data members of the derived class consist of the data members inherited from the base class and newly added data members in the derived class. If the new data members of the derived class include inline objects of other classes, the data members of these object members are also indirectly included in the data members of the derived class. Therefore, **data members of the base class, new data members, and data members of object member should all be initialized when creating an object of the derived class.** Since the constructor of the base class is not inherited, in order to implement the initialization of objects of the derived class, we must add a new constructor to the derived class. The constructor of the derived class needs appropriate initial values as arguments. Some of the arguments are used to initialize the new members in the derived class, while others are used to pass on to the constructors of the base class and the inline object members so as to initialize the corresponding members. When creating an object of the derived class, the constructors of the base class and the inline object members are first called implicitly to initialize the corresponding data members; then the function body of the derived class constructor is executed.

The syntax form of the definition of a derived class constructor is as follows:

```
name of the derived class:: name of the derived class
        (argument list):name of base class 1(argument list 1), ...,
        name of base class n(argument list n),
    name of inline object 1(argument list of inline object 1), ...,
        name of inline object m(argument list of inline object m)
{

    statements to initialize new members of the derived class;

}
```

Here, the name of the constructor is the same as the name of the derived class. The argument list of the constructor should provide all the arguments needed to initialize the base class data, new inline object data, and newly-added member data. Following the argument list, the names of the base class and the inline members that need arguments for initializations, along with their associated argument lists, should be listed. Each item is separated by commas. The order of the names of base classes and of objects does not matter: they can appear in any order. When generating an object of the derived class, the system will first use the arguments listed here to call the constructors of the base classes and of the inline object members.

If a derived class has more than one base class, then for all the base classes and all the inline object members that need arguments for initializations, their names and argument lists should be given explicitly. For those base classes that use default constructors, their names and argument lists need not be given. As for single inheritance, we need to give the name and argument list of only one base class.

Now, let us discuss when we should declare the construction of the derived class. **If the base class declares a constructor with formal arguments, then the derived class should declare its constructor.** This provides a way to pass arguments to the constructor of the base class, ensuring that the base class can get necessary data during its initialization. If the base class does not declare a constructor, the derived class can choose not to declare its constructor. In such a case, the default constructor will be used and the task of initializing new members can be done by other public functions.

The common execution order of calling constructor of a derived class is as follows:
1. Call the constructors of the base classes. The calling order is the same as the order of these base classes appearing in the definition of the derived class (from left to right).

2. Call the constructors of the inline object members. The calling order is the same as the declaration order of these object members in the body of the derived class.
3. Execute the constructors of the derived class.

Only when the new members of the derived class contain inline objects will the second step be executed. Otherwise, the second step is skipped and the constructor of the derived class is executed immediately after the first step. The calling order of the constructors of the base classes is the order of these base classes appearing in the definition of the derived class, and the calling order of the constructors of inline object members is the declaration order of these object members in the body of the derived class. Note that the execution order of these constructors has nothing to do with the order listed in the constructor of the derived class.

Example 7.5: Example of constructor of derived class (multiple inheritance, has inline object members).
This is an example with general features. There are three base classes *B1*, *B2*, and *B3*. The only member of class *B3* is a default constructor. The only member of both class *B1* and class *B2* is a constructor with one argument. Class *C* is derived publicly from the three base classes. The derived class has three private object members, which are objects of class *B1*, *B2*, and *B3* respectively. The program is as follows:

```cpp
//7_5.cpp
#include <iostream>
using namespace std;
class B1      //Base class B1. Its constructor has arguments
{
public:
    B1(int i) {cout<<"constructing B1 "<<i<<endl;}
};
class B2      //Base class B2. Its constructor has arguments
{
public:
    B2(int j) {cout<<"constructing B2 "<<j<<endl;}
};
class B3      //Base class B3. Its constructor doesn't have arguments
{
public:
    B3(){cout<<"constructing B3 *"<<endl;}
};
class C: public B2, public B1, public B3 //Derived class C
//pay attention to the order of the appearances of the base classes
```

```
{
public:        //public members of the derived class
    C(int a, int b, int c, int d):B1(a),memberB2(d),memberB1(c),B2(b){}
    //pay attention to the number and the order of the base classes
    //pay attention to the number and the order of the object members
private:       //Private object members in the derived class
    B1 memberB1;
    B2 memberB2;
    B3 memberB3;
};
int main()
{
    C obj(1,2,3,4);
}
```

Let us analyze the characteristics of the constructor of the derived class. Because the base classes and the inline object members all have nondefault constructors, a nondefault constructor (i.e., a constructor with arguments) is required in the derived class. The main task of the constructor of the derived class is to initialize the base classes and the inline object members, by the rules we mentioned before. The definition of the constructor of the derived class constructor is:

```
C(int a, int b, int c, int d):B1(a),memberB2(d),memberB1(c),B2(b){}
```

The argument list of the constructor provides all the arguments needed for the initialization of the base classes and the inline object members. Following the colon are the names of the base classes and the inline objects together with their arguments lists. Here, we should notice two things. Firstly, we do not list all the base classes and the member objects. Because class *B3* has a default constructor and there is no need to pass arguments to it, we need not list class *B3* and the object *memberB3* here. Secondly, the order of the base classes and the object members in the argument list is arbitrary. The body of the constructor of this derived class constructor is empty, so it is only used to call the constructors of the base classes and the inline object members and pass on arguments to them.

The *main()* declares an object *c* of the derived class *C*. The constructor of the derived class is called when *c* is created. Let us consider the execution of the constructor of class *C*. Firstly the constructors of the base classes should be called; then the constructors of the inline object members should be called. The calling order of the constructors of the base classes is the order of these base classes appearing in the definition of the derived class, i.e., *B2*, *B1*, and then *B3*. The calling order of the constructors of the inline object members is the declaration order of these object members in the body of the derived class, i.e., *B1*, *B2*, and then *B3*. The execution result proves the above analysis, which is as below:

```
constructing B2 2
constructing B1 1
constructing B3 *
constructing B1 3
constructing B2 4
constructing B3 *
```

In the declaration of the constructor of the derived class, the names of class *B3* and the object *memberB3* of class *B3* are not listed explicitly, so the system will call the default constructor of class *B3* automatically. If a base class declares both the default constructor and constructor with arguments, then in the declaration of the constructor of the derived class, we can either list the name and corresponding arguments of the base class or not, depending on the actual needs.

7.4.2 Copy Constructor

How does write copy constructor when there is an inheritance? For any class, if the programmer does not write a copy constructor, then the compiler will generate a default copy constructor when necessary. If the default copy constructor is called when creating an object of a derived class, then the compiler will automatically call the copy constructor of the base class.

If we want to write a copy constructor for the derived class ourselves, we need to pass arguments to the copy constructor of the base class. For example, suppose class *C* is a derived class from class *B*. The copy constructor of class *C* is as follows:

```
C::C(C &c1):B(c1)
{...}
```

Readers might get confused by the fact that the argument type of class *B*'s copy constructor should be the reference of class *B*'s objects, but here the reference *c1* of class *C*'s objects is used as the argument of class *B*'s copy constructor. This is because of the type compatible rule: we can use the reference of the derived class to initialize the reference of the base class. So when the formal argument is a reference of the base class, the actual argument can be a reference of the derived class.

7.4.3 Destructor

The destructor of a derived class is used to do necessary cleanup work before an object of the derived class disappears. Destructor has neither type nor arguments. So it is simpler than the constructor.

The destructor of the base class cannot be inherited in the derivation. A new destructor should be declared in the derived class if needed. The method of declaring a destructor in the derived class is the same as that in an ordinary class without any inheritance relationships. The only responsibility of the destructor of a derived class is to clean up the new nonobject members of the derived class in its body. The system will call the destructors of the base classes and the object members automatically. The execution order of destructors is just the opposite of that of the constructors. Firstly the new ordinary members of the derived class should be cleaned up, and then the new object members, and finally the members inherited from the base class. This cleanup work is accomplished by executing the destructors of the derived class, the object members, and the base classes respectively.

In previous examples in this chapter, we have not declared destructors of any class explicitly. In such cases, the compiler will generate a default destructor for each class, which will be called at the end of the object's life period. Such a destructor does nothing but formally complete the destruction process.

Example 7.6: An example of destructor of derived class (multiple inheritances, has inline object members).

We modified Example 7.5 by adding destructors to all the base classes. The program is shown below:

```cpp
//7_6.cpp
#include <iostream>
using namespace std;
class B1                                    //define base class B1
{
public:
    B1(int i) {cout<<"constructing B1 "<<i<<endl;}
                                            //constructor of class B1
    ~B1() {cout<<"destructing B1 "<<endl;}  //destructor of class B1
};
class B2                                    //define base class B2
{
public:
    B2(int j) {cout<<"constructing B2 "<<j<<endl;}
                                            //constructor of class B2
    ~B2() {cout<<"destructing B2 "<<endl;}  //destructor of class B2
};
class B3                                    //define base class B3
{
public:
    B3(){cout<<"constructing B3 *"<<endl;}  //constructor of class B3
    ~B3() {cout<<"destructing B3 "<<endl;}  //destructor of class B3
};
```

```
class C: public B2, public B1, public B3    //define derived class C
{
public:
   C(int a, int b, int c, int d):B1(a),memberB2(d),memberB1(c),B2(b){}
                           //define constructor of the derived class
private:
      B1 memberB1;
      B2 memberB2;
      B3 memberB3;
};
int main()
{ C obj(1,2,3,4);
}
```

In this program, we add destructors to all the three base classes, but make no changes to the derived class. The derived class will still use the default destructor provided by the system. The *main()* also remains the same. During the execution, the constructor of the derived class will be executed first, then the destructor of the derived class. We discussed constructors in the previous section. The default destructor of the derived class in turn calls the destructors of the member objects and the base classes. The calling order is just the opposite of that of the constructors. The execution result is as follows:

```
constructing B2 2
constructing B1 1
constructing B3 *
constructing B1 3
constructing B2 4
constructing B3 *
destructing B3
destructing B2
destructing B1
destructing B3
destructing B1
destructing B2
```

The output proves our analysis. Here we only illustrate the syntax rules of constructors and destructors of derived class using a simple example. In latter examples we will continue to discuss them, combining their uses.

7.5 Identification and Access of Derived-Class Member

We have learned the syntax rules of class inheritance and derivation around three procedures: accepting base class members, modifying base class members, and adding new members. A class family is formed through class derivation. In this section, we will focus on some issues in the uses of derived classes, including the identification and access of the derived class and its object members (including members inherited from the base class and newly added members).

In the derived class, members can be classified into four groups according to their access attributes:

Inaccessible Members
These members are inherited from the private members of the base class. Neither the derived class nor the modules creating objects of the derived class can access them. If the derived class continues to derive new class, these members remain inaccessible.

Private Members
These members can be inherited from the base class or newly added members. They are accessible inside the derived class, but are inaccessible in the modules establishing objects of the derived class. Further derivation will make these private members become inaccessible members in newly derived classes.

Protected Members
These members can be inherited from the base class or newly added members. They are accessible inside the derived class, but are inaccessible in the modules establishing objects of the derived class. Further derivation will make these protected members become private or protected members in newly derived classes.

Public Members
These members can be accessed by the derived class or the modules establishing objects of the derived class. Further derivation will make these public members become private, protected, or public members in newly derived classes.

Two problems remain to be solved in accessing a derived class. The first one is about unique identifiers and the other is about the access attributes of class members, or more specifically, their visibility. We can only access visible members with their unique identifiers. If more than one member can be referred to by one expression, then this case is called ambiguity. The ambiguity problem is the unique identifier problem that will be discussed in this section.

7.5.1 Scope Resolution

The scope qualifier is represented by the symbol ":.". It is used to specify the class to which the member we want to access belongs. The general syntax form of its use is:

```
name of the base class::name of the member;        //data member
name of the base class::name of the member ( argument list);
                                                //function member
```

Next, we will see how the scope qualifier uniquely identifies members in the class family's hierarchy.

For identifiers declared in different scopes, the visibility rule is as follows: For two or more scopes that have inclusion relationships, if an identifier is declared in the outer layer and there is no homonymic identifier declared in the inner layer, then the outer layer's identifier is visible in the inner layer; if a homonymic identifier is declared in the inner layer, then the outer layer's identifier is invisible in the inner layer: at this time, the inner layer's variable **hides** the outer layer's homonymic variable, and this is called the **name hiding rule**.

In the hierarchy of class derivation, both the base class members and the new members in the derived class have class scopes, while the two scopes are different and have inclusion relationships. The derived class is in the inner scope. If the derived class declares a new member whose name is the same as a member in the base class, then the new member of the derived class will hide the homonymic member inherited from the base class. Using the name directly can only access the newly declared member of the derived class. If a new function, whose name is the same as a function in the base class, is declared in the derived class, even if it has a different argument list from those declared in the base class, all the overloading forms of the homonymic functions inherited from the base class will be hidden. To access the hidden members, we should use the scope qualifier to qualify the name of the homonymic function of the base class.

For multiple inheritance, let us first consider a simple case where there are no inheritance relationships among the base classes and there is no common base class. The most typical case is that no base class has a superior base class. Suppose two or more base classes of a derived class have members with the same name; if the derived class has a new homonymic member, then the derived class's member will hide all members with the same name in the base classes. The new member in the derived class can be uniquely identified and accessed through the form "object name. member name". The members in the base class can be accessed by the name of the base class and the scope qualifier; if there is no new member declared in the derived class that has the same name as the homonymic members of the based classes, then "object name. member name" cannot uniquely identify a member. At this time, all the members inherited from the different base classes have the same name and same scope, and thus the system cannot judge which class member should be called. This problem can also be solved by using the name of the base class together with the scope qualifier. See the following example.

Example 7.7: Example of name hiding in multiple inheritance.
In the following program, two base classes, *B1* and *B2*, are defined. A new class *D1* is

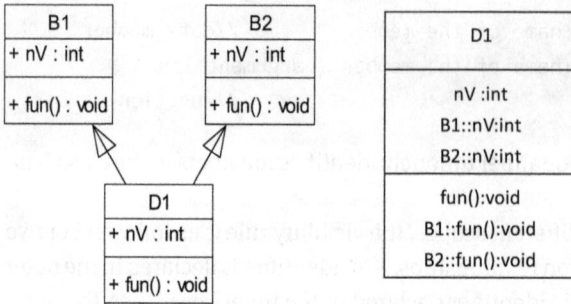

Fig. 7.6: The derivation relations of derived class *D1* in multiple inheritance and *D1*'s member structure.

derived publicly from base classes *B1* and *B2*. The two base classes both declare data member *nV* and function *fun*. Two new members are added to the derived class, one named *nV* and the other named *fun*. So class *D1* has six members, and each group of three has the same name. Figure 7.6 shows the derivation relationships among the classes and the structure of the derived class.

Now we will analyze the access issues of the derived class. The new members in the derived class have a smaller class scope, so in the derived class and the module creating the derived-class objects, the new members in the derived class hide the homonymic members derived from the base class. We can access new members of the derived class by using the term "object name . member name". The members derived from the base class can be accessed by using the name of the base class and the scope qualifier, telling the system which member of which class is to be called. The source program is as below:

```
//7_7.cpp
#include <iostream>
using namespace std;
class B1                          //define base class B1
{
public:                           //external interfaces
    int nV;
    void fun(){cout<<"Member of B1"<<endl;}
};
class B2                          //define base class B2
{
public:                           //external interfaces
    int nV;
    void fun(){cout<<"Member of B2"<<endl;}
};
class D1: public B1, public B2  //define derived class D1
{
```

```
public:
    int nV;                         //data member with the same name
    void fun(){cout<<"Member of D1"<<endl;}
                                    //function member with the same name
};
int main()
{
    D1 d1;
    d1.nV=1;                        //object name.member name
    d1.fun();                       //access the member in class D1

    d1.B1::nV=2;                    //scope qualifier
    d1.B1::fun();                   //access the member of base class B1

    d1.B2::nV=3;                    //scope qualifier
    d1.B2::fun();                   //access the member of base class B2
}
```

An object *d1* of the derived class *D1* is created in *main()*. According to the hiding rule, if we call a homonymic member in the derived class only through the member name, then only the new member declared in the derived class will be accessed, and the members inherited from the base classes will be hidden because they are in the outer layer. To access the homonymic member inherited from a base class, we must use the name of the base class and the scope qualifier. The statements at the end of the program aim at accessing the members inherited from base class *B1* and *B2* respectively. The result of execution is:

```
Member of D1
Member of B1
Member of B2
```

By using the scope qualifier, we can specify the base class from which the member in the derived class is inherited, and thus solve the problem of member hiding.

In this example, if the derived class does not declare a member with the same name as any member inherited from the base classes, then no member can be accessed by using the term "object name. member name". The homonymic members inherited from class *B1* and from *B2* have the same scope, so the system cannot identify uniquely which member is to be called. In such a case, it is necessary to use the scope qualifier.

If no new member is added to the derived class in the program of Figure 7.6, then the definition of the derived class is modified as follows.

```
class D1: public B1, public B2                    //define derived class D1
{
};
```

In this case, if the rest of the program remains unchanged, then using "object name . member name" to access class members in *main()* will result in errors.

```
int main()
{
    D1 d1;
    d1.nV=1;          //error, ambiguity of "object name . member name"
    d1.fun();         //error, ambiguity of "object name . member name"
    d1.B1::nV=2;      //scope qualifier
    d1.B1::fun();     //access a member of base class B1
    d1.B2::nV=3;      //scope qualifier
    d1.B2::fun();     //access a member of base class B2
}
```

We assume there is no inheritance relationship among the base classes in the above example. What if this assumption is not satisfied? If some or all of a derived class's direct base classes are derived from another common base class, then in these direct base classes, all the members inherited from the upper base class will have the same names. In this case we must also use a scope qualifier to identify unique members, which also have to be defined by the direct base class.

Consider the following example. A data member *nV* and a function *fun* are declared in the base class *B0*. Class *B1* and *B2* both are derived publicly from class *B0*, and class *D1* is derived publicly from both class *B1* and *B2*. There is no new member with the same name as any member inherited from the base classes in the derived class (if there is, it should obey the hiding rule). In this case, class *D1* has members *nV* and *fun* inherited from both class *B1* and *B2*. The derivation relations among the classes and the structure and memory allocation of the derived class are shown in Figure 7.7.

Now let us focus on the issues of identification and the access of member *nV* and *fun*. Each of the two members of the indirect base class *B0* appears as two homonymic members in derived class *D1* through different paths after two derivations. At this time, even if we use the indirect base class name *B0* to qualify an inherited member, it is still unclear whether the member is inherited from class *B1* or from *B2*. In this case, we must use the direct base class name to qualify the inherited member, as shown in the following source code.

```
#include <iostream>
using namespace std;
class B0                                    //define base class B0
{
```

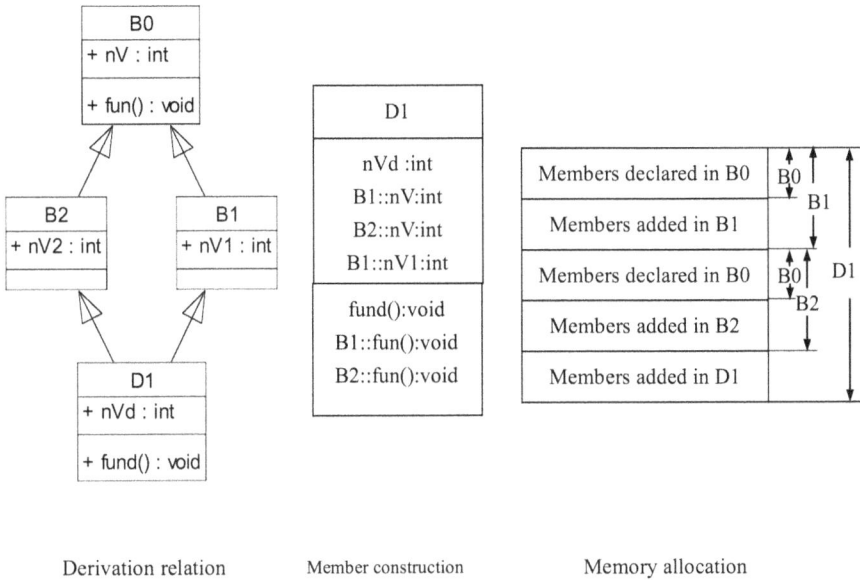

BO + nV : int + fun() : void		

D1
nVd :int B1::nV:int B2::nV:int B1::nV1:int
fund():void B1::fun():void B2::fun():void

Members declared in BO	BO B1	
Members added in B1		
Members declared in BO	BO B2	D1
Members added in B2		
Members added in D1		

B2 + nV2 : int	B1 + nV1 : int

D1 + nVd : int + fund() : void

Derivation relation   Member construction   Memory allocation

Fig. 7.7: The derivation relations among the classes and the structure and memory allocation of the derived class.

```
public:                            //external interface
    int nV;
    void fun(){cout<<"Member of B0"<<endl;}
};
class B1: public B0                //define base class B1
{
public:                            //new external interfaces
    int nV1;
};
class B2: public B0                //define base class B2
{
public:                            //new external interfaces
    int nV2;
};
class D1: public B1, public B2     //define derived class D1
{
public:                            //new external interfaces
    int nVd;
    void fund(){cout<<"Member of D1"<<endl;}
};
```

```
int main()                          //main()
{
    D1 d1;                          //declare object d1 of class D1
    d1.B1::nV=2;                    //use a direct base class
    d1.B1::fun();
    d1.B2::nV=3;                    //use a direct base class
    d1.B2::fun();
}
```

In *main()*, an object *d1* of the derived class *D1* is created. The system cannot uniquely identify which member is to be accessed only through the object name. In this case, the scope qualifier should be used. Using the name of the direct base class to qualify a member can determine which member inherited from the base class is to be accessed. The result of execution is:

```
Member of B0
Member of B0
```

In this case, there are two copies of member *nV* and of member *fun* with the same names in the memory of a derived-class object. The two *nV* can be initialized by the constructor of *B0* called by *B1* and *B2* respectively, and thus the two *nV* can store different values. They can also be separately accessed by using the direct base class name to qualify the name *nV*. However, in most cases we only need one copy of the base-class members. Multiple copies will only result in more memory cost. This problem can be solved by the virtual class mechanism provided by C++.

7.5.2 Virtual Base Class

If some or all of a derived class's direct base classes are derived from the same base class, then the members of the direct base classes inherited from the upper base class share the same names. Then the data members declared in the indirect base class will have multiple copies in memory for a derived class object and each function declared in the indirect base class will have multiple mappings. We can utilize the scope qualifier to access them separately, or we can also **set the common base class as a virtual base class**. In the latter case, there will be only one copy in memory for data members with the same name inherited from different paths and only one map for each function name. This solves the unique identification problem for the members with the same name.

Virtual base class is declared during the definition of the derived class. Its syntax form is:

```
class derived-class name: virtual inheritance mode base-class name
```

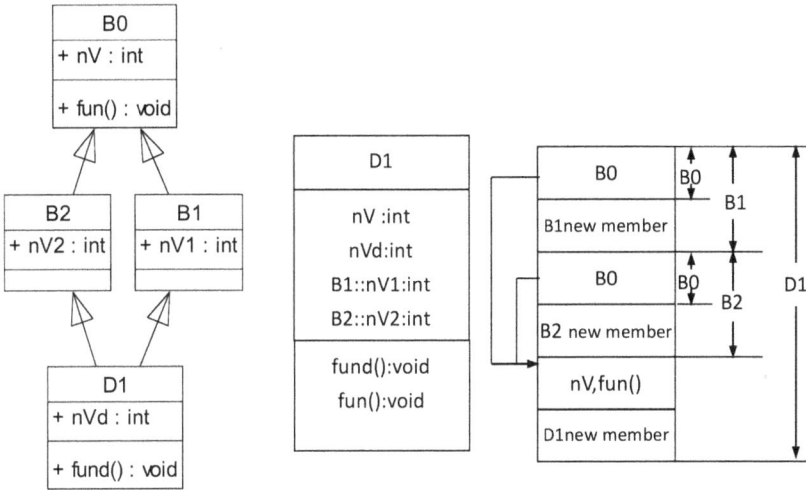

Fig. 7.8: The derivation relations among the classes, and the structure and memory allocation of the derived class.

The above statement declares that the base class of the derived class is a virtual base class. In multiple inheritance, as the specified inheritance mode, the key word "virtual" takes effect only on the base class that follows it closely. After declaring the virtual base class, the members of the virtual base class will maintain the same data copy in memory as the derived class in further derivations.

Example 7.8: Example of virtual base class.
Let us consider the problem mentioned before. Data member nV and function fun are declared in the base class $B0$. Class $B1$ and class $B2$ both are derived publicly from $B0$. The difference from the previous example is that $B0$ is declared as a virtual base class during the derivations. A new class $D1$ is derived from $B1$ and $B2$ publicly. We do not add new members with the same name in class $D1$. (If there is a new member with the same name, it should obey the hiding rule.) So in class $D1$, members nV and fun in base class $B0$ will have only one copy respectively. The derivation relations among the classes and the structure and memory allocation of the derived class are shown in Figure 7.8.

There is only one copy of data member nV and function fun in the derived class $D1$ after using the virtual base class mechanism. In the module, when creating objects of class $D1$, the members are accessible by using the term "object name . member name".

```
//7_8.cpp
#include <iostream>
using namespace std;
class B0                    //define base class B0
{
```

```
public:                          //external interfaces
    int nV;
    void fun(){cout<<"Member of B0"<<endl;}
};
class B1: virtual public B0      //class B0 is a virtual base class of
                                 //the derived class B1

{
public:                          //new external interface
    int nV1;
};
class B2: virtual public B0      //class B0 is a virtual base class of
                                 //the derived class B2

{
public:                          //new external interface
    int nV2;
};
class D1: public B1, public B2 //define derived class D1
{
public:                          //new external interfaces
    int nVd;
    void fund(){cout<<"Member of D1"<<endl;}
};
int main()                       //main()
{
    D1 d1;                       //declare object d1 of class D1
    d1.nV=2;                     //use direct base class
    d1.fun();
}
```

Note: the declaration of a virtual base class just uses the key word **virtual** during the class derivation. In *main()*, a derived-class object *d1* is created and *d1's* members *nV* and *fun* can be accessed by the member names. The execution result is:

```
Member of B0
```

Consider the personnel information management problem mentioned at the beginning of this chapter. In the system, we need to take into account four groups of people. In Section 7.1, we defined the base class *employee* and derived the class *technician*. Now let us consider the definitions of other groups. Both part-time salesmen and managers should be inherited from the base class *employee*. Since sales manager belongs to both the manager group and salesman group, it has the characteristics of the two groups. For example, a sales manager's monthly salary is composed of two parts: the fixed salary and sales commissions. This clearly shows that the sales manager should be derived from both the manager group and the salesman group. The definitions of the classes are:

```
class salesman:virtual public employee //part-time salesman
{
protected:
    float CommRate;              //percentage of the sales commissions
    float sales;                 //current sales
public:
    salesman();                  //constructor
    void Setsales(float sl);     //set sales
    void pay();                  //calculate monthly salary
};

class manager:virtual public employee //manager
{
protected:
    float monthlyPay;            //fixed monthly salary
public:
    manager();                   //constructor
    void pay();                  //calculate monthly salary
};

class salesmanager:public manager,public salesman //sales manager
{
public:
    salesmanager();              //constructor
    void pay();                  //calculate monthly salary
};
```

Here both *salesman* and *manager* are inherited from the virtual base class *employee*. So in the further derived class *salesmanager*, there is only one copy of base class *employee*'s members derived from different paths, to avoid redundant copies. Each class has the function *pay()*. The base class *employee* only declares the function to unify the interface of the class family. Because different derived classes have different characteristics (e.g., different ways of calculating monthly salary), the function *pay()* declared in class *employee* cannot apply to every derived class. The derived classes must declare their own function *pay()* to hide the function declared in the base class. You will have a better understanding of it after reading the entire program in Section 7.7.

Let us compare the two examples, which respectively use scope qualifier and virtual class mechanism. In the former case, the derived class has multiple copies of the members with the same name inherited from the base classes, which are uniquely identified through the scope qualifiers of the direct base classes. These different copies can save different data values or do different operations. In the latter case, only one copy of the members inherited from the base classes is saved in the memory of the derived class. So, the former can store more data information while the latter is more precise and reduces memory cost. Programmers ought to choose appropriate approaches according to actual needs.

7.5.3 Constructors of Virtual Base Class and Derived Class

In Example 7.8, the use of virtual base class is convenient and easy because all the classes use default constructors automatically generated by the compiler. If the virtual base class declares a nondefault constructor (i.e., with arguments) instead of the default constructor, things will be more complicated. In this case, all the derived classes directly and indirectly derived from the virtual base class must explicitly list the initialization of the virtual base class in the member initialization lists of their constructor's. For example, if in Example 7.8 the virtual base class declares a constructor with arguments, then the program should be modified as follows:

```
#include <iostream>
using namespace std;
class B0                           //define base class B0
{
public:                            //external interfaces
    B0(int n){ nV=n;}
    int nV;
    void fun(){cout<<"Member of B0"<<endl;}
};
class B1: virtual public B0        //class B0 is a virtual base class of
                                   //the derived class B1

{
public:                            //new external interfaces
    B1(int a) : B0(a) {}
    int nV1;
};
class B2: virtual public B0        //class B0 is a virtual base class of
                                   //the derived class B2

{
public:                            //new external interfaces
    B2(int a) : B0(a) {}
    int nV2;
};
```

```
class D1: public B1, public B2 //define derived class D1
{
public:                           //new external interfaces
    D1(int a) : B0(a), B1(a), B2(a){}
    int nVd;
    void fund(){cout<<"Member of D1"<<endl;}
};
int main()                        //main()
{
    D1 d1(1);                     //declare object d1 of class D1
    d1.nV=2;
    d1.fun();
}
```

Some readers may have the concern that when creating object *d1* of class *D1*, not only the constructor of virtual base class *B0* is directly called to initialize the member *nV* inherited from class *B0*, but the constructors of the direct base classes *B1* and *B2* are also called, which also call the constructor of base class *B0* for initialization. This seems to suggest that the member *nV* inherited from the virtual base class is initialized three times. The C++ compiler has an elegant way to solve this problem, so we can write programs like the above example without worry. Now let us see how the C++ compiler deals with this problem. For convenience, we refer to the class to which the created object belongs as the furthest derived class. Using the above program as an example, class *D1* is the furthest derived class when creating object *d1*. If the object has members inherited from a virtual base class, then the members of the virtual base class are initialized by the constructor of the virtual base class, which is called by the constructor of the furthest derived class. Only the constructor of the furthest derived class can call the constructor of the virtual base class. Calls on the constructor of the virtual base class from other base classes of the furthest derived class (e.g., class *B1* and *B2*) will automatically be ignored.

7.6 Program Example: Solving Linear Equations using Gaussian Elimination Method

Many problems in natural science and engineering may come down to the solving of linear equations. The Gaussian elimination method is a classical algorithm to solve linear equations. The complete pivoting elimination method, which is the improvement and deformation of Gaussian elimination method, is a common and efficient method for solving linear equations.

7.6.1 Fundamental Principles

Suppose there are n linear equations, (to conveniently represent an array in C++, the suffix in equations starts from 0)

$$\begin{cases} a_{00}x_0 + a_{01}x_1 + \cdots + a_{0,n-1}x_{n-1} = b_0 \\ a_{10}x_0 + a_{11}x_1 + \cdots + a_{1,n-1}x_{n-1} = b_1 \\ \cdots \\ a_{n-1,0}x_0 + a_{n-1,1}x_1 + \cdots + a_{n-1,n-1}x_{n-1} = b_{n-1} \end{cases} \tag{7.1}$$

The matrix form of the above equations is $Ax = b$, where A is the coefficient matrix, x is the column vector, which is the solution of the equations, and b is also a column vector. Generally, we can assume that A is a nonsingular matrix. For more knowledge about matrices, please refer to books on linear algebra.

$$a = \begin{bmatrix} a_{00} & a_{01} & \cdots & a_{0,n} \\ a_{10} & a_{11} & \cdots & a_{1,n} \\ \vdots & \vdots & \ddots & \vdots \\ a_{n-1,0} & a_{n-1,1} & \cdots & a_{n-1,n-1} \end{bmatrix}, \quad x = \begin{bmatrix} x_0 \\ x_1 \\ \vdots \\ x_{n-1} \end{bmatrix}, \quad b = \begin{bmatrix} b_0 \\ b_1 \\ \vdots \\ b_{n-1} \end{bmatrix} \tag{7.2}$$

Put the coefficient matrix A and vector b together to make an augmented matrix B.

$$B = (A, b) = \begin{bmatrix} a_{00} & a_{01} & \cdots & a_{0,n} & b_0 \\ a_{10} & a_{11} & \cdots & a_{1,n} & b_1 \\ \cdots & a_{i1,j1} & \vdots & \cdots & \vdots \\ a_{n-1,0} & a_{n-1,1} & \cdots & a_{n-1,n-1} & b_{n-1} \end{bmatrix} \tag{7.3}$$

The complete pivoting elimination is carried out on matrix B. The whole process can be divided into two steps:

1. Elimination
For k starting from 0 to $n - 2$, do the following three steps:
a) Select the element with the largest absolute value in the submatrix, which starts at row k and column k of A, as the pivot element. For example,

$$|a_{i1,j1}| = \max_{\substack{k \le i < n \\ k \le j < n}} |a_{ij}| \neq 0 \tag{7.4}$$

Then swap the k-th row and the i_1-th row, as well as the k-th column and the j_1-th column. So the element with the largest absolute value in this submatrix is moved to the k-th row and k-th column.
b) Normalization. The method is:

$$a_{kj} = a_{kj}/a_{kk}, \quad j = k + 1, \cdots, n - 1$$
$$b_k = b_k/a_{kk} \tag{7.5}$$

c) Elimination.

$$a_{ij} = a_{ij} - a_{ik}a_{kj}, \qquad j, i = k+1, \cdots, n-1$$
$$b_i = b_i - a_{ik}b_k, \qquad i = k+1, \cdots, n-1 \tag{7.6}$$

2. Back Substitution

$$x_{n-1} = b_{n-1}/a_{n-1,n-1}$$

$$x_i = b_i - \sum_{j=i+1}^{n-1} a_{ij}x_j, \qquad i = n-2, \cdots, 1, 0 \tag{7.7}$$

Here, we only list the steps of the complete pivoting elimination algorithm. The derivation and detailed process of the algorithm can be found in books on numeric calculation.

7.6.2 Analysis of the Program Design

We can see from the above algorithm analysis that the main task in this example is the matrix calculation. We can define a class *Matrix* as the base class, and then derive a linear equation class *Linequ* from class *Matrix*. The class *Matrix* only deals with $n \times n$ square matrices and stores square matrices using a one-dimensional array. The data members of class *Matrix* include the starting address of the one-dimensional array and the variable n. The functions of class *Matrix* include *setMatrix()* for setting the matrix value, *printM()* for displaying the matrix, and so on.

According to the analysis, besides the coefficient matrix *A* inherited from class *Matrix*, the linear equation class *Linequ* should also include the starting address of solution vector *x* and vector *b*. The primary functions of class *Linequ* include *setLinequ()* for setting equations, *printL()* for displaying equations, *Solve()* for solving equations, and *showX()* for outputting the solution. We can define new members in class *Linequ* to implement these functions for solving equations.

The composition of classes *Matrix* and *Linequ* and their relations are shown in Figure 7.9.

The member function *Solve* of class *Linequ* needs to access the data members of base class *Matrix* when solving the equations. We use public derivation and set the access attributes of the data members in class *Matrix* as protected. Thus, after the public derivation, protected members in the base class are still protected members in the derived class and can be accessed by derived-class functions.

7.6.3 Source Code and Explanation

Example 7.9: Use complete pivoting elimination method to solve linear equations. The whole program contains three files: *linequ.h*, *linequ.cpp*, and *liqumain.cpp*. Classes

```
┌─────────────────────────────────────┐
│                Matrix                │
├─────────────────────────────────────┤
│ # index : int                        │
│ # MatrixA : double*                  │
├─────────────────────────────────────┤
│ + Matrix(dims : int = 2)             │
│ + ~Matrix()                          │
│ + setMatrix(rmatr : double*) : void  │
│ + printM() : void                    │
└─────────────────────────────────────┘
```

```
┌──────────────────────────────────────────────┐
│                    Linequ                      │
├──────────────────────────────────────────────┤
│ - sums : double *                              │
│ - solu : double *                              │
├──────────────────────────────────────────────┤
│ + Linequ(dims : int = 2)                       │
│ + ~Linequ()                                    │
│ + setLinequ(a : double*, b : double *) : void  │
│ + printL() : void                              │
│ + Solve() : int                                │
│ + showX() : void                               │
└──────────────────────────────────────────────┘
```

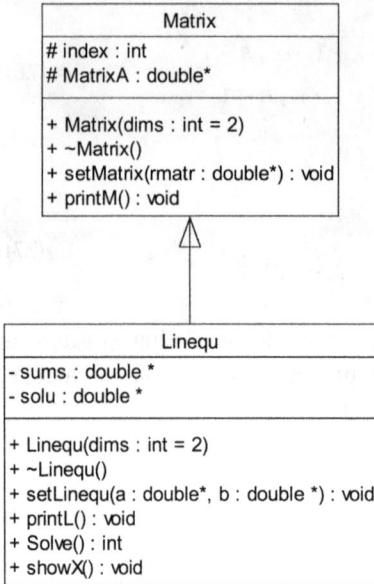

Fig. 7.9: The derivation relations between class *Matrix* and class *Linequ*.

Matrix and *Linequ* are defined in *linequ.h*. The member functions of the two classes are implemented in *linequ.cpp*. The *main()* is in *leuqmain.cpp*. An object of class *Linequ* is defined in *main()*, which we can use to solve the linear equations with four variables.

```cpp
//linequ.h file 1, defining classes
#include <iostream>
#include <cmath>
using namespace std;
class Matrix              //define base class Matrix
{
public:                   //external interfaces
    Matrix(int dims=2);   //constructor
    ~Matrix();            //destructor
    void setMatrix(double* rmatr); //set initial value for matrix
    void printM();        //display matrix
protected:                //protected data members
    int index;            //dimension of the matrix
    double* MatrixA;      //starting address of the matrix in memory
};
class Linequ: public Matrix //define publicly derived class Linequ
{
public:                   //external interface
    Linequ(int dims=2);   //constructor
    ~Linequ();            //destructor
```

```
        void setLinequ(double* a, double *b); //assign values to equations
        void printL();              //display equations
        int Solve();                //use complete pivoting elimination to
                                    //solve equations
        void showX();               //display the solution
    private:                        //private data
        double *sums;               //the vector on the right side of the
                                    //equations
        double *solu;               //the solution
    };
    //End of file linequ.h
```

Through public derivation, class *Linequ* inherits all the members in class *Matrix* except for the constructor and the destructor. Because all the base-class members are public or protected, they are accessible in the function members of the derived class. The protected members of the base class, however, are not accessible in the module creating objects of class *Linequ*. By using the protected access attributes and public derivation, we realize efficient sharing and reliable protection of data of the base class *Matrix*. In the program, we store the coefficient matrix, the solution vector, and the vector on the right side of the equations all through dynamic memory allocation, which are implemented in the constructors of the base class and the derived class. The cleanup work is done in destructors.

```
//lineequ.cpp file 2, class implementation
#include "linequ.h" //header file which includes class definitions
//implementation of the function member of Class Matrix
//Public Function member No.1: Set Matrix value
void Matrix::setMatrix(double* rmatr) //set the matrix
{
    for(int i=0;i<index*index;i++){
    *(MatrixA+i)=rmatr[i];      //set initial value of the matrix
    }
}
//Public Function member No.2 Constructor
Matrix::Matrix(int dims)          //constructor of class Matrix
{
    index=dims;                   //protected data assignment
    MatrixA=new double[index*index]; //dynamic memory allocation
}
//Public Function member No.3 Destruction function
Matrix::~Matrix()                 //destructor of class Matrix
{
    delete[] MatrixA;             //free memory
}
```

```
//Public Function member No.4 Display Matrix function
void Matrix::printM()              //display matrix's elements
{
    cout<<"The Matrix is:"<<endl;
    for(int i=0;i<index;i++){
     for(int j=0;j<index;j++)
       cout<<*(MatrixA+i*index+j)<<" ";
     cout<<endl;
    }
}
//implementation of the function member of Class Linequ
//Public Function member No.1 Constructor
Linequ::Linequ(int dims):Matrix(dims)
                                 //constructor of derived class Linequ
{                                //call base-class constructor, pass
                                 //arguments
    sums=new double[dims];       //dynamic memory allocation
    solu=new double[dims];
}
//Public Function member No.2 Destruction function
Linequ::~Linequ()                //destructor of derived class Linequ
{                                //call destructor of base class
    delete[] sums;               //free memory
    delete[] solu;
}
//Public Function member No.3 Set Line Equation function
void Linequ::setLinequ(double *a,double *b) //set the linear equations
{
    setMatrix(a);                //call base-class functions
    for(int i=0;i<index;i++)
     sums[i]=b[i];
}
//Public Function member No.4 Display Line Equation function
void Linequ::printL()            //display linear equations
{
    cout<<"The Line equation is:"<<endl;
    for(int i=0;i<index;i++){
     for(int j=0;j<index;j++)
       cout<<*(MatrixA+i*index+j)<<" ";
     cout<<" "<<sums[i]<<endl;
    }
}
```

```
//Public Function member No.5 Display the solution
void Linequ::showX()              //output the solution
{
    cout<<"The Result is:"<<endl;
    for(int i=0;i<index;i++){
     cout<<"X["<<i<<"]="<<solu[i]<<endl;
    }
}
//Public Function member No.6 Constructor
int Linequ::Solve()                    //use complete pivoting elimination
                                       //method to solve linear equations
{
    int *js,l,k,i,j,is,p,q;
    double d,t;
    js=new int[index];
    l=1;
    for (k=0;k<=index-2;k++)      //elimination
    {
     d=0.0;
     for (i=k;i<=index-1;i++)
         for (j=k;j<=index-1;j++)
         { t=fabs(MatrixA[i*index+j]);
           if (t>d)
           { d=t; js[k]=j; is=i; }
         }
     if (d+1.0==1.0) l=0;
     else
     { if (js[k]!=k)
           for (i=0;i<=index-1;i++)
           { p=i*index+k; q=i*index+js[k];
             t=MatrixA[p]; MatrixA[p]=MatrixA[q]; MatrixA[q]=t;
           }
           if (is!=k)
           { for (j=k;j<=index-1;j++)
             { p=k*index+j; q=is*index+j;
               t=MatrixA[p]; MatrixA[p]=MatrixA[q]; MatrixA[q]=t;
             }
             t=sums[k]; sums[k]=sums[is]; sums[is]=t;
           }
     }
     if (l==0)
     { delete[] js; cout<<"fail"<<endl;
```

```
        return(0);
    }
    d=MatrixA[k*index+k];
    for (j=k+1;j<=index-1;j++)
    { p=k*index+j; MatrixA[p]=MatrixA[p]/d;}
    sums[k]=sums[k]/d;
    for (i=k+1;i<=index-1;i++)
    { for (j=k+1;j<=index-1;j++)
        { p=i*index+j;
        MatrixA[p]=MatrixA[p]-MatrixA[i*index+k]*MatrixA[k*index+j];
        }
        sums[i]=sums[i]-MatrixA[i*index+k]*sums[k];
    }
    }
    d=MatrixA[(index-1)*index+index-1];
    if (fabs(d)+1.0==1.0)
    { delete[] js; cout<<"fail"<<endl;
        return(0);
    }
    solu[index-1]=sums[index-1]/d; //back substitution
    for (i=index-2;i>=0;i--)
    { t=0.0;
        for (j=i+1;j<=index-1;j++)
            t=t+MatrixA[i*index+j]*solu[j];
        solu[i]=sums[i]-t;
    }
    js[index-1]=index-1;
    for (k=index-1;k>=0;k--)
        if (js[k]!=k)
        { t=solu[k]; solu[k]=solu[js[k]]; solu[js[k]]=t;}
    delete[] js;
    return(1);
}
//End of file linequ.cpp
```

In the process of implementing class member functions, the constructor of the derived class calls the constructor of the base class to pass arguments and it dynamically allocates memory space for the matrix. The destructor of the derived class also calls the destructor of the base class. The entire calling procedure is completed within the system automatically. After public derivation, protected base-class members remain as protected members in the derived class, which can be accessed by the member functions of the derived class.

The return type of the function implementing the complete pivoting elimination approach is an integer. If the program terminates normally, the return value is 1; otherwise the return value is 0. According to the return value, we can determine the completion status of the solving process.

```
//7_9.cpp file 3, main()
#include "linequ.h" //header file which includes class definitions
int main()              //main()
{
    double a[]=                         //coefficient matrix
    {
        0.2368,0.2471,0.2568,1.2671,    //the first row
        0.1968,0.2071,1.2168,0.2271,    //the second row
        0.1581,1.1675,0.1768,0.1871,    //the third row
        1.1161,0.1254,0.1397,0.1490};   //the fourth row
        double b[4]=                     //the vector on the right side
                                         //of the equations

        {1.8471,1.7471,1.6471,1.5471};
        Linequ equ1(4);                  //define an object of the
                                         //equation class
        equ1.setLinequ(a,b);             //set the equations
        equ1.printL();                   //output the equations
        if(equ1.Solve())                 //solve the equations
            equ1.showX();                //output the solution
        else
            cout<<"Fail"<<endl;
}
//End of file lequmain.cpp
```

In *main()*, we use a quaternion equation to test our algorithm. Both the coefficients and the vector on the right side of the equations are stored in one-dimensional arrays. Firstly, an object *equ1* of quaternion equations is created. During the creation process, the constructor of the derived class is called. The constructor of the derived class in turn calls the constructor of the base class, and then dynamically allocates memory spaces. Next, the coefficients and the vector on the right side of the equations are initialized, where the selected equations are input into the object *equ1*. The member functions *printL*, *solve*, and *showX* of the object complete the tasks of displaying equations, solving equations, and displaying the solution, respectively.

7.6.4 Execution Result and Analysis

The result of the program is as follows.

```
The Line equation is: //equations
0.2368 0.2471 0.2568 1.2671 1.8471
0.1968 0.2071 1.2168 0.2271 1.7471
0.1581 1.1675 0.1768 0.1871 1.6471
1.1161 0.1254 0.1397 0.149 1.5471
The Result is: //solution
X[0]=1.04058
X[1]=0.987051
X[2]=0.93504
X[3]=0.881282
```

The equations that this example uses come from the book *C Programs of Common Algorithms* written by Mr Xu Shiliang. The calculation result here is exactly the same as in the book. The selected equations are:

$$\begin{cases} 0.2368x_0 + 0.2471x_1 + 0.2568x_2 + 1.2671x_3 = 1.8471 \\ 0.1968x_0 + 0.2071x_1 + 1.2168x_2 + 0.2271x_3 = 1.7471 \\ 0.1581x_0 + 1.1675x_1 + 0.1768x_2 + 0.1871x_3 = 1.6471 \\ 1.1161x_0 + 0.1254x_1 + 0.1397x_2 + 0.1490x_3 = 1.5471 \end{cases} \tag{7.8}$$

The matrix is stored in a one-dimensional array through dynamic memory allocation.

This is an example of solving practical problems through the derivation hierarchy of classes. The base class deals with the matrix. The publicly derived class *Linequ* is designed to deal with linear equations. In addition to the members inherited from the base class, new members are added to class *Linequ* according to actual needs. In this way, we detail and specialize the base class *Matrix* to describe and solve the problem more efficiently.

The access control is also designed according to actual needs. The matrix stored in and maintained by the data members of the base class, which is the coefficient matrix in the derived class, must be accessed by the functions of the derived class. We take advantage of the characteristics of protected members, setting the access attributes of the base-class members to be protected. Thus the protected members inherited from the base class can be accessed in the publicly derived class *Linequ*, while they are inaccessible by other modules outside the class. In this way, we find an appropriate balance between data sharing and data hiding.

New constructors and destructors should be added to the derived class to do the initialization and cleaning up work in the derived class because the constructor and destructor of the base class cannot be inherited. The constructor of the derived class initializes the data inherited from the base class by calling the constructor of the base class. In this example, the constructor of the derived class *Linequ* calls the constructor of the base class *Matrix* and passes on the initialization arguments. The destructor of the derived class also calls the destructor of the base class to do the cleaning up work.

7.7 Program Example: Personnel Information Management Program

In this section, we will take the personnel information management of a small corporation as an example to further illustrate the procedure of derivation and the applications of virtual functions and virtual base classes.

7.7.1 Problem Description

In Section 7.1.1, we analyzed the problem of the personnel information management system that had been discussed in Chapters 4.6. In Section 7.1.3 we proposed an improvement of the program. Here, we implement the salary calculating function mentioned in Section 7.1.1 using class inheritance and derivation. For example, we assume the salary calculating method to be: a manager's fixed salary is 8,000 RMB; a part-time technician gets his salary by the hour and the hourly pay is 100 RMB; a part-time salesman's salary includes commissions, which are 4% of his sales; a sales manager takes both his fixed salary of 5,000 RMB and sales commissions, which are 5% of his department's sales in a current month.

7.7.2 Class Design

According to the above needs, we design a base class *employee*, from which we derive the classes *technician* (part-time technician), *manager* (manager), and *salesman* (part-time salesman). Because a sales manager is both a manager and a salesman, we design the class *salesmanager* derived from both class *manager* and *salesman* for this group of people.

In the base class *employee*, aside from the constructor and destructor, the operations on information of all kinds of people should also be defined uniformly, to regulate the basic behaviors in all the derived classes of the class family. Since the salary calculation methods vary for different kinds of people, they cannot be defined uniformly in the base class *employee*. Therefore, we can set the function body of salary calculating in the base class as empty, and implement specific functionalities in the homonymous functions in different derived classes according to the hiding rule. The class design is shown in Figure 7.10.

Since the two base classes of the class *salesmanager* have a common base class *employee*, we design the class *employee* as virtual here to avoid ambiguity.

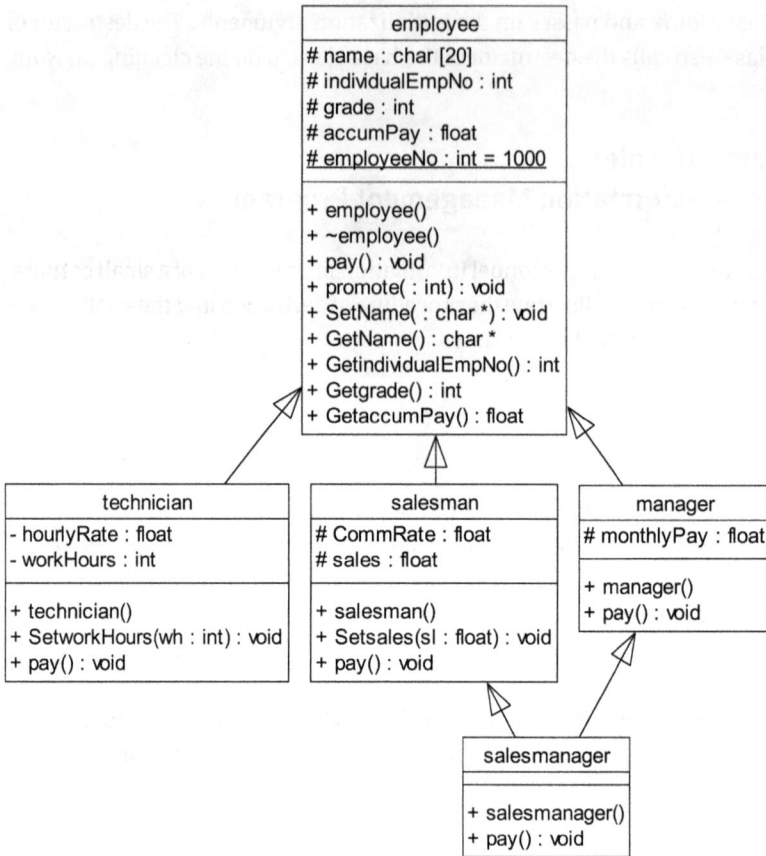

Fig. 7.10: UML of personnel information management system of a small corporation.

7.7.3 Source Code and Explanation

Example 7.10: Personnel information management system.
The entire program is divided into three files: *employee.h* is a header file for class definitions; *employee.cpp* is a file in which function members of the classes are implemented; and *7_10.cpp* contains the main function *main()*. After compiling, *7_10.cpp* and *employee.cpp* are linked together. In the VC++ development environment, they should be placed in one project.

```
//employee.h
class employee
{
protected:
    char name[20];          //name
    int individualEmpNo;    //employee number
```

```
    int grade;                     //grade
    float accumPay;                //total salary in current month
    static int employeeNo;         //largest employee number in the
                                   //company
public:
    employee();                    //constructor
    ~employee();                   //destructor
    void pay();                    //monthly salary calculating function
    void promote(int);             //promotion function
    void SetName(char *);          //function to set name
    char * GetName();              //function to get name
    int GetindividualEmpNo();      //function to get individual employee
                                   //number
    int Getgrade();                //function to get grade
    float GetaccumPay();           //function to get salary
};

class technician:public employee //part-time technician
{
private:
    float hourlyRate;              //hourly pay
    int workHours;                 //work hours in current month
public:
    technician();                  //constructor
    void SetworkHours(int wh);     //function to set work hours
    void pay();                    //function to calculate monthly salary
};

class salesman:virtual public employee //part-time salesman
{
protected:
    float CommRate;                //commissions rate
    float sales;                   //total sales in current month
public:
    salesman();                    //constructor
    void Setsales(float sl);       //set total sales
    void pay();                    //calculate monthly salary
};

class manager:virtual public employee //manager
{
```

```
protected:
    float monthlyPay;              //fixed salary
public:
    manager();                     //constructor
    void pay();                    //calculate monthly salary
};

class salesmanager:public manager,public salesman //sales manager
{
public:
    salesmanager();                //constructor
    void pay();                    //calculate salary
};

//employee.cpp
#include<iostream>
#include<cstring>
#include"employee.h"
using namespace std;
int employee::employeeNo=1000;  //the basic employee number is 1000

employee::employee()
{ individualEmpNo=employeeNo++;  //new employee number is the current
                                 //largest employee number plus one
    grade=1;                     //initial grade is 1
    accumPay=0.0; }              //initial salary is 0

employee::~employee()
{}

void employee::pay()             //calculate salary, empty function
{}

void employee::promote(int increment)
{ grade+=increment;}             //promote

void employee::SetName(char* names)
{ strcpy(name,names); }          //set name

char* employee::GetName()
{ return name;}                  //get name
```

```
int employee::GetindividualEmpNo()
{ return individualEmpNo;}      //get employee number

int employee::Getgrade()
{ return grade;}                //get grade

float employee::GetaccumPay()
{ return accumPay;}             //get monthly salary

technician::technician()
{ hourlyRate=100;}              //hourly pay is 100 RMB

void technician::SetworkHours(int wh)
{ workHours=wh;}                //set work hours

void technician::pay()
{ accumPay=hourlyRate*workHours;} //calculate monthly salary by hour

salesman::salesman()
{ CommRate=0.04;}               //commission rate is 4%

void salesman::Setsales(float sl)
{ sales=sl;}                    //set sales

void salesman::pay()
{ accumPay=sales*CommRate;}     //salary = sales commissions

manager::manager()
{ monthlyPay=8000;}             //fixed salary is 8000 RMB

void manager::pay()
{ accumPay=monthlyPay;}         //total salary is fixed salary

salesmanager::salesmanager()
{ monthlyPay=5000 ;
   CommRate=0.005;}

void salesmanager::pay()
{ accumPay=monthlyPay+CommRate*sales; }
                     //total salary = fixed salary + sales commission
```

```
//7_10.cpp
#include<iostream>
#include<cstring>
#include"employee.h"
using namespace std;
int main()
{
    manager m1;
    technician t1;
    salesmanager sm1;
    salesman s1;
    char namestr[20];              //the employee name is stored in
                                   //namestr temporarily

    cout<<"Please input next employee's name:";
    cin>>namestr;
    m1.SetName(namestr);           //set the name of employee m1

    cout<<" Please input next employee's name:";
    cin>>namestr;
    t1.SetName(namestr);           //set the name of employee t1

    cout<<" Please input next employee's name:";
    cin>>namestr;
    sm1.SetName(namestr);          //set the name of employee sm1

    cout<<" Please input next employee's name:";
    cin>>namestr;
    s1.SetName(namestr);           //set the name of employee s1

    m1.promote(3);                 //promote manager m1 by 3 grades
    m1.pay();                      //calculate the salary of m1

    cout<<"Please input part-time technician"<<t1.GetName()<<"work
        hours in current month:";
    int ww;
    cin>>ww;                       //input work hours for t1
    t1.SetworkHours(ww);           //set work hours for t1
    t1.promote(2);                 //promote t1 by 2 grades
    t1.pay();                      //calculate salary for t1

    cout<<"Please input sales manager"<<sm1.GetName()<<"total sales
        of his department in current month:";
```

```
        float sl;
        cin>>sl;                        //input total sales
        sm1.Setsales(sl);               //set total sales
        sm1.pay();                      //calculate salary for sm1
        sm1.promote(2);                 //promote sm1 by 2 grades

        cout<<"Please input salesman"<<s1.GetName()<<"current sales:";
        cin>>sl;                        //input current sales for s1
        s1.Setsales(sl);                //set current sales for s1
        s1.pay();                       //calculate monthly pay for s1

        //show m1's information
        cout<<m1.GetName()<<"employee number is"<<m1.GetindividualEmpNo()
         <<"grade is"<<m1.Getgrade()<<",current salary is
            "<<m1.GetaccumPay()<<endl;

        //show t1's information
        cout<<t1.GetName()<<"employee number is"<<t1.GetindividualEmpNo()
         <<"grade is"<<t1.Getgrade()<<",current salary is
            "<<t1.GetaccumPay()<<endl;

        //show sm1's information
        cout<<sm1.GetName()<<"employee number "<<sm1.GetindividualEmpNo()
         <<"grade is "<<sm1.Getgrade()<<",current salary is
            "<<sm1.GetaccumPay()<<endl;

        //show s1's information
        cout<<s1.GetName()<<"employee number "<<s1.GetindividualEmpNo()
         <<" grade is "<<s1.Getgrade()<<",current salary is
            "<<s1.GetaccumPay()<<endl;
    }
```

7.7.4 Execution Result and Analysis

The execution result is as follows.

```
Please input next employee's name: Zhang
Please input next employee's name: Wang
Please input next employee's name: Li
Please input next employee's name: Zhao
Please input part-time technicianWang current work hours: 40
```

```
Please input sales manager Li total sales of his department in
current month: 400000
Please input salesman Zhao current sales: 40000
Zhang employee number1000 grade is4, current salary is 8000
Wang employee number 1001 grade is 3, current salary is 4000
Li employee number 1002 grade is 3, current salary is 7000
Zhao employee number 1003 grade is 1, current salary is 1600
```

In the above program, each derived class only defines its own new members, while retaining the members inherited from the base class without change. The derived-class constructor only needs to initialize new members. When creating a derived-class object, the system will first call the base-class constructor to initialize the members inherited from the base class and then call the derived-class constructor to initialize new data members.

Each derived class has the function *pay()*. In *main()*, when calling the function *pay()* through a derived-class object, according to the hiding rule, the system will call the function declared in the derived class. The empty function in the base class only regulates the basic behaviors of the derived-classes in the class family.

The employee number starts from 1,000 and increases by 1 each time. The static data member *employeeNo* is initialized outside the class and is shared by all objects of the entire class family.

The program has two shortcomings:

Firstly, the function *fun()* declared in the base class is to be empty, but we still need to write the empty function body as its implementation, which seems redundant. However, we should keep it to uniformly regulate the basic behaviors of the class family. This problem can be solved by using virtual functions, which will be introduced in the next chapter.

Secondly, in *main()*, four objects of different classes are created. To perform similar operations on these objects (e.g., input name, output basic personnel information) we have to write similar statements four times. Can we use the base-class pointer array to point to multiple derived-class objects and deal with the objects in a loop structure, according to the type compatible rule? From what we have learned so far, this is impossible since a base-class pointer can only point to base-class members, while here we need to access the *pay()* functions declared in different classes. Again, this problem can be solved by using the virtual functions introduced in the next chapter.

7.8 Summary

In this chapter, we first introduced the concept of class inheritance. Class inheritance allows programmers to give more specific and detailed class definitions based on the characteristics of the original class. A new class is generated from the original class, i.e., the new class inherits the characteristics of the original class, or the original class derives the new class. The procedure of deriving a new class includes three steps: accepting members inherited from the original class, modifying existing members, and adding new members. We focus on the access controls of base-class members and the addition of constructors and destructors, under different kinds of derivations. We then discuss the unique identification and access of derived-class members in more complicated inheritance relationships. Finally, we discuss the use scope of derived-class objects. Two examples, using Gaussian elimination method to solve linear equations and a personnel information management system, are presented as a review and conclusion of the chapter.

Inheritance is to obtain features from one's ancestor. Class inheritance refers to when a new class inherits characteristics from an existing class. Class derivation is the process of creating a new class from an existing class. A derived class can also serve as a base class to derive new classes, which form a class hierarchy. Class derivation is a process of evolution and development, i.e., through extension, modification, and specification to create a new class from an existing class. Class derivation creates a class family that has common characteristics, to realize code reuse. The inheritance and derivation mechanism greatly facilitates the development and improvement of existing programs.

In the class hierarchy, the top layer represents the most abstract and common concept. A lower layer keeps the characteristics of its upper layer, while having its own characteristics. In the class hierarchy, it is a specialization process from top to bottom and an abstraction process from bottom to top.

A new class can be derived in three steps: accepting base-class members, modifying base-class members, and adding new members. In C++ inheritance, a derived class inherits all the members of its base classes except for the constructor and destructor. Modifications to base-class members concern two issues. The first one is the access control of base-class members, which depends on the inheritance mode specified in the definition of the derived class. The other is the overriding of the data and function members of the base class. Adding new members in a derived class is the key to the inheritance and derivation mechanism, and it is crucial for the development of functionalities in derived classes. We can add appropriate data and function members to the derived class according to actual needs. The constructor and destructor of the base class cannot be inherited, so we should add a new constructor and destructor to the derived class to do specific initialization and cleanup work.

After discussing the derivation procedure, we focus on the issues of the identification and access of the members (including members inherited from the base class and new members) of a derived class and its object. There are two problems to be solved in an accessing process. The first one is regarding unique identification and the other is regarding the access attributes, i.e., the visibility, of a class member. We introduce several methods, including the hiding rule, scope qualifier, and virtual base class, to solve these unique identification problems.

The type compatible rule is about the use scope of derived-class objects. After public derivation, a derived class has all the functionalities of its base class. We can use a derived class to substitute for the base class wherever the latter one is needed. This characteristic lays the foundation for polymorphism, which will be discussed in the next chapter.

Exercises

7.1 Compare the three inheritance modes: public, protected, and private.

7.2 What is the execution order of a derived-class constructor?

7.3 If member function *fn1()* declared in base class *A* has already been overridden in derived class *B*, while member function *fn2()* declared in *A* has not, then how does one call the base-class members functions *fn1()* and *fn2()* in a derived class, respectively?

7.4 What is a virtual base class? What can it do?

7.5 Define a base class *Shape*, from which to derive two classes *Rectangle* and *Circle*. Both of the derived classes use function *GetArea()* to calculate the area. Derive another class *Square* from *Rectangle*.

7.6 Define a class *Mammal*, which stands for mammals, from which to derive a new class *Dog*. Define an object of class *Dog*. Observe the calling orders of the constructors and the destructors of both the base class and derived class, respectively.

7.7 Define a base class and a derived class, and output some prompt messages in both constructors. Create a derived-class object and observe the execution order of the constructors.

7.8 Define a class *Document* that has a data member, *name*. Derive a new class *Book* from the *Document* class and add a new member, *PageCount*, in class *Book*.

7.9 Define a base class *Base* that has two public member functions, *fn1()* and *fn2()*. Then privately derive a class *Derived*. How does one call the base-class function *fn1* through a derived object?

7.10 Define a class *object* that has a data member *weight* and some function members operating *weight*. Derive a class *box* from the class *object*. Add new data members *Height* and *width*, and some function members operating the two new members, to the derived class. Declare an object of class *box*. Observe the calling orders of constructors and destructors.

7.11 Define a base class *BaseClass*, and derive class *DerivedClass* from the class *BaseClass*. Class *BaseClass* has member functions *fn1()* and *fn2()*. Class *DerivedClass* also declare functions *fn1()* and *fn2()* in its definition. Declare an object of *DerivedClass* in *main()*. Call *fn1()* and *fn2()* through the object of *DerivedClass*, a *BaseClass* pointer, and a *DerivedClass* pointer respectively. Observe the execution results.

8 Polymorphism

The power of object-oriented programming lies not only in inheritance, but also in its ability to treat a derived-class object like a base-class object. It is polymorphism and dynamic binding that support this mechanism.

8.1 An Overview of Polymorphism

Polymorphism means that different objects behave differently when they are given the same message. The call by member functions is the 'message' and different behaviors are due to different implementations, i.e., calling different functions. Polymorphism is quite often used in programming. The most common example is the math operator. We use the same plus sign "+" to implement adding operation between integers, floating numbers, and double precision floating numbers. The same message, adding, is accepted by different objects or variables, and different variables carry out the adding operation in different ways. If the adding operation is performed on variables of different types, e.g., a floating and an integer, then the integer will first be converted to a floating point before adding. This is a typical polymorphism.

8.1.1 Types of Polymorphism

Object-oriented polymorphism can be divided into four types: overload polymorphism, coercion polymorphism, inclusion polymorphism, and argument polymorphism. The former two fall into the category of special polymorphism, while the latter two, general polymorphism. Overloads of ordinary functions and overloads of class member functions are both overload polymorphism. We will learn operator overloading in this chapter. The example of the add operation between floating numbers and integers is an example of overload. Coercion polymorphism is converting the type of a variable to meet the requirement of the function or operation. When adding a floating number and an integer, first we should do type coercion to convert an integer to a floating number. This is an example of coercion polymorphism.

Inclusion polymorphism is investigating polymorphic behaviors of the member functions with the same name in different classes within a class family. It is implemented by using virtual functions. Argument polymorphism and class templates (to be introduced in Chapter 9) are related to each other. This polymorphism must be assigned an actual type before realization. So, all classes instantiated from the class template have the same operations, but the types of operands are different.

This chapter mainly introduces overloading and inclusion polymorphisms. Function overloading has been elaborated in Chapters 3 and 4. Here we mainly introduce operator overload. Virtual function is the main issue of polymorphism.

https://doi.org/10.1515/9783110471977-008

8.1.2 Implementation of Polymorphism

Polymorphism can be divided into two groups in terms of implementation: **compiling polymorphism** and **executing polymorphism**. For the former group, the operands in the same operation are determined during compiling while for the latter group, they are determined dynamically during execution. The process of determining the operands is **binding**. Binding is a procedure in which computer programs relate to each other by themselves. It also means combining the identifier and memory address. In object-oriented programming, **binding is the process of connecting a message with a function of an object.** According to the different stages of binding, there are two ways of binding: static binding and dynamic binding, corresponding to two methods of polymorphism implementation.

   A static binding is a binding during the compiling and linking processes. Because binding is done before the execution, it is also called early binding. During compiling and linking, the system can determine the relation between the operation and the code for the operation according to the features such as type matching. In other words, it determines the proper code for a certain identifier. The operands with the same operation name can be decided during compiling and linking for some polymorphism types. It is done by static binding, such as overloading, coercion, and argument polymorphism.

   If binding is performed during the execution, such a binding is called dynamic binding. In some cases, binding cannot be performed during compiling or linking and instead, it is performed during the execution. It is through dynamic binding that objects are determined if they have polymorphism operations.

8.2 Operator Overload

Operands of the predefined operators in C++ are only basic data types. In fact, for many user-defined types (such as classes), similar operations are also needed. For example, the following program defines a class of a complex number.

```
class complex                    //define a complex number
{
public:
    complex(double r=0.0,double i=0.0){real=r;imag=i;} //constructor
    void display();                 //show the value of complex number
private:
    double real;
    double imag;
};
```

We can then define an object of the complex number class with the following state-ment:

```
complex a(10,20), b(5,8);
```

The question is how to perform the add operation between *a* and *b*. Naturally, we would like to use the operator "+" and to write the expression "a+b", but such expres-sion will render an error during compiling because the compiler does not know how to perform the add operation between two complex numbers. In this case, we must write a program to clearly specify the operation '+' when it operates on complex number objects. This is called operator overload. Operator overload makes existing operators more versatile and, with overload, an operator can act on different types of data and have different behaviors.

Operator overload is essentially function overload. We should first convert the expression to the call of an operator function. The operands are converted to actual arguments of the operator function. And then the function to be called is determined according to the type of actual arguments, which is completed in the compilation process.

8.2.1 Rules of Operator Overload

The rules of operator overload are as follows:
1. All operators in C++ can be overloaded except a few exceptions and only those existing operators in C++ can be overloaded.
2. After overloading, the priority and **associability are still the same.**
3. Operator overload meets the actual needs of new types of data and makes appro-priate modifications to the original operator. Generally speaking, an overloaded function should be similar with the original function. The number of operands cannot be changed and at least one operand should be a user-defined type.

Only five operators cannot be overloaded. They are the genetic relation operator ".", member pointer operator ".*", scope resolution operator "::", *sizeof* operator, and ternary operator "?:". The first two operators ensure the meaning of accessing mem-bers in C++ will not be changed. The operands of the scope resolution operator and *sizeof* operator are types, not regular expressions, so they do not have the overloading feature.

There are two types of operator overload: overloading as member functions and overloading as friend functions. The syntax of overloading as member functions is:

```
function type operator operatorname(argument list)
{
    function body;
}
```

The prototype of a friend function should be declared in the class if the operator is overloaded as a friend function:

```
friend function type operator operatorname (argument list);
```

The *function type* is the type of return value of the overloaded operator, i.e., the type of the result of the operation. The term *operator* is the key word in defining operator overload. operatorname is the name of the operator to be overloaded. It must refer to an operator that can be overloaded, such as "+", the add sign. The *argument list* lists the arguments and their types needed for the operator. If the operator is to be overloaded as a friend function, then the key word *friend* should be declared in the function in the class. The function is implemented outside the class.

If the operator is overloaded as a member function, the number of arguments is one less than the number of operands (not applicable to "++" or "−−"). If the operator is overloaded as a friend function, then the two numbers are the same. The reason is that if the operator overloaded as a member function and an object uses the overloaded member function, then the data of the object can be accessed directly, so there is no need to pass it by the argument list. The missing operand is the object itself. But when the operator is overloaded as a friend function, and the friend function operates on the data of an object, it must work through the object name. So the number of operands does not change.

The main advantage of operator overloading is that we can change the operations of existing operators so they can operate on a user-defined class type.

8.2.2 Operator Overloaded as Member Function

Operator overload is essentially function overload. When an operator is overloaded as a member function, it can freely access data members in the class. We always use an object of the class to access overloaded operators. If it is a binary operator, an operand is the object's data, pointed by the pointer *this*, and the other operand is passed by an argument list of the overloaded function. If the operator is unary, the operand is pointed by pointer *this* of the object, so it does not need any argument. These two cases are illustrated below.

For binary operator *B*, if it is overloaded as a member function in order to indicate the expression *oprd1 B oprd2*, where *oprd1* is an object of class *A*, then B should be overloaded as a member function of *A* and the function has one formal argument, whose type is the type of *oprd2*. After overloading, expression *oprd1 B oprd2* is equivalent to calling function *oprd1.operator B (oprd2)*.

For a prefix operator *U*, such as "−" (minus sign), if it is to be overloaded as a member function in order to indicate expression *U oprd*, where *oprd* is an object of class *A*, then operator *U* should be overloaded as a member of class *A*, which has no argument list. After overloading, the expression *U oprd* is equivalent to calling function *oprd.operator U()*.

For postfix operators "++" and "--", if they are to be overloaded as member functions in order to indicate expression *oprd++* or *oprd--*, where *oprd* is an object of class *A*, then the operator should be overloaded as a member function of class *A* and the function has an integer (*int*) as formal argument. After overloading, the expressions *oprd++* and *oprd--* is equivalent to calling function *oprd.operator++ (0)* and *oprd.oprator--(0)* respectively. Here, the integer argument does not play any useful roles. It is used to differentiate prefix ++, -- and postfix ++, --.

In UML language, the representations of overloaded operators are similar to that of other member functions, which is "*operator* operatorname (argument list): function type".

Example 8.1: Operator (add and minus) overload for complex number class as member functions.

This is an example of binary operators overloaded as member functions. The rule of addition and subtraction is to separately add and subtract the real part and imaginary part respectively. The two operands must be objects of a complex number class. So operators "+" and "-" can be overloaded as member functions. The overloaded function has only one formal argument, an object of a complex number class. In the example, the UML representation of the complex number class with operators overloading is shown in Figure 8.1.

```
//8_1.cpp
#include<iostream>
using namespace std;
class complex              //define complex number class
{
public:                    //external interface
    complex(double r=0.0,double i=0.0){real=r;imag=i;} //constructor
    complex operator + (complex c2);
                           //member function to overload operator +
    complex operator - (complex c2);
                           //member function to overload operator -
    void display();        //output the complex number
```

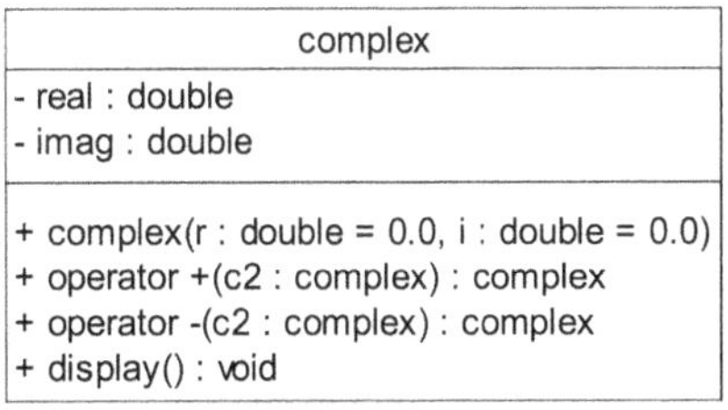

complex
- real : double - imag : double
+ complex(r : double = 0.0, i : double = 0.0) + operator +(c2 : complex) : complex + operator -(c2 : complex) : complex + display() : void

Fig. 8.1: The UML representation of a complex number class with overloaded operators "+" and "-".

```
    private:                   //private data
        double real;           //real part of a complex number
        double imag;           //imaginary part of a complex number
    };
    complex complex::operator +(complex c2)
                               //implementation of overload function


    {
        return complex(real+c2.real, imag+c2.imag);
                               //create a temporary object to return value
    }
    complex complex::operator -(complex c2)
                               //implementation of overload function
    {
        return complex(real-c2.real, imag-c2.imag);
                               //create a temporary object to return value
    }
    void complex::display()
    {
        cout<<"("<<real<<","<<imag<<")"<<endl;
    }
    int main()                 //main()
    {
        complex c1(5,4),c2(2,10),c3; //declare objects of class complex
        cout<<"c1=";c1.display();
        cout<<"c2=";c2.display();
        c3=c1-c2;              //complete complex numbers' subtraction by
                              //operator overload
        cout<<"c3=c1-c2=";
        c3.display();
        c3=c1+c2;             //complete complex numbers' addition by
                             //operator overload
        cout<<"c3=c1+c2=";
        c3.display();
    }
```

In the example, the addition and subtraction of complex numbers are overloaded as member functions of the *complex* class. We can see that operator overload member functions are almost the same as the ordinary member functions except the key word *operator* is used in the declaration and implementation. We can call the function by using the operator and operands. The original functions of operator "+" and "−" are still the same, which means for data of basic types such as floating numbers and integers, the operators still obey the predefined rules in C++, but they have new functions for operating on complex numbers. Operator "+", when acting on different objects, will have different behaviors, and hence it has polymorphic features.

In this example, temporary objects are created for returning values in the overload functions of "+" and "−":

```
return complex(c.real,c.imag);
```

This statement appears to be "calling the constructor function". In reality, this is only a temporary object syntax, which means to "create a temporary object and return it". We can also use the following statements to return the function value:

```
complex complex::operator +(complex c2)
                        //implementation of overload operator
{
    complex c(real+c2.real, imag+c2.imag);
    return c;
}
```

The efficiencies of these two methods are different. The latter execution includes the following steps. First a local object c (the constructor is called here) is created, then the copy-constructor is called when executing return statement, copy the value of c to a temporary object in *main()*. When the function operator "+" ends, the destructor is called to destroy object c. The former method is much more efficient, which creates a temporary object in *main()*.

The result of the program is:

```
c1=(5,4)
c2=(2,10)
c3=c1-c2=(3,-6)
c3=c1+c2=(7,14)
```

Example 8.2: Overload unary operator ++ as member function.
This example is to overload unary operator ++ as a member function. Here we use the example of class *Clock*. The operands of unary operator prefix ++ and postfix ++ are both objects of class *Clock*. We can overload the operator as a member function of class *Clock*. For the prefix unary operator, there is no formal argument in the overload function but for the postfix unary operator, there is an integer in the formal argument list.

```
//8_2.cpp
#include<iostream>
using namespace std;
class Clock                      //define class Clock
{
```

```
    public:                              //external interface
        Clock(int NewH=0, int NewM=0, int NewS=0);
        void ShowTime();
        Clock& operator ++();            //overload prefix unary operator
        Clock operator ++(int);          //overload postfix unary operator
    private:                             //private data
        int Hour,Minute,Second;
    };
    Clock::Clock(int NewH, int NewM, int NewS) //constructor
    {
        if(0 <= NewH && NewH < 24 && 0 <= NewM && NewM < 60 && 0 <= NewS
            && NewS < 60)
        { Hour=NewH;
            Minute=NewM;
            Second=NewS;
        }
        else
            cout<<"Time error!"<<endl;
    }
    void Clock::ShowTime()               //function to show the time
    {
        cout<<Hour<<":"<<Minute<<":"<<Second<<endl;
    }
    Clock& Clock::operator ++()          //overload function of prefix
                                         //unary operator

    {
        Second++;
        if(Second>=60)
        {
            Second=Second-60;
            Minute++;
            if(Minute>=60)
            {
                Minute=Minute-60;
                Hour++;
                Hour=Hour%24;
            }
        }
        return *this;
    }
    Clock Clock::operator ++(int)        //overload function of postfix
                                         //unary operator
```

```
{                                       //note the integer in argument list
    Clock old=*this;
    ++(*this);
    return old;
}
int main()
{
    Clock myClock(23,59,59);
    cout<<"First time output:";
    myClock.ShowTime();
   cout<<"Show myClock++:";
    (myClock++).ShowTime();
   cout<<"Show ++myClock:";
    (++myClock).ShowTime();
}
```

In the example, we overload the prefix ++ and postfix ++ for time increments as member functions of class *Clock*. The most important difference between the overloads of the prefix operator and the postfix operator is the formal arguments of the overload functions. According to the syntax, the member function of a prefix unary operator has no formal argument, while for a postfix unary operator, an integer formal argument is required. The integer argument is not used in the function body. It is only for differentiating the prefix and postfix. Therefore the argument list can contain only the type name without the argument name. The execution result of the program is as follows.

```
First time output:23:59:59
Show myClock++: 23:59:59
Show ++myClock: 0:0:1
```

8.2.3 Operator Overloaded as Friend Function

The operator can also be overloaded as a friend function of the class. Thus, it can freely access any data member of the class. Here, all the operands need to be passed by a formal argument list. The argument order from left to right in the argument list is the order of operands.

For binary operator *B*, if it has an operand that is an object of class *A*, then *B* can be overloaded as a friend function of class *A*. The function has two formal arguments and the type of one argument is class *A*. After overloading, expression *oprd1 B oprd2* is equivalent to calling function *operator B(oprd1, oprd2)*.

For prefix unary operator *U*, e.g., "–", to realize operation *U oprd*, where *oprd* is an object of class *A*, *U* can be overloaded as a friend function of class *A*. The formal argument is the object *oprd* of class *A*. After overloading, the expression *U oprd* is equivalent to calling function operator *U(oprd)*.

For postfix operators ++ and --, to realize expression *oprd++* or *oprd--*, where *oprd* is an object of class *A*, the operators can be overloaded as friend functions of class *A* and there are two formal arguments: one is object *oprd* and the other is an integer. The second argument is used to distinguish itself from prefix operators. After overloading, the expression *operd++* and *oprd--* is equivalent to calling function *operator++ (oprd, 0)* and *operator--(oprd,0)*.

Example 8.3: Overload complex operators + and – as friend functions.
In the example, operators + and – are overloaded as friend functions of class *complex* for implementing complex addition and subtraction. The problem is the same as the one in Example 8.1. Since both of the operands are complex objects, the overload function has two complex numbers as formal arguments. In the example, the UML representation of overloading operator + and – as friend functions of the class *complex* is shown in Figure 8.2.

```
//8_3.cpp
//If readers use earlier VC++ 6.0 compiler, then there will be
//compiling errors in this program
//fatal error C1001: INTERNAL COMPILER ERROR
//The reason is there is a bug in VC++6.0, in which "using namespace
//std;" cannot be written before the declaration of operator overload
//You need to download Microsoft Visual Studio 6.0 Service Pack 5 and
//install it to solve the problem.
#include<iostream>
using namespace std;
class complex                      //define class complex
{
public:                            //external interface
    complex(double r=0.0,double i=0.0){real=r;imag=i;} //constructor
```

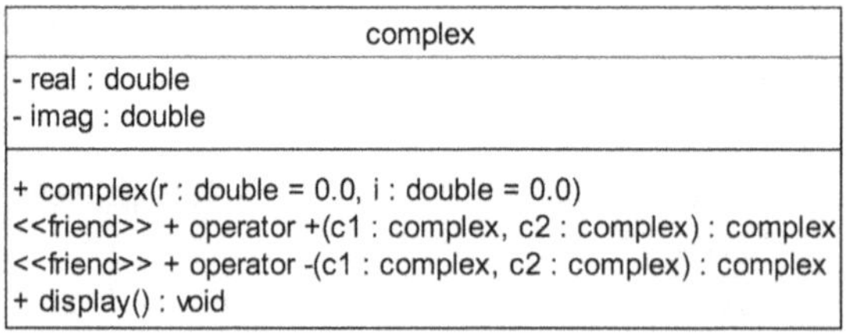

complex
- real : double - imag : double
+ complex(r : double = 0.0, i : double = 0.0) <<friend>> + operator +(c1 : complex, c2 : complex) : complex <<friend>> + operator -(c1 : complex, c2 : complex) : complex + display() : void

Fig. 8.2: The UML representation of overloading operator + and – as friend functions of the class *complex*.

```
    friend complex operator + (complex c1,complex c2);
                              //friend function for operator +
    friend complex operator - (complex c1,complex c2);
                              //friend function for operator -
    void display();           //show the value of the complex number
private:                      //private data members
    double real;
    double imag;
};                            //implementation of display function
void complex::display()
{ cout<<"("<<real<<","<<imag<<")"<<endl;}
complex operator +(complex c1,complex c2)
              //implement the friend function for operator overload
{ return complex(c2.real+c1.real,c2.imag+c1.imag);}
complex operator -(complex c1,complex c2)
              //implement the friend function for operator overload
{ return complex(c1.real-c2.real,c1.imag-c2.imag);}
int main()                    //main()
{
    complex c1(5,4),c2(2,10),c3;
    cout<<"c1=";c1.display();
    cout<<"c2=";c2.display();
    c3=c1-c2;                 //use overloaded operator
    cout<<"c3=c1-c2=";
    c3.display();
    c3=c1+c2;                 //use overloaded operator
    cout<<"c3=c1+c2=";
    c3.display();
}
```

If the operator is overloaded as a friend function, then all operands must be passed to operator overload function by formal arguments. Compared to Example 8.1, no change is made in *main()*. The change is mainly in the members of the class *complex*. The execution results are the same.

Here, we only introduce several simple operator overload. Overloading of certain operators, such as [], =, and casting is to some degree different. They are omitted in this chapter but will be introduced in Chapter 9 where the example "safe array class template" is used to demonstrate the concept.

8.3 Virtual Function

In Section 7.7, we introduced a program for a staff information management system. A problem remains unsolved from that example, i.e., how to utilize iteration to deal with different objects of the same class. To do that, we now change the *main()* in Example 7.10 into the following form and observe the outcome of the program.

```
#include<iostream>
#include"employee.h"
using namespace std;
int main()
{
    manager m1;
    technician t1;
    salesmanager sm1;
    salesman s1;
    employee *emp[4]={&m1,&t1,&sm1,&s1};
    //store the addresses of the objects in pointer array

    int i;
    for(i=0;i<4;i++)
    {
        emp[i]->pay();
            cout<< "employee number"<<emp[i]->GetindividualEmpNo()
        <<"current salary"<<emp[i]->GetaccumPay()<<endl;
    }
}
```

The execution result is:

```
employee number 1000 current salary 0
employee number 1001 current salary 0
employee number 1002 current salary 0
employee number 1003 current salary 0
```

From the execution result, function *pay()* in the derived classes is not executed. Readers can execute the program step-by-step and it will be clear that every time the base-class object pointer calls the derived-class member function, it actually calls the base-class member function instead of the new function in the derived class. Function *pay()* in the base class does not work. To solve this problem, we can use a virtual function to implement polymorphism.

Virtual functions are the basis of dynamic binding. A virtual function must be a non-static member function. After being overloaded, the virtual function can implement the execution polymorphism in a class family.

According to the type compatibility rule, we can use derived-class objects to replace base-class objects. If the base-class pointer points to a derived-class object, then we can access the object by the pointer. The problem is that what we access is the member inherited from the base class. One way to solve the problem is that if a base-class pointer points to a derived-class object, and we want to access a derived-class member whose name is the same as that of a base-class member, then the function in the base class should be declared a virtual function. By doing so, different objects of different derived classes will have different behaviors and the execution polymorphism can be realized.

8.3.1 Ordinary Virtual Function Member

The syntax for declaring a virtual member function is as follows:

```
virtual function type function name(argument list)
{
function body
}
```

The keyword *virtual* is to restrict the member function in the class definition. The declaration of a virtual function can only appear in the function prototype declaration in the class definition, but not in the implementation of the member function.

Polymorphism must satisfy three conditions during execution. The first condition is having a **compatible assignment rule** among classes. The second one is the declaration of the **virtual function**, and the third is that **the virtual function is called by a member function, pointer, or reference**. If the virtual function is accessed by an object name, then binding can be completed during compiling (static compiling), and there is no need to do it during execution.

In UML representation, an ordinary virtual function is represented by adding *<<virtual>>* in front of the member function.

Example 8.4: Virtual member function.
This program is a modified version of Example 7.4's "compatible type rule" in Chapter 7. The member function *display()* is declared virtual in base class *BO*. There is no modification to other parts. The difference between this program and the one in Example 7.4 is that the virtual member function of the derived-class object pointed by the base-class pointer can be accessed by the base-class pointer. The derivation relation is shown in Figure 8.3 in a UML representation where class *BO* has a virtual function *display()*.

```
//8_4.cpp
#include <iostream>
using namespace std;
```

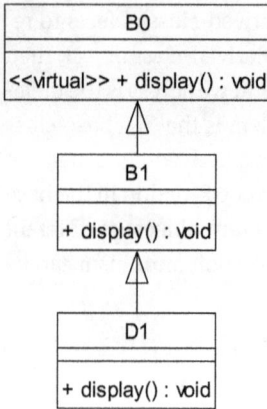

Fig. 8.3: UML of derivation relation of class *B0* with a virtual function.

```
class B0                 //define base class B0
{
public:                  //external interface
    virtual void display(){cout<<"B0::display()"<<endl;}
                         //virtual member function
};
class B1: public B0      //public derivation
{
public:
    void display(){cout<<"B1::display()"<<endl;}
                         //virtual member function
};
class D1: public B1      //public derivation
{
public:
    void display(){cout<<"D1::display()"<<endl;}
                         //virtual member function
};
void fun(B0 *ptr)        //ordinary function
{
    ptr->display();
}

int main()              //main()
{
    B0 b0,*p;           //declare base-class object and pointer
    B1 b1;              //declare derived-class object
```

```
D1 d1;                  //declare derived-class object
p=&b0;
fun(p);                 //call the member function of class B0
p=&b1;
fun(p);                 //call the member function of derived class B1
p=&d1;
fun(p);                 //call the member function of derived class D1
}
```

Class *B0*, *B1*, and *D1* belong to the same class family. They are derived in a public way so they satisfy the compatible type rule. At the same time, member function *display()* in base class *B0* is declared as virtual. The member function is accessed by an object pointer in the program, so the binding is completed in execution, thus implementing execution polymorphism. We can access the members of the pointed objects using a base-class pointer, which allows objects of the same class family to be processed uniformly. The program is more succinct and efficient. The execution result of the program is as follows:

```
B0::display()
B1::display()
D1::display()
```

In the program, the derived class does not declare the virtual function explicitly. The system will follow the following rules to judge whether a derived-class member function is virtual.
–   If the function has the same name as some base-class virtual function
–   If the function has the same number of arguments and a corresponding argument type with the base-class virtual function
–   If the function has the same return value or the same return value of the pointer and reference as the base-class virtual function, satisfying the compatible assignment rule

After examining the name, arguments, and return value, the derived class is recognized as a virtual function if it satisfies all the above conditions. Here, the virtual function of the derived class overtakes the virtual function of base class. And the virtual function of the derived class also hides all other forms of overloading by the function with the same name.

When the base-class constructor calls a virtual function, the derived-class virtual function will not be called. Suppose there is a base class *Base* and a derived class *Derived*. They both have the virtual function *virt()*. If *Base::Base()* calls virtual function *virt()*, then it is *Base::virt()* that is called, not *Derived::virt()*. This is because when the base class is constructed, the object is not a derived-class object yet.

Similarly, when the base class is destructed, the object is no longer a derived-class object. So if *Base::~Base()* calls *virt()*, then what is actually called is *Base::virt()*, not *Derived::virt()*.

Only virtual functions are bound dynamically. If the derived class needs to modify base-class behaviors (i.e., override the function with the same name), then the function should be declared virtual in the base class. Those functions that are not virtual functions cannot be modified by the derived class. They cannot become polymorphic. So, one usually should not override the nonvirtual functions inherited from the base class although the syntax does not prevent the programmer from doing so.

When the virtual function inherited from the base class is overloaded, and the function has a default formal argument value, one should never redefine different values. The reason is that the default formal argument value is bound statically, although the virtual function is bound dynamically. That is to say, the virtual function in a derived class can be accessed by a base-class pointer pointing to a derived-class object. The default formal argument value, however, can only be defined in the definition of the base class.

8.3.2 Virtual Destructor

In C++, one is not allowed to declare a virtual constructor, but it is legal to declare a virtual destructor. Destructors do not have types or arguments. Compared to ordinary member functions, destructors are simpler.

The syntax of a virtual destructor's declaration is as follows.

```
virtual~class name();
```

If the destructor of a class is a virtual one, then all child classes' destructors are all virtual destructors. After setting a destructor to be a virtual one, the pointer and reference are bound dynamically to implement execution polymorphism. And the base classes' pointer can be used to call an appropriate destructor to clean up according to different objects.

To sum up, if it is possible to call an object's destructor by a base-class pointer (by *delete*), and an object to be destructed is an object of the class that has an important overloaded destructor, then the base-class destructor should be a virtual function.

Example 8.5: Example of virtual destructor.
Note that the following program does not have a virtual destructor.

```
//8_5.cpp
#include <iostream>
using namespace std;
class Base
{
```

```
public:
    ~Base(){ cout<< "Base destructor\n";}
};

class Derived: public Base
{
public:
    Derived();
    ~Derived();
private:
    int *i_pointer;
};

Derived::Derived()
{ i_pointer=new int(0); }

Derived::~Derived()
{
    cout<< "Derived destructor\n";
    delete i_pointer;
}

void fun(Base* b)
{ delete b; }

int main()
{
    Base *b=new Derived();
    fun(b);
}
```

The output message during execution is:

```
Base destructor
```

This illustrates that it is the base-class destructor, rather than the derived-class destructor, that is called when deleting a derived-class object by a base-class pointer. So the memory dynamically allocated to derived-class objects is not freed and this causes memory leak. That is to say that the memory that *i_pointer* points to is not used or freed after the disappearance of the object. For a program that needs a large memory and long running time, it is dangerous to repeat the error. It may eventually cause insufficient memory error and the program will be terminated.

An effective way to avoid this error is to declare the destructor to be a virtual function:

```
class Base
{
public:
    virtual ~Base(){ cout<< "Base destructor\n";}
};
```

The output message during the execution is:

```
Derived destructor
Base destructor
```

In this way, the derived-class destructor is called, the dynamically allocated memory is freed properly, and the virtual function implements polymorphism.

8.4 Abstract Classes

An abstract class is a special class, which provides uniform interface to a class family. An abstract class is designed to abstract and design. The member functions can be called in a polymorphic way by abstract classes. An abstract class lies in an upper layer of classes. An abstract class cannot be instantiated, which means we cannot directly define an abstract-class object. An abstract class has to be inherited and derived from a nonabstract derived class before it can be instantiated.

An abstract class is a class with pure virtual function. To understand abstract classes, we must first learn pure virtual functions.

8.4.1 Pure Virtual Functions

In Section 7.7, a problem remains unsolved in the staff management program. The problem is that the body of base-class member function *pay()* is empty but it is necessary, though cumbersome, to include it. The question for such functions is whether we can just declare the interface in the base class for the whole class family and implement it in the derived classes. This in fact can be accomplished by using pure virtual functions in C++.

A pure virtual function is a virtual function declared in the base class. It does not declare specific operations in the base class. All the derived classes will have their own version of definition according to their needs. The syntax of a pure virtual function declaration is:

```
virtual function type function name (argument list) =0;
```

In fact, it only differs from the ordinary virtual function by a "=0" in the syntax. **After declaring a pure virtual function, the function should not be implemented in the base class but rather in the derived class.**

In UML, a pure virtual function is also called an abstract function, which is represented by adding <<*abstract*>> before the italicized function name.

Please note the difference between an empty virtual function and pure virtual function. A pure virtual function does not have a body, but the empty virtual function has an empty function body. The former is in an abstract class that cannot be initialized directly, while the latter can. The common features they share are that they both can derive new classes, they are implemented in the new class, and the implementation can be polymorphic.

8.4.2 Abstract Classes

A class with a pure virtual function is an abstract class. The primary role of an abstract class is to establish a common interface for a class family and to enhance its polymorphic characteristics. An abstract class declares a common interface for a derived class family. The implementation of the interface, i.e., the body of the pure virtual function, is to be defined by the derived class.

After the abstract class derives a new class, and the derived class has implemented all pure virtual functions, then the derived class can define its own objects and the derived class is no longer an abstract class. Also, if the derived class does not implement all pure virtual functions, then it is still an abstract class.

An abstract class cannot be instantiated. An object of an abstract class cannot be defined. We can, however, declare an abstract-class pointer and reference, by which derived-class objects can be accessed. This kind of access is polymorphic.

In UML language, the name of an abstract class is written in italics.

Example 8.6: Example of an abstract class.
This program is a modified version of the program in Example 8.4. Member function *display()* is declared to be a pure virtual function in base class *B0*, so *B0* is an abstract class and we cannot declare any objects of *B0*. We can declare pointers and references of *B0*. Class *B1* is derived publicly from *B0*, and *B1* derives class *D1* as a new base class. When a pointer of the abstract class *B0* is pointed to a derived-class object, we can access the virtual function of the object using the pointer. The UML representation of the abstract class and virtual function in this example is shown in Figure 8.4.

Source code:

```
//8_6.cpp
#include <iostream>
using namespace std;
class B0                    //define an abstract base class B0
{
```

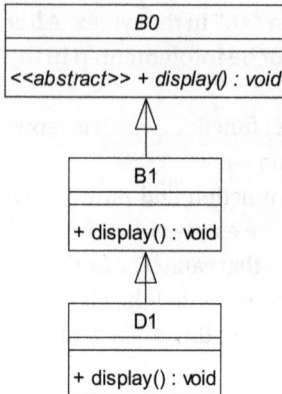

Fig. 8.4: The UML representation of the abstract class and virtual function.

```
public:                       //external interface
    virtual void display()=0; //pure virtual member function
};
class B1: public B0    //public derivation
{
public:
    void display(){cout<<"B1::display()"<<endl;}
                              //virtual member function
};
class D1: public B1    //public derivation
{
public:
    void display(){cout<<"D1::display()"<<endl;}
                              //virtual member function
};
void fun(B0 *ptr)      //ordinary function
{
    ptr->display();
}

int main()            //main()
{
    B0 *p;            //declare an abstract base class pointer
    B1 b1;            //declare a derived-class object
    D1 d1;            //declare a derived-class object
    p=&b1;
    fun(p);           //call the member function of derived class B1
    p=&d1;
    fun(p);           //call the member function of derived class D1
}
```

In this program, classes *B0*, *B1*, and *D1* belong to the same class family. Abstract class *B0* provides a general external interface for the whole class family via a pure virtual function. The child class derived by public derivation implements the pure virtual function, so it is not an abstract class and we can define derived-class objects. According to the compatible assignment rule, the abstract-class pointer of *B0* can also point to any derived classes' object. We can access the objects of derived-classes *B1* and *D1* through the pointer of base class *B0*. This is an implementation of polymorphism of uniformly processing objects in a class family. The execution result of the program is:

```
B1::display()
D1::display()
```

Note that the key word *virtual* is not indicated explicitly in the virtual function of the derived class because it has the same name, argument, and return value as the pure virtual function of the base class. The system automatically recognizes it as a virtual function.

8.5 Program Instance: Variable Stepwise Trapezoid Method to Calculate Functional Definite Integral

In many applications, definite integrals are evaluated by using numerical approximation methods. The reason is that many functions only have values at discrete points or the integrand cannot be represented by fundamental functions. In this example, we will introduce a basic variable step size trapezoid method to calculate a functional definite integral.

8.5.1 Basic Principle

We only consider the simplest situation. Suppose the integrand is a function of one variable. And the expression of definite integral is:

$$I = \int_a^b f(x)dx \tag{8.1}$$

The meaning of the integral is the area under the graph of the function $f(x)$ over the interval between a and b as shown in Figure 8.5.

If the integral is integrable for any integer n, let $h = (b - a)/n$ and

$$X_k = a + k \times h$$

$$I_k = \int_{X_{k-1}}^{X_k} f(x)dx$$

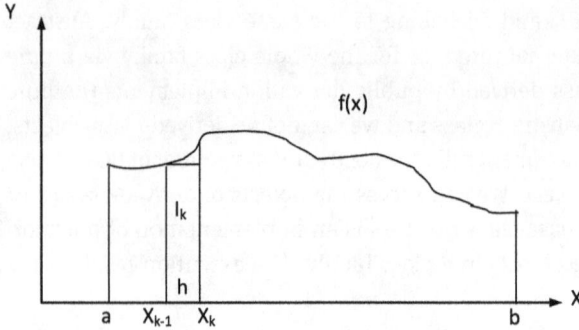

Fig. 8.5: Principle of trapezoid integral.

then we have $I = \sum_{k=1}^{n} I_k$

In the small interval $[X_{k-1}, X_k]$, we take an approximate value of I_k and calculate the approximate value of I.

In the interval $[X_{k-1}, X_k]$, let $I_k = (f(X_{k-1}) + f(X_k)) \times h/2$ for the trapezoid integral. An easy way to understand the trapezoid integral is to see that the original interval is divided into a series of small intervals and in each small interval, we approximate the integral of the original function by the area of a trapezoid. If the interval is small enough, a close approximation of the value of the original integral can be achieved. Here, the integral can be approximated by:

$$T_n = \sum_{k=0}^{n-1} \frac{h}{2}[f(x_k) + f(x_{k+1})] \tag{8.2}$$

Before applying the integral formula, an appropriate step length must be given. If the step is too big, then the precision cannot be guaranteed. Therefore, we often use a variable step size method. We apply the integral formula repeatedly and in each integration, the step size is halved. This procedure is applied until the integral result meets the precision requirement.

Dividing the integral interval $[a, b]$ into n equal intervals, we get $n + 1$ points of division. According to formula (8.2), we ought to calculate the function value $n + 1$ times. If the integral interval is halved, then the number of points of division reaches $2n + 1$. We analyze the recursive relation between these two integrals as follows:

After halving, each subinterval $[x_k, x_{k+1}]$ has one more point of division $x_{k+1/2} = (x_k + x_{k+1})/2$. So the integral value after halving is:

$$\frac{h}{4}[(f(x_k) + 2f(x_{k+\frac{1}{2}}) + f(x_{k+1})] \tag{8.3}$$

Note that here $h = (b - a)/n$ is still the step before halving. Adding each interval's integral together, we get the integral result:

$$T_{2n} = \frac{h}{4} \sum_{k=0}^{n-1} [f(x_k) + f(x_{k+1})] + \frac{h}{2} \sum_{k=0}^{n-1} f(x_{k+\frac{1}{2}}) \tag{8.4}$$

We can get the recursive formula by exploiting the integral result before halving (8.2):

$$T_{2n} = \frac{1}{2}T_n + \frac{h}{2}\sum_{k=0}^{n-1} f(x_{k+\frac{1}{2}}) \tag{8.5}$$

For practical problems, we often take the following steps:

First, let $n = 1$, apply formula (8.2) to calculate the integral value.

Second, halve and apply recursive formula (8.5) to calculate the new integral value.

Third, judge if the difference between the two integral values is within the given error tolerance, and if so, then the integral value after halving is the expected result and we can stop the integration. Otherwise, go back to the second step and continue execution.

Note that this integral method has certain restrictions on the integrand. If a function happens to be 0 on the boundaries and center, but not 0 between these points, then the results of the first and the second step are both 0. In this case, the procedure is concluded with 0 as the final result, which is obviously wrong.

8.5.2 Analysis of Program Design

From the above analysis, it is obvious that the two problems we face are: the calculation of the integrand values where we need to evaluate the function value over a very small interval at every step, and the implementation of the variable step size of a trapezoid integral.

Two abstract classes are defined: function class F and integral class $Integ$. They have virtual functions:

```
virtual double operator ()(double x) const=0;
                        //pure virtual function overload operator()
virtual double operator ()(double a,double b,double eps) const=0;
```

They are both overload operators (). The former calculates the function value at point x while the latter calculates the integral value with an error less than eps in interval [a,b]. The specific implementations are given by their derived classes. The advantage of doing so is that when the derived class offers different implementations, it can calculate different integrals using different methods (here we only use the variable step size trapezoid method, but we can also use new methods by deriving new classes). Figure 8.6 illustrates the classes we designed and their relations.

When calculating the integral, the member function in class $Trapz$ needs to access the member function in class Fun. Data member f (reference of class F) is added to class $Trapz$. According to the features of virtual functions and the rule of compatible assignments, we can access the member function in the object of the derived class of class F using the pointer.

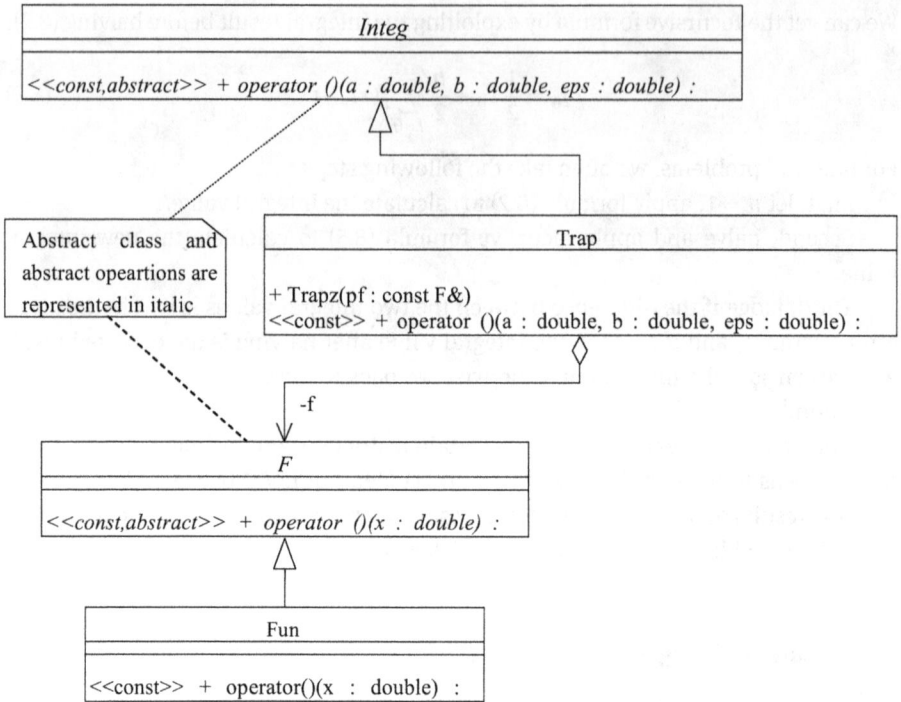

Fig. 8.6: The classes designed for the variable step size trapezoid method and their relations.

8.5.3 Source Code and Explanation

Example 8.7: Variable step size trapezoid method to calculate functional definite integral.

The program has three independent files. File *Trapzint.h* has the class definitions. File *Trapzint.cpp* includes implementations of member functions. File *intmain.cpp* includes the *main()*. The *main()* defines objects of class *Fun* and *Trapz*. We calculate the integral of a test function in a given interval using these objects, and the error *eps* is 10^{-7}.

$$I = \int_{1}^{2} \frac{\log(1 + x)}{1 + x^2} dx \tag{8.6}$$

```
//Trapzint.h file 1, definitions of classes
#include <iostream>
#include <cmath>
using namespace std;
class F                 //define abstract class F
{
```

```
public:
    virtual double operator ()(double x)const=0;
                        //pure virtual function overload operators()
};
class Fun:public F     //define public derived class Fun
{
public:
    double operator()(double x) const
                        //inline implementation of abstract class F
    {
     return log(1.0+x)/(1.0+x*x); //the integrand
    }
};
class Integ              //define abstract class Integ
{
public:
    virtual double operator ()(double a,double b,double eps) const=0;
};
class Trapz:public Integ //define public derived class Trapz
{
public:
    Trapz(const F&pf):f(pf){}     //constructor
    double operator ()(double a,  double b,double eps) const;
private:
    const F &f;         //private member, pointer of class F's objects
};
//End of file Trapzint.h
```

After public derivation, class *Fun* has all members of class *F* except the constructor and destructor. Because the base class has a pure virtual function, it is an abstract class. So the member function in the derived-class is a specific implementation of the pure virtual function in the base class. The integrand is shown in expression 8.6.

$$f(x) = \frac{\log(1 + x)}{1 + x^2} \qquad (8.7)$$

Because the member function has the same name, argument, and return value as that of the base-class function, the system recognizes it as a virtual function. So there is no need to declare it explicitly. If we calculate the integral of another function, we only need to derive a new class from base class *F*, e.g., *Fun1*, and implement the function as a pure virtual function of class *Fun1*.

After public inheritance, class *Trapz* inherits members of class *Integ*. The base class is a virtual class. The pure virtual functions are implemented in member functions in the derived class. The function in file *Trapzint.cpp* is an implementation of the variable step size trapezoid integral algorithm.

```cpp
//Trapzint.cpp, file 2, class implementation
#include "Trapzint.h"        //header file
double Trapz::operator ()(double a,double b,double eps) const
{                //the integral calculate process, overload operator ()
    int done(0);             //a virtual member function of class Trapz
    int n;
    double h,Tn,T2n;
    n=1;
    h=b-a;
    Tn=h*(f(a)+f(b))/2.0;   //calculate integral when n=1
    while(!done)
    {
        double temp(0.0);
        for(int k=0;k<n;k++)
        {
            double x=a+(k+0.5)*h;
            temp+=f(x);
        }
        T2n=(Tn+h*temp)/2.0; //variable stepwise trapezoid method
        if(fabs(T2n-Tn)<eps) done=1; //integral error
        else                     //next calculation
        {
            Tn=T2n;
            n*=2;
            h/=2;
        }
    }
    return T2n;
}
//End of file Trapzint.cpp
```

The above function calculates the integral result of integrand f in interval $[a, b]$ using the overloading operator (). The integral error is controlled by *eps*. Function f is a reference of abstract class F, whose implementation is given by derived class *Fun* and whose return value is the integral result.

```cpp
//8_7.cpp main()
#include "Trapzint.h"                //header file of class definition
#include <iomanip>
using namespace std;
```

```
int main()                      //main()
{
    Fun f;                      //declare an object of class Fun
    Trapz trapz1(f);            //declare an object of class Trapz
    cout<<"TRAPZ Int:"<<setprecision(7)<<trapz1(0,2,1e-7)<<endl;
                                //calculate and output the result
}
```

In *main()*, an object *f* of class *Fun* and an object *trapz1* of class *Trapz* are defined and *trapz1* is initialized by the object of class *Fun*. A data member of class *Trapz*, the reference of abstract class *F* becomes an alias of object *f*. A reference operation on base class *F* in object *trapz1* was performed on object *f* of class *Fun*. Through *trapz1*'s calling the overloaded operator *()*, calculation was implemented in interval [0,2] with an error of less than 1e–7.

8.5.4 Execution Result and Analysis

The execution result is:

```
TRAPZ Int:0.5548952 <
```

To calculate another function's integral, we can modify the program as follows. The new integrand should be given in class *Fun* and then point out the interval *a* and *b* and error control especially when object *trapz1* calls the overloaded operator *()*. If there are other integral algorithms, such as the variable step size Simpson algorithm, then we should derive a new class, e.g., a class named *Simpson*, and change the overload function of operator *()* to a Simpson algorithm. In main function, we also need to define a *Simpson* object.

This is a complicated example where we solve a practical problem involving almost all important aspects of object-oriented programming, such as inheritance, operator overload, abstract classes, and so on. It implements polymorphism using abstract classes. It is worthwhile for readers to carefully analyze this program and to test and run this program.

8.6 Program Instance: Improvement on Staff Information Management System for a Small Corporation

In Chapter 7, we used the staff information management system as an example to illustrate derivation, virtual functions, and virtual base classes. There are two drawbacks to the program of Example 7.10:

First, the base-class member function *pay()* is empty. It is necessary but cumbersome to implement its body.

Second, similar operations are performed on the four different objects in main() by repeating similar statements four times. This is not succinct.

In this section, we take advantage of virtual functions and abstract classes to improve the program.

The class design is the same as that in Example 7.10 of Chapter 7. The only difference is that the member function *pay()* is designed to be a pure virtual function in base class employee. Then, we can use a base-class pointer array to process different derived-class objects according to the compatible assignment rule in *main()*. This is because the system will execute the pointed object's member function when calling the virtual function using a base-class pointer.

Because different actual arguments are needed to pass the function *promote()* when called by objects of different classes, it is hard to process different objects uniformly in the iteration. So function *promote()* is declared to be a virtual function in base class *employee*. The derived classes then declare functions with the same name. The member function *promote()* in the base class is called with different formal arguments in derived classes. The derivation relation is shown in Figure 8.7.

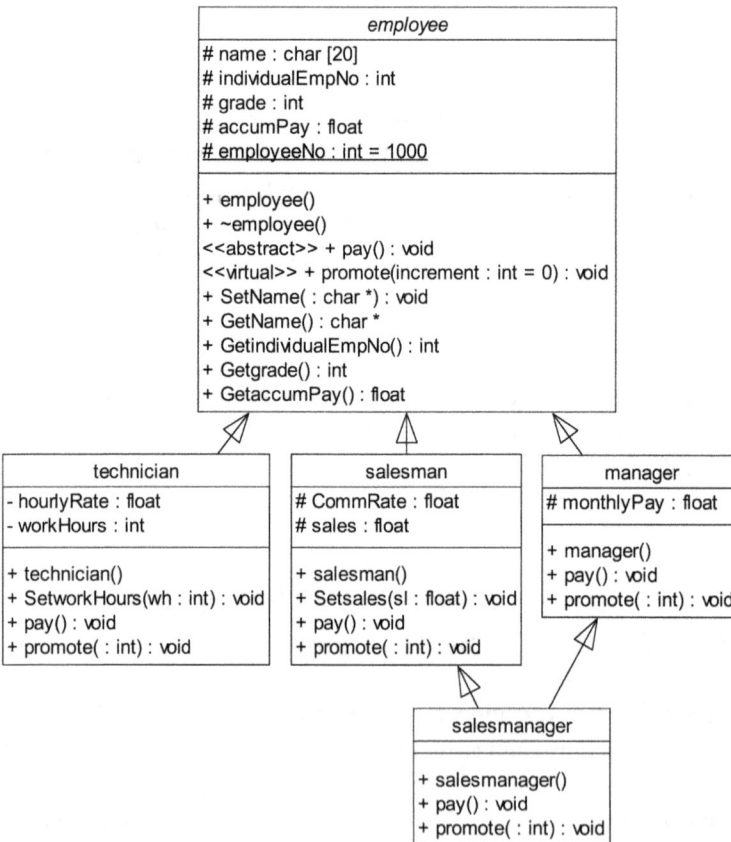

Fig. 8.7: The UML representation of the derivation relation in Example 8.8.

Example 8.8: Staff information management.

As in Example 7.10, the program has three files: *employee.h* is the header file of class definitions, *employee.cpp* is the file of class implementation, and *8_8.cpp* is the file of the main functions. File *8_8.cpp* and *employee.cpp* are linked together after compiling. These two files should be in one project if developed in VC++.

```cpp
//employee.h
class employee
{
protected:
    char name[20];                  //name
    int individualEmpNo;            //employee number
    int grade;                      //grade
    float accumPay;                 //monthly pay
    static int employeeNo;          //largest employee number in the
                                    //corporation
public:
    employee();                     //constructor
    ~employee();                    //destructor
    virtual void pay()=0;           //calculate salary (pure virtual
                                    //function)
    virtual void promote(int increment=0);
                                    //promote (virtual function)
    void SetName(char *);           //set name
    char * GetName();               //get name
    int GetindividualEmpNo();       //get employee number
    int Getgrade();                 //get grade
    float GetaccumPay();            //get salary
};

class technician:public employee //part-time technician
{
private:
    float hourlyRate;               //hourly pay
    int workHours;                  //current work hours in a month
public:
    technician();                   //constructor
    void SetworkHours(int wh);      //set work hours
    void pay();                     //calculate salary
    void promote(int);              //promote
};
```

```
class salesman:virtual public employee //part-time salesman
{
protected:
    float CommRate;                   //commission rate
    float sales;                      //current sales
public:
    salesman();                       //constructor
    void Setsales(float sl);          //set sales
    void pay();                       //calculate salary
    void promote(int);                //promote
};

class manager:virtual public employee //manager
{
protected:
    float monthlyPay;                 //fixed salary
public:
    manager();                        //constructor
    void pay();                       //calculate salary
    void promote(int);                //promote
};

class salesmanager:public manager,public salesman //sales manager
{
public:
    salesmanager();                   //constructor
    void pay();                       //calculate salary
    void promote(int);                //promote
};

//employee.cpp
#include<iostream>
#include<cstring>
#include"employee.h"
using namespace std;
int employee::employeeNo=1000;    //the basic employee number is 1000

employee::employee()
{ individualEmpNo=employeeNo++;
      //the number of new employee is one larger than current largest
number
    grade=1;                          //initial grade is 1
    accumPay=0.0;}                    //initial salary is 0
```

```
employee::~employee()
{}

void employee::promote(int increment)
{ grade+=increment; }              //promote, the increment is decided
                                   //by increment

void employee::SetName(char* names)
{ strcpy(name,names); }            //set name

char* employee::GetName()
{ return name;}                    //get name

int employee::GetindividualEmpNo()
{ return individualEmpNo;}         //set employee number

int employee::Getgrade()
{ return grade;}                   //get grade

float employee::GetaccumPay()
{ return accumPay;}                //get salary

technician::technician()
{ hourlyRate=100;}                 //hourly pay is 100

void technician::SetworkHours(int wh)
{ workHours=wh;}                   //set work hours

void technician::pay()
{ accumPay=hourlyRate*workHours;} //calculate salary by hourly pay

void technician::promote(int)
{ employee::promote(2); }     //call promote function with increment 2

salesman::salesman()
{ CommRate=0.04;}                  //commission rate is 4%

void salesman::Setsales(float sl)
{ sales=sl;}                       //set sales

void salesman::pay()
{ accumPay=sales*CommRate;}        //salary = sales commission
```

```
void salesman::promote(int)
{ employee::promote(0); }
                    //call base-class promote function with increment 0

manager::manager()
{ monthlyPay=8000;}              //fixed salary 8000

void manager::pay()
{ accumPay=monthlyPay;}          //total salary is fixed salary

void manager::promote(int )
{ employee::promote(3);}
                    //call base-class promote function with increment 3

salesmanager::salesmanager()
{ monthlyPay=5000;
   CommRate=0.005;}

void salesmanager::pay()
{ accumPay=monthlyPay+CommRate*sales; }
                        //salary = fixed salary + sales commission

void salesmanager::promote(int)
{ employee::promote(2);}
                    //call base-class promote function with increment 2

//8_8.cpp
#include<iostream>
#include<cstring>
#include"employee.h"
using namespace std;
int main()
{
    manager m1;
    technician t1;
    salesmanager sm1;
    salesman s1;
    char namestr[20];               //the input employee names are
                                    //stored in namestr

    employee *emp[4]={&m1,&t1,&sm1,&s1};
    int i;
```

```
for(i=0;i<4;i++)
{
   cout<<"Please input next employee's name:";
   cin>>namestr;
   emp[i]->SetName(namestr);   //set name for each employee
   emp[i]->promote();
    //promote, access derived-class function by base-class pointer
}
cout<<"Please input part-time technician"<<t1.GetName()<<"current
   work hours:";
int ww;
cin>>ww;
t1.SetworkHours(ww);             //set work hours

cout<<"Please input sales manager"<<sm1.GetName()<<"current sales
   in his department:";
float sl;
cin>>sl;
sm1.Setsales(sl);               //set sales
cout<<"Please input salesman"<<s1.GetName()<<"current sales:";
cin>>sl;
s1.Setsales(sl);                //set sales
for(i=0;i<4;i++)
{
   emp[i]->pay();
   //calculate salary, access derived-class function by base-class
   //pointer
   cout<<emp[i]->GetName()<<"employee number"<<emp[i]->
      GetindividualEmpNo()
    <<"grade is"<<emp[i]->Getgrade()<<",salary is"<<emp[i]->
      GetaccumPay()<<endl;
}
}
```

The execution result is:

```
Please input next employee's name:Zhang
Please input next employee's name:Wang
Please input next employee's name:Li
Please input next employee's name:Zhao
Please input part-time technician Wang current work hours:40
Please input sales manager Li current sales in his department:400000
```

```
Please input salesman Zhao current sales:40000
Zhang employee number 1000 grade is 4, salary is 8000
Wang employee number 1001 grade is 3, salary is 4000
Li employee number 1002 grade is 3, salary is 7000
Zhao employee number 1003 grade is 1, salary is 1600
```

We can see that the execution result is the same as in Example 7.10. But because base class *employee* has virtual functions, it is the derived-class member functions that are accessed when using the base-class pointer array to process objects of different classes. So we can use an iterative structure in *main()* and, in the iterations, functions of different classes are called uniformly to fulfill different actions.

8.7 Summary

We introduced an important feature of class: polymorphism. Polymorphism means that different objects behave differently when they are given the same message. It is another abstraction of member functions. The call by member functions is the 'message' and different behaviors are due to different implementations, i.e., calling different functions.

The polymorphism in C++ can be divided into four groups: overload polymorphism, coercion polymorphism, inclusion polymorphism, and argument polymorphism. The former two fall into the category of special polymorphism while the latter two are general polymorphisms. Overloads of ordinary functions and member functions belong to overload polymorphism. Overload is when a function or procedure can act on objects of different types. Coercion polymorphism converts the type of a variable by semantic operation to meet the requirement of a function or an operation. Inclusion polymorphism investigates polymorphic behaviors of member functions with the same name defined in different classes of the same class family. It is implemented by virtual functions. Argument polymorphism is related to class attributes, which are class templates that can be parameterized. The types related to the included operations must be instantiated by type arguments. Different classes instantiated by class attributes have the same operation but the types of the objects are different. This chapter mainly introduced overload and inclusion polymorphisms. Operator overload polymorphism and virtual function are key learning objectives of this chapter.

Polymorphism can be divided into two groups in terms of implementation: compiling polymorphism and executing polymorphism. For the former group, the specific operation objects are determined during compiling while for the latter group they are decided dynamically during execution. The process of determining operation objects is called 'binding.'

Operator overload makes existing operators more versatile and allows them to operate on user-defined types (such as class). Operator overload is essentially function overload. We should first convert the expression to calling an operator function. The operands are converted to arguments of the operator function. And then the function to be called is determined according to the type of the arguments, which is completed in the compilation process.

Virtual functions are nonstatic member functions declared by the keyword *virtual*. According to the compatible assignment rule, we can use base-class pointers to point to derived-class objects. If the member function of the object is an ordinary member function, then using base-class pointers, we can only access base-class members. If the function with the same name in the base class is a virtual one, then we can access derived-class functions by base-class pointers. Objects of different classes have different behaviors if they are called by base-class pointers, thus executing polymorphism.

The variable step size trapezoid method is a common method for calculating functional definite integrals. In many practical applications, the function only has values at a discrete point or the integral of the function cannot be represented by elementary functions. In these cases, definite integrals are evaluated by numerical approximation methods. In the example of the variable step size trapezoid method, the concepts of inheritance, operator overload, and derived class are applied.

An improved version of the staff information management system is included at the end of the chapter to better illustrate the effect of virtual functions.

Exercises

8.1 What is polymorphism? How is it implemented in C++?

8.2 What is an abstract class? What is its function? Does the class derived from an abstract class have to implement the pure virtual function?

8.3 Declare a virtual function with no return value, whose argument is an integer and name is *fn1*.

8.4 Can a virtual constructor be declared in C++? Why? What about a virtual destructor? What is its application?

8.5 Write four overload functions *Double(x)*. The return value is twice the input argument. The types of arguments are *int, long, float*, and *double* respectively. The type of return value is the same as that of the argument.

8.6 Write a class *Rectangle*, with data members *itsLength* (length), *itsWidth*(width) and so on. It has overloaded constructors *Rectangle()* and *Rectangle(int width, int length)*.

8.7 Write a counter class *Counter* and overload the operator +.

8.8 Write a mammal class *Mammal*, then derive the dog class *Dog* from *Mammal*. Both declare the member function *Speak()*, which is declared as a virtual function in the base class. Define an object of class *Dog*. Call function *speak* through the object, and observe the execution result.

8.9 Write an abstract class *Shape* and derive classes *Rectangle* and *Circle* from it. Both *Rectangle* and *Circle* have function *GetArea()* to calculate the area of the object and function *GetPerim()* to calculate the perimeter.

8.10 Overload operators ++ (self increment) and – (self decrement) for class *Point*.

8.11 Define a base class *BaseClass* and derive class *DerivedClass* from it. Class *Base-Class* has member functions *fn1()* and *fn2()*, and *fn1()* is a virtual function. Class *DerivedClass* also has member functions *fn1()* and *fn2()*. Define an object of *DerivedClass*. Let two pointers, a *BaseClass* pointer and a *DerivedClass* pointer, point to the object. Call *fn1()* and *fn2()* through the pointers and observer the result.

8.12 Define a base class *BaseClass* and derive class *DerivedClass* from it. Declare a virtual destructor in *BaseClass*. In *main()*, assign a *BaseClass* pointer with the address of a *DerivedClass* object. Then free the memory through the pointer and observe the result.

8.13 Define class *Point* with data members *X* and *Y*. Overload operator + as its friend function.

9 Collections and Their Organization

We have introduced basic data types and user-defined types (array, structures, etc.) in Chapters 2 and 6. Basic data types are predefined by the C++ compiler system, and user-defined data types consist of elements of base types and user-defined types. We call the data **collections**. In many cases, system-defined operations aren't enough and user-defined operations are required to deal with specific problems. A collection class can be defined by encapsulating data and operations with the object-oriented method.

There are two types of collections: linear collections and nonlinear collections. **A node in a linear collection can be specified by its position**. It is possible to determine the order of the elements in a linear collection. An array is a good example of a linear collection (as shown in Figure 9.1). **In a nonlinear collection, a node cannot be specified by its position.** For example, a tree is a nonlinear collection (as shown in Figure 9.2). This chapter will introduce several commonly used collections and their related operations.

Organizing data in a collection is of interest in the study of data structure, which is described briefly in this chapter. Two types of commonly used algorithms are introduced: sorting and searching.

Sorting is the process of ordering all elements in a collection. There are two basic operations in sorting algorithm: comparing two elements and adjusting the position of an element. In this chapter, we introduce three sorting methods: direct insertion sorting, direct selection sorting, and bubble sorting.

Searching is the process of locating a specific element in an array by following a certain procedure. Looking up a word in a dictionary is a good example of searching.

| 1st Element | 2nd Element | 3rd Element | | Last Element |

Fig. 9.1: A linear collection.

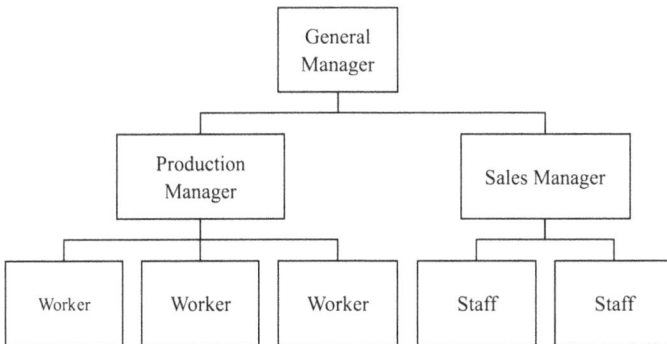

Fig. 9.2: A nonlinear collection.

https://doi.org/10.1515/9783110471977-009

In this chapter, we only introduce the two most basic searching algorithms: sequential searching and binary searching.

In this chapter, the concept of templates will be introduced, and this concept will be used to describe linear collections and the organization of collections in later chapters.

9.1 Function Templates and Class Templates

Code reuse is the most important feature in C++. Code has to be written in the most generic form in order for it to be reusable. A generic code can adapt to various data types automatically. This type of programming is called parameterized programming. C++ provides templates as a tool to support parameterized programming. By **declaring the object types as parameters, a code segment can be used for various object types.**

9.1.1 Function Template

Function overloading was introduced in Chapter 3. Function overloading can be used to perform similar actions on different data types. In many cases, the algorithm is the same but the operations are performed on different data types. Even with the help of function overloading, identical codes are often repeated many times. The following program is an example of such cases.

```
int abs(int x)
{
      return x<0 ? -x:x;
}
double abs(double x)
{
      return x<0 ? --x:x;
}
```

These two functions are identical except that the parameter types differ. In this case, a generic code can efficiently deal with both types of parameters. In C++, programmers only need to write a function template once, and then the compiler will generate corresponding functions for executing the algorithm on specific data types when the function template is called.

The definition of a function template is:

```
template <class T> Or template <typename T>
DataType FunctionName(ParameterList)
{Definition of Function Body}
```

The definition of function templates begins with the keyword *template* and is followed by a type parameter list embraced by angular brackets. Each parameter (e.g., T in the above example) specifies a data type with a leading keyword, *class* or *typename*. The parameter can be referred to as the type of function formal parameter, the type of return value, or the type of local variable. The body of a function template is similar to an ordinary function. The following is an example that calculates absolute value:

```
#include<iostream>
using namespace std;
template<typename T>
T abs(T x)
{ return x<0?-x:x;
}

int main()
{
    int n=-5;
    double d=-5.5;
    cout<<abs(n)<<endl;
    cout<<abs(d)<<endl;
}
```

The compiler infers the types of parameters in the template when it finds an invocation of *abs()*. For example, the compiler infers the type T as *int* when it tries to compile the expression *abs(n)*, in which *n* is an *int* variable.

The compiler instantiates the template after determining the types of parameters in the template and generates a new function:

```
int abs(int x)
{ return x<0?-x:x;
}
```

Similarly, the compiler infers T as *double* when it tries to compile *abs(d)*, in which *d* is a *double* variable. Then it generates the following function based on the template:

```
double abs(double x)
{ return x<0?-x:x;
}
```

Therefore, the main function actually calls the following function when the function *abs(n)* is executed

```
int abs(int x)
```

and the main function calls the function

```
double abs(double x)
```

when the function abs(d) is executed.

Example 9.1: An example of a function template.

```cpp
//9_1.cpp
#include <iostream>
using namespace std;
template< class T >//Declaration of function template
void outputArray( const T *P_array, const int count )
                                    //Definition of function body
{
   for ( int i = 0; i < count; i++ )
      cout << P_array[ i ] << " ";
   cout << endl;
}

int main()                                //main function
{
   const int aCount = 8, bCount =8, cCount = 20;
   int aArray[ aCount ] = {1, 2, 3, 4, 5,6,7,8};
                                    //Define an int array
   double bArray [ bCount ] = {1.1, 2.2, 3.3, 4.4, 5.5, 6.6, 7.7,8.8};
                                    //Define a double array
   char cArray [ cCount ] = "Welcome to see you!";
                                    //Define a char array
   cout << " a Array contains:" << endl;
   outputArray( aArray, aCount );       //Invoke the function template
   cout << " b Array contains:" << endl;
   outputArray( bArray, bCount );       //Invoke the function template
   cout << " c Array contains:" << endl;
   outputArray( cArray, cCount );       //Invoke the function template
}
```

The result from executing this program is as follows:

```
a Array contains:
1 2 3 4 5 6 7 8
b Array contains:
1.1 2.2 3.3 4.4 5.5 6.6 7.7 8.8
c Array contains:
W e l c o m e   t o   s e e   y o u !
```

The function template declares the type parameter T an abstract type. When the compiler compiles the call *outputArray*, it replaces T as the type of the first parameter in the call, then it instantiates the template and compiles the result of instantiation.

The main program defines three types of array, *aArray*(an *int* array), *bArray*(a *double* array), and *cArray*(a *char* array), whose lengths are 8, 8, and 20 respectively. The main function invokes the function template *outputArray* to print out the elements in the array. Below are the functions generated during the compilation:

```
outputArray( aArray, aCount );
                    //outputArray Template instance for int type
outputArray( bArray, bCount );
                    //outputArray Template instance for double type
outputArray( cArray, cCount );
                    //outputArray Template instance for char type
```

As shown above, function template and overloading are closely related. Functions generated from a specific template have the same function name, since the compiler invokes the corresponding function in the form of overloading. Note that there are many other ways to overload a function template.

9.1.2 Class Template

Class template allows programmers to parameterize the class and set the type of the members of the class, the parameters in class methods, and the return value of the methods to any types (including both primitive and user-defined).

A class template is a higher level of abstraction. A class is an abstraction of common properties of objects, and a class template is an abstraction of common properties of classes; thus a class template is also called a parameterized class because it needs one or more type parameters.

The form of a class template is:

```
template <TypeParameterList>
class ClassName
{ClassDefinition}
```

The declaration of template classes is nearly identical to that of ordinary classes except that the type parameter T is often used in members of template classes.

When defining class methods outside the class template, the following form should be used:

```
template < TypeParameterList>
TypeName ClassName<T>::FunctionName(ParameterList)
```

"TypeParameterList" is a list of type identifiers or constant expressions separated by commas, including:
1. **Class** (or **typename**) **Identifier**, indicating the template is able to accept a type parameter
2. **TypeName Identifier**, indicating the template is able to accept a constant with the type *TypeName*

Parameters should be separated by commas if there is more than one parameter in the list. Moreover, **member functions of a template class have to be function templates.**

The compiler does not generate codes immediately when it sees declarations of class templates, which only declare a series of classes. The compiler generates codes on demand when it figures out a template is referenced.

The form for using a template class is as follows:

```
Template<ParameterList> Object1, ...Object n;
```

Figure 9.3 demonstrates how to represent template classes in a UML graph, in which T is a formal parameter indicating the type information in the class.

The compiler generates concrete classes by binding actual types to formal type parameters, which is often called "instantiation". The UML represents the dependency of instantiation by the <<*bind*>> operation. There are two forms of showing binding elements, as in Figure 9.4:

Each parameter in the *ParameterList* corresponds to the parameter in the class template declaration. The compiler generates a class based on the constants and the types of parameter, then instantiates the class to generate an instance. That is to say, the compiler instantiates the class template to generate a concrete class and instantiates the concrete class to produce an object.

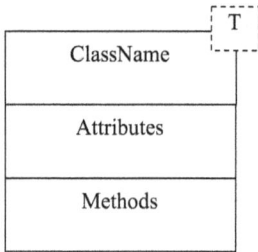

Fig. 9.3: Parameterized class with explicit attributes and methods.

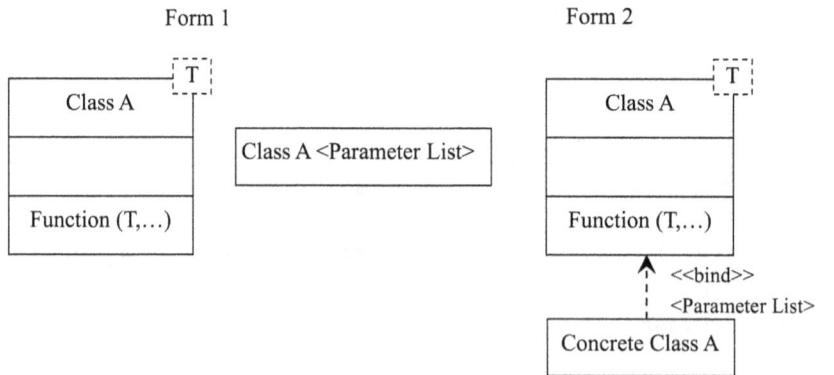

Fig. 9.4: Forms of binding elements in parameterized class.

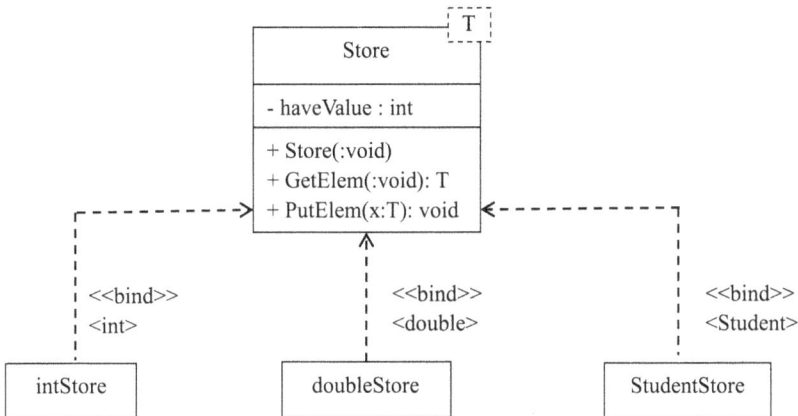

Fig. 9.5: UML of template class *Store* and concrete classes.

Example 9.2: Example of class template.
In this example, the program declares a class template *Store* to implement a wrapper to store / load data. The template is instantiated as concrete classes based on the given parameters, which are instantiated as objects S1, S2, S3, and D. However, the instantiation of the class template (as shown in Figure 9.5) is hidden. We call these concrete classes *intStore / doubleStore / StudentStore* (which do not occur in the program) in order to represent them in the UML graph.

```cpp
//9_2.cpp
#include <iostream>
#include <cstdlib>
using namespace std;

struct Student            //Structure Student
{
    int id;               //Student ID
    float gpa;            //Student GPA
};
template <class T>        //Class Template: Load/store with any data
                          //type
class Store
{
    private:
        T item;           //item is used to hold any type of data
        int haveValue;    //haveValue indicates item is holding data
                          //or not
```

```
    public:
        Store(void);        //Default constructor(no argument)

        T GetElem(void);    //Function to get data
        void PutElem(T x);  //Function to store data
};

//Implementation of member functions
/* Notice: member functions of template class must be implemented as
    template function out of the definition of class */
template <class T>          //Implementation of default constructor
Store<T>::Store(void): haveValue(0)
{}
template <class T>          //Implementation of function to get data
T Store<T>::GetElem(void)
{
    if (haveValue == 0)    //End the program if it wants to get data
                           //when there is no data
    {
        cout << "No item present!" << endl;
        exit(1);                //Exit the program and back to the
                                //operating system
            //The parameter could be used to express the reason of exit
            //to the operating system
    }
    return item;                //Return the data held in item
}
template <class T>          //Implementation of function to store data
void Store<T>::PutElem(T x)
{
    haveValue++;                //Set haveValue to non-zero, which
                                //indicates item has held data
    item = x;                   //Store x into item
}

int main()
{
    Student g= {1000, 23}; //Define a Student type variable, with
                                //initialization
    Store<int> S1, S2;      //Define 2 objects of class Store<int>,
                                //with int as data type
    Store<Student> S3;      //Define object of class Store<Student> S3,
                                //with Student as data type
```

```
    Store<double> D;      //Define object of class Store<double> D,
                          //with double as data type
    S1.PutElem(3);        //Store data into object S1(initialization)
    S2.PutElem(-7);       //Store data into object S2(initialization)
    cout<<S1.GetElem()<<" "<<S2.GetElem()<<endl; //Output data member
                                                 //of S1 and S2
    S3.PutElem(g);        //Store data into object D(initialization)
    cout <<"The student id is "<<S3.GetElem().id << endl;
                          //Output data member of S3
    cout << "Retrieving object D " ;
    cout << D.GetElem() << endl; //Output data member of D
    /* D has not been initialized, so program will be terminated
        during the routine of function D.GetElement().*/
}
```

Running result:

```
3  -7
The student id is 1000
Retrieving object D  No item present!
```

9.2 Linear Collection

9.2.1 Definition of Linear Collection

The order and the position of an element are directly related in a linear collection. There are three access methods in linear collection: direct access, sequential access, and indexed access. In this section, we only introduce direct access and sequential access.

Programmers can directly access any element in a linear collection that supports the direct access method. For instance, programmers can access any element in an array through the subscripts. But programmers can only traverse the collection to access an element in a linear collection that only supports sequential accesses.

There are two special linear collections – stacks and queues.

To introduce stacks, let's consider a pile of dishes in a restaurant: we can only grab the dish on the top, and only put a dish on the top of the pile. This is exactly what a stack does as shown in Figure 9.6. A stack is a linear collection that only can be accessed from one side. The accessible side is called the top of the stack, while the other side is called the bottom of the stack. Adding / removing elements to the top of the stack is called pushing and popping, respectively. As we can see, elements in stacks are "Last In, First Out" (LIFO).

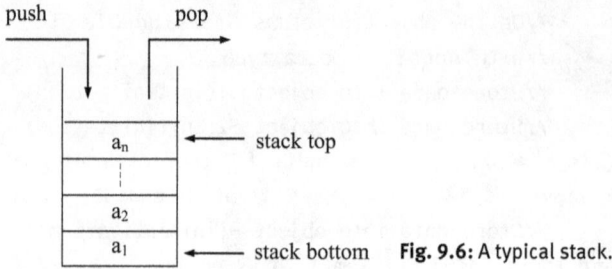

Fig. 9.6: A typical stack.

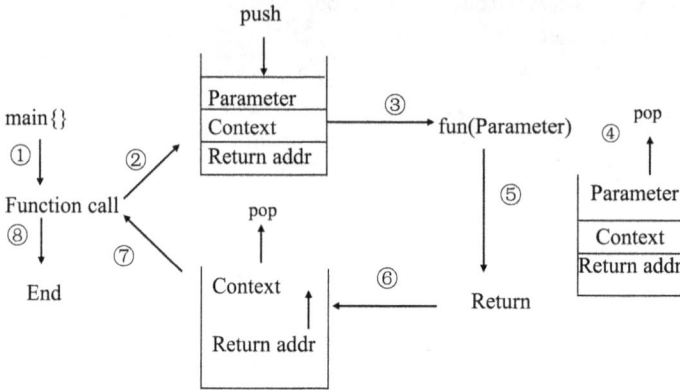

Fig. 9.7: How a stack works in a function call.

The stack is a basic and widely used linear collection in computer programs. For example, the compilation system uses stacks to implement function calls.

Programmers only need to write a simple statement to call a function in C++ and the compiler does the rest. Figure 9.7 shows how function calls are implemented. Before a function call, the compiler generates codes to push the return address, calling contexts and actual parameters into the stack. The function pops necessary information out from the stack to initialize formal parameters. Return addresses and contexts are restored from the stack when the function returns.

The compiler also parses expressions in the programs using stacks. We can see expressions such as the following one in almost all programs: $a/b+c*d$.

Let's examine how the compiler parses these expressions. The compiler establishes two stacks: an operand stack (ODS) and an operator stack (OPS) to parse them. An operand or an operator is represented by a token. Figure 9.8 shows the algorithm for parsing expressions. Figure 9.9 shows the process of parsing the expression $a/b+c*d$.

The queue is also a basic and widely used linear collection in computer programs. Elements are only added to one side (which is called the tail), and are only removed at the other side (which is called the head). Elements in the queue are served in a "First In, First Out" (FIFO) manner. Figure 9.10 shows the logical structure of a queue.

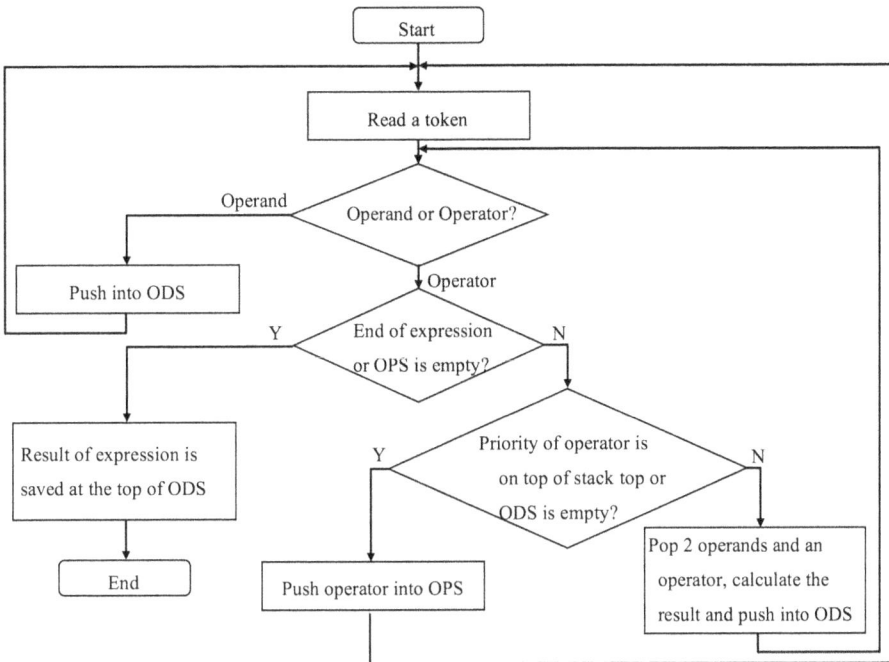

Fig. 9.8: Algorithm of parsing expressions.

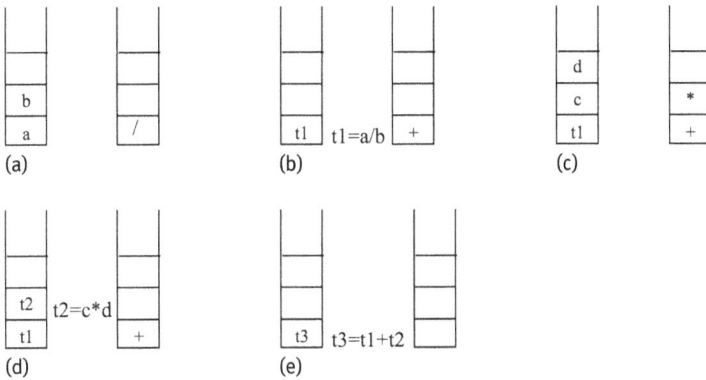

Fig. 9.9: Using a stack to parse the expression a/b+c*d.

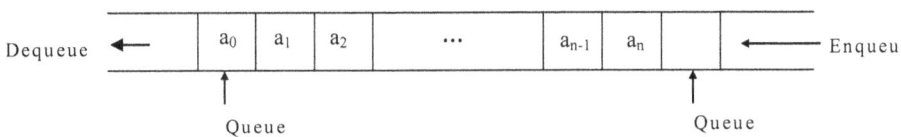

Fig. 9.10: A typical queue.

Queues are widely used in request scheduling, like processing client requests in the bank, or processing printing jobs in a computer system.

9.2.2 Direct Accessible Linear Collection – Array

Static arrays were discussed in Chapter 6. The static array has a fixed number of elements, which can be accessed directly with subscripts. It is impossible to modify the size of a static array and there is no built-in mechanism to deal with the out-of-bound problem.

Now we propose a class template *Array* to deal with these problems. *Array* contains a number of consecutive elements of the same type, and its size can be changed on demand.

Example 9.3: Class Array.
The definition and implementation of template class *Array* is in the file below:

```
//9_3.h
#ifndef ARRAY_CLASS
#define ARRAY_CLASS

#include <iostream>
#include <cstdlib>
using namespace std;

#ifndef NULL
const int NULL = 0;
#endif //NULL

//Set of errors: Array size error, Memory allocation error, Index out
//of bound error
enum ErrorType
  {invalidArraySize, memoryAllocationError, indexOutOfRange};

//Error message
char *errorMsg[] =
{
    "Invalid array size", "Memory allocation error",
    "Invalid index: "
};

//Definition of template class Array
template <class T>
class Array
```

```
{
    private:
      T* alist; //Pointer of type T, used to store memory address of
                //dynamic array
      int size; //Array size(number of elements)
      void Error(ErrorType error,int badIndex=0) const;
                            //Function to handle errors
    public:
      Array(int sz = 50);        //Constructor
      Array(const Array<T>& A); //Copy constructor
      ~Array(void);              //Deconstructor
      Array<T>& operator= (const Array<T>& rhs);
                        //Overload "=" to allow assignment of Array
      T& operator[](int i);      //Overload "[]", make Array similar
                                 //to C++ array
      operator T* (void) const; //Overload T*, make Array similar
                                 //to C++ array
      int ListSize(void) const; //Get the size of array
      void Resize(int sz);       //Set the size of array
};


//Implementation of member functions
//Template function Error implements the function of outputting error
//messages
template <class T>
void Array<T>::Error(ErrorType error, int badIndex) const
{
//Header files may be contained by many other source files, so it is
//not suitable to use the namespace std as default. In other words,
//"using namespace std;" should not appear in header files.
//In order to use identifier in namespace std, here the program uses
//"std::"
    std::cout << errorMsg[error]; //According to the error type,
                                  //output the corresponding error
                                  //message.
    if (error == indexOutOfRange)
        std::cout << badIndex;    //If the error is index out of
                                  //range, output the index which
                                  //cause the error
    std::cout << endl;
    exit(1);
}
```

```
//Constructor
template <class T>
Array<T>::Array(int sz)
{
//sz is the size of array(number of elements). If it's equal or less
//than 0, output error message
    if(sz<=0)
       Error(invalidArraySize);
    size = sz;                   //Assign the size of array to
                                 //variable size
    alist = new T[size];         //Allocate memory space for size
                                 //elements with type T
    if (alist == NULL)           //If the allocation is failed,
                                 //output error message

       Error(memoryAllocationError);
}


//Deconstructor
template <class T>
Array<T>::~Array(void)
{ delete [] alist; }


//Copy constructor
template <class T>
Array<T>::Array(const Array<T>& X)
{
    //Get the array size from object X, assign it to current object
    int n = X.size;
    size = n;
    //Check errors during memory allocation
    alist = new T[n];            //Allocate memory space for
                                 //n elements with type T
    if (alist == NULL)           //Output error message if the
                                 //allocation is failed
        Error(memoryAllocationError);
    //Copy elements of array from object X to current object
    T* srcptr = X.alist;         //X.alist is the address of array
                                 //in object X
    T* destptr = alist;          //alist is the address of array in
                                 //current object
    while (n--)                  //Copy elements one by one
```

```
        *destptr++ = *srcptr++;
}


/* Overload operator "=", assign object rhs to current object.
Implement the whole assignment between objects*/
template <class T>
Array<T>& Array<T>::operator= (const Array<T>& rhs)
{
    int n = rhs.size;              //Get the size of array in rhs
/*If the size of array in current object is different from the one
in rhs, free the existing memory and reallocate it */
    if (size != n)
    {
        delete [] alist;          //Free the existing memory of array
        alist = new T[n];         //Reallocate the memory of n elements
        if (alist == NULL)        //Output error message if the
                                  //allocation is failed
            Error(memoryAllocationError);
        size = n;                 //Save the size of array in current
                                  //object
    }
    //Copy elements from object rhs to current object
    T* destptr = alist;
    T* srcptr = rhs.alist;
     while (n--)
        *destptr++ = *srcptr++;
     return *this;                //Return the reference of current
                                  //object
}


/* Overload the index operator, make it be able to access the
elements by index like a common array, and have the function of
index check */
template <class T>
T& Array<T>::operator[] (int n)
{
    if (n < 0 || n > size-1)      //Check whether the index is out of
                                  //range
        Error(indexOutOfRange,n);
    return alist[n];              //Return the element which has an
                                  //index of n
}
```

```
/*Overload the pointer operator, convert the object of Array to a
pointer of T, which pointed to the private array of the object. Thus
it is able to use object of Array like the address of common array*/
template <class T>
Array<T>::operator T* (void) const
{
    return alist;                    //Return the private array of the
                                     //current object
}


//Get the size of array
template <class T>
int Array<T>::ListSize(void) const
{
    return size;
}


//Change the size of array to sz
template <class T>
void Array<T>::Resize(int sz)
{
    if (sz <= 0)                     //Check whether sz <= 0
        Error(invalidArraySize);
    if (sz == size)                  //If the size specified is equal to
                                     //the original size, do nothing
        return;
    T* newlist = new T[sz];          //Allocate the memory of new array
    if (newlist == NULL)             //Check whether the allocation is
                                     //succeed
        Error(memoryAllocationError);
    int n = (sz <= size) ? sz : size;
                                     //Assign the smaller one of sz and size to n
    //Copy the first n elements of the original array to the new array
    T* srcptr = alist;               //The address of the original array
                                     //alist
    T* destptr = newlist;            //The address of the new array newlist
    while (n--)                      //Copy the elements of array
        *destptr++ = *srcptr++;
    delete[] alist;                  //Free the original array
    alist = newlist;                 //Let alist pointed to the new array
    size = sz;                       //Update size
}
#endif //ARRAY_CLASS
```

Array does an out-of-bound check before accessing an element, and its size can be changed during the runtime. Programmers can use *Array* as a normal static array, since *Array* overloads the subscript operator [] and dereference operator *. Programmers can replace static arrays with *Array* to perform bounds checking during the runtime.

There are three design issues in the *Array* template: 1) Why is the copy constructor so complicated, rather than just a simple assignment? 2) Why do some functions return a reference of an object, rather than the value of the object? 3) Why does *Array* overload the type-cast pointer? The following section addresses these problems.

1. Shallow Copy vs Deep Copy

This problem was discussed in Section 6.4. Shallow copy only copies the references of elements, and not the contents of elements in *Array*. Here is an example of shallow copy:

```
template <class T>
Array<T>::Array(const Array<T>& X)
{
    size = X.size;
    alist= X.alist;
}
```

Consider the following main function:

```
int main()
{
    Array<int> A(10);
    ......
    Array<int> B(A);
    ......
}
```

Figure 9.11 shows the effects of shallow copy.

As the figure shows, the copy constructor does not copy the elements in the array, and instead, A and B share the same array. The program will generate a serious error during the execution of the destructors. Here is the destructor function in *Array*:

```
template <class T>
Array<T>::~Array(void)
{ delete [] alist; }
```

At the end of the program, the destructor will be invoked twice and free the same memory twice, once for A and once for B. This, of course, is not allowed and will certainly generate a runtime error.

The correct way of doing it is 'deep copy' as shown in the following scenario:

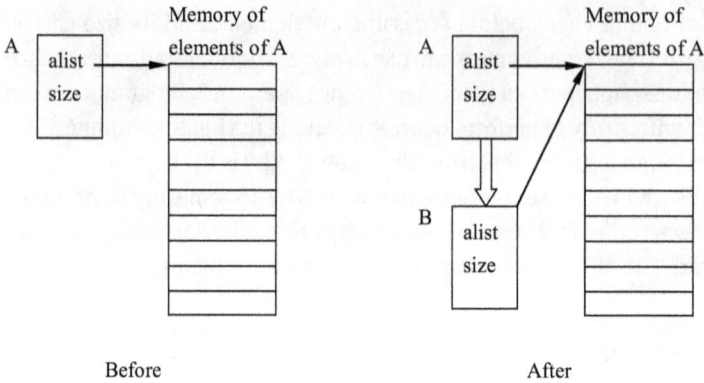

Fig. 9.11: Shallow copy.

```
template <class T>
Array<T>::Array(const Array<T>& X)
{
    //Get the size of array in object X and assign it to current
    //object
    int n = X.size;
    size = n;
    //Error check of allocation
    alist = new T[n];      //Allocate the memory of n elements with
                           //type T
    if (alist == NULL)     //Output error message if the allocation is
                           //failed
        Error(memoryAllocationError);
    //Copy elements from array in object X to current object
    T* srcptr = X.alist; //X.alist is the address of array in object X
    T* destptr = alist;  //alist is the address of array in current
                         //object
    while (n--)                //Copy elements one by one
        *destptr++ = *srcptr++;
}
```

Figure 9.12 shows the effects of deep copy. That is what we want to do.

2. Special Operators

In this example, the overloaded operator = and [] return the reference of the object instead of the value of it. Readers might wonder why it is done this way.

Notice that in a program, an arithmetic expression can be used in further computation or as the value of a variable (on the right side of an assignment operator), but it

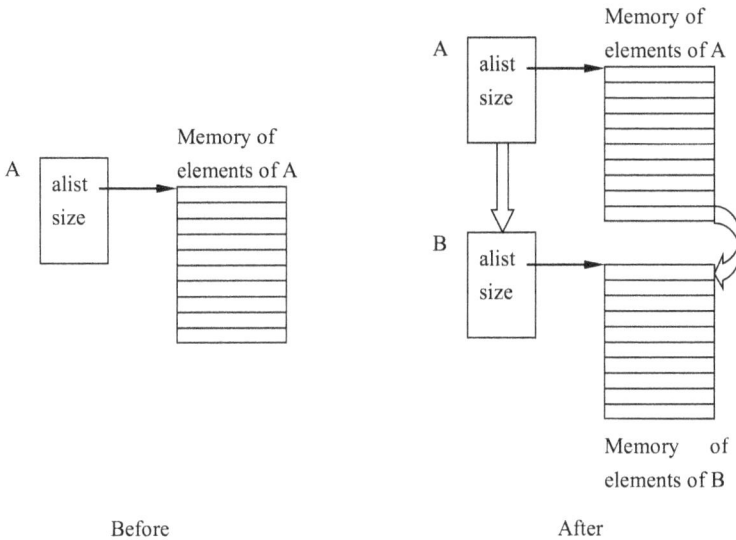

Fig. 9.12: Deep copy.

cannot be placed on the left of an assignment operator. C++ does not allow expressions like "a+b=c".

Programmers often write statements like: "a[3] = 5", in which the result of operator [] is placed on the left of the assignment operator. We call it a left value (lvalue) by convention.

As discussed above, the result of arithmetic operators should be a constant so that it cannot be used as a lvalue, but the situation differs in operator [] – it is desirable that we can write statements like "a[3]=5". That is why the operator [] returns a reference rather than a constant value.

The operator = is just a convention for compatibility. As a convention, C++ requires that the result of an assignment operator can be used as an lvalue. The following statements are valid in C++:

```
int a, b=5;
(a=b)++;
```

The value of A is 6 after running these statements.

Moreover, the syntax of C++ requires operators = / [] / () / –> to be member functions of a class, and the assignment operator is not inheritable.

3. The Type-Cast Operator
Let's consider the following program:

```
#include <iostream>
using namespace std;
```

```
int main()
{
    int a[10];
    void read(int *p, int n);
    read(a, 10);
}
void read(int *p, int n)
{
    for (int i=0; i<n; i++)
        cin>>p[i];
}
```

There is no problem in this program. Now consider replacing *a* with the *Array* class:

```
int main()
{
    Array<int> a(10);
    void read(int *p, n);
    read(a, 10);
}
```

When the compiler detected the mismatch between the type of formal parameter and actual parameter, it will try to perform a type cast, i.e., converting *a* into a variable with type *int**. However, we need to override the type-cast operator to help the compiler to cast *a* into an int* variable.

Some reader might find that the type-cast operator does not declare the type of return value. It is in fact a C++ syntax, which requires that the type of return value should not be declared (including void) for overloading a type-cast operator.

Example 9.4: An example of an array.
The problem is to find all prime numbers between 2 and *N* where *N* is provided by users during runtime.

Primes are integers greater than or equal to 2 that can only be divided by itself and 1. We have to use a dynamic array since *N* is provided at runtime. Here is the program:

```
//9_4.cpp
#include <iostream>
#include <iomanip>
#include "9_3.h"
using namespace std;

int main()
{
    Array<int> A(10);               //Array to store primes, initialized
                                    //with 10 free elements
```

```
    int n;                              //Upper bound of prime, inputted
                                        //during run time
    int primecount = 0, i, j;

    cout << "Enter a value >= 2 as upper limit for prime numbers: ";
    cin >> n;

    A[primecount++] = 2;                //2 is a prime
    for(i = 3; i < n; i++)
    {
        //If the prime table is full, acquire 10 more free elements
        if (primecount == A.ListSize())
            A.Resize(primecount + 10);
        //Skip evens greater than 2, none of them is prime
        if (i % 2 == 0)
            continue;
        //Check whether 3,5,7,..., i/2 is a factor of i
        j = 3;
        while (j <= i/2 && i % j != 0)
            j += 2;
        //If none of them is a factor of i, i is a prime
        if (j > i/2)
            A[primecount++] = i;
    }
    for (i = 0; i < primecount; i++) //Output primes
    {
        cout << setw(5) << A[i];
        if ((i+1) % 10 == 0)        //Start a new line after every
                                    //10 primes
            cout << endl;
    }
    cout << endl;
}
```

Running result:

```
Enter a value >= 2 as the upper limit for prime numbers: 100
  2   3   5   7  11  13  17  19  23  29
 31  37  41  43  47  53  59  61  67  71
 73  79  83  89  97
```

9.2.3 Sequential Access Collection – Linked List

A linked list is another linear collection and it is used as an example of a sequential access collection. A linked list consists of a number of nodes, which are generated at runtime. There are two fields in each node: a payload and a pointer pointing to the next node. If a node has one field pointing to the next node, the list is called a single linked list. If a node has two fields connecting to other nodes, one pointing to its previous node and the other pointing to its next node, then the list is called a double linked list. Figure 9.13 is an example of a single linked list.

1. Node Class

The node, the basic component of a linked list, consists of a data member and a pointer pointing to the next node. It should also contain methods to initialize the node, to remove the node, or to add a new node into the list. Figure 9.14 and Figure 9.15 show the procedure of adding and removing nodes. Example 9.5 is the node template class.

Example 9.5: Node template class.
Source code:

```
//9_5.h
#ifndef NODE_CLASS
#define NODE_CLASS
```

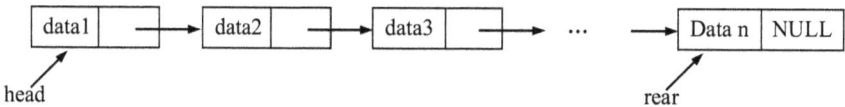

Fig. 9.13: A typical single linked list.

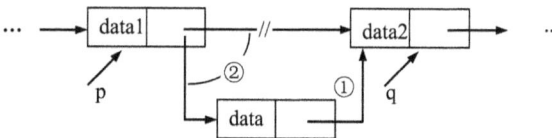

Fig. 9.14: Insert a node after *p*.

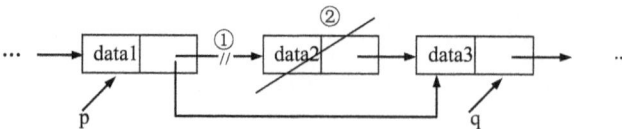

Fig. 9.15: Delete a node after *p*.

```
//Definition of class
template <class T>
class Node
{
    private:
        Node<T> *next;     //Point to the next node
    public:

        T data;            //Data area
        Node (const T& item, Node<T>* ptrnext = NULL);
                           //Constructor
        void InsertAfter(Node<T> *p); //Insert node p after self
        Node<T> *DeleteAfter(void);
                           //Delete the next node, return its address
        Node<T> *NextNode(void) const; //Get pointer of the next node
};


//Implementation of class
//Constructor, initialize data and pointer member
template <class T>
Node<T>::Node(const T& item, Node<T>* ptrnext) : data(item),
    next(ptrnext)
{}


//Return the pointer of next node
template <class T>
Node<T> *Node<T>::NextNode(void) const
{ return next; }


//Insert node p after self
template <class T>
void Node<T>::InsertAfter(Node<T> *p)
{
    p->next = next;        //Assign pointer of p the next node of self
    next = p;              //Let p be the next node
}


//Delete the next node and return its address
template <class T>
Node<T> *Node<T>::DeleteAfter(void)
{
Node<T> *tempPtr = next;
    //Save the address of the node which is about to delete to tempPtr
```

```
        if (next == NULL)      //If the next node is not exist, return NULL
            return NULL;
        next = tempPtr->next;//Let the next node of tempPtr be next node
                             //of self
        return tempPtr;        //Return the address of deleted node
    }


    #endif //NODE_CLASS
```

2. Linked List Class Template

Many applications use linked lists. It is beneficial to abstract common linked list operations, like creating or removing nodes, and traversing through a linked list in an object-oriented manner.

a) Data Member of Linked List

A sequence of nodes linking sequentially makes a linked list. All operations of a linked list start from its head node. It is essential to have a pointer pointing to the head node in the linked list class, and a pointer for the last node is also valuable information to the program.

The linked list class needs to manage the nodes at runtime since it is a dynamic data structure.

The traversal operation requires two pointers, one pointing to the current visiting node, and the other pointing to the predecessor. Both inserting and deleting nodes use the pointer of predecessor.

Therefore, the linked list class needs to manage these data:
- Pointer to the head node
- Pointer to the last node
- The number of nodes
- Current position of traversal

b) Methods of a Linked List Class

The linked list class should provide these primitives:
- Creating a node
- Inserting a node into the list
- Removing a node
- Access and modification of the data of a node
- Traversal

All of them should be wrapped into the methods of the class. The linked list class also overloads the "=" operator to behave correctly in assignments.

The declaration of the linked list class is shown in Example 9.6. The implementation is left as an exercise.

Example 9.6: The declaration of the linked list class.

```
//9_6.h
#ifndef LINKEDLIST_CLASS
#define LINKEDLIST_CLASS
#include <iostream>
#include <cstdlib>
using namespace std;

#ifndef NULL
const int NULL = 0;
#endif //NULL

#include "9_5.h"

template <class T>
class LinkedList
{
   private:
   //Data members:
     Node<T> *front, *rear;     //Pointer of list head and list tail
     Node<T> *prevPtr, *currPtr; //Pointer of current position, will
                                 //be updated by insertion and deletion
     int size;                   //Number of elements in the list
     int position;               //Index of current element, used by
                                 //function Reset

   //Function members:
   //Generate a new node, the data is assigned to item and the
   //pointer is assigned to ptrNext
     Node<T> *GetNode(const T& item,Node<T> *ptrNext=NULL);

     //Release a node
     void FreeNode(Node<T> *p);

     //Copy linked list L to current list(assume that the current list
     //is empty)
     //Will be called by constructor and operator =
     void CopyList(const LinkedList<T>& L);
   public:
     LinkedList(void);            //Constructor
     LinkedList(const LinkedList<T>& L); //Copy constructor
     ~LinkedList(void);           //Deconstructor
```

```
        LinkedList<T>& operator= (const LinkedList<T>& L);
                              //Overload operator "="


    int ListSize(void) const; //Return the number of elements in the
                              //list(size)
    int ListEmpty(void) const; //Return TRUE when size is equal to 0,
                              //otherwise return FALSE


    void Reset(int pos = 0);    //Move pointer currPtr to the element
                                //whose index is pos, prevPtr changes
                                //relatively position records the index
                                //of current node
    void Next(void);            //Let prevPtr and currPtr move to
                                //next node
    int EndOfList(void) const; //Return TRUE when currPtr is equal
                                //to NULL, otherwise return FALSE
     int CurrentPosition(void) const; //Return data member position


    void InsertFront(const T& item); //Insert node at list head
    void InsertRear(const T& item);  //Insert node at list tail
    void InsertAt(const T& item); //Insert node before current node
    void InsertAfter(const T& item); //Insert node after current node


    T DeleteFront(void);        //Delete the list head
    void DeleteAt(void);        //Delete current node


    T& Data(void);              //Return the reference of data member
                                //of current node(let the data member
                                //able to be accessed or modified)


    //Clear the linked list: release the memory space of every node.
    //Will be called by deconstructor and operator =
    void ClearList(void);
};
#endif //LINKEDLIST_CLASS
```

3. Application

Example 9.7: Application of a linked list.

This program is to perform the following operations: get 10 integers from the keyboard; create a linked list whose nodes hold these integers, and output the numbers in order.

Then get another number from the keyboard, delete all nodes containing the number and output the data in the linked list, lastly clearing the linked list before exiting.

```cpp
//9_7.cpp
#include <iostream>
#include "9_6.h"
#include "9_6.cpp"
using namespace std;

int main()
{
    LinkedList<int> Link;
    int i, key, item;
    //Input 10 integers and insert them to the head of list one by one
    for (i=0;i < 10;i++)
    {
        cin>>item;
        Link.InsertFront(item);
    }
    //Output the linked list
    cout << "List: ";
    Link.Reset();
    //Output data of every node, until the end of the linked list
    while(!Link.EndOfList())
    {
        cout <<Link.Data() << " ";
        Link.Next(); //Let currPtr pointed to the next node
    }
    cout << endl;

    //Input the number to delete
    cout << "Please input the number to delete: ";
    cin >> key;

    //Find and delete the node
    Link.Reset();
    while (!Link.EndOfList())
    {
     if(Link.Data() == key)
        Link.DeleteAt();
     Link.Next();
    }
```

```
        //Output the linked list
        cout << "List: ";
        Link.Reset();
        //Output data of every node, until the end of the linked list
        while(!Link.EndOfList())
        {
            cout <<Link.Data() << " ";
            Link.Next(); //Let currPtr pointed to the next node
        }
        cout << endl;
}
```

Running result:

```
3 6 5 7 5 2 4 5 9 10
List: 10 9 5 4 2 5 7 5 6 3
Please input the number to delete: 5
List: 10 9 4 2 7 6 3
```

9.2.4 Stack

As mentioned in 9.2.1, a stack is a special linear collection with restricted access. It is possible to implement stacks in arrays or linked lists. However, the access pattern of a stack is a restricted one, so we need a different interface for the stack class.

In order to represent the states of a stack, the stack class should contain data elements and the pointer to the top of the stack. There are two types of implementation: one is based on arrays (either static or dynamic) and the other is based on linked lists.

There are three states of a stack: normal, empty and full. A stack is full when the number of elements reaches the number in the declaration. In the implementation based on dynamic arrays or linked lists, it is possible to set the number as unlimited.

A stack should provide interfaces of these operations:
- Initialization
- Push data into the stack
- Pop data out of the stack
- Clear the stack
- Access the top of the stack
- State detection

Figure 9.16 shows a stack implemented via arrays.

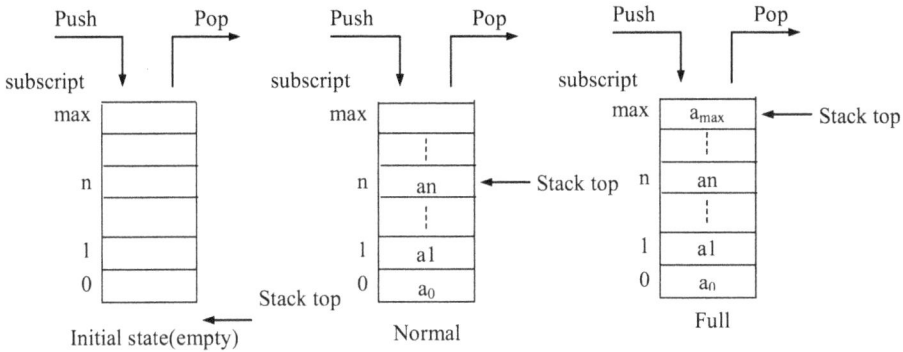

Fig. 9.16: Stack implemented via array.

Example 9.8: Implementation of stack.

```
//9_8.h
#ifndef STACK_CLASS
#define STACK_CLASS
#include <iostream>
#include <cstdlib>
using namespace std;

const int MaxStackSize = 50;        //Size of the stack, the maximum
                                    //number of elements in the stack

//Definition of class
template <class T>
class Stack
{
    private:
        T stacklist[MaxStackSize]; //The array used to store elements
                                    //of the stack
        int top;                   //Position of stack top(index)
    public:
        Stack (void);               //Constructor, initialize the stack
        void Push (const T& item); //Push the element item
        T Pop (void);               //Pop the element on stack top
        void ClearStack(void);      //Clear the stack
        T Peek (void) const;        //Access the element on stack top

        int StackEmpty(void) const; //Test whether the stack is empty
        int StackFull(void) const; //Test whether the stack is full
};
```

```cpp
//Implementation of class
template <class T>
Stack<T>::Stack (void) : top(-1)   //Constructor, stack top is
                                   //initialized to -1


template <class T>
void Stack<T>::Push (const T& item)
                                   //Push the element item in the stack
{
    if (top == MaxStackSize-1)     //Terminate the program if the
                                   //stack is full
    {
        std::cerr << "Stack overflow!" << endl;
        exit(1);
    }
    top++;                         //Increase the pointer of stack top by 1
    stacklist[top] = item;         //Push the new element to stack top
}


template <class T>
T Stack<T>::Pop (void)             //Pop the element on stack top
{
    T temp;
    if (top == -1)                 //Terminate the program if the stack is empty
    {
        std::cerr << "Attempt to pop an empty stack!" << endl;
        exit(1);
    }
    temp = stacklist[top];         //Get the element on stack top
    top--;                         //Decrease the pointer of stack top
    return temp;                   //Return the element on stack top
}
template <class T>
T Stack<T>::Peek (void) const      //Access the element on stack top
{
    if (top == -1)                 //Terminate the program if the stack is empty
    {
        std::cerr << "Attempt to peek at an empty stack!" << endl;
        exit(1);
    }
    return stacklist[top];         //Return the element at stack top
}
```

```
template <class T>
int Stack<T>::StackEmpty(void) const //Test whether the stack is empty
{ return top == -1; }                //return TRUE if stack is empty,
                                     //otherwise return FALSE
template <class T>
int Stack<T>::StackFull(void) const //Test whether the stack is full
{ return top == MaxStackSize-1; } //return TRUE if stack is full,
                                     //otherwise return FALSE


template <class T>
void Stack<T>::ClearStack(void)    //Clear the stack
{ top = -1; }


#endif //STACK_CLASS
```

The example shows how to implement a stack in arrays. It is also possible to implement a stack in a linked list, which is left as an exercise.

Example 9.9: Application of stacks – a simple calculator.
In this example, we implement a simple calculator that is capable of addition, subtraction, multiplication, and powers. The input expressions are in suffix form, with each operand and operator separated by a space. For example, the user should input "3 5 +" in order to calculate the value of "3+5". The power operator is "^". Each calculation is based on the previous result. "c" means clear the result and "q" means exit.

In 9.2.1, we introduced how to use stacks to evaluate an expression. A calculator needs two stacks, one for operands and one for operators to calculate complex expressions. However, the simple calculator can only use one stack to store the operands since it does not need to deal with the precedence of operators.

The main operation of the program is:
- When the input is an operand, push it into the stack.
- When the input is an operator, pop two operands out of the stack, calculate the result and push the result back to the stack
- When the input is "c", clear the stack
- When the input is "q", clean up and exit the program.

We implement a calculator class to model all operations stated above.

```
//9_9.h
#include <iostream>
#include <cmath>
#include <cstdlib>
#include <cstring>

using namespace std;
```

```
enum Boolean {False, True};
#include "9_8.h"                //Include the header file of template
                               //class stack
class Calculator               //Class calculator
{
    private:
        Stack<int> S;                  //Stack of operands
        void Enter(int num);           //Push operand num into the stack
        //Pop 2 operands out of stack, store them into opnd1 and opnd2
        Boolean GetTwoOperands(int& opnd1, int& opnd2);
        void Compute(char op);     //Commit calculation of operator op
    public:
        Calculator(void);              //Constructor
        void Run(void);                //Run the calculator
        void Clear(void);              //Clear the stack of operands
};
```

```
void Calculator::Enter(int num) //Push operand num into the stack
{ S.Push(num); }
```

```
//Pop 2 operands out of stack, store them into opnd1 and opnd2
//If the stack does not contain enough operands, return False and
//output the message
Boolean Calculator::GetTwoOperands(int& opnd1, int& opnd2)
{
    if (S.StackEmpty())            //Check whether the stack is empty
    {
        cerr << "Missing operand!" << endl;
        return False;
    }
    opnd1 = S.Pop();               //Pop the right operand
    if (S.StackEmpty())            //Check whether the stack is empty
    {
        cerr << "Missing operand!" << endl;
        return False;
    }
    opnd2 = S.Pop();               //Pop the right operand
    return True;
}
```

```
void Calculator::Compute(char op) //Commit calculation
```

```
{
    Boolean result;
    int operand1, operand2;
    result = GetTwoOperands(operand1, operand2); //Pop 2 operands
    if (result == True)          //If succeed, commit the calculation
                                 //and push the result to the stack
    {
        switch(op)
        {
            case '+': S.Push(operand2+operand1);
                    break;
            case '-': S.Push(operand2-operand1);
                    break;
            case '*': S.Push(operand2*operand1);
                    break;
            case '/': if (operand1 == 0)
                                //Check whether the divisor is 0
                        {
                            cerr << "Divide by 0!" << endl;
                            S.ClearStack();
                                //Clear the stack if the divisor is 0
                        }
                        else
                            S.Push(operand2/operand1);
                        break;
            case '^': S.Push(pow(operand2,operand1));
                    break;
        }
        cout<<'='<<S.Peek()<<' '; //Output the result of calculation
    }
    else
        S.ClearStack();          //No enough operands, clear the stack
}

Calculator::Calculator(void)     //Constructor
{}

void Calculator::Run(void)       //Read and process a postfix notation
{
    char c[20];

    while(cin >> c, *c != 'q')   //Read an expression end with 'q'
```

```
        switch(*c)
        {
          case 'c': S.ClearStack();
                           //Clear the stack of operands when 'c' occurs
                    break;
          case '-':     //Judge a '-' is a minus or a subtraction sign
                    if (strlen(c)>1)
                                     //If the length of string is larger
                                     //than 1, the '-' is a minus
                      Enter(atoi(c));
                                     //Convert the string to an integer
                                     //and push it into the stack
                    else
                      Compute(*c);//Commit calculation if the '-' is a
                                  //subtraction sign
                    break;
          case '+':                  //Other operator occurs
          case '*':
          case '/':
          case '^':
                    Compute(*c);  //Commit calculation
                    break;
          default:                   //If the string is an operand,
                                     //convert it to an integer and push
                                     //it into the stack
                    Enter(atoi(c));
                    break;
        }
}


void Calculator::Clear(void)      //Clear the stack of operands
{ S.ClearStack(); }


//9_9.cpp
#include "9_9.h"
int main()
{
    Calculator CALC;
    CALC.Run();
}
```

Running result:

```
10 20 +
=30 15 /
=2 c
2 8 *
=16 2 ^
=256 c
4 +
Missing operand!
4 6 +
=10 q
```

9.2.5 Queues

Similar to stacks, queues are also linear collections with a restricted access pattern. We can only add elements on one side (head), and only remove elements on the other side (tail). It is also possible to implement queues in both arrays and linked lists. The definition of the status of a queue is similar to the one for stacks.

A queue should provide a queue element, head pointer, and tail pointer as data members, and it also needs to provide the interfaces of these operations:
- Initialization
- Enqueue / dequeue
- Clear the stack
- Access the head of the queue
- State detection

Figure 9.17 shows a trivial implementation in static arrays. We can see all elements must be moved towards the head of the queue when dequeuing an element, which is very inefficient.

A clever way to design a queue is to make it a circular one. The idea is shown in Figure 9.18. The queue maintains two pointers pointing to the head and the tail of the queue respectively. The queue changes these pointers when enqueuing and dequeuing elements. The important part is to use a modular operation to wrap the queue, ensuring the pointers are reset to zero when they cross the boundary. The queue also needs to count the elements. Example 9.10 is an implementation using this method.

Example 9.10: Implementation of queues.

```
//9_10.h
#ifndef QUEUE_CLASS
#define QUEUE_CLASS
```

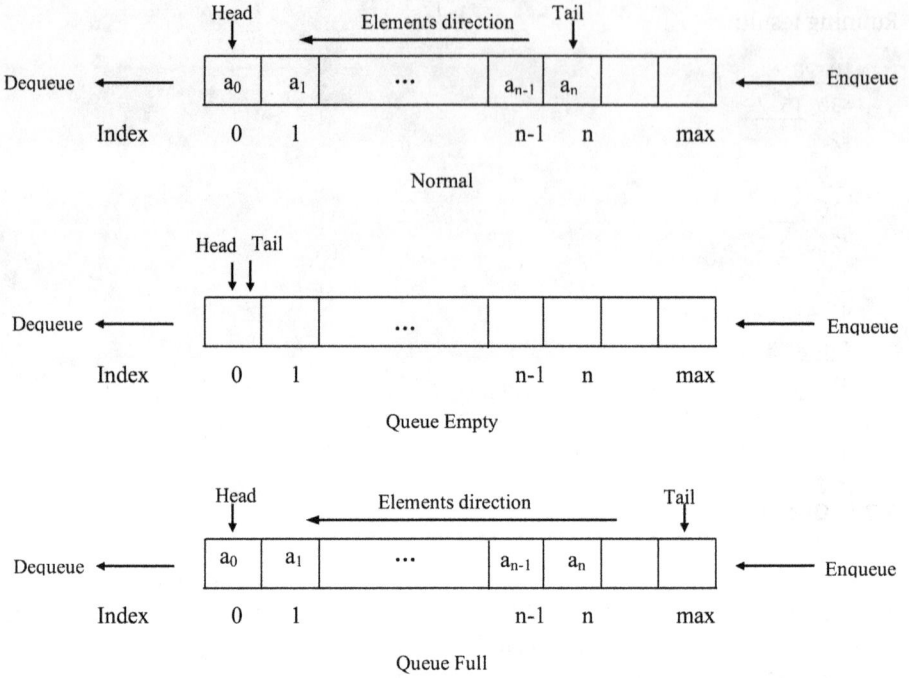

Fig. 9.17: States of a queue.

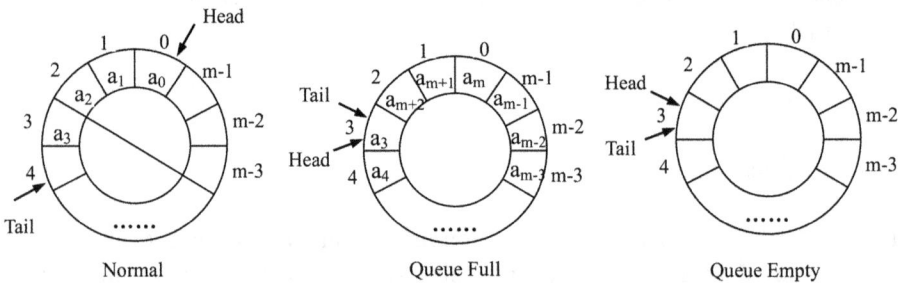

Fig. 9.18: States of a circular queue.

```
#include <iostream>
#include <cstdlib>
using namespace std;

const int MaxQSize = 50;          //Maximum elements in queue

//Definition of class
template <class T>
class Queue
```

```
{
    private:
        int front, rear, count;  //Pointer of queue head and tail,
                                  //number of elements
        T qlist[MaxQSize];        //Array of elements of queue

    public:
        Queue (void);             //Constructor, initialize queue head,
                                  //tail and number of elements
        void QInsert(const T& item); //Enqueue new element
        T QDelete(void);          //Dequeue element
        void ClearQueue(void);    //Clear the queue

        T QFront(void) const;     //Get the element of queue head

        //Test the status of queue
        int QLength(void) const;  //Get the length of queue
                                  //(number of elements)
        int QEmpty(void) const;   //Check whether queue is empty
        int QFull(void) const;    //Check whether queue is full
};

//Constructor, initialize queue head, tail and number of elements
template <class T>
Queue<T>::Queue (void) : front(0), rear(0), count(0)
{}

template <class T>
void Queue<T>::QInsert (const T& item)
                        //Insert element to the queue tail(enqueue)
{
    if (count == MaxQSize) //Terminate the program if queue is full
    {
        std::cerr << "Queue overflow!" << endl;
        exit(1);
    }
    count++;                     //Increase the number of elements
    qlist[rear] = item;          //Insert the element to queue tail
    rear = (rear+1) % MaxQSize;  //Increase the pointer of queue tail
                                 //by 1, implement circular queue by
                                 //reminder
}
```

```
template <class T>
T Queue<T>::QDelete(void)            //Delete the queue head, return its
                                     //value(Dequeue)
{
    T temp;
    if (count == 0)            //Terminate the program if queue is empty
    {
        std::cerr << "Deleting from an empty queue!" << endl;
        exit(1);
    }
    temp = qlist[front];            //Save the value of queue head
    count--;                        //Decrease the number of elements
    front = (front+1) % MaxQSize; //Increase the pointer of queue head
                                    //by 1, implement circular queue by
                                    //reminder
    return temp;                    //Return the value of queue head
}


template <class T>
T Queue<T>::QFront(void) const    //Return the value of queue head
{ return qlist[front]; }


template <class T>
int Queue<T>::QLength(void) const //Return the number of elements
{ return count; }


template <class T>
int Queue<T>::QEmpty(void) const //Check whether the queue is empty
{ return count == 0; }           //Return the boolean value of count ==0


template <class T>
int Queue<T>::QFull(void) const //Check whether the queue is full
{ return count == MaxQSize; }
                        //Return the boolean value of count == MaxQSize


template <class T>
void Queue<T>::ClearQueue(void) //Clear the queue
{
    count = 0;
    front = 0;
    rear = 0;
}
```

```
#endif //QUEUE_CLASS
```

Implementing queues via linked list is also left as an exercise.

9.3 Organizing Data in Linear Collections

In this section, we discuss how to organize data in linear collections, introducing how to sort collections and find a particular element in a collection.

9.3.1 Insertion Sort

The basic idea of insertion sort is to insert one unsorted element at a time into the correct position (in the sorted subcollection) until the collection is completely sorted. For example, if we need to sort an *n*-element array *a*, we can consider *a[0]* a sorted subcollection and *a[1:n−1]* as the subcollection to be sorted. The procedure is shown in Figure 9.19. There are some variants of the algorithm using different ways to find the position in which to insert the element. Here we only introduce the simplest one, the direct insertion sort.

Example 9.11: Implementation of direct insertion sort.

```
//9_11.h
#ifndef ARRAY_BASED_SORTING_FUNCTIONS
#define ARRAY_BASED_SORTING_FUNCTIONS

//Use direct insertion sort to sort the n elements in array A
template <class T>
```

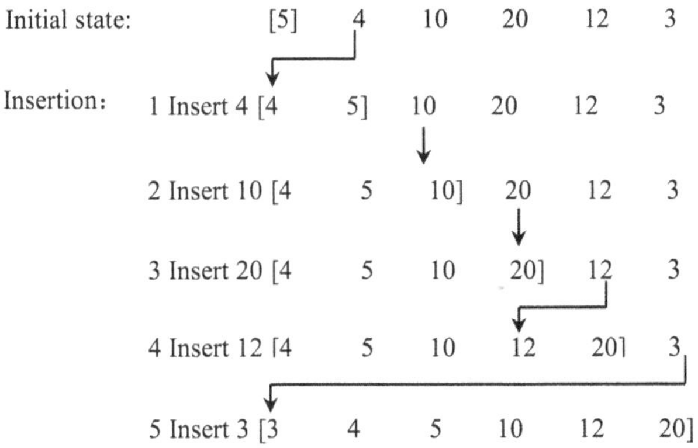

```
Initial state:           [5]    4     10    20    12    3

Insertion:    1 Insert 4 [4      5]    10    20    12    3

              2 Insert 10 [4     5     10]   20    12    3

              3 Insert 20 [4     5     10    20]   12    3

              4 Insert 12 [4     5     10    12    20]   3

              5 Insert 3 [3      4     5     10    12    20]
```

Fig. 9.19: Procedure of insertion sort.

```
void InsertionSort(T A[], int n)
{
    int i, j;
    T temp;

    //Insert the elements with index 1~n-1 to the appropriate position
    //in the sorted sequence
    for (i = 1; i < n; i++)
    {
        //Scan elements from A[i-1] to A[0], find the appropriate
        //position to insert A[i]
        j = i;
        temp = A[i];
        while (j > 0 && temp < A[j-1])
        { //Compare them one by one until temp>=A[j-1], j is the
          //position to insert
          //If j==0, 0 is the appropriate position
            A[j] = A[j-1];   //Move elements forward one by one, make it
                             //possible to insert immediately when the
                             //appropriate is found

            j--;
        }
        //The position is found, insert immediately
        A[j] = temp;
    }
}
#endif
```

9.3.2 Selection Sort

The basic idea of the selection sort is to select the minimum element in the subcollection to be sorted and put it at the end of the sorted subcollection. There are also some variants of it based on different ways to find the minimum element. The simplest one is to scan through the collection, which is the so-called direct selection sort as shown in Figure 9.20.

Example 9.12: Implementation of direct selection sort.

```
//9_12.h
#ifndef ARRAY_BASED_SORTING_FUNCTIONS
#define ARRAY_BASED_SORTING_FUNCTIONS
```

Initial state: [5   4   10   20   12   3]

1. Pick 3 [5   4   10   20   12   3]

2. Pick 4 3 [4   10   20   12   5]

3. Pick 5 3   4 [10   20   12   5]

4. Pick 10 3   4   5 [20   12   10]

5. Pick 12 3   4   5   10 [12   20]

After sort: 3   4   5   10   12 [20]

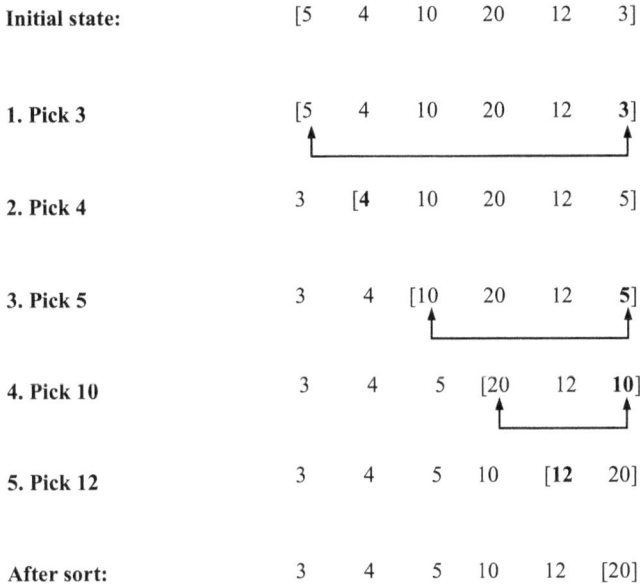

Fig. 9.20: Procedure of direct selection sort.

```
//Tool function: swap the value of x and y
template <class T>
void Swap (T &x, T &y)
{
    T temp;

    temp = x;
    x = y;
    y = temp;
}

//Use selection sort to sort the n elements in array A
template <class T>
void SelectionSort (T A[], int n)
{
    int smallIndex;              //Select the index of minimum
                                 //element every turn
    int i, j;

    for (i = 0; i < n-1; i++)
    {
        smallIndex = i;          //The initial index of minimum
```

```
                                              //element is set to i
            for (j = i+1; j < n; j++)         //Compare between A[i+1]..A[n-1],
                                              //get the minimum one
               if (A[j] < A[smallIndex]) //smallIndex always stores the
                                              //index of minimum element
                  smallIndex = j;
               Swap(A[i], A[smallIndex]);     //Swap the minimum element this
                                              //turn and A[i]
        }
    }
    #endif
```

9.3.3 Exchange Sort

The idea of the exchange sort is to pair up elements in the collections and exchange them if they are disordered. Bubble sort is a good example.

The following is the algorithm of bubble sort for operating on an array with n elements:

1. Check the first and the second element, and exchange them if they are not in the right order. Then do this similarly for the second and the third one, and so on until the last one is reached. The whole procedure is called the first stage of bubble sort. After the procedure, the maximum is at the n-th position.
2. Repeat the first step with the first $n-1$ elements. After the procedure, the maximum of these $n-1$ elements is at $n-1$-th position.
3. Repeat the second step until no exchange appears in a stage of bubbling sort. For an n-element collection, bubbling sort requires $n-1$ stages at most.

Figure 9.21 shows the procedure of the bubble sort.

Example 9.13: Implementation of bubble sort.

```
//9_13.h
#ifndef ARRAY_BASED_SORTING_FUNCTIONS
#define ARRAY_BASED_SORTING_FUNCTIONS

//Tool function: swap the value of x and y
template <class T>
void Swap (T &x, T &y)
{
    T temp;
    temp = x;
    x = y;
```

```
      y = temp;
}


//Use bubbling sort to sort the n elements in array A
template <class T>
void BubbleSort(T A[], int n)
{
   int i,j;
   int lastExchangeIndex;      //Record the index of smaller elements
                               //in the last pair of elements in
                               //every swap
   i = n-1;                    //i is the largest index of the
                               //elements which will take place in
                               //next turn
   while (i > 0)               //Keep sorting, until no swap occurred
                               //in the last turn or n-1 turn has
                               //been done
   {
      lastExchangeIndex = 0;   //Set swap signal 0 before every
                               //turn(no swap)
      for (j = 0; j < i; j++)  //Compare and swap between A[0]..A[i]
                               //in every turn
        if (A[j+1] < A[j])     //If element A[j+1] < A[j], swap them
        {
          Swap(A[j],A[j+1]);
          lastExchangeIndex = j; //Record the smaller index in the swap
        }
      i = lastExchangeIndex;   //Set i to the smaller index in the
                               //last swap
```

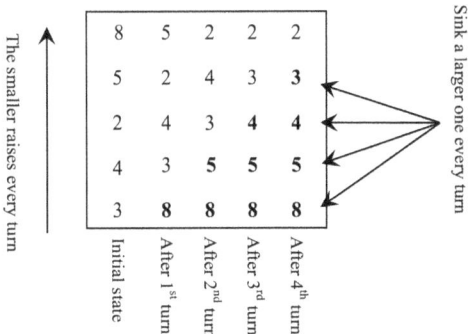

Fig. 9.21: Procedure of bubble sort.

```
    }
}
#endif
```

9.3.4 Sequential Search

Sequential search is a basic search method. It scans through the array, and compares each element with the desired one until it finds the match. The search is unsuccessful if there is no element that matches the desired one.

Example 9.14: Sequential search.

```
//9_14.h
#ifndef SEARCH_METHODS
#define SEARCH_METHODS

//Find element with value key in the array list using sequential
//search
//Return the index of the element if found, otherwise return -1
template <class T>
int SeqSearch(T list[], int n, T key)
{
    for(int i=0;i < n;i++)
        if (list[i] == key)
            return i;
    return -1;
}

#endif //SEARCH_METHODS
```

9.3.5 Binary Search

We can use binary search if we search a sorted collection. The idea of binary search is that a comparison splits the sequence into two parts of equal size and only one of them can contain the desired one. Figure 9.22 shows the procedure of a binary search.

Example 9.15: Binary search.

```
//9_15.h
#ifndef SEARCH_METHODS
#define SEARCH_METHODS
```

5	13	19	21	37	56	64	75	80	88	92

↑ low=0   ↑ high=10

↑ mid=(low+high)/2=5   21< list[mid]

5	13	19	21	37

↑ low=0   ↑ high=mid-1=4

↑

mid=(low+high)/2=2   21>list[mid]

21	37

low=mid+1 ↑   ↑ high

↑

mid=(low+high)/2=3   21==list[mid]   Found the element 21, index is 3

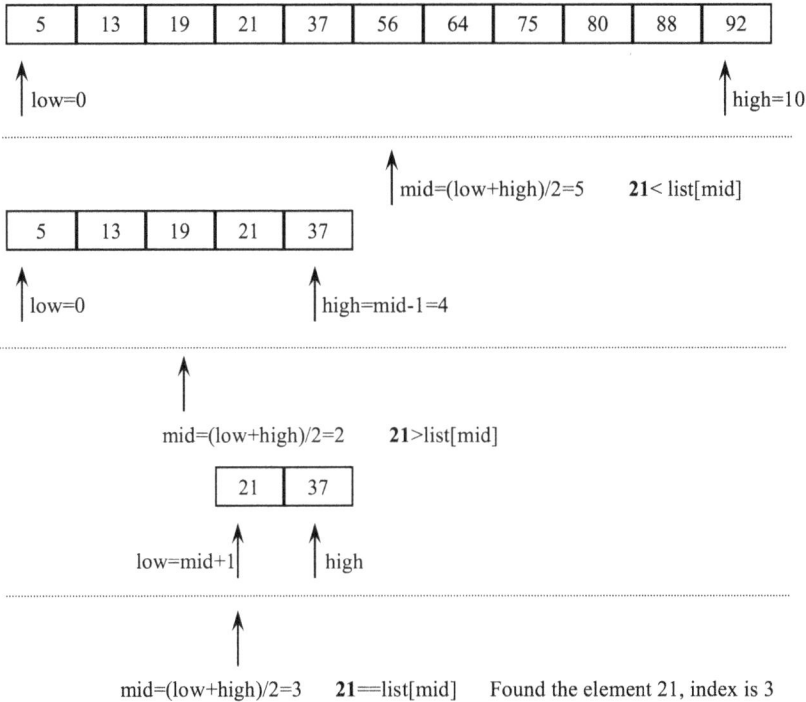

Fig. 9.22: Procedure of a binary search.

```
//Use binary search to find the element with key as value in a
//ascending array list
template <class T>
int BinSearch(T list[], int n, T key)
{
    int mid, low, high;
    T midvalue;

    low=0;
    high=n-1;
    while (low <= high)                 //low <= high indicates the array
                                        //haven't been searched through

    {
        mid = (low+high)/2;             //Get the index of the element at
                                        //the center
        midvalue = list[mid];           //Get the value of the element
        if (key == midvalue)
            return mid;                 //If found, return the index
```

```
        else if (key < midvalue)
            high = mid-1;                //If key < midvalue, set the search
                                         //range to the first half

        else
            low = mid+1;                 //Otherwise, set the search range to
                                         //the second half

    }
    return -1;                           //Return -1 if not found
}


    #endif                               //SEARCH_METHODS
```

9.4 Application – Improving the HR Management Program of a Small Company

We demonstrated how to use polymorphism in Chapter 8. Now we use the dynamic array to implement the same functionality.

Example 9.16: Improving the HR management program.
There are four files in the program: *employee.h, employee.cpp* in Chapter 8, *9_3.h* in this chapter, and a modified *9_16.cpp* derived from *8_8.cpp*, with slight modifications.

```
//9_16.cpp
#include<iostream>
#include<string>
#include"employee.h"
#include "9_3.h"       //Include the header file of template class Array
using namespace std;

int main()
{
    manager m1;
    technician t1;
    salesman s1;
    salesmanager sm1;
    char namestr[20];               //The employee names will be saved
                                    //into namestr temporary

    //Changed part
    Array<employee*> emp(4);
    emp[0]=&m1;
```

```
emp[1]=&t1;
emp[2]=&sm1;
emp[3]=&s1;

//The following part is the same with 8_8.cpp completely, omitted
int i;
for(i=0;i<4;i++)
{
cout<<"Please input the name of next employee: ";
      ......
```

Running result:

```
Please input the name of next employee: Zhang
Please input the name of next employee: Wang
Please input the name of next employee: Li
Please input the name of next employee: Zhao
Please input the part-time technicians Wang's working hours this
week: 40
Please input the sales manager Li's total sales this month of his
department: 400000
Please input the salesman Zhao's sales this month: 40000
Zhang ID 1000 Level 4, salary this month 8000
Wang ID 1001 Level 3, salary this month 4000
Li ID 1003 Level 3, salary this month 7000
Zhao ID 1002 Level 1, salary this month 1600
```

9.5 Summary

This chapter introduces the concept of templates, and several commonly used linear collections: arrays, linked lists, stacks, and queues. Methods for sorting and searching a linear collection are also discussed.

The template is a powerful tool for describing parameterized polymorphism. Templates allow programmers to write features (like searching), without considering the underlying implementation (like, searching an array or a linked list).

The access order of an element and the position of it are directly related in a linear collection. There are three ways to access a linear collection: direct access, sequential access, and indexed access. In this chapter, we introduce the linear collections that support direct access and sequential access.

The basic idea of insertion sort is to repeatedly insert an unsorted element into the correct position in the sorted subcollection until the complete collection is sorted.

The basic idea of selection sort is to select the minimum element in the unsorted subcollection and put it to the end of the sorted subcollection.

The idea of exchange sort is to pair up elements in the collections and exchange them if they are disordered. Bubble sort is a good example.

The idea of sequential search is to scan through the array and compare each element with the desired one until finds the matched one. The search is unsuccessful if there are no element matches with the desired one.

The idea of binary search is that a comparison can split the sequence into two parts of equal size and only one of them can possibly contain the desired one.

There are many algorithms for sorting and searching linear collections. Readers can refer to books of data structure for advanced topics in this area.

Exercises

9.1 There are N students in a class. Write a program to calculate the average score of course A of the class. Please use the *Array* template to define a *float* type array to store the scores.

9.2 What elements at least should be in the *Node* class in a linked list? What are the differences between a single-linked list and a double-linked list?

9.3 What is the maximum number of elements in a linked list?

9.4 What are the differences of the *Node* class used in a double-linked list and single-linked list? Try to declare the *Node* class DNODE used in a double-linked list.

9.5 Declare two linked lists A and B with type *int* using the template provided in this chapter. Insert five elements respectively and then append all elements in B to the tail of A.

9.6 Derive an ordered linked list class *OrderList* from the class *LinkedList*, and add a new method *InsertOrder* to insert elements in order. Declare two ordered linked lists A and B with type *int* using the template provided in this chapter. Insert five elements in order respectively, and then add all elements to B, keeping A ordered.

9.7 What is a stack? What is the access pattern of a stack?

9.8 What is a queue? What is the access pattern of a stack?

9.9 Describe the idea of insertion sort.

9.10 Initialize an *int*-type array

```
data1[]={1,3,5,7,9,11,13,15,17,19,2,4,6,8,10,12,14,16,18,20}.
```

Sort it with the direct insertion sort algorithm. Modify the implementation slightly to show the whole array after each insertion, and observe the changes of the data.

9.11 Describe the idea of selection sort.

9.12 Initialize an *int*-type array

data1[]={1,3,5,7,9,11,13,15,17,19,2,4,6,8,10,12,14,16,18,20}.

Sort it with the direct selection sort algorithm. Modify the implementation slightly to show the whole array after each insertion, and observe the changes of the data.

9.13 Describe the idea of bubble sort.

9.14 Initialize an *int*-type array

data1[]={1,3,5,7,9,11,13,15,17,19,2,4,6,8,10,12,14,16,18,20}.

Sort it with the bubbling sort algorithm. Modify the implementation slightly to show the whole array after each insertion, and observe the changes of the data.

9.15 All sorting algorithms described in this chapter are sorting in ascending order. Modify the bubbling sort algorithm slightly to perform a descending sort. Initialize an *int*-type array

data1[]={1,3,5,7,9,11,13,15,17,19,2,4,6,8,10,12,14,16,18,20}.

Sort it with the descending bubble sort algorithm. Modify the implementation slightly to show the whole array after each insertion, observe the changes of the data.

9.16 Describe the idea of sequential search.

9.17 Initialize an *int*-type array

data1[]={1,3,5,7,9,11,13,15,17,19,2,4,6,8,10,12,14,16,18,20}.

Let the user input a number and search it in the array, using the sequential search algorithm.

9.18 Describe the idea of binary search.

9.19 Initialize an *int*-type array

data1[]={1,3,5,7,9,11,13,15,17,19,2,4,6,8,10,12,14,16,18,20}.

Let the user input a number and search it in the array, using the binary search algorithm.

10 Generic Programming and the Standard Template Library

In Chapter 9, we introduced several basic collections and related algorithms. There are many other types of commonly used collections and complex algorithms. The study of these issues is the subject of data structure. It is not necessary for programmers to develop every class and algorithm from scratch. In fact, the standardization and modulization of commonly used algorithms are the keys to fast software production. To achieve this, we need to use not only concepts from object-oriented programs but also those from generic programming. The Standard Template Library (STL) in C++ is a good example of integrating these two concepts.

In this chapter we introduce the concepts, the structures, and the usage of STL. We briefly introduce the basic applications of containers, iterators, algorithms, and function objects to get an overall picture of STL. We recommend that readers refer to other books for other topics in STL and generic programming. Grasping some basic knowledge in data structure helps to understand the materials in this chapter.

10.1 Generic Programming

10.1.1 Introduction

The goal of generic programming is to represent abstract concepts and algorithms in generic codes without losing efficiency. Generic programming is a different technique from object-oriented programming. In some cases, there are even conflicts between good generic programming design and good object-oriented programming design. But the combination of these two techniques results in a powerful tool for building complex software systems. STL is an excellent example of it. For example, with the help of STL, programmers do not need to write array classes for integers, reals, and characters; writing a generic template is sufficient. These techniques allow heavy code reuses and improve the efficiency of software production.

Recall the array, linked list, and the queues template implementation, searching, and sorting algorithm discussed in Chapter 9. In object-oriented programming, it is good practice to encapsulate these algorithms into classes. However, a better solution is to write generic algorithms independent of implementation such as "finding an element sequentially in a linear collection". That is the goal of generic programming.

The iterator is the adaptive layer between the algorithms and the data structure. Algorithms can use the iterator interface to access the data structure to perform specific operations. That is the key scheme for decoupling the data structure and the algorithm used by generic programming.

https://doi.org/10.1515/9783110471977-010

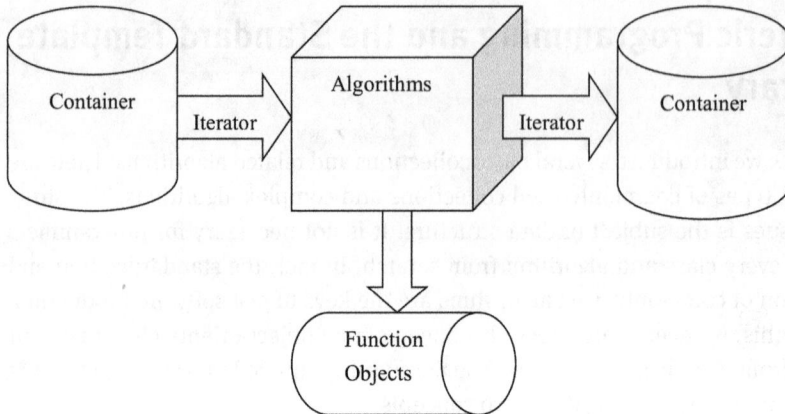

Fig. 10.1: Relationship between STL components.

STL is the core component of the C++ standard library. STL implements general containers and iterators, which are the basis of algorithm templates. There are four key components in STL: containers, iterators, algorithms, and function objects as shown in Figure 10.1. As indicated, the algorithm is in the center of the structure. The algorithm uses iterators to obtain data from the container, operates on it with the function objects, and then sends the result to another container through another iterator.

10.1.2 Namespace

There are many modules in complex software, including different libraries and classes provided by different programmers. These might contain naming conflicts among these modules, i.e., different things represented by the same identifier. A namespace is the way of resolving this problem in C++.

A namespace restricts a set of identifiers in a named scope. So it is possible to have the same identifier in a different named scope. Programmers use "the name of namespace" + "::" to refer an object in the named scope. For example, the following code declares a namespace *NS* and some identifiers in it:

```
namespace NS {
class File;
void Fun();
}
```

The way to refer to these identifiers is the following:

```
NS:: File obj;
NS:: Fun();
```

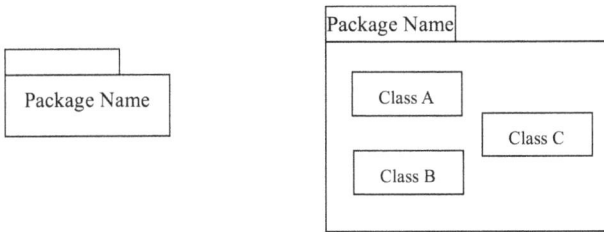

Fig. 10.2: UML graph of packages.

There is a special anonymous namespace that can be used directly. Most examples in this book do not declare namespace explicitly, so the identifiers in these examples are in the scope of the default anonymous namespace.

Programmer can write the *"using"* statement to avoid writing the lengthy prefixes of the identifiers. For example, if programmer writes the following statement in the code:

```
using NS::File;
```

then all references of *File* in the current scope mean *NS::File*.

However, if the programmer writes the following statement:

```
using namespace NS;
```

then the program can use all identifiers in the named scope of *NS* without any prefixes.

The standard library in C++ is in the namespace *"std"*. Programmers can refer to identifiers in the standard library directly with the *"std::"* prefix, e.g., *"std::cout"*, or use the *"using"* statement to enable the program to use these identifiers directly.

Namespaces are represented in a package graph in UML. A package contains classes and other elements, whose identifiers must be unique. All elements in the package are destroyed if the package is destroyed.

Packages are represented by folders in a UML graph. The inner classes of the package can be hidden by writing the package name in the middle of the folder. To show the details of the package, the package name should be written at the label part of the folder. Figure 10.2 shows how to represent a package in these two ways.

The dependencies between packages represent the references among objects in different namespaces. The access dependency describes a package with the privilege of accessing all public interfaces in another package. For example, objects in package *P2* are able to access class *C* in *P1* if class *C* is in the public interface. The relationship between *P2* and *C* is an access dependency, as shown in Figure 10.3.

Import dependency represents merging the public interfaces between two packages. For example, if there is an import dependency between *P1* and *P2*, then *P2* can use class *C* directly, i.e., adding *"using namespace P1"* in *P2*'s codes.

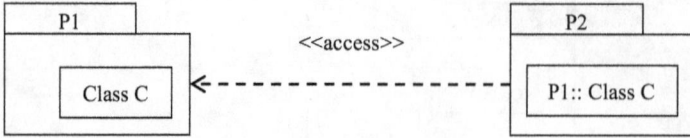

Fig. 10.3: UML graph for packages.

10.1.3 Differences of Naming Conventions Between C/C++

The C++ standard library declares all identifiers in the namespace *"std"*. There is no extension name in the header filename; for example, the following statement includes the string library in the program:

```
#include <string>
```

It also works for *C*'s standard library, but the programmer should add the prefix "c" rather than the suffix ".h":

```
#include <cstdlib> //refer to <stdlib.h>
#include <cstring> //refer to <string.h>
```

The old style of the include statement still works in order to be backwards compatible with *C*:

```
#include <stdlib.h>
```

Notice that the header declares the identifiers in both the global namespace and the *"std"* namespace.

The STL library is scattered in a series of header files. Here is a quick reference of objects in STL:

1. Vector, lists, and double queues are in *<vector>/<list>/<deque>* respectively.
2. Sets and multisets are in *<set>*, maps and multimaps are in *<map>*.
3. Stacks are in *<stack>*. Queues and priority queues are in *<queue>*.
4. Basic algorithms are in *<algorithm>*, some generic numeric algorithms are in *<numeric>*.
5. Iterators and the adapters of iterators are in *<iterator>*.
6. Function objects and function adapters are in *<functional>*.

10.1.4 Concepts of STL

10.1.5 Containers

Containers are objects that contain a set of objects. There are two kinds of containers: heterogeneous containers where the container can hold elements of different types;

and homogenous containers where the container can only hold elements of the same type.

There are seven types of containers in the STL library: vector, double queue, list, set, multiset, map, and multimap. They can be divided into two groups: sequential containers and associative containers. Sequential containers, such as vectors, double queues, and lists organize elements linearly, while associative containers, such as sets, multisets, maps, and multimaps organize elements based on indexes.

10.1.6 Adapters

Adapters provide new interfaces for existing classes and enable two classes to work co-operatively. There are three types of adapters in STL: adapters of containers, adapters of iterators, and adapters of function objects. Adapters are very powerful tools for code reuse. For example, STL uses adapters of containers to implement stacks, queues, and priority queues based on corresponding containers.

10.1.7 Iterators

Iterators can be seen as pointers in an object-oriented view. Iterators provide methods like *current()*, *previous()*, and *next()* to allow programmers to access the container via the iterators.

10.1.8 Algorithms

There re more than 70 algorithm implementations in STL, including sorting, eliminating, counting, comparing, transforming, and container managing, which covers a wide range of applications. The implementations are generic so that they can be applied to different objects and primitive types.

10.1.9 Interfaces of Containers

There are several common interfaces in the STL containers. These containers overload the comparison operator to perform comparison between containers (Table 10.1). There are also methods to access iterators (Table 10.2) and methods to access the status of the container (Table 10.3).

Tab. 10.1: All Operators in STL Containers.

General Container Operator	Description
a==b	Equal operation for same type container
a!=b	Unequal operation for same type container, the same as !(a==b)
a>b	If $b<a$, return boolean type "true"
a>=b	If !($a<b$), return boolean type true
a<b	If $a<b$, return boolean type true
a<=b	If !($b<a$), return boolean type true
r=b	Assign value operation for a container

Note: x is a container class, and a and b are instances of class x, r is the value of type $x\&$.

Tab. 10.2: Iterator and Access Methods of Each Container.

Iteration Function	Description
begin()	Return an iterator pointing to the first element in this container
end()	Return an iterator pointing to the last element in this container
rbegin()	Return reverse_iterator(end()), a reverse iterator which points to the first element of the reversed elements.
rend()	Return reverse_iterator*(begin()), a reverse iterator which points to the last element of the reversed elements

Access Methods	Description
size()	Return the number of elements
max_size()	Return the maximum amount of elements that the container could hold
swap()	Swap two containers which are of the same type
empty()	If the container is empty or size()==0, return true

Tab. 10.3: Immutable Access to Container Elements.

Immutable Method	Description
front()	To access the header element of the container
back()	To access the tail element of the container
[] operand	To access any element in the container directly

10.2 Containers in STL

STL containers have been introduced briefly in the previous section. This section will discuss containers in detail.

Sequential containers organize elements linearly, meaning that the program can define the positions of elements as well as the top/bottom of the container. You can see sequential containers as an implementation of linear collection. It is a totally different story for associative containers, which organize elements based on indexes.

There are two access patterns in sequential containers: sequential access and random access. You have to access the element sequentially in a container that only supports sequential access, i.e., you have to access the first and the second element before accessing the third one. However, you can access the elements directly if the container supports random access. Vectors and double queues are random-access containers while lists are sequential-access containers.

There are four associative containers: set, multiset, map, and multimap. An element can be accessed based on its key. Interested readers can refer to books about data structure and STL for more details.

There are seven containers in STL, and they provide the functions of storing, searching, and accessing elements. Besides, stacks, queues, and priority queues are standard data structures, and are necessary in many applications. STL provides three kinds of module called adaptors. Combining adaptors and sequential containers can provide the functions of stacks, queues, and priority queues.

10.2.1 Sequential Containers

The most widely used sequential container in C++ is the array. However, sometimes more powerful tools are needed. To meet this need, STL implements three sequential containers: **vectors, lists, and double queues**.

The vector is a powerful extension of the static array. It is very similar to the static array, but it can enlarge its storage on demand at runtime.

The list is an implementation of the double-linked list. It is quick to add or remove an element to or from a list.

The double queue is an extension of the data structure queue. Compared to a standard queue, it can add or remove elements from both ends of the queue.

1. Common Interfaces of Sequential Containers
a) Adding Elements

There are a number of ways to insert elements into a container. The first one is to use the *push_front()* or *push_back()* methods, which add an element at the top or at the end of the container respectively.

The second way is to use the *insert()* method. It has some variants in different containers. *Insert (L, O)* adds element O before location L. *Insert (L, N, O)* inserts element O before location L N times. *Insert (L, i, j)* adds all element between location i and location j before location L. It is worth mentioning that the *insert()* method will possibly invalidate all iterators in vectors and double queues, so iterators and *insert()* methods should be used with care.

The third way is to use the assignment operator to add all elements in a container into an empty container.

These three ways are standard ways to add elements into a sequential container.

Calling push_front() or push_back, using insert(), and using the assignment operator are the three standard ways to add elements to a sequential container.

b) Removing Elements

There are also a number of ways to remove elements in a container. We should notice that to remove elements, the destructor of elements should be called rather than the container's destructor. The first method is to call *pop_front()* or *pop_back()*. They remove the element at the head and the element at the tail of the container, respectively.

The second way is to call the *erase()* method. *Erase(L)* removes the element at location *L*; *erase(L1, L2)* removes all elements between locations L1 and L2.

The third way is to call the *clear()* method, which removes all elements in the container.

Removing elements will also invalidate the iterators. *Erase()* and *clear()* will invalidate the iterators pointing to the deleted elements in list container. The effect of removing elements from the head or the tail of the double queue is the same as the one in the list, but removing an element from the middle of a double queue will invalidate all iterators. Removing elements in vectors also invalidate all iterators.

c) Traversing the Sequential Container

The iterator is the object-oriented approach to traverse a container. It overloads the dereference operator "*" to return the reference of the element that it points to, just as a normal pointer.

d) Other Ways to Access Elements in a Sequential Container

Programmer can use methods *front()* and *back()* to access the element at the head or at the tail of the container respectively. Subscript operator "[]" can also be used to directly access elements in the container, which is only available in vectors and double queues. For example, in a double queue A that holds 15 elements, A[7] points to the seventh element in the queue, and A[N] points to the *N*-th element in A. Table 10.3 demonstrates these methods.

2. Vectors

The vector is a variable length linear collection designed to provide rapid random access for objects. It is very similar to the static array, but vectors can change their storage size on demand at runtime.

Vectors are powerful containers. They can be used to implement queues, stacks, lists, or other complicated data structures.

a) Constructors and Destructors

There are four default constructors in a vector:

```
vector(); //default constructor, create a vector container of size 0
vector(size_type n,const T&value=T()); /*initialize a vector of
    size n, the second parameter is the initial value of any object,
    which is by default an object constructed by T()*/
vector(const vector& x);//copy constructor, initialized with vector x
vector(const_iterator first, const_iterator last); /*create a new
    vector from part of a container which supports const_iterator*/
```

As in all containers in STL, vectors accommodate the object-oriented mechanism for memory management. All memory used by the vector itself, and the memory used by elements in the vector, are reclaimed by calling their destructors appropriately when the instance is out of scope.

One thing to notice is that removing an element from a vector just removes the element from the vector. It only calls its destructor but does not reclaim the memory used by the element.

b) Using Vector

1. Querying Status of Vector

There are four methods for querying the status of a vector: *size()*, *max_size()*, *capacity()*, and *empty()*. Here are their prototypes:

```
size_type size() const;      //Returns the size of the vector
size_type max_size() const;  //Returns the largest possible size of
                             //the vector
size_type capacity() const;  //Number of elements for which memory has
                             //been allocated
bool empty() const;          //returns true if the vector's size is 0
```

2. Adding Elements into a Vector

There are a number of ways to add an element into a vector: the constructor, *push_back()*, *insert()*, and *swap()* methods, the subscript operator, and the assignment operator. We have introduced some methods before. Here are the prototypes of *push_back()*, *insert()*, and *swap()*:

```
void push_back(const T& x); /* Inserts a new element at the end,
    memory would be requested if lacked */
iterator insert(iterator it, const T& x = T()); //Inserts x before it
void insert(iterator it,size_type n,const T& x);
                    //Inserts n copies of x before it
void insert(iterator it, const_iterator first, const_iterator last);
                    //Inserts the range [first, last) before it
void swap(vector x);      //Swaps the contents of two vectors
```

The *reverse()* method reserves memory space to hold a certain number of elements. The *reverse()* method reallocates memory only if it finds its need is beyond the current capacity of the vector. Please notice that reallocation invalidates all references and iterators of a vector.

3. Deleting Elements from Vector

Programmers can use *pop_back()*, *erase()*, or *clear()* methods to remove an element from a vector. Here are their prototypes:

```
void pop_back();           //Removes the last element
iterator erase(iterator it); //Erases the element at position it
iterator erase(iterator first,iterator last);
                           //Erases the range [first, last)
void clear();              //Erases all of the elements, but the buffer
                           //area is kept
```

4. Accessing Elements in Vector

Methods *front()* and *back()* return the first and the last element in the vector respectively. The subscript operator can access the elements via the position directly.

c) Application

Example 10.1: Find all primes between 2 – N.

We now use a vector to rewrite the program in Example 9.4 and here is the program:

```
//10_1.cpp
#include <iostream>
#include <iomanip>
#include <vector>                  //include the header of vector
using namespace std ;
int main()
{
    vector<int> A(10);             //used to store prime numbers,
                                   //initialized with 10 elements
    int n;                         //upper limit for the numbers,
                                   //inputted by user
    int primecount = 0, i, j;
    cout << "Enter a value >= 2 as upper limit for prime numbers: ";
    cin >> n;
    A[primecount++] = 2;           //2 is a prime number
    for(i = 3; i < n; i++)
    {
        if (primecount == A.size())//if prime number table is full,
                                   //10 more spaces are requested
```

```
                A.resize(primecount + 10);
            if (i % 2 == 0)                    //even numbers larger than 2 is not
                                               //prime numbers.
                continue;
            //check whether 3,5,7,...,i/2 are factors of i
            j = 3;
            while (j <= i/2 && i % j != 0)
                j += 2;
            if (j > i/2)                       //if all such number are not factors
                                               //of i, i is a prime number
                A[primecount++] = i;
        }
        for (i = 0; i < primecount; i++) //print the prime number
        {
            cout << setw(5) << A[i];
            if ((i+1) % 10 == 0)         //10 numbers per line
                cout << endl;
        }
        cout << endl;
    }
```

The result of the program is as follows:

```
Enter a value >= 2 as upper limit for prime numbers: 100
  2   3   5   7 11 13 17 19 23 29
31 37 41 43 47 53 59 61 67 71
73 79 83 89 97
```

3. Double Queues

A double queue is an extension of the queue data structure. Elements can be added or removed at both ends of double queues. Programmers can use the subscript operator "[]" to access an element directly.

a) Constructors and Destructors

There are four constructors in a double queue:

```
deque();                            //Creates an empty deque
deque(size_type n, const T& v = T());
                                    //Creates a deque with n copies of v
deque(const deque& x);              //The copy constructor
deque(const_iterator first, const_iterator last);
                                    //Creates a deque with a copy of a range
```

b) Using a Double Queue
1. Query the Status of a Double Queue
The *size()* method returns the number of elements in the double queue. The *max_size()* method returns the maximum number of elements that the double queue can hold. Method *empty()* tests whether the double queue is empty or not.

2. Adding Elements into the Double Queue
Adding elements into a double queue is very similar to adding them into a vector. Programmers can add elements via the constructor, *push_back()/insert()/swap()* methods, the subscript operator, and the assignment operator. Moreover, double queue provides an additional *push_front()* method to add an element at the head of the queue:

```
void push\_front(const T\& x);  //Inserts a new element at the
                               //beginning
```

3. Removing Elements in the Double Queue
Methods *pop_back()/pop_front()/erase()/clear()* can remove elements in a double queue. Their semantics are the same as the ones for vectors. Moreover, double queues provide an additional method *pop_front()* for removing the first element of the double queue:

```
void pop\_ front();  //Removes the first element
```

4. Access Elements
There are a number of ways to access elements in a double queue. Programmer can use methods like *pop_front()/pop_back()/front()/back()* to access an element in a queue. They can also use iterators to traverse the queue and access the element directly via subscript operator.

c) Application
Example 10.2: Store doubles with a double queue.

```
//10_2.cpp
#include <iostream>
#include <deque>                //include deque header file
#include <algorithm>            //include algorithm header file
using namespace std;

int main()
{
    deque< double > values;        //define a double deque
    ostream_iterator< double > output( cout, " " );
    values.push_front( 2.2 );      //use push_front to add an element at
                                   //the beginning
    values.push_front( 3.5 );
```

```
values.push_back( 1.1 );        //use push_back to add an element at
                                //the end
cout << "values contains: ";
for ( int i = 0; i < values.size(); ++i )
   cout << values[ i ] << ' ';
values.pop_front();             //use pop_front to delete the first
                                //element
cout << "\nAfter pop_front values contains: ";
copy ( values.begin(), values.end(), output );
values[ 1 ] = 5.4;              //use operator [] to re-assign values
cout << "\nAfter values[ 1 ] = 5.4 values contains: ";
copy ( values.begin(), values.end(), output );
cout << endl;
}
```

Results:

```
values contains: 3.5 2.2 1.1
After pop_front values contains: 2.2 1.1
After values[ 1 ] = 5.4 values contains: 2.2 5.4
```

4. Lists

A list is a sequential container designed for adding/removing elements quickly. It supports splicing, which adds all elements in a list to another one. Lists do not support random access, so some algorithms do not work on lists. Lists are implemented as double-linked lists in STL, so they can be traversed in both directions.

a) Constructors and Destructors

There are four constructors in a list:

```
list();                             //create an empty list
list(size_type n, const T& v = T());
                                    //Creates a list with n copies of v
list(const list& x);                //The copy constructor
list(const_iterator first, const_iterator last);
                                    //Creates a list with a copy of a range
```

b) Using Lists

1. Accessing the List

There are some minor differences between the interfaces of lists and vectors. There are no *capacity()/subscript* operators and *at()* methods, since lists do not support random access. Other interfaces are the same.

2. Adding Elements

The semantics of the method *insert()* are the same as the ones for vectors and queues but the *insert()* method in lists does not affect any iterators of a list. The *splice()* method can also add elements to a list:

```
void splice(iterator it, list& x);
        //All of the elements of x are inserted before it and removed
        //from x.
        //Notice: it must be a valid iterator in *this, and x must be a
        //list that is distinct from *this
void splice(iterator it, list& x, iterator first);
        //Move the element by first from x to *this, inserting it
        //before it.
        //x could be *this
        //If it == first or it == ++first, this method is a null
        //operation x
void splice(iterator it, list& x, iterator first, iterator last);
        //Move the elements in [first, last) from x to *this, inserting
        //them before it
        //x could be *this, when [first, last] can not include element
        //pointed by it
```

3. Removing Elements

The *erase()* method removes both the element and the iterator pointing to it. The *remove()* method removes all elements equal to *x* in a list. Here is the prototype of *remove()*:

```
void remove(const T& x);    //Removes all elements that compare equal
                            //to x
```

c) Application

Example 10.3: Rewrite Example 9.7 with a list in STL.

Read 10 integers from the keyboard, create a linked list whose nodes hold these integers, and output the numbers in order. Then get another number from the keyboard, delete all nodes containing the number and output the data in the linked list. Clear the linked list before exiting.

Here is the program:

```
//10_3.cpp
#include <iostream>
#include <list>
using namespace std ;
```

```
int main()
{
    list<int> Link;        //create a list to store integer linked list
    int i, key, item;
    for (i=0;i < 10;i++)  //insert 10 integers at the beginning
    {
      cin>>item;
      Link.push_front(item);
    }
    cout << "List: ";      //print the linked list
list<int>::iterator p=Link.begin();
                            //Iterator p is used to traverse the list
    while(p!=Link.end())  //print data of each element until the end
    {
        cout <<*p << " ";
        p++;                //p points to the next element
    }
    cout << endl;

    cout << "Please input an integer to delete: ";
                            //input an integer to delete
    cin >> key;
    Link.remove(key);
    cout << "List: ";      //print the list
    p=Link.begin();        //p points back to the beginning
    while(p!=Link.end())  //print data of each element until the end
    {
        cout <<*p << " ";
        p++;                //p points to the next element
    }
    cout << endl;
}
```

Results:

```
3 6 5 7 5 2 4 5 9 10
List: 10 9 5 4 2 5 7 5 6 3
Please input an integer to delete: 5
List: 10 9 4 2 7 6 3
```

10.2.2 Adapters of Containers

Adapters of containers do not implement the mechanism of storing the data and other functionalities like iterators. They just implement different interfaces based on the containers provided by STL.

1. Stacks

A stack is a linear collection with restricted access. Elements can only be added or removed from one end of a stack. Such operations are called push and pop respectively. In theory, there is no limit on the number of elements in a stack. In practice, a stack will overflow if it exceeds the memory limit of the computer, and it will underflow if one tries to pop an element from an empty stack. STL catches these exceptions to keep the program from crashing.

Stacks are based on the implementation of a certain container, which is specified at the declaration. Here is an example of declaration of a stack using a deque as its underlying implementation of storage:

```
stack<int, deque<int>> myStack;
```

Stacks only implement the primitives of the stack data structure. Methods *push()/pop()* add or remove an element at the top of stack, respectively. The method *top()* returns the reference of the element at the top of the stack. The method *empty()* checks whether a stack is empty. The method *size()* returns the number of elements in the stack. The underlying storage can be a vector, list, or deque, and the deque is the default implementation. Please refer to related documents like MSDN for detailed information. Here is a simple example of a stack.

Example 10.4: Initialize a stack holding integers.

```
//10_4.cpp
#include <iostream>
#include <stack>                    //include stack adapter header file
using namespace std;

template< class T >
void popElements( T &s );

int main()
{
    stack< int > intDequeStack;     //use deque as the default container
    for ( int i = 0; i < 10; ++i ) {
        intDequeStack.push( i );    //push the integer in deque as the
                                    //top of the stack
    }
```

```
      cout << "Popping from intDequeStack: ";
      popElements( intDequeStack ); //pop the element in stack
      cout << endl;
   }

   template< class T >
   void popElements( T &s )           //define a template function
   {
      while ( !s.empty() ) {
         cout << s.top() << ' ';      //get the top element of stack and
                                      //print
         s.pop();                     //use pop to remove the top element
      }
   }
```

Results:

```
   Popping from intDequeStack: 9 8 7 6 5 4 3 2 1 0
```

2. Queues

Queue adapters provide interfaces for First In First Out (FIFO) services, i.e., adding an element to the tail of the container (enqueuing) and removing the first element of the container (dequeuing). Queues are implemented based on an underlying storage, typically a list or deque. The default underlying implementation of storage is the deque. Here is an example of a declaration of a queue, using the deque as the underlying storage implementation:

```
   queue<int, deque<int>> myQueue;
```

The method *push()* adds an element to the tail of the queue, the method *pop()* removes the first element of the queue, and the methods *front()* and *back()* return the reference of the head and the tail of the queue respectively. The method *empty()* checks whether the queue is empty, and the method *size()* returns the number of elements in the queue. Please refer to related documents like MSDN for detailed information. Here is a simple example of using a queue.

Example 10.5: Initialize a queue with integers.

```
   //10_5.cpp
   #include <iostream>
   #include <queue>                   //include queue adapter header file
   using namespace std;

   template< class T >
   void popElements( T &s );
```

```
int main()
{
    queue< int > intDequeQueue;       //use queue as the default container
    for ( int i = 0; i < 10; ++i ) {
        intDequeQueue.push( i );      //push the integer in deque as the
                                      //top of the queue
    }
    cout << "Popping from intDequeQueue: ";
    popElements( intDequeQueue );  //pop the top element of the queue
                                   //and print
    cout << endl;
}


template< class T >
void popElements( T &s )             //define a template function
{
    while ( !s.empty() ) {
        cout << s.front() << ' ';    //use front to get top element of
                                     //Queue and print
        s.pop();                     //use pop to remove the top element
    }
}
```

Results:

```
Popping from intDequeQueue: 0 1 2 3 4 5 6 7 8 9
```

Similar to stacks and queues, a priority queue is another adapter for implementing an advanced data structure. Priority queues are designed as ordered queues, which are able to extract the highest priority element from a queue.

10.3 Iterators

Iterators are an object-oriented version of a pointer. They provide a uniform mechanism with which to traverse through a container. Pointers point to a memory location, so that program is able to access the object at the memory location through the pointer. You can see iterator as a type-safe pointer – it points to an object of a specific type.

The iterator is a common design pattern for bridging algorithms and containers. Real algorithms need to traverse a linear collection, like traversing a linked list through a pointer or traversing an array though subscripts. It is good to write an algorithm that works for all linear collections, so that you do not have to implement an algorithm many times for every type of linear collections. Therefore, the algorithm needs an abstraction layer to handle things like "get me the next element", or "is it the end?". In theory, pointers can handle this issue, but make the implementation of algorithms and containers more complicated. For an object-oriented pointer, an iterator is included in STL to enable writing abstract algorithms that works on all containers.

10.3.1 Types of Iterators

There are five basic types of iterators: the **input iterator, output iterator, forward iterator, bidirectional iterator, and random access iterator.** There are two iterator adapters: the **reverse iterator adapter and insert iterator adapter.**

1. Categories
An input iterator can read data from a collection and an output iterator can write data to a collection.

A forward iterator is both an input iterator and output iterator, and it can traverse through the collection in a certain direction. A bidirectional iterator can traverse the collection in both directions. A random access iterator can access any position in a collection.

2. Iterator Adapters
An iterator adapter is an adapter that extends or adjusts the functions of an iterator. There are two types of iterator adapters:

The reverse iterator adapter reverses the functionalities of the increment operator and decrement operator, so that the algorithm processes the elements in a reversed order. All standard containers can be used with reverse iterators.

The insert iterator adapter overloads the assignment operator and turns it into insertions, so algorithms running on it inserts elements into the collections rather than overwriting the value of the elements. There are three types of insert iterators: back inserters, front inserters, and general inserters. Back inserters append an element to the end of a collection, and front inserters add an element at the head of a collection. General inserters decide the inserting position based on its parameters. Vectors, deques, links, and strings support back inserters, while deques supports front inserters, and all standard collections support general inserters.

Here is an example of an iterator adapter.

Example 10.6: Example of using iterator adapter.

```cpp
//10_6.cpp
#include <iostream>
#include <vector>
#include <algorithm>
using namespace std;

int main()
{
  int A[] = {1, 2, 3, 4, 5};
  const int N = sizeof(A)/sizeof(int);
  vector<int> col1(A,A+N);
  ostream_iterator< int > output( cout, " " );

  cout << "List col1 contains: ";
  copy( col1.begin(), col1.end(), output );
                              //print all elements in col1

  vector<int>::iterator pos=col1.begin();
                              //declare the iterator pointing to the
                              //first element of col1
  cout<<"\nThe fist element is: "<<*pos; //print the first element

  vector<int>::reverse_iterator rpos=col1.rbegin();
                  //use reversed iterator to point to the last element
  cout<<"\nThe last element is: "<<*rpos<<endl;
                              //print the last element

  back_insert_iterator<vector<int> > iter(col1);
                              //declare back insert iterator
  *iter=66;                   //insert element 66
  back_inserter(col1)=88;     //use function to back insert element 88
  copy( col1.begin(), col1.end(), output );
                              //print all elements in col1 after the
                              //back insert operation
  cout<<endl;
}
```

Results:

```
List col1 contains: 1 2 3 4 5
The fist element is: 1
```

```
The last element is: 5
1 2 3 4 5 66 88
```

10.3.2 Auxiliary Functions in Iterators

There are three auxiliary functions in iterators: *advance()*, *distance()*, and *iter_swap()*. *advance()* and *distance()* emulate the power of random access iterators such as advancing and going back for several positions and calculating the distances of two iterates, through basic iterator primitives. *Iter_swap()* allows programmers to swap the values that the two iterators are pointing to.

1. *advance()* move the position of an iterator forward or backward by *n* position. Here is the prototype:

```
void advance (InputIterator & pos, Dist n);
```

In bidirectional or random access iterators, *n* can be negative so that the iterator goes back for *n* elements.

2. *distance()* calculates the distances between two iterators:

```
Dist distance (InputIterator pos1, InputIterator pos2);
```

pos1 and *pos2* should point to the same container. If the iterators are not random access iterates, then *pos1* must be able to reach *pos2* via advancing *pos1*.

3. *iter_swap()* swaps the values that two iterators are pointing to:

```
void iter_swap (ForwardIterator1 pos1, ForwardIterator2 pos2);
```

pos1 and *pos2* may point to different containers, but the elements they are pointing to must be able to be assigned to each other.
    Here is an example:

Example 10.7: Example of auxiliary function of adapters.

```
//10_7.cpp
#include <iostream>
#include <list>
#include <algorithm>
using namespace std;

int main()
{
   int A[] = {1, 2, 3, 4, 5};
   const int N = sizeof(A)/sizeof(int);
```

```
list<int> col1(A,A+N);
ostream_iterator< int > output( cout, " " );

cout << "List col1 contains: ";
copy( col1.begin(), col1.end(), output );
                                //print all elements in col1

list<int>::iterator pos=col1.begin();
                                //declare the iterator pointing to
                                //the first element of col1

cout<<"\nThe fist element is: "<<*pos; //print the first element
advance(pos,3);                 //step forward 3 elements,
                                //pointing to the 4th element
cout<<"\nThe 4th element is: "<<*pos; //print the 4th element

cout<<"\nThe advanced distance is: "<<distance(col1.begin(),pos);
                                //print the distance between current
                                //iterator and initial position

iter_swap(col1.begin(),--col1.end());
                                //swap the first and last elements
cout << "\nAfter exchange List col1 contains: ";
copy( col1.begin(), col1.end(), output );
                                //print elements in col1 after swap
cout<<endl;
}
```

Results:

```
List col1 contains: 1 2 3 4 5
The fist element is: 1
The 4th element is: 4
The advanced distance is: 3
After exchange List col1 contains: 5 2 3 4 1
```

10.4 Algorithms in STL

STL implements generic algorithms via function templates. Generic algorithm gets an element with an input iterator, performs the operation with a function object, then outputs the result through an output iterator. The algorithm only specifies the semantics of the algorithm. Details of the implementation, like how to load/store data from/to containers are hidden in the implementation of iterators. The design splits functionalities into different components that are joined via a function template. Programmers are free to change any part of the whole link to implement new functionalities, such as working on a different type of container. That is the goal of generic programming.

There are four types of STL algorithms: Nonmutating Sequence Algorithms, Mutating Sequence Algorithms, sorting algorithms, and numerical algorithms. They cover a wide range of applications. This chapter focuses on the usage of these algorithms. The design and implementation of these algorithms are out of the scope of this chapter; please refer to advanced materials for more information.

10.4.1 Using the Algorithms

We have used the copy algorithm in Section 10.3; here is the prototype of it:

```
template <typename InputIterator, typename OutputIterator>
OutputIterator copy(InputIterator first, InputIterator last,
                    OutputIterator result);
```

The algorithm copies all elements in range [*first*, *last*) to [*result*, *result* + (*last* – *first*)), and it returns *result* + (*last* – *first*).

Here is the related code from Example 10.7:

```
ostream_iterator< int > output( cout, " " );
                            //create an output stream iterator
cout << "List col1 contains: ";
copy( col1.begin(), col1.end(), output ); //print elements in col1
```

Line 1 initializes an output stream iterator *output* and transfers all elements in *col1* to the *output* iterator, which outputs the data to the console. *Col1.begin()* and *col1.end()* points to the first and the last element of *col1* respectively.

Many algorithms take function objects as an input parameter for customizing the behaviors of the algorithms. Here are two prototypes of the sort algorithm:

```
template<typename RandomAccessIterator>
void sort(RandomAccessIterator first, RandomAccessIterator last);
template<typename RandomAccessIterator, typename Compare>
void sort(RandomAccessIterator first, RandomAccessIterator last,
          Compare comp);
```

The first prototype uses the operator < for comparison, so the result is in ascending order. The second prototype compares the elements with the function object *comp*, so that programmers can write their own rules for sorting, making the implementation flexible.

Here is an example of the sort algorithm:

Example 10.8: Example of sort algorithm.

```
//10_8.cpp
#include <iostream>
#include <vector>
#include <algorithm>
#include <functional>
using namespace std;

int main()
{
  int A[] = {1, 4, 3, 2, 5};
  const int N = sizeof(A)/sizeof(int);
  vector<int> col1(A,A+N);
  ostream_iterator< int > output( cout, " " );

  cout << "Vector col1 contains: ";
  copy( col1.begin(), col1.end(), output );    //print elements in col1
  sort(col1.begin(),col1.end());               //first way to call
  cout << "\nAfter sorted in ascending order col1 contains: ";
  copy( col1.begin(), col1.end(), output );
                        //elements in col1 after ascending sort
  sort(col1.begin(),col1.end(),greater<int>());
                        //second way, to use standard functional object
  cout << "\nAfter sorted in descending ordercol1 contains: ";
  copy( col1.begin(), col1.end(), output );
                        //elements in col1 after descending sort
  cout<<endl;
}
```

Results:

```
Vector col1 contains: 1 4 3 2 5
After sorted in ascending order col1 contains: 1 2 3 4 5
After sorted in descending ordercol1 contains: 5 4 3 2 1
```

10.4.2 Nonmutating Sequence Algorithms

Nonmutating Sequence Algorithms do not modify the elements of the input containers, such as algorithms for finding an element in a container, checking whether two sequences are equal, and counting the occurrence of elements.

Tab. 10.4: List of Nonmutating Sequence Algorithms in STL.

Name	Function
for_each	Apply a function to each element in a sequence
find	Find the first matching element in a sequence
find_if	Find the first matching element in a sequence according to some conditions
adjacent_find	Find two adjacent matching elements
find_first_of	Return the first iterator in a matching sequence
find_end	Return the last iterator in a matching sequence
count	Count the number of matching elements
count_if	Count the number of matching elements according some conditions
mismatch	Find the first two mismatched elements
equal	Test two sequences for equality
search	Search for a sequence
search_n	Search for a sequence that happens n times

Table 10.4 lists Nonmutating Sequence Algorithms in STL.

Here is an example of using Nonmutating Sequence Algorithms:

Example 10.9: An example of using Nonmutating Sequence Algorithms.

```
//10_9.cpp
#include <iostream>
#include <algorithm>
#include <functional>
#include <vector>
using namespace std;

int main()
{
    int iarray[]={0,1,2,3,4,5,6,6,6,7,8};
    vector<int> ivector(iarray,iarray+sizeof(iarray)/sizeof(int));
    int iarray1[]={6,6};
    vector<int> ivector1(iarray1,iarray1+sizeof(iarray1)/sizeof(int));
    int iarray2[]={5,6};
    vector<int> ivector2(iarray2,iarray2+sizeof(iarray2)/sizeof(int));
    int iarray3[]={0,1,2,3,4,5,7,7,7,9,7};
    vector<int> ivector3(iarray3,iarray3+sizeof(iarray3)/sizeof(int));

    //find the first element in adjacent element of the same value in
    //ivector
    cout<<*adjacent_find(ivector.begin(),ivector.end())<<endl;

    //count the number of elements in ivector having the value of 6
    cout<<count(ivector.begin(),ivector.end(),6)<<endl;
```

```
    //count the number of elements in ivector whose value is less
    //than 7
    cout<<count_if(ivector.begin(),ivector.end(),
        bind2nd(less<int>(),7))<<endl;

    //find the first position of elements in ivector whose value is 4
    cout<<*find(ivector.begin(),ivector.end(),4)<<endl;

    //find the first position of elements in ivector whose value is
    //larger than 2
    cout<<*find_if(ivector.begin(),ivector.end(),
        bind2nd(greater<int>(),2))<<endl;

    //find the last position of elements in subsequence ivector1, then
    //get the element after stepping forward 3 position
    cout<<*(find_end(ivector.begin(),ivector.end(),
        ivector1.begin(),ivector1.end())+3)<<endl;

    //find the first position of elements in subsequence ivector1,
    //then get the element after stepping forward 3 position
    cout<<*(find_first_of(ivector.begin(),ivector.end(),ivector1.
        begin(),ivector1.end())+3)<<endl;

    //the first element in subsequence ivector2 which appears
    //in ivector
    cout<<*search(ivector.begin(),ivector.end(),
        ivector2.begin(),ivector2.end())<<endl;

    //search the first element in which 3 consecutive 6 appears
    cout<<*search_n(ivector.begin(),ivector.end(),3,6,equal_to<int>())
        <<endl;

    //whether ivector and ivector3 are equal(0 is false, 1 is true)
    cout << equal(ivector.begin(), ivector.end(), ivector3.begin())
        << endl;

    //find the range that ivector3 and ivector mismatch
    pair<int*,int*>result=mismatch(ivector.begin(),ivector.end(),
        ivector3.begin());
    cout<< result.first - ivector.begin() << endl;
}
```

Results:

```
6
3
9
4
3
8
7
5
6
0
6
```

10.4.3 Mutating Sequence Algorithms

Mutating Sequence Algorithms change the elements in the input containers. Table 10.5 lists Mutating Sequence Algorithms in STL.

Here is an example of a mutating algorithm.

Example 10.10: An example of mutating algorithm.

```cpp
//10_10.cpp
#include <iostream>
#include <algorithm>
#include <functional>
#include <vector>
using namespace std;

class even_by_two{        //Function object by a class
public:
    int operator()() const
    {return _x+=2;}
private:
    static int _x;
};
int even_by_two::_x=0;    //Initialization of static member

int main()
{
    int iarray[]={0,1,2,3,4,5,6,6,6,7,8};
    int iarray1[]={0,1,2,3,4,4,5,5,6,6,6,6,6,7,8};
```

Tab. 10.5: Mutating Sequence Algorithms.

Name	Function
copy	Copy the elements in the interval
copy_n	Copy first *n* elements in the interval
copy_backward	Copy the elements in the interval in reverse order
fill	Replace the elements in the interval with a specified value
fill_n	Replace first *n* elements in the interval with a specified value
generate	Call the function object repeatedly, replace the elements in the interval with the return value
generate_n	Call the function object repeatedly, replace first *n* elements in the interval with the return value
partition	Put the elements that satisfy the condition by a function object before the other elements
stable_partition	Put the elements that satisfy the condition by a function object before the other elements, and keep the relative order
unique	Remove the adjacent elements that have the same value, make the value unique
unique_copy	Remove the adjacent elements that have the same value, make the value unique, and copy the result into another container
random_shuffle	Shuffle the elements in the interval randomly
remove	Remove all elements with the specified value in the interval
remove_if	Remove all elements that satisfy the condition in the interval
remove_copy	Remove all elements with the specified value in the interval and copy the result into another container
remove_copy_if	Remove all elements that satisfy the condition in the interval and copy the result into another container
replace	Replace a certain kind of elements
replace_copy_if	Replace a certain kind of elements conditionally and copy the result into another container
reverse	Reverse the order of elements in the interval
reverse_copy	Reverse the order of elements in the interval and copy the result into another container
rotate	Rotate two parts of elements in the interval
rotate_copy	Rotate two parts of elements in the interval and copy the result into another container
swap	Swap two elements using references
iter_swap	Swap two elements using iterator
swap_ranges	Swap elements in two intervals
transform	Make a new sequence using an existing sequence and a function object, or using two existing sequences and a function object

```
vector<int> ivector(iarray,iarray+sizeof(iarray)/sizeof(int));
vector<int> ivector1(iarray+6,iarray+8);
vector<int> ivector2(iarray1,iarray1+sizeof(iarray1)/sizeof(int));
ostream_iterator< int > output( cout, " " );
                    //Define stream iterator used to output data
```

```
//Traverse ivector1, commit even_by_two on every element
generate(ivector1.begin(),ivector1.end(),even_by_two());
copy(ivector1.begin(),ivector1.end(),output);
cout<<endl;

//Traverse the specified interval of ivector(by starting point
//and length), commit even_by_two on every element
generate_n(ivector.begin(),3,even_by_two());
copy(ivector.begin(),ivector.end(),output);
cout<<endl;

//Delete the 6th element
remove(ivector.begin(),ivector.end(),6);
copy(ivector.begin(),ivector.end(),output);
cout<<endl;

//Delete the 6th element and put the result into another interval
//(the original sequence has not been changed)
vector<int> ivector3(12);
remove_copy(ivector.begin(),ivector.end(),ivector3.begin(),6);
copy(ivector3.begin(),ivector3.end(),output);
cout<<endl;

//Delete the elements which are less than 6
remove_if(ivector.begin(),ivector.end(),bind2nd(less<int>(),6));
copy(ivector.begin(),ivector.end(),output);
cout<<endl;

//Delete the elements which are less than 7 and put the result
//into another interval (the original sequence has not been
//changed)
remove_copy_if(ivector.begin(),ivector.end(),ivector3.begin(),
    bind2nd(less<int>(),7));
copy(ivector3.begin(),ivector3.end(),output);
cout<<endl;

//Modify the value of elements which have a value of 6 to 3
replace(ivector.begin(),ivector.end(),6,3);
copy(ivector.begin(),ivector.end(),output);
cout<<endl;
```

```
//Modify the value of elements which have a value of 3 to 5 and
//put the result into another interval
replace_copy(ivector.begin(),ivector.end(),ivector3.begin(),3,5);
copy(ivector3.begin(),ivector3.end(),output);
cout<<endl;

//Modify the value of elements which have a value less than 5 to 2
replace_if(ivector.begin(),ivector.end(),
    bind2nd(less<int>(),5),2);
copy(ivector.begin(),ivector.end(),output);
cout<<endl;

//Modify the value of elements which have a value of 8 to 9 and
//put the result into another interval
replace_copy_if(ivector.begin(),ivector.end(),ivector3.begin(),
    bind2nd(equal_to<int>(),8),9);
copy(ivector3.begin(),ivector3.end(),output);
cout<<endl;

//Reverse all elements
reverse(ivector.begin(),ivector.end());
copy(ivector.begin(),ivector.end(),output);
cout<<endl;

//Reverse all elements and put the result into another interval
reverse_copy(ivector.begin(),ivector.end(),ivector3.begin());
copy(ivector3.begin(),ivector3.end(),output);
cout<<endl;

//Rotate(swap) the interval [first,middle) and [middle,end)
rotate(ivector.begin(),ivector.begin()+4,ivector.end());
copy(ivector.begin(),ivector.end(),output);
cout<<endl;

//Rotate(swap) the interval [first,middle) and [middle,end) and
//put the result into another interval
rotate_copy(ivector.begin(),ivector.begin()+5,ivector.end(),
    ivector3.begin());
copy(ivector3.begin(),ivector3.end(),output);
cout<<endl;
}
```

Results:

```
2 4
6 8 10 3 4 5 6 6 6 7 8
8 10 3 4 5 7 8 6 6 7 8
8 10 3 4 5 7 8 7 8 0 0 0
8 10 7 8 6 6 7 8 6 7 8
8 10 7 8 7 8 7 8 8 0 0 0
8 10 7 8 3 3 7 8 3 7 8
8 10 7 8 5 5 7 8 5 7 8 0
8 10 7 8 2 2 7 8 2 7 8
9 10 7 9 2 2 7 9 2 7 9 0
8 7 2 8 7 2 2 8 7 10 8
8 10 7 8 2 2 7 8 2 7 8 0
7 2 2 8 7 10 8 8 7 2 8
10 8 8 7 2 8 7 2 2 8 7 0
```

10.4.4 Sorting Related Algorithms

There are a number of sorting related algorithms in STL, including sorting a sequence, merging two sorted sequences, setting algorithms, and heaping algorithms for sorted sequences. Here is an overview of these algorithms:

Four sorting algorithms: *sort, partial_sort, partial_sort_copy*, and *stable_sort*;
Four binary searching algorithms: *binary_search, lower_bound, upper_bound*, and *equal_range*;
Two algorithms of merging two sorted sequences: *merge* and *inplace_merge*;
Four algorithms to find maximum/minimum:
min, max, min_element and max_element;
Three sorting related algorithm:
lexicographical_compare, next_permutation, and *prev_permutation*;
Five set algorithms:
includes, set_union, set_intersection, set_difference, and *set_symmetric_difference*;
Four heap algorithms: *make_heap, pop_heap, push_heap*, and *sort_heap*.

Algorithm *nth_element* resorts the sequence based on a particular rule. Table 10.6 lists sorting-related algorithms.

Tab. 10.6: STL Sorting-Related Algorithms.

Name	Function
sort	Sort the elements in the interval
stable_sort	Sort the elements in the interval and keep the relative order of elements that have same values
partial_sort	Sort the elements in the interval locally
partial_sort_copy	Sort the elements in the interval locally and copy them to another place
nth_element	Reorder the elements on the left side and the right side of the n-th element in the interval
upper_bound	Find the elements that have a value equal to the specified value in the ordered interval [first, last) using binary search, return the last insertable iterator
lower_bound	Find the elements that have a value equal to the specified value in the ordered interval [first, last) using binary search, return the first insertable iterator
binary_search	Find the elements that have a value equal to the specified value in the ordered interval using binary search
equal_range	Find the elements that have a value equal to the specified value in the ordered interval using binary search, return the result interval
merge	Merge two ordered intervals and put the result into an interval that is not overlapped with the two inputted intervals
inplace_merge	Merge two ordered intervals, replace the original interval with the result
min	Return the minimum element
max	Return the maximum element
min_element	Return the position of minimum element
max_element	Return the position of maximum element
lexicographical_compare	Compare two intervals in lexicographical way
next_permutation	Get the next permutation of the interval in lexicographical way
prev_permutation	Get the previous permutation of the interval in lexicographical way
includes	Check whether the elements of an interval are included in another interval
set_union	Return the union set of two sets using intervals. The set contains either the first set or the second set
set_difference	Return the difference set of two sets using intervals. The elements in the result belong to the first set but do not belong to the second set
set_intersection	Return the intersection of two sets using intervals. The elements in the result belongs to the first set and the second set
set_symmetric_diffference	Return the symmetric difference of two sets using intervals. The elements in the result only belong to one of two inputted sets
make_heap	Reorder the elements in the interval, make it a heap
pop_heap	Assume the interval is a heap, get the top of it
push_heap	Assume the interval is a heap, insert a element into it
sort_heap	Assume the interval is a heap, sort the elements in it

Here is an example of these algorithms:

Example 10.11: Example of sorting related algorithms.

```cpp
//10_11.cpp
#include <iostream>
#include <algorithm>
#include <functional>
#include <vector>
using namespace std;

int main()
{
  int iarray[]={26,17,15,22,23,33,32,40};
  vector<int> ivector(iarray,iarray+sizeof(iarray)/sizeof(int));

  //Find and output the maximum element and the minimum element
  cout<<*max_element(ivector.begin(),ivector.end())<<endl;
  cout<<*min_element(ivector.begin(),ivector.end())<<endl;

  //Sort the elements between ivector.begin()+4 and
  //ivector.begin(), put the result into interval
  //[ivector.begin(),ivector.begin()+4]. It is not guaranteed
  //that the order of remaining elements is kept.
  partial_sort(ivector.begin(),ivector.begin()+3,ivector.end());
  copy(ivector.begin(),ivector.end(),ostream_iterator<int>(cout," "));
  cout<<endl;

  //Sort locally and copy the result to another place
  vector<int> ivector1(5);
  partial_sort_copy(ivector.begin(),ivector.end(),ivector1.begin(),
      ivector1.end());
  copy(ivector1.begin(),ivector1.end(),ostream_iterator<int>
      (cout," "));
  cout<<endl;

  //Sort, using ascending order as default
  sort(ivector.begin(),ivector.end());
  copy(ivector.begin(),ivector.end(),ostream_iterator<int>(cout," "));
  cout<<endl;

  //The insertion of elements does not affect the location of the
  //minimum element and the maximum element
```

```
cout<<*lower_bound(ivector.begin(),ivector.end(),24)<<endl;
cout<<*upper_bound(ivector.begin(),ivector.end(),24)<<endl;

//Using binary search to find an element in the ordered interval
cout<<binary_search(ivector.begin(),ivector.end(),33)<<endl;
cout<<binary_search(ivector.begin(),ivector.end(),34)<<endl;

//Get the next permutation
next_permutation(ivector.begin(),ivector.end());
copy(ivector.begin(),ivector.end(),ostream_iterator<int>(cout," "));
cout<<endl;

//Get the previous permutation
prev_permutation(ivector.begin(),ivector.end());
copy(ivector.begin(),ivector.end(),ostream_iterator<int>(cout," "));
cout<<endl;

//Merge 2 sequences ivector and ivector1, put the result into
//ivector2
vector<int> ivector2(13);
merge(ivector.begin(),ivector.end(),ivector1.begin(),ivector1.end(),
    ivector2.begin());
copy(ivector2.begin(),ivector2.end(),ostream_iterator<int>
    (cout," "));
cout<<endl;

//Put all elements which are less than *(ivector.begin()+5) on
//the left side ofit, put the other elements on the right side of
//it. It is not guaranteed that the relative order is kept during
//the operation
nth_element(ivector2.begin(),ivector2.begin()+5,ivector2.end());
copy(ivector2.begin(),ivector2.end(),ostream_iterator<int>
    (cout," "));
cout<<endl;

//Sort and keep the relative order
stable_sort(ivector2.begin(),ivector2.end());
copy(ivector2.begin(),ivector2.end(),ostream_iterator<int>
    (cout," "));
cout<<endl;
```

```
//Find a sub-interval in an ordered interval, make sure all
//elements in the sub-interval are equal to a specified value
pair<vector<int>::iterator,vector<int>::iterator> pairIte;
pairIte=equal_range(ivector2.begin(),ivector2.end(),22);
cout<<*(pairIte.first)<<endl;
cout<<*(pairIte.second)<<endl;

//Merge 2 ordered sequences and replace the original sequences
int iarray3[] = { 1, 3, 5, 7, 2, 4, 6, 8 };
vector<int> ivector3(iarray3,iarray3+sizeof(iarray3)/sizeof(int));
inplace_merge(ivector3.begin(), ivector3.begin()+ 4,
    ivector3.end());
copy(ivector3.begin(),ivector3.end(), ostream_iterator<int>
    (cout, " "));
cout<<endl;

//Compare sequence ivector3 and ivector4 in lexicographical way
int iarray4[] = { 1, 3, 5, 7,1, 5, 9, 3 };
vector<int> ivector4(iarray4,iarray4+sizeof(iarray4)/sizeof(int));
cout<< lexicographical_compare(ivector3.begin(),ivector3.end(),
    ivector4.begin(),ivector4.end()) << endl;
}
```

Results:

```
40
15
15 17 22 26 23 33 32 40
15 17 22 23 26
15 17 22 23 26 32 33 40
26
26
1
0
15 17 22 23 26 32 40 33
15 17 22 23 26 32 33 40
15 15 17 17 22 22 23 23 26 26 32 33 40
15 15 17 17 22 22 23 23 26 26 32 33 40
15 15 17 17 22 22 23 23 26 26 32 33 40
22
23
1 2 3 4 5 6 7 8
1
```

10.4.5 Numerical Algorithms

There are four generic numerical algorithms; Table 10.7 lists numerical algorithms in STL.

Here is an example of numerical algorithms in STL:

Example 10.12: An example of numerical algorithms.

```
//10_12.cpp
#include <iostream>
#include <numeric>
#include <functional>
#include <vector>
using namespace std;

int main()
{
    int iarray[]={1,2,3,4,5};
    vector<int> ivector(iarray,iarray+sizeof(iarray)/sizeof(int));

    //Accumulation of elements
    cout<<accumulate(ivector.begin(),ivector.end(),0)<<endl;

    //Inner product of vectors
    cout<<inner_product(ivector.begin(),ivector.end(),ivector.begin(),
        10)<<endl;

    //Sum of part of elements in a vector
    partial_sum(ivector.begin(),ivector.end(),ostream_iterator<int>
        (cout," "));
    cout<<endl;

    //Difference of adjacent elements in a vector
```

Tab. 10.7: STL Numerical Algorithms.

Name	Function
accumulate	Calculate the sum of all elements in a sequence
partial_sum	Add parts of the elements in a sequence, save them into another sequence
adjacent_difference	Calculate the differences of adjacent elements in a sequence, save them into another sequence
inner_product	Add the corresponding elements of two sequences (inner product of vectors)

```
    adjacent_difference(ivector.begin(),ivector.end(),ostream_iterator
        <int>(cout," "));
    cout<<endl;
}
```

Results:

```
15
65
1 3 6 10 15
1 1 1 1 1
```

10.5 Function Objects

Many algorithms use a function object to abstract the operation of the algorithm, in order to provide additional flexibility. In this section, we introduce the design and usage of function objects in STL.

1. Function Objects

A function object is a design pattern used in STL for maximal flexibility. **Function objects are an abstraction layer to hide the implementation detail.** They behave like functions; they can return a value or perform some operations with side effects (like opening a file). In C++, all functions and any classes overloading the operator *()* can be used as function objects.

Now we use the numerical algorithm *accumulate()* as an example to discuss the design and usage of function objects. There are two prototypes of *accumulate()*: one uses the addition operator "+" to calculate the sum of the sequence, the other uses a customized function object to calculate the result.

Here is an example of using a function as a function object to implement a multiplication operation:

Example 10.13: Use a function as a function object.

```
//10_13.cpp
#include <iostream>
#include <numeric>        //Include header file of numerical algorithms
using namespace std;

int mult(int x, int y) { return x*y; }; //Define a common function
int main()
{
    int A[] = {1, 2, 3, 4, 5};
    const int N = sizeof(A)/sizeof(int);
```

```
    cout << "The result by multiplying all elements in A is "
        << accumulate(A, A + N, 1, mult)
                            //Pass function mult to the generic function
        << endl;
}
```

Results:

The result by multiplying all elements in A is 120

Besides functions, function objects could be objects of a class that overloaded the operator doing the calling . The following example is another implementation of Example 10.13. In this example, the object of a class is used instead of a function.

Example 10.14: Define function objects using classes.

```
//10_14.cpp
#include <iostream>
#include <numeric>       //Include header files of numerical algorithm
using namespace std;

class multclass         //Define class multclass
{
public:
    int operator()(int x, int y) const {return x*y;}
                        //Overload operator()
};

int main()
{
  int A[] = {1, 2, 3, 4, 5};
  const int N = sizeof(A)/sizeof(int);
  cout << "The result by multiplying all elements in A is "
      << accumulate(A, A + N, 1, multclass())
                        //Pass multclass to the generic algorithm
      << endl;
}
```

Results:

The result by multiplying all elements in A is 120

The class *multclass* overloads the operator *()* to implement the multiplication. The compiler generates an instance of *multclass* with its default constructor and passes it to the *accumulate()* algorithm. The programmer can create a customized instance to provide additional information for the algorithm.

Tab. 10.8: STL Function Objects in Standard Library.

STL Function Object	Type	Description
Plus<T>	Numeric	Input two operands with a type of T, return their sum
Minus<T>	Numeric	Input two operands with a type of T, return the result of subtracting the second operand from the first operand
Multiplies<T>	Numeric	Input two operands with a type of T, return their product
Divides<T>	Numeric	Input two operands with a type of T, return the result of dividing the second operand by the first operand
Modulus<T>	Relation	Input two operands x and y with a type of T, return result of $x\%y$
Negate<T>	Numeric	Input an operand with a type of T, return its opposite number
Equal_to<T>	Relation	Input two operands x and y with a type of T, return true if $x==y$
Not_equal_to<T>	Relation	Input two operands x and y with a type of T, return true if $x!=y$
Greater<T>	Relation	Input two operands x and y with a type of T, return true if $x>y$
Less<T>	Relation	Input two operands x and y with a type of T, return true if $x<y$
Greater_equal<T>	Relation	Input two operands x and y with a type of T, return true if $x>=y$
Less_equal<T>	Relation	Input two operands x and y with a type of T, return true if $x<=y$
Logical_and<T>	Logical	Input two operands x and y with a type of T, return the result of logical and: $x\&\&y$
Logical_or<T>	Logical	Input two operands x and y with a type of T, return the result of logical or: $x\|\|y$
Logical_not<T>	Logical	Input a operand x with a type of T, return the result of logical not: $!x$

STL defines a number of standard function objects, including arithmetic operations, boolean operations, and logical operations (as shown in Table 10.8). All of them are defined as inline functions to maximize the performance.

You can also use the multiplication function object provide by STL to implement the same functionalities. Here is the program:

Example 10.15: Using the STL function object multiplies to implement multiplication.

```
//10_15.cpp
#include <iostream>
#include <numeric>       //Include header file of numerical algorithms
#include <functional>    //Include header file of STL function objects
using namespace std;

int main()
{
  int A[] = {1, 2, 3, 4, 5};
  const int N = sizeof(A)/sizeof(int);
  cout << "The result by multiplying all elements in A is "
   << accumulate(A, A + N, 1, multiplies<int>())<< endl;
                   //Pass STL function object to the generic algorithm
}
```

Everything is the same except we changed the *multclass* in Example 10.14 to *multiplies<int>*.

STL defines two basic classes of function objects, one for unary functions and one for binary functions for simplifying the design of function objects. For advanced topics please refer to related materials.

2. Function Adapters

Using function adapters is an easier way to create function objects. Interested readers might refer to advanced materials for details

10.6 Application – Improving the HR Management Program of a Small Company

In this section, we demonstrate how to use STL's vectors to simplify storing objects in the application.

There are three files in the program: *employee.h, empfunc.cpp*, and *10_16.cpp*. *10_16.cpp* is derived from Example 9.16.

Example 10.16: Improving the HR management program.

```
//10_16.cpp
#include<iostream>
#include"employee.h"
#include<vector>
using namespace std;

int main()
{
    manager m1;
    technician t1;
    salesmanager sm1;
    salesman s1;
    char namestr[20];
            //The employee names will be saved into namestr temporary

    vector <employee *> vchar;          //Define vector container
                                        //for member elements
    vchar.push_back(&m1);
    vchar.push_back(&t1);
    vchar.push_back(&sm1);
    vchar.push_back(&s1);
```

```
   int i;
   for(i=0;i<4;i++)
   {
     cout<<" Please input the name of next employee:";
     cin>>namestr;
     vchar[i]->SetName(namestr);           //Set name of every employee
     vchar[i]->promote();                  //Promote
   }
   cout<<"Please input the part-time technicians "<<t1.GetName()<<"'s
       working hours this week:";
   int ww;
   cin>>ww;
   t1.SetworkHours(ww);                    //Set working hours

   cout<<"Please input the sales manager "<<sm1.GetName()<<"'s total
       sales this month of his department:";
   float sl;
   cin>>sl;
   sm1.Setsales(sl);                       //Set total sales

   cout<<"Please input the salesman "<<s1.GetName()<<"'s sales this
       month:";
   cin>>sl;
   s1.Setsales(sl);                        //Set sales

   for(i=0;i<4;i++)
   {
     vchar[i]->pay();                      //Calculate salary
     cout<<vchar[i]->GetName()<<" ID "<<vchar[i]->
        GetindividualEmpNo()<<" Level "
     <<vchar[i]->Getgrade()<<", salary this month "
     <<vchar[i]->GetaccumPay()<<endl;
   }
}
```

Results:

```
Please input the name of next employee: Zhang
Please input the name of next employee: Wang
Please input the name of next employee: Li
Please input the name of next employee: Zhao
Please input the part-time technicians Wang's working hours this
week:40
```

> Please input the sales manager Li's total sales this month of his
> department: 400000
> Please input the salesman Zhao's sales this month: 40000
> Zhang ID 1000 Level 4, salary this month 8000
> Wang ID 1001 Level 3, salary this month 4000
> Li ID 1002 Level 3, salary this month 7000
> Zhao ID 1003 Level 1, salary this month 1600

10.7 Summary

This chapter introduced the concepts of containers, container iterators, iterators, iterator adapters, generic algorithms, function objects, and function adapters; and discussed a number of collections (vectors, deques, and lists) and container iterators (stacks, queues, priority queues). This chapter also discussed four generic algorithms, iterators, and function objects, and demonstrates how to use them.

STL is a powerful tool for simplifying the development of applications. Readers can refer to Appendix C of the student book for the prototypes of generic algorithms. Interested readers can refer to the MSDN of SGI's documents to understand STL.

Exercises

10.1 In STL's implementation of stacks, the method *push()* adds an element at the top of the stack, the method *pop()* removes an element from the top of the stack, the method *empty()* checks whether the stack is empty, the method *top()* return the top element of a non-empty stack, and the method *size()* returns the number of elements in the stacks. Please construct a stack with type *int* that calls the above functions to learn about the stack and the usage of these functions.

10.2 STL's implementation of stack overload operators ==, !=, >, >=, <, <= for comparison between two stacks. Please construct two stack with type *int* and compare them with operator == and <. Observe the result.

10.3 In STL's implementation of queues, the method *push()* adds an element at one end of the queue, the method *pop()* removes the last element from a nonempty queue, the method *empty()* checks whether the queue is empty, the method *back()/front()* returns the last element and the first element of a non-empty queue respectively, and the method *size()* returns the number of elements in the queue. Please construct two queues with type *int* and type *char*, respectively, and then apply the above methods to the queue to learn about the characteristics of the queue and the usage of these functions.

10.4 In STL's implementation of deques, the method *assign()* reassigns values to a deque, the method *swap()* swaps elements of two deque, and the method *begin()/end()* return the iterators pointing to the first/last element. Please construct a deque with *int* type and apply these functions to the deque to learn more about deques and the usage of these functions.

10.5 In STL's implementation of deque, the methods *front()/back()* return the first/ last element of the deque. Please construct a deque with type *char* and apply these functions to the deque to learn more about deques and the usage of these functions.

10.6 In STL's implementation of deque, method *insert()* inserts an element into a deque, the methods *push_front()/pop_front()* add /remove an element at the head of the deque, and *push_back()/pop_ back()* add /remove an element at the end of the deque. Please construct a deque with type *char* and apply these functions to the deque to lean more about the usage of these functions.

10.7 The length of a deque is variable. The method *resize()* resets the size of a deque, the method *size()* returns the number of elements in a deque, and the method *max_size()* returns the available size of the queue. Please construct a deque with type *char* and apply these functions to the deque to lean more about the usage of these functions.

10.8 What are the two types of containers? What are the five types of iterators? What are three types of container adapters? What mechanism does STL use to access the elements in containers?

10.9 Write a program to use the fill function in STL to set a certain range of container to a certain value, then use the generate function to generate a sequence of value.

10.10 Write a program to use *swap()*, *iter_swap()*, and *swap_ranges()* to swap elements in an array.

10.11 Write a program to use *inplace_merge()* to merge two sorted sequences in the same container, then use *reverse_copy()* to copy elements reversely into another container, and at last use *unique_copy()* to copy elements into another container uniquely.

10.12 Write a program to use *set_difference()* to find elements in the first sequence but not in the second sequence, then use *set_intersection()* to find elements occurring in both sequences, and at last use *set_union()* to find the union of the elements of both sequences.

10.13 Write a program to run *count()* and *for_each()* on a vector.

10.14 Write a program to run *swap()* and *replace()* on a vector.

10.15 Write a program to run *sort()*, *binary_search()*, *merge()*, and *includes()* on a vector to implement basic sorting, finding, merging, and set operations.

10.16 Write a program to run *swap()*, *rotate()*, *partition()*, *erase()*, *fill()*, and *shuffle()* on a collection.

10.17 Use heap-related algorithms to perform operations on a heap.

10.18 Use set-related algorithms to perform operations on a set.

11 The I/O Stream Library and Input/Output

As in the C language, there is no input/output statement in C++. However, there is an object-oriented input/output software package in C++, i.e., the **I/O stream library**. Stream is the key concept of an I/O stream. In this chapter, the concept of stream and then the structure and the use of stream library will be introduced. A more detailed explanation and description of classes and the members of the stream library can be found in the reference book of the running libraries of compiler system.

11.1 I/O Stream's Concept and the Structure of a Stream Library

An I/O stream library is a replacement product of the C language I/O function in object-oriented program design.

As introduced in Chapter 2, we conceptualize the flow from one object to another as "stream" in C++. The operation of getting data from a stream is called extraction, and adding data into a stream is called insertion. Data input and output is realized through an I/O stream. We will give a detailed introduction of it in the following paragraphs.

When a program exchanges information with the external environment, there are two objects: one is the object in the program, and the other is the file object. Stream is a kind of abstract, which is responsible for establishing the connection between the producer of data and the consumer of data, and managing the flow of data. A program generates a stream object and designates this stream object to be associated with a file object, the program operates the stream object, and the stream object affects the connected file object through the file system. Since a stream object is the exchanging interface between objects in the program and file objects, and a stream object has all the properties of a file object, **programs regard a stream object as a form of file object.**

Operating systems handle the keyboard, screen, printer, and communication port as extended files by using a device driver. Therefore, for a C++ programmer, these devices are the same as disk files. Data exchange with these devices is achieved by using an I/O stream.

Stream is not limited to I/O operations. Every operation of transmitting data from one place to another is a stream operation. For example, both Internet data exchange and process data exchange are stream operations. Therefore, reading an operation is called **extraction** in stream data abstraction, and writing an operation is called **insertion**.

The basis of an I/O stream library is class templates. Class templates provide most of the functions in the library, and they can operate on different types of elements. All these templates have "basic_" as the prefix in their names.

There are two kinds of template in an I/O stream: wide-character-oriented and narrow-character-oriented. The wide-character-oriented class supports multibyte charac-

https://doi.org/10.1515/9783110471977-011

ters, and the narrow-character-oriented class supports single-byte characters. The following instantiation types are defined in head file <*iosfwd*>:

```
//char TYPEDEFS
typedef basic_ios<char, char_traits<char> > ios;
typedef basic_streambuf<char, char_traits<char> > streambuf;
typedef basic_istream<char, char_traits<char> > istream;
typedef basic_ostream<char, char_traits<char> > ostream;
typedef basic_iostream<char, char_traits<char> > iostream;
typedef basic_stringbuf<char, char_traits<char>, allocator<char> >
    stringbuf;
typedef basic_istringstream<char, char_traits<char>, allocator<char>
    > istringstream;
typedef basic_ostringstream<char, char_traits<char>, allocator<char>
    > ostringstream;
typedef basic_stringstream<char, char_traits<char>, allocator<char>
    > stringstream;
typedef basic_filebuf<char, char_traits<char> > filebuf;
typedef basic_ifstream<char, char_traits<char> > ifstream;
typedef basic_ofstream<char, char_traits<char> > ofstream;
typedef basic_fstream<char, char_traits<char> > fstream;
//wchar_t TYPEDEFS
typedef basic_ios<wchar_t, char_traits<wchar_t> > wios;
typedef basic_streambuf<wchar_t, char_traits<wchar_t> > wstreambuf;
typedef basic_istream<wchar_t, char_traits<wchar_t> > wistream;
typedef basic_ostream<wchar_t, char_traits<wchar_t> > wostream;
typedef basic_iostream<wchar_t, char_traits<wchar_t> > wiostream;
typedef basic_stringbuf<wchar_t, char_traits<wchar_t>,
    allocator<wchar_t>> wstringbuf;
typedef basic_istringstream<wchar_t, char_traits<wchar_t>,
    allocator<wchar_t>>
wistringstream;
typedef basic_ostringstream<wchar_t, char_traits<wchar_t>,
    allocator<wchar_t> >
wostringstream;
typedef basic_stringstream<wchar_t, char_traits<wchar_t>,
    allocator<wchar_t> >
wstringstream;
typedef basic_filebuf<wchar_t, char_traits<wchar_t> > wfilebuf;
typedef basic_ifstream<wchar_t, char_traits<wchar_t> > wifstream;
typedef basic_ofstream<wchar_t, char_traits<wchar_t> > wofstream;
typedef basic_fstream<wchar_t, char_traits<wchar_t> > wfstream;
```

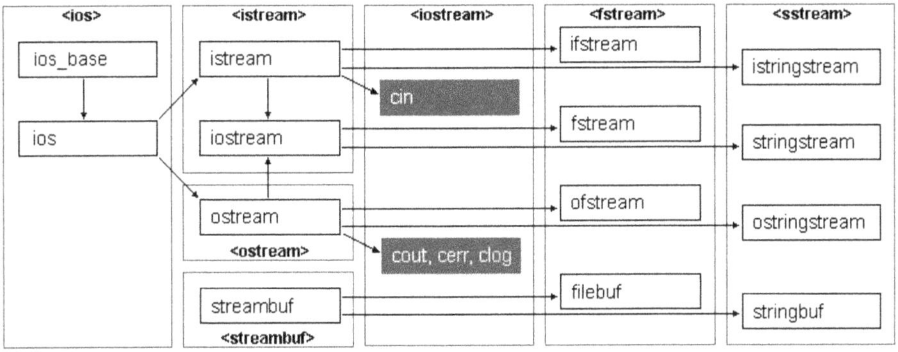

Fig. 11.1: Hierarchy chart of I/O stream class.

It is unnecessary to include the head file *<iosfwd>* explicitly, because *<iosfwd>* is already included in other related head files. *<iosfwd>* is necessary only when a specific type definition is needed, but the corresponding class definition is not needed.

In an I/O stream library, the head file *<iostream>* declared eight reprocessing stream objects for accomplish input/output operations on standard devices. These objects are *cin, out, cerr, clog, wcin, wcout, wcerr, and wclog*.

Figure 11.1 shows the relationship among the narrow-character-oriented classes in an I/O stream library. Table 11.1 shows descriptions of these classes and the name of the head file that contains the corresponding class definition. The relation among wide-character-oriented classes is similar to narrow-character-oriented classes, but due to space limitation, we will only introduce the narrow-character-oriented I/O stream class in this chapter.

The head files *<ios>*, *<istream>*,*<ostream>*,*<streambuf>*, and *<iosfwd>* in Table 11.1 usually will not be shown in the source program explicitly, because all of them describe the basic types in class hierarchy structure, and they are already included in the head files of other derived classes.

11.2 Output Stream

An output stream object is the target of information flow. The three most important output streams are *ostream, ofstream*, and *ostringstream* respectively.

The predefined *ostream* class object is used to accomplish the output to standard devices:

cout standard output

cerr standard error output. It has no buffer area, and outputs the content sent to it
immediately.

clog is similar to *cerr*, but it has a buffer area. It outputs the content when the buffer
area is full.

Tab. 11.1: I/O Stream Class List.

Class name	Description	File included
Abstract stream basic type		
Ios	Stream base type	*ios*
Input stream class		
Istream	Common use input stream class and other input stream basic class	*istream*
Ifstream	Input file stream class	*fstream*
Istringstream	Input character string stream class	*sstream*
Output stream class		
Ostream	Common use output stream class and other output stream basic class	*ostream*
Ofstream	Output file stream class	*fstream*
Ostringstream	Output character string stream class	*sstream*
Input/output stream class		
Iostream	Common use input/output stream class and other input/output stream basic class	*istream*
Fstream	Input/output file stream class	*fstream*
Stringstream	Input/output character string stream class	*sstream*
Stream buffer class		
Streambuf	Abstract stream buffer basic class	*streambuf*
Filebuf	Stream buffer class of disk files	*fstream*
Stringbuf	Stream buffer class of character string	*sstream*

ofstream class supports disk file output. An *ofstream* class object can be constructed for an output-only disk file. An *ofstream* object can be designated to receive binary or text data before or after opening a file. Many format options and member functions of *ofstream* objects can be used, including all the functions in the basic classes *ios* and *ostream*.

When a file name is included in the constructor of *ofstream*, the file will be opened automatically when constructing this *ofstream* object. You can also use the member function *open* to open the file after calling the default constructor, or construct an *ofstream* object based on an opened file that is marked by a file identifier.

11.2.1 Construct Output Object

If only the predefined objects of *cout, cerr,* or *clog* are used, it is not necessary to construct an output stream. For example, in the examples of the previous chapter, we use *cout* to output the information to standard output devices. To use file stream to output information to a file, a constructor should be used to establish stream objects.

An often-used method to construct output file stream is to use the default constructor, and then call the member function *open* as shown in the following example:

```
ofstream myFile; //define an ofstream object
myFile.open("filename",iosmode);        //open file, link stream object
                                        //and file
```

or:

```
ofstream* pmyFile = new ofstream; //new an ofsteam object
pmyFile\textminus>open("filename",iosmode); //open file, link stream
                                        //object and file
```

Specify file name and mode when calling constructor:

```
ofstream myFile("filename",iosmode);
```

You can also use one stream to open different files one after another (only one is opened at the same time):

```
ofstream ofile;
ofile.open("FILE1", iosmode); //open file "FILE1"
//...... output to file "FILE1"
ofile.close();                    //close FILE1
ofile.open("FILE2", iosmode); //open file "FILE2"
//...... output to file "FILE2"
ofile.close();                    //close FILE2
//object ofile will disappear when it leaves its scope
```

We will introduce the member functions *open()*, *close()*, and the modes of opening files later in this chapter.

11.2.2 The Use of Inserter and Manipulator

In this section, we will introduce how to control the form of output and how to build inserter operators for a user defined class. Operator << is predefined to all standard C++ data types and is used to transmit bytes to an output stream object. Using << with predefined manipulators can control the output form.

A lot of manipulators are defined in class *ios_base* (such as *hex()*) and the head file of *<iomanip>* (such as *setprecision()*).

1. Output Width
To modulate output, we can insert the manipulator *setw* in the stream or call member function *width* to specify the output width of each item. The following example is of output data with a width of 10 characters and a right-aligned mode:

Example 11.1: Use function *width* to control output width.

```cpp
//11_1.cpp
#include <iostream>
using namespace std;
int main()
{
    double values[] = {1.23,35.36,653.7,4358.24};
    for(int i=0;i<4;i++)
    {
        cout.width(10);
        cout << values[i] <<'\n';
    }
}
```

The result of the program is as follows:

```
      1.23
     35.36
     653.7
   4358.24
```

From the results we can see that the program added leading space before values that are less than 10 characters wide.

Blank is the default filler. When the output data cannot satisfy the specified width, the system will fill it with blanks automatically. By using the member function *fill*, other characters can be set as the filler to fill. To use an asterisk to fill the row, for example, we changed the *for* loop in Example 11.1 to the following:

```cpp
for(int i=0; i<4; i++)
{
    cout.width(10);
    cout.fill('*');
    cout << values[i]<< endl;
}
```

The result of the program is as follows:

```
******1.23
*****35.36
*****653.7
***4358.24
```

The manipulator *setw* can be used to specify the width for different data items in the same row, as shown in the following example.

Example 11.2: Use manipulator *setw* to appoint width.

```
//11_2.cpp
#include <iostream>
#include <iomanip>
using namespace std;
int main()
{
    double values[] = {1.23,35.36,653.7,4358.24};
    char *names[] = {"Zoot", "Jimmy", "Al", "Stan"};
    for (int i=0;i<4;i++)
        cout << setw(6) << names[i] << setw(10) << values[i] << endl;
}
```

The member function *width* is declared in *iostream*. If *setw* is used with parameters or any other manipulators, it must include *iomanip*. On the output line, the width of a character string is set to six and that of an integer is set to 10, as shown below.

```
  Zoot 1.23
 Jimmy 35.36
    Al 653.7
  Stan 4358.24
```

Neither *setw* nor *width* can truncate values. If there are more digits than the specified width, all digits will be displayed with the proper precision set of the stream. *setw* and *width* only affect the scope of the first output after the instruction is executed. After the first output, the width reverts back to its default value. All other stream form options remain effective until they are changed.

2. Alignment

The default output is right-aligned text. The following program is modified in order to achieve an output with left-aligned names and right-aligned values.

Example 11.3: Set alignment.

```
//11_3.cpp
#include <iostream>
#include <iomanip>
using namespace std;
int main()
{
    double values[] = {1.23,35.36,653.7,4358.24};
    char *names[] = {"Zoot", "Jimmy", "Al", "Stan"};
    for (int i=0;i<4;i++)
        cout << setiosflags(ios_base::left)
```

```
                << setw(6) << names[i]
                << resetiosflags(ios_base::left)
                << setw(10) << values[i] << endl;
    }
```

Result:

```
    Zoot 1.23
    Jimmy 35.36
    Al 653.7
    Stan 4358.24
```

This program used manipulator *setiosflags* with parameters to set left alignment. *setiosflags* is defined in *<iomanip>*. Parameter *ios_base::left* is an enumeration constant; it is defined in class *ios_base*, therefore needs to include *ios_base::*prefix when quoting. Manipulator *resetiosflags* is used to close the left alignment label here. Unlike *width* and *setw*, *setiosflags* remains effective until *resetiosflags* resumes the default value.

The parameter of *setiosflags* is the format designator of the stream and its value is specified by the mask code (*ios_base* enumeration type constant) shown below. The value can be combined by using bitwise *or* the (|) operator.

ios_base::skipws skip the blanks in input

ios_base::left display left-alignment value, and use filler character to fill the right

ios_base::right display right-alignment value, and use filler character to fill the left (default alignment)

ios_base::internal insert specified filler inside the specified width, after the specified prefix symbol, before the value.

ios_base::dec format the value in decimal form (default form)

ios_base::oct format the value in octal form

ios_base::hex format the value in hexadecimal form

ios_base::showbase insert prefix symbol to represent the form (decimal, octal, or hexadecimal) of integrals.

ios_base::showpoint display the decimal point and tail 0s of float value

ios_base::uppercase display capital letters A~F for hexadecimal form, and display capital letter E for scientific form

ios_base::showpos display the positive sign (+) for nonnegative numbers

ios_base::scientific display float numbers in scientific form

ios_base::fixed display float numbers in fixed-point form (no index part)

ios_base::unitbuf dump and delete the contents in buffer after each insertion

3. Precision

The default value of a float number output precision is 6. For example, 3466.9768 is displayed as 3466.98. We can use the manipulator *setprecision* (defined in head file *<iomanip>*) to change the precision by using either the label, *ios_based::fixed* or *ios_based::scientific*. If it is set to *ios_base::fixed*, the output will be 3466.976800; if it is set to *ios_base::scientific*, the output will be 3.4669773+003. The program above can be modified to display floating point numbers with a precision of 1 as shown in the following example.

Example 11.4: Control output precision.

```cpp
//11_4.cpp
#include <iostream>
#include <iomanip>
using namespace std;
int main()
{
    double values[] = {1.23,35.36,653.7,4358.24};
    char *names[] = {"Zoot", "Jimmy", "Al", "Stan"};
    for (int i=0;i<4;i++)
        cout << setiosflags(ios_base::left)
            << setw(6)<< names[i]
            << resetiosflags(ios_base::left)
            << setw(10) << setprecision(1) << values[i] << endl;
}
```

The result of the program is as follows:

```
Zoot        1
Jimmy    4e+001
Al       7e+002
Stan     4e+003
```

To use the fixed-point format instead of the scientific form, the following statement should be inserted before the *for* loop:

```cpp
cout << setiosflags(ios_base::fixed);
```

The result of the program using a fixed-point format with a precision of 1 is shown below:

```
Zoot       1.2
Jimmy     35.4
Al       653.7
Stan    4358.2
```

If *ios_base::fixed* is changed to *ios_base::scientific*, the result is as follows:

```
Zoot    1.2e+000
Jimmy   3.5e+001
```

```
A1      6.5e+002
Stan    4.4e+003
```

Note that this program outputs one digit after the decimal point. This indicates that when either *ios_base::fixed* or *ios_base::scientific* is used, the precision value is the number of digits after the decimal point. In other cases, the precision value is the number of all the effective digits. Manipulator *reseriosflags* can be used to delete these labels.

4. Notation

dec, oct, and *hex* manipulators set the default notation of input and output. For example, if the manipulator *hex* is inserted into the output stream, the output will be in a hexadecimal format. If *ios_base::uppercase* (default) label is cleared, the hex numbers *a* through *f* are displayed in lowercase; otherwise they are displayed in uppercase. The default notation is *dec* (decimal).

11.2.3 Output File Stream Member Function

There are three types of member functions in the output stream classes:
1. Member functions equivalent to manipulators;
2. Member functions executing unformatted write operations;
3. Other member functions that modify stream state and are not equal to manipulators or inserters.

Inserters and manipulators can be used in ordinal formatted outputs. For random binary disk outputs, other member functions should be used.

1. Function *open* of output stream

To use an output file stream (*ofstream*), the stream should be related to a specified disk file in the constructor or function *open*. In both cases, the parameters of the described files are the same.

When a file related to an output stream is opened, an *open mode* label is often needed as shown in Table 11.2. These labels can be combined by using a bitwise *or* (|) operator. They are defined as enumeration constant in class *ios_base*.

2. Function *close* of output stream

Member function *close* closes a disk file related to an output file stream. To complete the disk output, the file must be closed after being used. Although an *ofstream* destructor will finish closing it automatically, if we want to open another file by the same stream object, we have to use the function *close*.

Tab. 11.2: Opening Model of Output File Stream File.

Label	Function
ios_base::app	Open an output file to add data at the bottom.
ios_base::ate	Open an extant file (used for input or output) and search its end.
ios_base::in	Open an input file, to *ofstream* files, use *ios_base::in* as an open mode to avoid deleting the contents of an extant file.
ios_base::out	Open a file used for output. To all *ofstream* objects, this mode is implicit.
ios_base::trunc	Open a file. If it already exists, delete the intrinsic content. If *ios_base::out is* appointed, but *ios_base::ate, ios_base::app* and *ios_base::in* are not appointed, then this mode is implicit.
ios_base::binary	Use binary mode to open a file (text mode is the default mode).

If the constructor or member function *open* is used to open this file, the destructor of the output stream will automatically close a stream's file.

3. Function *put*

Function *put* writes a character to the output stream. The default of the following two statements are the same, but the second one is impacted by the format parameter of the stream:

```
cout.put('A'); //output a character precisely
cout << 'A';   //output a character, the width and filling method
               //installed before does its work
```

4. Function *write*

Function *write* writes a part of memory content to the output file stream. The length parameter indicates the number of bytes. The following example builds an output file stream and writes the binary value of structure *Date* into a file.

Example 11.5: Output to a file.

```
//11_5.cpp
#include <fstream>
using namespace std;
struct Date
{
    int mo,da,yr;
};
int main()
{
    Date dt = {6,10,92};
    ofstream tfile("date.dat",ios_base::binary);
```

```
        tfile.write((char *) &dt,sizeof dt);
        tfile.close()
    }
```

Function *write* will not stop when it encounters space characters and therefore it can read-in a whole class structure. This function has two parameters: one *char* pointer (indicates the starting address of memory data) and the number of bytes that need to be written. Note that you need *char** to cast type before the address of the structure object.

5. Function *seekp* and *tellp*

An output file stores an internal pointer to indicate the location of the next read/write operation. Member function *seekp* is used to set this pointer so it can output to a random location in a disk file. Member function *tellp* returns the value of the pointer of this file location.

6. Error Handling Function

The role of error handling function is to handle errors when writing a stream. Table 11.3 shows the functions and their effects.

Operator *!* has been reloaded. Its role is the same as function *fail*, therefore expression *if (!cout)* equals *if (cout.fail())*...

Operator *void*()* has also been reloaded. It does the opposite of what the operator *!* does. The expression *if (cout)* has the same effect as the expression *if (!cout.fail())*...

Operator *void*()* is not equivalent to *good* because it does not detect the ending of a file.

Tab. 11.3: Error Handling Functions and Their Effects.

Function	Effect and return value
bad	If an error appeared and cannot be recovered, then return a non-0 value.
fail	If an error that cannot be recovered or an expected condition appeared, for example, a conversion error or cannot find file, then return a non-0 value. Error label will be deleted after call *clear* using zero parameter.
good	If all the error labels and file ending labels have been cleared, then return a non-0 value.
eof	Meet the file ending condition, and return a non-0 value.
clear	Set the state of internal errors, if called by default parameters, then clear all the error digits.
rdstate	Return the current error state.

11.2.4 Binary Output File

The original purpose of stream was to use it to process text and therefore the default output mode is text. In text mode output, a line break (decimal 10) will be extended to a new line break (decimal 13) automatically. This can cause problems shown in the following program.

```
#include <fstream>
int iarray[2] = {99,10};
int main()
{
    ofstream os("test.dat");
    os.write((char *) iarray, sizeof(iarray));
}
```

When 10 is output to a file, it will be converted to 13 automatically. However, this conversion is not needed here. To solve this problem, we have to use binary mode output. The characters are not converted while using binary mode output. There are two ways to use binary mode to output to a file as shown below:

1. Use the mode parameter in *ofstream* constructor to specify binary output mode as shown in the following example:

```
#include <fstream>
using namespace std;
int iarray[2] = {99,10};
int main()
{
    ofstream ofs("test.dat",ios_base::binary);
    ofs.write((char *)iarray,4);
                            //read-in a 4-byte data into the binary file
}
```

2. Use function *open* with a binary mode label to open a file as shown in the following example:

```
#include <fstream>
using namespace std;
int iarray[2] = {99,10};
int main()
{
    ofstream ofs();
    ofs.open("test.dat",ios_base::binary);
    ofs.write((char *)iarray,4);
                            //read-in a 4-byte data into the binary file
}
```

11.3 Input Stream

An input stream object is the source of a data flow. The three most important input streams are *istream, ifstream,* and *istringstream.*

Class *istream* is most suitable for ordered text mode input. All the functions of the basic class *ios* are included in *istream.* We rarely need to construct objects from class *istream.* We usually use predefined a *cin* object, which is actually an object of class *istream_withassign.*

Class *ifstream* supports disk file input. For an input-only disk file, one can construct a class *ifstream* object, and set its mode to text or binary. If a file name is specified in the constructor, the file will be opened automatically when constructing this object or the member function *open* can be used to open the file after calling the default constructor. Many format options and member functions of *ifstream* objects can be used, including all the functions in the basic classes *ios* and *istream.*

11.3.1 Construct Input Stream Object

It is unnecessary to construct an input stream object if only the predefined object *cin* is used. If a file stream is needed to read information from file, a constructor should be used to establish a stream object. Two commonly used methods for constructing input file streams are shown below:

1. Use the default constructor, and then call member function *open* to open the file as shown in the following example:

```
ifstream myFile;                        //define a file stream object
myFile.open("filename",iosmode);        //open file "filename"
```

or:

```
ifstream* pmyFile = new ifstream;       //new a file stream object
pmyFile->open("filename",iosmode);      //use object pointer to call
                                        //function open to open the file
```

2. Specify the file name and mode when calling the constructor to build a file stream object, and open the file during constructing:

```
ifstream myFile("filename",iosmode);
```

11.3.2 Extraction Operator

The extraction operator (>>) has been predefined for all standard C++ data types. It is the easiest way to get bytes from an input stream object.

The extraction operator (>>) is used to form text input. The space character is used as a delimiter when extracting data. For a text passage with the space character, it is inconvenient to use the extraction operator. In such a case, unformatted input member function *getline* can be used to read a block of text for analysis. Another method is to derive an input stream class that has a member function like *GetNextToken* and use it to call *istream* member to extract and form character data.

The error handling functions of an output stream can also be applied to an input stream. It is very important to test errors in extraction.

11.3.3 Input Stream Manipulator

Manipulators defined in the class *ios_base* and head file *<iomanip>* can be applied to the input stream. However, only a few manipulators can really impact input stream objects. The most important ones are notation manipulators *dec, oct,* and *hex.*

The *hex* manipulator can receive and handle many different kinds of input stream forms in extraction. For example *c, C, 0xc, 0xC, 0Xc,* and *0XC* can all be interpreted as 12 in hexadecimals. Any character except 0~9, A~F, a~f, and X can lead to the termination of a change in value. For example, sequence *124n5* can change into value 124, and the sets *ios_base::fail.*

11.3.4 Input Stream Member Function

Input stream member functions can be used to input disk files. These member functions include:
- function *open*
- function *get*
- function *getline*
- function *read*
- function *seekg* and function *tellg*
- function *close*

1. Function *open* of input stream
To use an input file stream (*ifstream*), the stream must be related to a special disk file through the constructor or by using function *open*. In either case, the parameters are the same.

When opening a file to be related to the input stream, a mode label is usually specified. Mode labels are shown in Table 11.4. Labels can be combined using bitwise *or* (|) operators.

2. Function *close* of input stream
The member function *close* closes the disk file related to an input file stream.

Tab. 11.4: Opening Mode of Input File Stream File.

ios_base::in	Open file used for input (default)
ios_base::binary	Use binary mode (the default mode is text mode) to open file

Although the destructor of the class *ifstream* can close files automatically, if the same stream object is used to open another file, the function *close* should be used to close the current file first.

3. Function *get*

The function of the unformatted function *get* is similar to the extraction operator (>>), the main difference being that the function *get* includes blanks while reading data, while the extraction operator refuses to receive blanks under the default condition. The following is an example of the function *get*.

Example 11.6: Example of the function *get*.

```
//11_6.cpp
#include <iostream>
using namespace std;
int main()
{
    char ch;
    while ((ch=cin.get())!=EOF)
        cout.put(ch);
}
```

If the following string is entered

```
abc xyz 123
```

the program generates the following output:

```
abc xyz 123
```

When entering "Ctrl+z", the value read by the program is EOF, which ends the program.

4. Function *getline*

The member function *getline* allows an input stream to read multiple characters, and it allows the programmer to specify the input termination character (the default value is a line feed character). The program will delete this termination character from the contents after reading. The following example shows a way to specify the termination character.

Example 11.7: Specification of termination character for input stream.
This program reads a string of characters continuously and stops when it encounters
the character 't'. The number of characters is limited to 99.

```cpp
//11_7.cpp
#include <iostream>
using namespace std;
int main()
{
    char line[100];
    cout << "Type a line terminated by 't' " << endl;
    cin.getline(line,100,'t');
    cout << line;
}
```

5. Function *read*

Member function *read* reads bytes from one file to a designated memory area. The number of bytes that need to be read is determined by the length parameter. If given a
length parameter, the read operation will end when the file ends or when the function
encounters a file-ending label character in the text mode files.

Example 11.8: Read a binary record from the file *payroll* into a structure.

```cpp
//11_8.cpp
#include<iostream>
#include <fstream>
#include<cstring>
using namespace std;
int main()
{
    struct
    {
        double salary;
        char name[23];
    } employee1, employee2;
    employee1.salary=8000;
    strcpy(employee1.name, "L Zheng");
    ofstream outfile("payroll",ios_base::binary);
    outfile.write((char *) &employee1,sizeof(employee1));
    outfile.close();
    ifstream is("payroll",ios_base::binary);
    if (is)
        {
```

```
        is.read((char *) &employee2,sizeof(employee2));
        cout << employee2.name << ' ' << employee2.salary << endl;
    }
    else
    {
        cout << "ERROR: Cannot open file 'payroll'." << endl;
    }
    is.close();
}
```

The data record here is formatted using the defined structure and there is no termination entered or new line character.

The result of the program is as follows:

```
John 8000
```

6. Functions *seekg* and *tellg*

The input file stream keeps an internal pointer that points to the position of the data that is to be read next. Function *seekg* is used to set this pointer.

Example 11.9: Use function *seekg* to set position pointer.

```
//11_9.cpp
#include<iostream>
#include <fstream>
using namespace std;
int main()
{
    char ch;
    ifstream tfile("payroll",ios_base::binary);
    if(tfile)
    {
        tfile.seekg(8);
        while (tfile.good())
        {//end read operation then file ends or read operation fails
            tfile.get(ch);
            if (!ch) break; //quit the loop if not reading
            cout << ch;
        }
    }
    else
    {
        cout << "ERROR: Cannot open file 'payroll'." << endl;
    }
```

```
        tfile.close();
}
```

The function *seekg* can be used to achieve an object-oriented data management system. The position of the last byte of the file can be determined by multiplying the fixed-length record size by the number of records. With this number, the record can be read by using *get*.

Member function *tellg* returns the position of the current reading pointer; the value is of the streampos type.

Example 11.10: Read a file and display the position of the blanks inside.

```
//11_10.cpp
#include<iostream>
#include <fstream>
using namespace std;
int main()
{
    char ch;
    ifstream tfile("payroll",ios_base::binary);
    if (tfile)
    {
        while (tfile.good())
        {
            streampos here = tfile.tellg();
            tfile.get(ch);
            if (ch==' ')
                cout << "Position " << here << " is a space\n";
        }
    }
    else
    {
        cout << "ERROR: Cannot open file 'payroll'." << endl;
    }
    tfile.close();
}
```

11.4 Input/output Stream

An *iostream* object can be the source or destination of data. The two important I/O streams *fstream* and *stringstream* are both derived from *iostream*. These classes inherit the functions *istream* and *ostream* described above.

Class *fstream* supports the input and output of disk files. To read or write a special disk file, an *fstream* object should be constructed. An *fstream* object is a single stream that has two logic substreams: one is used for input and the other is used for output. A detailed explanation can be found from online help or reference books of a running library.

11.5 Example-improve Employee Information Management System

We have used an employee information management system in examples in the previous chapters. In those examples, the relevant information was stored in the memory at all times and, therefore, the information would be lost when the program ends. How can we save the information permanently? For this, we need to use files. Example 11.11 shows an improved program that can permanently store the information into a file.

Example 11.11: Employee information management.
The program includes three files: class definition head file *employee.h*, class implementation file *empfunc.cpp*, and main function file *11_11.cpp*. *11_11.cpp* and *employee.cpp* are linked after compiling. If the development environment is VC++, *11_11.cpp* and *employee.cpp* should be put in the same project. The following code is the source code of *11_11.cpp*:

```
//11_11.cpp
#include<iostream>
#include<fstream> //include file stream head file
#include"employee.h"
#include<vector>   //include vector head file
using namespace std;

int main()
{
    manager m1;
    technician t1;
    salesmanager sm1;
    salesman s1;
    char namestr[20];             //store the employee name in namestr
                                  //temporarily

    vector <employee *> vchar;    //declare the vector used to store
                                  //member objects
    vchar.push_back(&m1);
    vchar.push_back(&t1);
```

```
vchar.push_back(&sm1);
vchar.push_back(&s1);

int i;
for(i=0;i<4;i++)
{
 cout<<"Please enter the next employee name:";
 cin>>namestr;
 vchar[i]->SetName(namestr); //set name
 vchar[i]->promote(i);       //promote
}

cout<<"Please enter the part-time technicist"<<t1.GetName()<<"'s
    work hours of this month:";
int ww;
cin>>ww;
t1.SetworkHours(ww);        //set work time

cout<<"Please enter sales manager"<<sm1.GetName()<<"'s department
    gross sales of this month:";
float sl;
cin>>sl;
sm1.Setsales(sl);           //set this month's gross sales

cout<<"Please enter salesman"<<s1.GetName()<<"'s sale of this
    month:";
cin>>sl;
s1.Setsales(sl);            //set the sale of this month

ofstream ofile("employee.txt",ios_base::out);
                           //establish an output file stream object
for(i=0;i<4;i++)
{ vchar[i]->pay();               //calculate monthly pay
 ofile<<vchar[i]->GetName()<<"Number"<<vchar[i]
    ->GetindividualEmpNo()
 <<"Level:"<<vchar[i]->Getgrade()<<",pay of this month:"<<vchar[i]
    ->GetaccumPay()<<endl;
}
ofile.close();
cout<<"Employee informations stored"<<endl;
cout<<"Read information from file and display:"<<endl;
char line[101];
```

```
        ifstream infile("employee.txt", ios_base::in);
                                //establish an input file stream object
        for(i=0;i<4;i++)
        {
          infile.getline(line,100);
          cout<<line<<endl;
        }
        infile.close();
    }
```

The result of the program is as follows:

```
Please enter the next employee name:Zhang
Please enter the next employee name:Wang
Please enter the next employee name:Li
Please enter the next employee name:Zhao
Please enter part-time technicist Wang's work hours of this month:40
Please enter sales manager Li's department gross sales of this
month:400000
Please enter salesman Zhao's sale of this month:40000
Employee information stored
Read information from file and display::
Zhang Number 1000 Level: 4, pay of this month: 8000
Wang Number 1001 Level:3, pay of this month: 4000
Li Number 1002 Level:3, pay of this month: 7000
Zhao Number 1003 Level:1, pay of this month: 1600
```

The program writes the employee information that is stored in the vector to a file, reads the file, and displays the information.

11.6 Summary

We first introduced the concept of stream in this chapter, and then introduced the structure and the use of a stream class library. There are no input/output statements in C++ language, but there is an I/O software package that is object-oriented in C++ compiling system, i.e., I/O stream class library. Stream is the central concept of I/O stream class. It is a kind of abstract. It is responsible for connecting the producers and the consumers of data and managing the flow of data. The program regards stream objects as forms of file objects.

An output stream object is the target of information flow. The three most important output streams are *ostream*, *ofstream*, and *ostringstream*.

An input stream object is the origin of data flow. The three most important input streams are *istream, ifstream*, and *istringstream*.

An *iostream* object is the origin or destination of data. The two important I/O stream classes *fstream* and *stringstream* are derived from *iostream*.

We only introduced the concept and simple applications of stream class library. Readers should refer to a class library reference manual or online help for more details.

Exercises

11.1 What is a stream? What is the extraction and insertion of a stream? What is the function of an I/O stream in C++?

11.2 What is the difference between *cerr* and *clog*?

11.3 Use an I/O stream text mode to create a file named *test1.txt*, write characters "Write files successfully!", and open it with other word processors (such as Notepad in Windows), see if it has been written correctly.

11.4 Use an I/O stream text mode to open the file *test1.txt* created above, read the content, and display it to see if it is right.

11.5 Use an I/O stream text mode to open the file *test1.txt* created above, add characters "Add characters successfully!" after the file, then read the whole file and display the content to see if it is right.

11.6 Define a class *dog*, including two member variables *weight, height* and their corresponding member functions, declare an example *dog1*, whose weight is 5 and age is 10, use an I/O stream to write *dog1* into the disk file, and then declare another example *dog2*, and assign the state of *dog1* to *dog2* by reading. Use text mode and binary mode to operate on the file respectively; analyze the difference of the result and the ASCII code of the disk file.

11.7 Observe the following program, explain the function of each statement, and write down the result of the program.

```
#include <iostream>
using namespace ::std;
int main()
{
    ios_base::fmtflags original_flags = cout.flags();      //1
    cout<< 812<<'|';
    cout.setf(ios_base::left,ios_base::adjustfield);       //2
    cout.width(10);                                        //3
    cout<< 813 << 815 << '\n';
```

```
        cout.unsetf(ios_base::adjustfield);                      //4
        cout.precision(2);
        cout.setf(ios_base::uppercase|ios_base::scientific);    //5
        cout << 831.0 ;

        cout.flags(original_flags);                              //6
    }
```

11.8 Write a program in which the user inputs a decimal integral and receives results in its decimal, octal and hex forms.

11.9 Write a program that achieves the following function: open a designated text file and add a row number before every line.

12 Exception Handling

When we write application software, we should ensure its correctness and robustness. In other words, the software should run correctly when conditions and user operations are correct. When an unexpected problem arises or users operate improperly, the program should behave properly and reasonably without causing system failure or catastrophic consequences. Because conditions and user operations cannot be guaranteed, we should consider all possible circumstances and take effective measures accordingly. This precautionary measure for dealing with runtime errors is called exception handling.

12.1 Basic Concepts of Exception Handling

Some unavoidable runtime errors can be anticipated, including insufficient memory, missing files on hard disks, and discounted printers. These errors are caused by the program running environment. When such errors arise, we should allow users to correct the environmental errors and allow the program to continue to run and we should show some error messages. This is the task of exception handlers.

In large-scale software, because each function has a specific purpose and the relationships between functions are complex, an individual function does not have the capacity of handling errors. When an error is detected by a function, it may trigger (or 'throw') an exception condition and expect its caller to handle this error. If the caller cannot handle the error, it should pass it to a higher-level caller. This propagation will continue until the exception is handled. If an exception cannot be handled by the program, it will be passed to the C++ running system, which will then terminate the program. Figure 12.1 shows the direction of exception propagation.

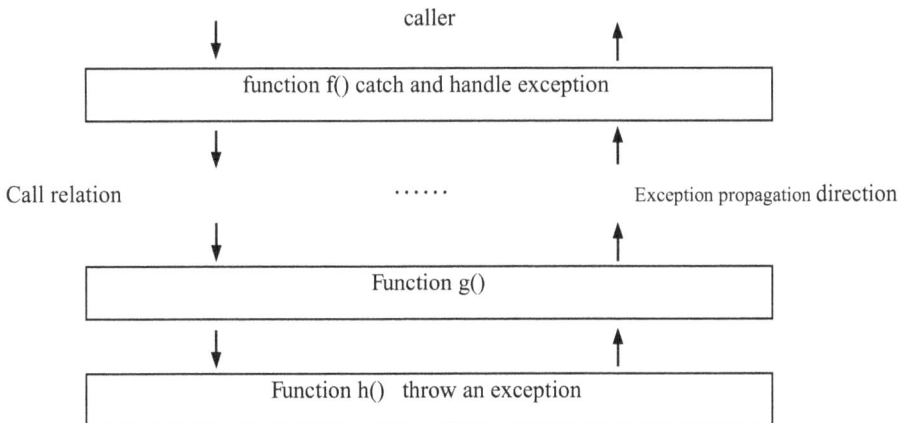

Fig. 12.1: Exception propagation direction.

https://doi.org/10.1515/9783110471977-012

The exception handling facility of C++ does not put the triggering (or throwing) and handling of exceptions in the same function, so that lower-level functions can focus on solving specific problems rather than dealing with exception handling unnecessarily. Higher-level callers can handle different exceptions at the right level.

12.2 The Implementation of Exception Handling in C++

C++ provides internal support for handling exceptions. The *try*, *throw*, and *catch* functions are the mechanism used for implementing exception handling. With C++ exception handling, the program can pass unexpected events to a higher-level execution context that can better recover from these unexpected events. The following section shows the proper syntax of exception handling functions.

12.2.1 The Syntax of Exception Handling

The syntax of the *throw* function is shown as follows:

```
throw expression
```

try block syntax:

```
try
    compound statement
catch (exception type declaration)
    compound statement
catch (exception type declaration)
    compound statement
    ...
```

If a program finds an exception that it cannot handle, it can use the *throw* expression to 'throw' this exception to its caller. The operands of *throw* are used to express exception type in a similar way to the operands of the *return* statement. If a program needs to throw an exception more than once, it should use different types of operands to differentiate different errors, and values of operands cannot be used to differentiate distinct exceptions.

The compound statement after the *try* clause is a protective segment of the code. If a program or a function is expected to encounter exceptions, we should put it after a *try* clause. If an exception occurs during the running of a program or a function, the *throw* expression will throw this exception to a handler.

The compound statement after the *catch* clause is the exception handler, which can "catch" exceptions thrown by the *throw* expression. The declaration part of exception types specifies the type of the exception handled by the clause. It is similar to formal parameters of a function and it can be values of some types or references. The type can be any valid data type, including classes of C++. When the exception is thrown, the *catch* clause will be checked one by one. If the exception type declaration of a *catch* clause matches the exception type being thrown, this exception handler will be executed. If the exception type declaration is an ellipsis (...), the *catch* clause will handle exceptions of any type, and this handler must be the last segment of a *try* block.

The execution process of exception handling is as follows:

1. Control reaches the *try* statement following the normal order, and then executes protective segment in the *try* block.

2. If there is no exception in the execution of a protective segment, the *catch* clause after the *try* block will not be executed. The program will continue from the statements after the last *catch* clause of the *try* block.

3. If there is an exception thrown during the period of executing a protective segment or any function called by the protective segment (direct or indirect call), the system will create an exception object using a *throw* operation (this implies that a copy constructor may be contained). At this point, the compiler will find a *catch* clause from a higher-level execution context that can handle the exception (or a catch handler that can handle exceptions of any type). The *catch* handler will be checked in the order of appearance after the *try* block. If there isn't any proper handler, it will continue to check the *try* block of the outer layer. This goes on until the outermost *try* layer is checked.

4. If no matched handler is found, the running function *terminate* will be called automatically. The default function of *terminate* is to call the *abort* terminator.

5. If a matched *catch* handler is found, it will be executed. Then the program jumps to statements after the last handler.

Example 12.1: Handle Exception of Dividing by Zero.

```cpp
//12_1.cpp
#include<iostream>
using namespace std;
int Div(int x,int y);
int main()
{
    try
    {
        cout<<"5/2="<<Div(5,2)<<endl;
        cout<<"8/0="<<Div(8,0)<<endl;
        cout<<"7/1="<<Div(7,1)<<endl;
    }
    catch(int)
```

```
        {
            cout<<"except of dividing zero.\n";
        }
        cout<<"that is ok.\n";
    }
    int Div(int x,int y)
    {
        if(y==0)
            throw y;
        return x/y;
    }
```

The result of the program is as follows:

```
5/2=2
except of dividing zero.
that is ok.
```

We can see from the result, when executing the following statement, the exception of dividing by zero will happen in function *Div*.

```
cout<<"8/0="<<Div(8,0)<<endl;
```

After the exception is thrown, it will be caught in the *main()* function. The exception handler outputs some relevant information, and then the program jumps to the last statement of the main function and outputs "that is ok". However, the following statement in function *Div* will not be executed.

```
cout<<"7/1="<<Div(7,1)<<endl;
```

The order of the *catch* handler is very important, because in a *try* block, exception handlers are checked by their appearance order. If a matched exception type is found in a catch clause, the subsequent catch clauses will be ignored. For example, in the exception handling block below, *catch (…)* appears firstly and it can catch any exceptions. So other *catch* clauses will never be checked. Therefore, *catch (…)* should always be put last.

```
//...
try
{
    //...
}
catch( ... )
{
    //handle all exceptions here
}
```

```
//error: two exception handlers behind will not be checked
catch( const char * str )
{
    cout << "Caught exception: " << str << endl;
}
catch( int )
{
    //handle int exception
}
```

In the VC++ 6.0 environment, we must set the following to use the exception handling facility:
1. Open "Project Settings" dialog;
2. Choose "C/C++" card;
3. Choose "C++ Language" in the Category box;
4. Choose "Enable Exception Handling".

12.2.2 Exception Interface Declaration

To make the program more readable, and to let the user know all possible exceptions that could be thrown by a function, we can list all possible exception types in the function declaration. For example,

```
void fun() throw(A, B, C, D);
```

indicates that *fun()* can, and can only, throw exceptions whose types are *A, B, C, D*, and their subtypes.

If there is no exception interface declaration in the function declaration, it can throw exceptions of any type. For example,

```
void fun();
```

A function that doesn't throw exceptions of any type can declare as follows:

```
void fun() throw();
```

12.3 Destruction and Construction in Exception Handling

The real capacity of exception handling in C++ lies in not only its ability to handle exceptions of various types, but also its ability to call destructors for all local objects constructed before throwing exceptions.

In a program, after a matched *catch* exception handler is found, if the exception type declaration of the *catch* clause is a value parameter, its initialization mode is to copy the thrown exception object; if the exception type declaration of the *catch* clause is a reference, its initialization mode is to make this reference point to the exception object.

After parameters of the exception type declaration are initialized, the unfolding process of the stack will begin. This contains the destruction of all automatic objects constructed (and not destructed yet) from the start of the *try* block to the place where the exception is thrown. The order of destruction is opposite to that of construction. And the program will resume execution after the last *catch* handler.

Example 12.2: Use C++ Exception Handling of Classes with Destructors.

```cpp
//12_2.cpp
#include <iostream>
using namespace std;
void MyFunc( void );
class Expt
{
  public:
    Expt(){};
    ~Expt(){};
    const char *ShowReason() const
    {
     return "Expt class is exceptional.";
    }
};
class Demo
{
  public:
    Demo();
    ~Demo();
};
Demo::Demo()
{
    cout << "construct Demo." << endl;
}
Demo::~Demo()
{
    cout << "destruct Demo." << endl;
}
void MyFunc()
{
    Demo D;
    cout<< "throw exception of Expt class in MyFunc()." << endl;
```

```
        throw Expt();
    }

    int main()
    {
        cout << "in the main function." << endl;
        try
        {
            cout << "call MyFunc() in the try block." << endl;
            MyFunc();
        }
        catch( Expt E )
        {
            cout << "in the catch exception handler." << endl;
            cout << "caught exception of Expt type: ";
            cout << E.ShowReason() << endl;
        }
        catch( char *str )
        {
            cout << "caught other exceptions. " << str << endl;
        }
        cout << "return to the main function and resume execution from
            here" << endl;
        return 0;
    }
```

The output of the program is as follows.

```
in the main function.
call MyFunc() in the try block.
construct Demo.
throw exception of Expt class in MyFunc().
destruct Demo.
in the catch exception handler.
caught exception of Expt type: Expt class is exceptional.
return to the main function and resume execution from here.
```

Note that in this example, the two *catch* handlers both specify exception parameters (parameters of the *catch* clause):

```
catch( Expt E )
{ //... }
catch( char *str )
{ //... }
```

In fact, we don't have to specify these parameters (*E* and *str*). In many cases, it is enough to notify that the handler has an exception of a certain type. But we do need to specify parameters when accessing exception objects. Otherwise, we cannot access the object in the *catch* clause. For example,

```
catch( Expt )
{
        //cannot access Expt exception object here
}
```

We can throw the exception being handled currently again by a *throw* expression without operands. This expression can only appear in a *catch* handler or the inner functions of the *catch* handler. The exception object being thrown again is the original exception object (not a copy). For example,

```
try
{
    throw CSomeOtherException();
}
catch(...) //handle all exceptions
{
    //response to exceptions (maybe only a part)
    //...

    throw; //pass the exception to some other handler
}
```

12.4 Exception Handling of Standard Library

The C++ standard provides a standard exception structure that begins with the base class *exception*. All exception handlings thrown by the standard library are derived from this base class. These classes are composed of derivation and inheritance relationships shown in Figure 12.2. The base class provides a *what()* service, redefines in each derived class, and sends an error message.

The immediately derived classes *runtime_error* and *logic_error* can be derived from the base class *exception* directly. Each derived class can be used for deriving other classes.

When the global operator *new* fails, the *bad_alloc* exception will be thrown. During the execution, when the dynamic type cast operation fails, *dynamic_cast* will throw a *bad_cast* exception. In the process of type identification, if the parameter of *typeid* is a zero or null pointer, the *bad_typeId* exception will be thrown. When unexpected exceptions happen, the system will call the *bad_exception* exception

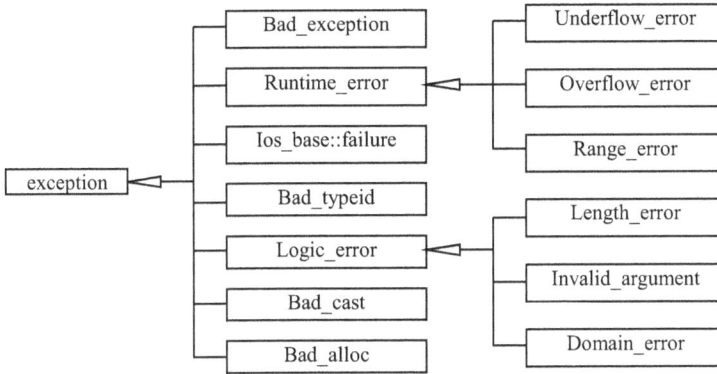

Fig. 12.2: Inheritance relationship between standard exception classes.

thrown by the function *unexpected()* if *std::bad_exception* is added in the throw list of the function, and won't terminate the program or call the function assigned by *set_unexpected*.

Exceptions of the C++ standard library are always derived from the *logic_error* logic class. It denotes logic errors in the program or violations of the invariance of the class, which can be avoided by writing correct codes. C++ standard library provides the following types of logic errors: *invalid_argument* denotes passing invalid arguments to functions. *Length_error* denotes that the length exceeds the maximum allowable length of the operational object. *Out_of_range* denotes that the value of the array subscript exceeds the defined range. *Domain_error* denotes invalid preprocessing errors. In addition, the stream class library of the standard library provides a special exception named *IOS_base::failure*. When the state of the data stream changes because of error or reaching the end of file, it will be thrown.

Exception classes derived from *runtime_error* are base classes of several other exception classes that denote errors that occur only in the program execution. *Range_error* denotes the interval error in internal computation, *overflow_error* denotes overflow errors in computation, and *underflow_error* denotes underflow error in computation.

To use exception classes, the corresponding header files should be contained. Exception base classes *exception* and *bad_exception* are defined in *<exception>*. *Bad_alloc* is defined in *<new>*. *Bad_cast* and *bad_typeid* are defined in *<typeinfo>*. *Iso_base::failure* is defined in *<ios>*. Other exception classes are defined in *<stdexcept>*.

C++ standard library guarantees that exceptions will not cause resource leak and the integrity of containers is maintained.

1. For base containers implemented by nodes, such as the list container, set container, multiset container, map container, and multimap container, if the construction of nodes fails, they should remain the same. Similarly, we should ensure that the move and remove operations of nodes are successful. When adding multiple

elements into the sequence associative container, in order to keep the ordered arrangement of the data, we should ensure that if the insertion fails, the container elements won't be changed. For the remove operation, we should guarantee the success of the operation. For example, to list a container, all operations besides *remove()*, *remove_if()*, *merge()*, *sort()*, and *unique()* should be successful, or they should ensure that the container remains the same.

2. For containers based on array implementation, such as vectors and deques, if the add operation of elements fails, we must make a backup of all elements after the insert point before the insertion to recover the initial state of the container. This can be time consuming. For functions *push()* and *pop()*, since they operate on the tail element of the container, we need not back up any element. Once the exception occurs, these two functions can ensure that the container returns to the original state.

12.5 Program Example Improvement to Personal Information Administration Program in a Small Company

As in the previous chapters, we take the personal information management program as an example. When accessing the disk file containing personal information, if the file does not exist, the problem cannot be processed. To handle this error condition, we add the exception handling facility to file access in Example 11.11 in Chapter 11. When accessing a file, if it does not exist, the program will throw an exception and quit. *12_3.cpp* and *employee.cpp* will be connected together after compiling. If we use a VC++ development environment, *12_3.cpp* and *employee.cpp* should be put in the same project.

Example 12.3: Personal Information Management.
Here, the program reads and displays the personal information stored in a disk file. If file access fails, we use the exception handling facility to solve the problem.

```
//12_3.cpp
#include<iostream>
#include<fstream>                //include the header file of file stream
#include"employee.h"
using namespace std;

class FileException {           //file exception handling class
public:
   FileException()
     : message( "File is not created!" ) { }
   const char *what() const { return message; }
private:
```

```
    const char *message;
};
int main()
{
    ifstream infile("employee.txt",ios::in);
                            //create an input file stream object
    try {
        if (!infile)
          throw FileException(); //throw an exception
    }
    catch ( FileException fe ) //catch the exception
    {
        cout<<fe.what()<<endl; //output the exception
    exit(0);                        //quit the program
}
cout<<"read information from the file and display as follows:"<<endl;
//read personal information from the file
    char line[101];
    for(int i=0;i<4;i++)
    {
        infile.getline(line,100);
        cout<<line<<endl;
    }
    infile.close();
    return 0;
}
```

If the specified file doesn't exist, the result is as follows:

```
read information from the file and display as follows:
File is not created!
```

If the specified file exists and is correct, the result is:

```
read information from the file and display as follows:
Zhang number 1000 grade is 4 grade, current month salary 8000
Wang number 1001 grade is 3 grade, current month salary 4000
Li number 1002 grade is 3 grade, current month salary 7000
Zhao number 1003 grade is 1 grade, current month salary 1600
```

12.6 Summary

Some unavoidable errors during program execution are to be expected. When such errors occur, we should allow the user to correct the environmental errors and allow the program to continue to run. This is the task of exception handlers. C++ language provides internal support for handling exceptions. The *try*, *throw*, and *catch* statements are the mechanism for implementing exception handling in C++.

To make the program more readable, and let the user know all possible exceptions that could be thrown by the function, we can list all possible exception types in the function declaration. This is the exception interface declaration.

The real capacity of exception handling in C++ lies in not only its ability to handle exceptions of various types, but also its ability to call destructors for all local objects constructed before the throwing of the exception.

In the last section of the chapter, we introduced the standard exception classes and their functions in the C++ standard library, and outlined a key property that is guaranteed by the exception handling in the C++ standard library. That is, exceptions will not cause resource leak and the integrity of containers is maintained.

Exercises

12.1 What is an exception? What is exception handling?

12.2 What are the advantages of the exception handling facility in C++?

12.3 Explain the use of *throw*, *try*, and *catch* statements by examples.

12.4 Design an exception abstract class *Exception*, and derive an *OutofMemry* class to respond to the out of memory situation, and a *RangeError* class to respond to the exception that input numbers are not in the specified range. Implement and test these classes.

12.5 Practice using *try* and *catch* statements. Use *new* to allocate memory in the program. If the operation fails, use a *try* statement to trigger an exception of the *char* type, and catch the exception using a *catch* statement.

12.6 Define an exception class *CException*, which has a member function *Reason()* to display the type of the exception. Define function *fn1()* to trigger an exception, call *fn1()* in the *try* module of the main function, and catch the exception in *catch* module. Observe the execution flow of the program.

Index

https://doi.org/10.1515/9783110471977-013